# When God Intervenes

## The Beginning of the End

**Douglas Berner**

*When God Intervenes: The Beginning of the End*
by Douglas C. Berner



Printed in the United States of America

ISBN 13: 978-1490944883
ISBN 10: 1490944885



V. 4 (July 2013)

Printed by CreateSpace

For more information: www.thesilenceisbroken.us

# Table of Contents

# List of Illustrations

# Introduction

> And I will show wonders in the heavens and in the earth, blood, and fire, and pillars of smoke. The sun shall be turned into darkness, and the moon into blood, before the great and the terrible day of the LORD come. (Joel 2:30-31)

This book is intended to be a companion to my book, *The Silence is Broken! God Hooks Ezekiel's Gog & Magog*, which was published in 2006. *The Silence is Broken!* comprises a close examination of the 38th and 39th chapters of the prophet Ezekiel which reveals the War of Gog and Magog. In the process of examining the character and timing of Gog and Magog in the context of the End Times, I also considered the issues of: "When does God finally break His silence that is so characteristic during this Age of Grace?" as well as, "When does God fully turn His face back toward Israel after having it facing towards the church during the Church Age?"

The conclusion of my study in *The Silence is Broken!* is that Ezekiel's prophecy of Gog and Magog will be fulfilled as a pretribulational event. It is not a war that takes place during either the first or second halves of Daniel's 70th Week. It is not the War of Armageddon. The Gog and Magog invasion of Israel comes exactly at a time of God's choosing. It marks the time when God both breaks His heavenly silence and returns His face towards Israel. It marks the time when God arises in supernatural judgment to shake the earth. Gog and Magog is the prophetic focal point for Israel that God uses to begin to get Israel's attention and to begin the process of returning the people and nation of Israel to an acceptable spiritual relationship with Him.

This book includes a chapter with an overview of the prophecy of Gog and Magog. It includes some arguments and material not included in *The Silence is Broken!* Some of the information is provided in chart and table format for easier comparison. This chapter provides a good introduction for those who have not intently studied the prophecy of Ezekiel 38 and 39, or a good review for those who have.

*When God Intervenes: The Beginning of the End* examines this point in time from the perspective of the larger prophetic puzzle. It comprises a close examination of the Day of the LORD: its character, its timing, and its design. The primary focus is on the beginning of the End Times. What are the conditions and events which begin the time of the end? How does the rapture of the church play into the picture of the prophetic puzzle? What is the timing of the rapture? If the rapture is a pretribulational event, what is the next event following the rapture? What is the primary character of this point in time? In the process of pursuing these questions, the characteristics of the beginning of the end will be compared and contrasted to the characteristics of the end of the end.

The gospel message of Christ is quite profound and quite simple. Unfortunately, this simplicity is not carried over into the study of eschatology. There is much confusion in the world of Bible prophecy. There are many contrasting and conflicting interpretations. Sides are taken and arguments ensue. While our salvation is not dependent upon the specific interpretations we make in terms of solving the prophetic puzzle, students of prophecy should do their best to rightly divide the word of God. We magnify God's holy name when we do so.

God could have made His prophetic plan for mankind very easy to interpret and comprehend. He could have made the pieces of the prophetic puzzle easily recognizable in their intersectional relationships. God could have given us "The Holy Bible for Dummies Version 101." We could have read it once, understood, and been satisfied.

God, in His infinite wisdom, chose depth and complexity over simplicity. Instead of a straightforward linear picture, He gave us the cryptic version. He gave us a crime scene which must be processed and interpreted with all the tools available to the crime scene investigator – CSI: The Prophetic Puzzle of the End Times. We need to examine, study, and ponder the meanings of individual prophetic passages. We need to follow the trail of the forensic evidence. God does leave fingerprints. There are footprints and blood splatter patterns. Hair, fiber, DNA, and other forms of trace evidence are woven into God's prophetic tapestry. The sciences of astronomy, physics, chemistry, and geology are all heavily involved in the solving of this puzzle.

While some portions of the puzzle will remain fuzzy, we can make educated conclusions regarding the intersection of a number of key pieces of the prophetic puzzle. We can solve significant portions of the puzzle. God will surprise all of us in some ways as to how His panoramic projection materializes. But His final solution will be completely in line with the scripture that He has given us and the context within which it has been given.

# 1

# The Beginning of the End

## Genesis to Revelation

It is often said that what begins in Genesis ends in Revelation. There is much truth in this statement. Genesis is the book of beginnings and Revelation is the book of endings and new beginnings. Genesis is the foundation stone of the Bible pyramid and Revelation is the capstone. Many themes in Revelation and in the teachings of Jesus and the prophets cannot be adequately understood without a good background from Genesis. Genesis begins the revelation of God's character and God's covenant promises to mankind through Adam, Noah, Abraham, Isaac, and Jacob (Israel).

The covenant promises that God initiated with mankind are the ultimate prophecies of the Bible. Each promise made by God is a prophecy which must be fulfilled and requires God's intervention in the affairs of this world. The progression of God's master plan down through the ages is a record of His remembrance of those covenant promises. One of the primary purposes for the climax of events during the End Times is to bring about the complete fulfillment of all of those covenant promises made by God.

Some of God's promises apply to all of humanity. Some of the promises apply only to the physical descendants of Abraham, through his son Isaac, through his son, Jacob – specifically targeting the nation of Israel. Other promises extend to the spiritual descendants of Abraham through faith in Jesus Christ as the promised Son of God – the Messiah. Jesus also made promises which apply to all mankind, some only to Israel, while other promises are limited to the church. It is important to reach a proper understanding of these promises and apply them to the appropriate groups in order to get an accurate picture of what God plans to accomplish during this Age of Grace and during the End Times.

Genesis introduces God with the presumption that God is. "In the beginning God created the heaven and the earth" (Gen 1:1). Revelation introduces Jesus Christ as Almighty God: the "Alpha and Omega, the beginning and the ending, … which is, and which was, and which is to come, the Almighty" (Rev 1:8). Thus, Revelation accurately describes the War of Armageddon as the "battle of that great day of God Almighty" (Rev 16:14). Revelation also depicts the destruction of the heaven and the earth and the creation of a new heaven and a new earth. Genesis introduces life, sin, and death, physically and spiritually. Revelation reveals the complete ending of sin and death and the reality of eternal life, physically and spiritually. Genesis reveals the desperate need of mankind for a savior and God's promise of a savior to come. Revelation portrays the final revelation of that savior in the person of Jesus Christ as the Lamb of God and as the King of Kings and Lord of Lords. Genesis leads us through a progression of patriarchs, twenty-four key elders of the entire human race, twenty-two of whom maintain the bloodline of the promised savior. Revelation depicts the twenty-four elders of the human race sitting on thrones in heaven surrounding the throne of God. Genesis reveals God's narrowed focus in His plan of salvation for mankind and in the bloodline of the Messiah upon a single nation of people – the twelve tribes of Israel. Revelation reveals God's renewed focus on the nation of Israel as His chosen servants on earth during the great day of God's wrath upon the earth through the supernatural sealing of 144,000 children of the tribes of Israel (Rev 7:1-8).

The entity that is a complete mystery in Genesis (and is still somewhat an enigma in Revelation) is the New Testament Church. Where God narrowed His focus to choose Israel from among the nations for Himself, God expanded His outreach to choose the church from all of the nations on earth for His Son. Where the tribes of Israel are the servants of God, church members are the servants of Christ. Where Israel is the chosen wife of God, the church is the bride of Christ. Where Israel had a tabernacle and later a temple in Jerusalem as the dwelling place for God within their midst, the church is indwelt by the Holy Spirit and is considered to be God's temple on earth during the present Age of Grace. Since Revelation reveals the presence of a Temple on earth again during the time of the Tribulation (Rev 11:1-2), the mystery temple that is the church must first be removed from the earth before that one can be rebuilt.

All of the beginnings in Genesis flow through the prophets and writings of the Old Testament into the gospels and epistles of the New Testament to reach final realization in Revelation. All of the prophecies are fulfilled. All of God's promises are realized. The twenty-four elders, Israel, and the church all achieve God's purposes in history, in redemption, in eternity. In the process the initial creation becomes contaminated, degraded, rundown, and old and is replaced with a new creation. The circle of life is completed – life, then death, followed by resurrection and new beginning.

God provides eternal life and vibrant fellowship with Him for all believers who trust God and Jesus Christ as God's Word – God's Messiah. For those who gain God's eternal presence, there is no curse, no death, no tears, no sorrow, and no pain. In contrast, God rejects all who reject Him. The Lake of Fire (second death and complete separation from God) becomes the everlasting prison for all unbelievers. Once cast into the Lake of Fire, there is no review board, no hope, no parole, no release, no escape – not even death or annihilation from the second death.

The story of Genesis has been created, lived, and progressed into both history and prophecy. The prophets have spoken. The vision of Revelation has been given, recorded, and studied. We are currently in the mystery Age of Grace. We look from the present latter days of the church through a cloudy but prophetic prism at a tapestry depicting a cataclysmic vortex, out of which emerges the future time of God's Messianic Kingdom. How do we get from the present age of the church to the End Times? How does the prophetic time of the end begin?

## The End Times

Many people in the secular environment share a fascination with the End Times, although their view tends to center on the concept of the End of the World or the Last Days of Planet Earth. Since they reject the literal interpretation of the scriptures of the Bible, they envision the pending total destruction of mankind. They focus on the potential catastrophic end that will come at the whim of nature or by man's own destructive hand. When people of the secular world consider how the world will end, they tend to visualize a great catastrophic war which is almost always referred to as the War of Armageddon. A few years ago, Elizabeth Vargas even made a passing reference to Armageddon in her introduction to the ABC network program focused on the Last Days of Planet Earth.

They are so focused on the pending total destruction of mankind that they completely miss the true hope and promise that the scriptures of the Bible provide – that man can receive salvation through faith in Jesus Christ and that Planet Earth will not be completely destroyed by either man or natural disaster, but will ultimately be the site of a glorious restoration. In their denial of God and His Holy Word, they completely miss that God has a master plan and that God is in complete control. In their ignorance of prophetic scripture any major disaster can become a catastrophe of biblical proportions, and the very next global scale war, regardless of what it is, will be the War of Armageddon.

They see the End Times as just an end, but the End Times in the Bible is less about an "end" as it is a new beginning. Actually, Bible prophecy deals with multiple end-time beginnings: the beginning of the church united with Christ, the beginning of Israel's Last Days, the beginning of the Messianic Kingdom, and the beginning of the Eternal State.

Israel's Last Days include the time of Jacob's trouble, which comes before the era of the Messianic or Millennial Kingdom. It comes as a period of judgment during God's Day of the LORD, which culminates with the coming of the Jewish Messiah (second coming of Jesus Christ), who ushers in the Messianic Kingdom.

For students of Bible prophecy, there is a considerable focus on understanding the events and chronology of the End Times. When many people initially approach the scriptures to study or teach Bible prophecy, they immediately begin with either the book of Revelation or the book of Daniel. The new student is plopped into a presentation of the progression of empires based upon the prophet Daniel's record of strange visions or is promptly immersed in the apocalyptic visions of the apostle John recorded in the Revelation of Jesus Christ. Before he knows it the student is sucked into the time and events of the Antichrist and the Tribulation without being given a solid foundation of how to understand these visions and revelations.

When the rapture of the church is taught as taking place first (pretribulational rapture), the teaching frequently jumps from the rapture to the Tribulation with no examination of how the one event leads to the other. Does the rapture really begin the Tribulation? Are the Antichrist and his final empire truly the central focus of Daniel and the book of Revelation? Frequently more time and effort is focused on teaching how everything ends rather than understanding how the end begins.

There are many different approaches to interpreting the beginning of the End Times. A number of different models have been proposed by different scholars to account for the sequence of events that will make up the time of the end. There are a number of issues that directly or indirectly relate to the beginning of the End for which there is no overall consensus. The timing and character of the rapture of the church is highly contested. The timing and length of the Day of the LORD is disputed. The relationship of the rapture to the Day of the LORD is questioned. The time that God's wrath begins is challenged. The timing and character of the War of Gog and Magog is a source of contention between certain camps of interpretation. The identity of the leader Gog is disputed. The Beginning of Sorrows is viewed in various ways regarding its length, timing, and character. The time period through which the seven seals are opened is also disputed. While many scholars link the opening of the first seal to the very beginning of Daniel's 70$^{th}$ Week as the seven-year Tribulation, what follows with the rest of the seals varies considerably. Many scholars link the beginning of birth pangs to at least the first four seals, while others separate the birth pangs from the seals and begin the birth pangs earlier in time. The student of Bible prophecy is left to try to make sense out of the various approaches and interpretations.

In the process of grappling with the End Times, many arguments ensue over the understanding of several key issues. In recent years, these include, among many others: the timing of the rapture of the church, the timing of Gog and Magog and its relationship to Armageddon, the nature of Psalm 83, the relevancy of the destruction of Damascus in Isaiah 17, the identity of the Antichrist, the role of Islam in Bible prophecy, the identity of the 24 Elders of Revelation 4, the character and timing of the wrath of God, and the timing of the Day of the LORD.

It is often said that interpreting Bible prophecy is like putting a puzzle together. When we study scripture we are examining different pieces of a puzzle that God has created – like a majestic tapestry woven together in intricate detail. The problem is that from our limited perspective many parts of the puzzle or tapestry are blurred and difficult to make out. Another problem is that some pieces of the puzzle seem to fit into the picture in multiple places. A slight misplacement of one or two pieces can make a huge difference in the outcome of the final picture that emerges. It is like we are traveling on a highway looking for key landmarks and intersections to tell us where we are and if we are headed in the right direction. There can be mountainous indicators as well as subtle details. A picture is made up of individual pixels. A painting is made up of brushstrokes. Both can have color and character, uniqueness and commonality. We are looking for identifying characteristics that will give us an exact match for an intersection. Short of that, we look at similarity between passages. However, similarity can be tricky. We also need to look closely for distinctions. Small but important distinctions can override similarity to the point of demonstrating significant differences in locations for passages within the larger prophetic puzzle.

Some conflicts and confusion of interpretation exist simply because of the shear number and variety of names and titles that the Bible and students of prophecy use when referring to the time of the end. There are many end-time titles. How do they relate? How do we sort them out? Which titles are important? Which ones coincide for the same period of time? Some of the many names and titles that the student of prophecy frequently encounters include:

- The Day of the LORD

- The Great & Terrible Day of the LORD
- The Tribulation
- The Great Tribulation
- Daniel's 70th Week
- The Time of Jacob's Trouble
- The Beginning of Sorrows
- The Day of Christ
- The Day of God
- Day of Wrath
- Day of Vengeance
- Great Day of God Almighty
- End Times
- The Hour of Temptation (Testing)
- Last Days
- Last Day
- End of Days
- The End
- The End of the world (Age)
- The Millennium
- Satan's Little Season

It is not uncommon for an author or teacher to use an end-time oriented title one way and have it interpreted another way by a reader or student if the author has not clearly defined his approach and use of the term. We will be examining several titles for end-time periods of time and how they relate to each other throughout the chapters of this book. One of the most important titles that we will deal with is "The Day of the LORD."

Many concepts of the interpretation of Bible prophecy are based upon assumptions. Many assumptions are not acknowledged as such, and thus are taught as fact. This often leads to confusion and frustration among casual Bible readers, students of prophecy, as well as established prophecy scholars. Some of the more common teachings by various scholars based upon assumptions include:

- That most of Bible prophecy has already been fulfilled in the first century or in history (Preterism & Historicism).
- That the church has replaced Israel as the true Israel (Replacement Theology).
- The rebirth of Israel as a modern nation has not fulfilled Bible prophecy.

- Israel has no future prophetic role – It is all about the church.
- That the church must be on earth to endure and persevere through the time of God's wrath.
- There are seven years between the rapture and the second coming of Jesus Christ.
- The pretribulational rapture leaves an undefined period of time after the rapture – before the Tribulation begins.
- The Day of the LORD and the seven-year Tribulation are the same time period.
- The Day of the LORD is a subset period of time to the seven-year Tribulation.
- The Great and Terrible Day of the LORD only applies to the very end of the Tribulation at the time of Christ's second coming.
- The apostle John's invitation to heaven in Revelation 4 directly signifies the timing of the rapture of the church to heaven.
- The 24 Elders in Revelation 4 comprise or directly represent the Christian church after it is raptured to heaven.
- The opening of the first seal in Revelation 6 signifies the ratification of the seven-year covenant of peace between the Antichrist and Israel.
- The opening of the first seal directly reveals the beginning of the seven-year Tribulation.
- There is an extended period of time between the breaking of the different seals in Revelation 6.
- The souls under the altar depicted in the fifth seal represent the souls of martyrs killed during the Tribulation.
- The Great Multitude wearing white robes in Revelation 7 represents tribulational believers who come out of the Great Tribulation over an extended period of time.
- The Great Multitude wearing white robes in Revelation 7 represents believers who are directly converted to faith by the evangelism of the 144,000 Jewish servants sealed to God in Revelation 7.
- There is only one incidence of major cosmic disturbances during the End Times.
- There is only one major war during the End Times and that is the War of Armageddon.
- There is only one incidence of God's inviting birds and or beasts to feast upon a battlefield of slain armies as a sacrifice or a supper table spread by God.

Students of prophecy try to make sense out of the prophetic passages in Daniel and the other Old Testament prophets, the Olivet Discourse of Jesus recorded in three of the four gospels, a few passages by the apostle Paul, and the extended prophecy that comprises the book of Revelation. They tend to focus on key characteristics of the Tribulation: the impact of the 7 Seals, 7 Trumpets, and 7 Bowl judgments in Revelation, the identity of the Antichrist, a seven-year covenant of peace with Israel, the abomination of desolation, the number 666 and the mark of the beast, the War of Armageddon, and the second coming of Christ. Many questions are asked. When is the rapture? What role does Islam play? Will Islam conquer the world? Does the Antichrist come out of Europe to the West or out of Islam to the East? One of the questions often asked is: How close are we to the Time of the End?

I do believe that the modern nation of Israel is a fulfillment of Bible prophecy. Israel has been reborn as a nation – a portion of the Jewish people brought back to a portion of the Promised Land, primarily under a condition of spiritual unbelief. While the birth of Israel in 1948, and Israel's recapture of Jerusalem in 1967, are highly significant, neither the nation of Israel, nor the world has yet entered the time of the end known as the Day of the LORD. The status of Jerusalem is a global issue. Israel is becoming the focal point of the world's focus on peace. God has a lot of unfinished prophetic work to do with the nation and people of Israel as opposed to the church before the Messianic Kingdom can be realized.

The unfulfilled prophetic events that directly involve the church center on the rapture of the church to heaven, the judgment seat of Christ, and the marriage of the church to Christ as His Bride. These are events of the Day of Christ. The Day of Christ does not relate to Israel. On earth, Israel and the nations will experience the Day-of-the-LORD judgments and God's refinement and purification by fire.

In several prophecies Israel appears as the target of military action and invasion. The Bible portrays Israel as sitting at the center of the world as the bull's-eye on a target. Israel is immediately surrounded by an inner circle of enemies, all of which directly border it. Outside of that circle is another ring of enemies we can call the outer circle or outer ring, as none of them actually share adjacent borders with Israel. Another circle of enemies surrounds that one as well. That is the outermost ring which comprises all the nations of the world. These rings of enemies will all attack Israel sometime during the time of the end. But they will not happen at the same time. Each circle will invade Israel at a different time. There will be a progression to these wars.

There are a few prophecies which relate to Israel that could be fulfilled prior to the rapture of the church. These events could be used by God to further set the stage and create the dynamics for the big event to follow in the wake of the rapture. These prophecies include Psalm 83 and Isaiah 17, which could in turn lead to Ezekiel 38–39. While there are events of prophecy that can take place before the rapture, there are no prophecies which we know of which must be fulfilled before the rapture can occur.

We are in the latter days of the dispensation of the church. The Bible gives us a clear characterization of the time that comprises the latter days of the Church Age. The world and the church will experience a period of social decline. This time is characterized by increasing apostasy (the departing away from faith), scoffers – deniers of the Word and of the coming of Christ, increased immorality and sexual immorality, deception, hypocrisy, following seducing spirits, increased demonic activity, self-idolatry, narcissism, covetousness, boasting, pride, greed, lust, pleasure seeking, self-gratification, disobedience, unthankfulness, self-righteousness, and self-centeredness (1 Tim 4:1-3; 2 Tim 3:1-9; 2 Pet 3:3-7; Rev 3:14-19). Much of the church which claims to be Christian has fallen or is falling away into apostasy. Instead of being separate from the world as a heavenly temple of God on earth, it seems that the majority of the church is uniting with the world – embracing the world's views and goals.

Comparing the characteristics of the time going into the time of the end with the characteristics predominate in the U.S.A. and major portions of the world in 2013, we can observe:

- The increasing apostasy of the church – the latter days of the Church Age.
- The downward spiral of western society – its morality and its economy.
- The nationalizing of sin – greed, hypocrisy, deception, sexual immorality – the Sin Bubble!
- The changing alignment of enemies surrounding Israel.
- The increasing alignment of nations for Ezekiel 38–39.
- The perceived increase and intensity of natural disasters – storms, drought, tornados, earthquakes, floods, and meteors.
- The global threat of war and rumors of war.
- The ongoing threat of Islamic terrorism.
- The issue of the need for peace and safety.
- The globalization of the issue of Middle Eastern peace centered on Israel, Jerusalem, and the Palestinians.
- The increasing threat of widespread famine.
- The increasing threat of widespread disease in the form of epidemics and pandemics.
- The potential threat of a major solar event, or an EMP (electromagnetic pulse) warfare event.

- The increasing threat of widespread computer hacking being used as a form of economic, political, or military warfare or terrorism.
- The increasing imposition of a surveillance society.

## The Beginning of the End

If God removes the church before the Tribulation, what is the impact of that removal on Israel and the nations? If the rapture is the next major prophetic event on the horizon for the church as the doctrine of imminence teaches, then what would logically follow the rapture in terms of God's prophetic puzzle?

- What will Israel's spiritual relationship be to God at that time?
- How will that spiritual condition impact Israel's role in end-time prophecy?
- When does God return His face to Israel?
- When and how does God let Israel know that He is still the God of Abraham, Isaac, and Jacob and that the people of Israel are still His chosen people?
- When and how does God inform the nations that Israel is the apple of God's eye?
- How does God get many more physical descendants of Israel to return to the Promised Land?
- How and when is the Palestinian issue resolved?
- How and when is Islam removed as an obstacle to Israel's control over Jerusalem and the Temple Mount?
- How and when does the Jewish temple in Jerusalem get rebuilt?
- How does the world get to the point where a seven-year covenant of peace can be formed with Israel?
- How does the government of the world come to be dominated by ten kings or kingdoms?
- How does the world get to the point where the Antichrist and the False Prophet essentially gain economic control over every nation and every person?
- When does God's wrath begin to manifest itself in judgments cast upon the earth?
- How does the beginning of the time of the End actually begin?

In 1972, Tim LaHaye authored a book, *The Beginning of the End*, in which he interpreted the first sign of the End Times to be the prophecy made by Jesus Christ in His Olivet Discourse (Mt 24:7) regarding the time when nation will rise against nation and kingdom against kingdom. LaHaye interpreted that this prophecy was fulfilled by the events of World War I between 1914 and 1918. LaHaye argued, "Until history produces a more acceptable fulfillment, it is reasonable to conclude that 1914 ushered in the beginning of the end." LaHaye also focused on the importance and meaning of Matthew 24:34, where Jesus declares that the particular generation that sees the signs of the beginning of the end will not pass away until all of the end-time events described in His Olivet Discourse are fulfilled. LaHaye described the length of a generation as seventy to eighty years, although he did allow that it could be longer. His emphasis was that the world would not see the complete passing away of the generation which was alive during 1914-1918 before the return of Jesus Christ.[1]

In 2013, we are now a full century past the year 1914. Was Tim LaHaye correct in his interpretation? Did World War I fulfill Christ's prophecy regarding nation rising against nation and kingdom against kingdom? It is true that World War I was a very devastating war involving a number of nations, which was accompanied by famine and a very serious pestilence in the form of a deadly influenza epidemic. But was that enough to fulfill Matthew 24:7? I think not.

What will happen when the world experiences the next great world war? It is only a matter of time before multiple nations will invade Israel and embroil the Middle East in a war which will threaten the safety of the entire world. While many people, world leaders and media outlets alike, act like they are in denial regarding the imminent danger of such a war, the prophecies of the Bible make it clear that a terrible war is in the making. But which war? Which prophetic war is going to be fulfilled next? How is the world going to interpret or understand that war?

The Bible provides several passages which describe end-time battles or wars which have yet to take place. Isaiah, Jeremiah, Ezekiel, and Zechariah all describe scenes of future military conflicts. Jesus Christ predicted that there would be wars and rumors of war (Mt 24:6). He also declares that there will be a time when nation will rise against nation and kingdom against kingdom (Mt 24:7). The prophet Daniel describes a war involving the king of the North and the king of the South (Dan 11:40-45). The apostle John observes that when Jesus Christ breaks the second seal on the scroll in heaven, peace will be taken from the earth (Rev 6:3-4). This war and its related aftermath will result in the destruction of one-fourth of the population of the earth (Rev 6:8). John also presents the setting for what has become to be popularly known as the War of Armageddon (Rev 16:12-16; 17:12-14; 19:11-21).

People ask, "How close are we to the End?" while looking for clues to decipher the signs. Frequently, people who ask this question are groping with the issue of, "How close are we to the War of Armageddon?" Unfortunately, people in the secular world and some students of Bible prophecy do not realize their search often focuses on characteristics that are not applicable to the beginning of the end. They are wondering how close the world is to the beginning of the end-time events, yet they are looking at the characteristics and events of the very end for their answer.

When most people consider how the world will end, they tend to visualize a great catastrophic war that is almost always referred to as the War of Armageddon. Armageddon! The concept of Armageddon as the final great holocaustic war of all times, accompanied by destructive natural disasters, has emerged in the form of a global mystique – the ultimate threat that hangs over the world.

The term Armageddon is derived from the reference to Har-Magedon (mountain of Megiddo) in Revelation 16:16 as the location in Israel where the armies of the world will gather for a great war. While the source of the reference to Armageddon is from the Christian New Testament, the entire world has come to accept the mystique of a future Armageddon. Fortunately, the End Times will not begin with the War of Armageddon. Unfortunately, that is a lesson the world will learn the hard way.

After the rapture of the church God's prophetic focus returns to Israel. What is the next event on God's agenda? What unfulfilled Old Testament prophecy or prophecies depict this exact point in time? What New Testament prophecies provide a parallel to this time frame?

In His prophetic Olivet Discourse Jesus plainly stated that there must be wars and rumors of war, but the end is not yet. "For nation shall rise against nation, and kingdom against kingdom: and there shall be famines, and pestilences, and earthquakes, in diverse places. All these *are* the **beginning** of sorrows" (Mt 24:6-8). The time of the end begins with war. Will it begin with a little military conflict? No. It will be a major conflict and it will be accompanied by famine, pestilence, and earthquakes – all at the same time. It may begin as a local event, but it will quickly spread out globally to encompass many "diverse places." This is not the war of Armageddon.

Do we see evidence of this war anywhere else in prophetic scripture? Yes. We see this evidence exactly where we should expect it to be – near the beginning of the opening of the seals of God's judgments by Jesus Christ in Revelation 6. The breaking of the second seal reveals a symbolic rider on a red horse who is given power by God to take peace from the earth by wielding a great sword. This is clearly symbolism for a great war. The breaking of the third seal reveals the accompanying famine and economic crisis, while the fourth seal informs us that one-fourth of the population of the earth will be killed during this series of events which make up the beginning of the Day of the LORD. The description of the sixth seal completes the picture with the impact of a global earthquake, the shaking and splitting of the heavens, and the realization by the peoples of the earth that the great day of God and Christ's wrath has finally come (the Day of the LORD). Is this Armageddon? No. Is this the second coming of Christ to the earth? No. This is not the end of either the Tribulation or God's Day of the LORD – it is just the beginning.

Jesus clearly teaches that the time of the end begins with a major war and it ends with a major war. Both wars are associated with global earthquakes. Are we to believe that God would be completely silent throughout Old Testament scripture regarding the war that will begin the judgments of the Day of the LORD? If not, what type of prophetic passage should we look for?

1. This prophecy will be focused on Israel. The message is to and about Israel – not the church.
2. It will be an Old Testament prophecy which predicts a war involving Israel.
3. The Day of the LORD begins with the end of the Church Age (Age of Grace). This prophecy will be about judgment, not grace. Yet it will also be about God's compassion and possessiveness regarding Israel.
4. This prophecy will deal with Israel's relationship to God and to the world. Since Israel, as a people and as a nation, is in rebellion against God (by largely denying God Himself, as well as by rejecting Jesus as God's Messiah), this prophecy should reflect Israel's rebellion against God. Israel will be profaning God's name.
5. God has hidden His face from Israel during this Church Age. This prophecy will be about God returning His face to Israel.
6. This passage will not characterize Israel as strong, militarily victorious on its own, but desperate for God's supernatural intervention.
7. This prophecy will reveal that God will intervene to save Israel from almost certain destruction.
8. This prophecy should reveal God's supernatural manner of intervention utilizing earthquakes, pestilence, and other natural disasters.
9. It would also be consistent for this prophecy to emphasize the realization on the part of Israel and the nations of the world that God has taken a stand and intervened in judgment.

These characteristics sound very much like the War of Armageddon, yet they are criteria for the beginning of the End Times. Since Israel will be profaning God's holy name at the time, Israel will not yet have accepted Jesus as the Messiah. Therefore, while this prophecy will be about God's intervention and presence, it will not be about the second coming of Christ and it will not depict the physical coming of the Messiah.

Can it possibly be that the beginning of the end is really so similar to the end of the end? Absolutely! Why do some scholars confuse the description of the events of the breaking of the sixth seal in the book of Revelation with the events involving the second coming of Christ? This is no coincidence or accident of prophecy. God has, for His own reasons, designed a prophetic plan where the beginning of the End Times mimics the end of the End Times.

The Day of the LORD will begin suddenly with catastrophe on a global scale, and the Tribulation will end with an even greater catastrophic finale at the time of Armageddon and the second coming of Christ. Where the sixth seal reveals a global earthquake and disasters impacting each and every person on earth (there are exactly seven categories of people identified in Rev 6:15), the earthquake that is part of the seventh bowl judgment will be the greatest earthquake ever to impact the earth throughout the history of man (Rev 16:18).

What Old Testament prophecy could possibly meet all of these criteria? There is one and only one such passage. That prophecy is the War of Gog and Magog described in Ezekiel 38–39. Therefore, it should be no surprise that there are many similarities between Gog and Magog and Armageddon. While some authors have gone to great lengths to note and list the similarities in an attempt to demonstrate that these are the same war, we should be very careful and realize that similarity does not necessarily make for sameness. It is not the similarities that are critical to understand in determining between these wars – it is the differences! In spite of the many similarities, there are several dynamic differences. We will examine those differences in a later chapter.

Ezekiel's prophecy is dominated by the first person presence of God. God makes a number of strong "I" statements like, "I am against you, O Gog, prince of Rosh, Meshech and Tubal." "I will turn you around and put hooks into your jaws, and I will bring you out, and all your army …" This prophecy is full of God's possessiveness for Israel and His relationship to Israel. God repeatedly refers to Israel in this prophecy as "My people Israel; My land; and My mountains." God very strongly declares that this prophecy is very much about His relationship to Israel and all the nations of the world. Where God's holy name is being profaned by Israel and the nations, God has a plan to change that by intervening and revealing Himself to the world. God presents Himself as the scriptwriter, the director, the producer, and the starring actor of this prophetic event that will become the invasion of Israel by the alliance of Gog and Magog. The entire situation is directly set up by God, so that He can manifest Himself through His intervention to save Israel.

Ezekiel 38–39 is a very different portrayal of war and God's intervention compared to other end time prophecies that are recorded by Daniel, Isaiah, Jeremiah, Zechariah, and the other prophets, as well as the prophecy recorded by the apostle John in the book of Revelation where we see the War of Armageddon. For example, when we look at the prophecy recorded in Daniel 11:40-45, which involves an end time war involving the king of the North and the king of the South attacking a leader who is frequently interpreted to be the future Antichrist, we do not see any first person presence or interest by God at all. The description of the prophecy is merely a matter of fact rendering from a heavenly perspective. Really, the same characteristic applies to the War of Armageddon. The War of Armageddon is about God's wrath – but God's own portrayal places a much stronger emphasis on Ezekiel's War of Gog and Magog – and we should too! This may be hard to understand, but Gog and Magog is God's war, while Armageddon is Satan's war. They occur at two different times and for very different reasons.

I believe the War of Gog and Magog is the most important war described in Bible prophecy. Here are several reasons why I believe Gog and Magog is so important.

First – In the context of God's Day of the LORD, Gog and Magog comes first. It comes before all of the other prophetic wars, including the battles described in Daniel 11:40-45 and the War of Armageddon.

Second – It has a probable relationship to the rapture of the church. It may immediately follow the rapture, or be an almost simultaneous event with the rapture. With God's removal of the church at the rapture and His supernatural destruction of Gog and Magog, God will have completely shifted His focus from the church during our current Age of Grace and returned His face to Israel. God's sudden and dramatic intervention will reveal His presence to Israel, and this is a very strong indication that the church is no longer on earth.

Third – Gog and Magog becomes a global event. It starts in Israel and expands outward through a global earthquake, fire from heaven, and quite possibly nuclear war throughout the world. God makes it very clear that every single person on earth will shake at His revealed presence – but this is not the second coming of Christ.

Fourth – It involves the largest human population of the world of any of the end-time wars. With the opening of the second seal and the fourth seal of Revelation – one-fourth of the world's population will be killed. Satan's all out assault against all followers of God and Christ during the Tribulation will result in many martyrs. Each subsequent war, natural disaster, and supernatural judgment from God will reduce the population of the world until the population has been significantly downsized by the time of the War of Armageddon.

Fifth – The War of Gog and Magog is going to catch the world by surprise. It is going to come suddenly and catastrophically upon both Israel and the world. It is going to come when the leaders of the world are proclaiming "Peace, Peace" – either calling for peace, or proclaiming a false peace. By the time Armageddon rolls around, the world will have been devastated by years of cataclysmic disasters and warfare. The War of Armageddon will come as no surprise to those people left alive towards the end of the Day of the LORD.

Sixth – The destruction caused by the War of Gog and Magog will be mistakenly attributed as the fulfillment of the War of Armageddon. This is going to create a power vacuum that will allow for the quick rise to power of the Antichrist. It will also create a situation where Israel and the world will be primed to accept a rising world leader as the real Messiah of God.

Gog and Magog is part of God's opening act to initiate His judgments during the Day of the LORD. Armageddon is Satan's desperate attempt to finally and completely destroy Israel and to hold onto a dying world by trying to prevent Christ's return to reclaim the earth for God.

God will supernaturally intervene in the affairs of men again. He has to because He has obligated Himself to do so. When God releases Christ to deal with His enemies, His time of intervention by wrath will be a marked contrast to the world as we know it today. This long awaited prophetic time will have both a beginning and an ending. The Beginning of the End will mark the end of the world as we know it. The End of the End will climax the time of God's wrath against the earth. It will also mark the beginning of the restoration of the world as it was in Genesis. We are embarking on a study of the Beginning of the End contrasted against the End of the End. We will set aside the fuzzy middle part of the Day of the LORD for another day.

**Notes: The Beginning of the End**

1. Tim LaHaye, *The Beginning of the End*, (Wheaton, IL: Tyndale House Publishers, 1972, Living Books edition 1981), pp. 35-39, 165-168.

# 2

# The Rapture of the Church

The rapture is the teaching that there will be a future event where all dead Christian believers will be simultaneously resurrected, all living believers along with the resurrected believers are instantly transformed into spiritually glorified bodies, and all of these glorified believers are "raptured" or caught up to meet Jesus Christ in the atmosphere above earth to be taken to heaven. The process of this event has Jesus bringing the souls of dead Christians with Him from heaven to the earth's atmosphere. Jesus does not come down to the surface of the earth but remains in the air as He calls up the collective body of church believers to be united with Him.

The word rapture is not found in an English translation of the Bible as it is a word derived from the Latin "raptus," which equates to the Greek word "harpazo," which means "to snatch or catch away" or "caught up." The concept of *harpazo* involves the forceful seizure or rescue of the church from the earth (1 Thes 4:15-18; 1 Cor 15:51-53). The rapture is a sudden dynamic event that takes place without warning.

## Issues Regarding the Rapture

### Literal vs. Allegorical Interpretation

Within Christianity several major schools of thought have developed regarding the understanding of the present Age of Grace and end-time prophecy. The differences between these perspectives are heavily influenced by whether they approach prophetic scripture from a literal versus an allegorical form of interpretation. The differences between major viewpoints also tend to revolve around the prophetic relationship of the church to Israel, as well as critical issues concerning the timing and characteristics of: Christ's second coming, the rapture of the church, and the Millennium or Messianic Kingdom.

The simplest and most direct method of understanding the language of the Bible is to interpret scripture literally whenever possible. A person who approaches the study of prophecy from the perspective of a literal hermeneutic seeks to understand the plain sense meaning of the scriptural passage, taking into consideration the grammatical meaning of the original language (Hebrew, Aramaic, or Greek) and the historical setting or context within which it was written. This literal approach is often called the grammatical-historical method of interpretation. The effect of this approach is to understand that God says what He means and God means what He says.

An allegorical approach is the exact opposite of the literal approach to understanding prophecy. Allegory seeks a hidden meaning in the prophetic passage. This approach spiritualizes the meaning of a passage by implying that even though it says one thing it actually means something else. In spite of the frequent use of symbols and visual images, do most prophetic passages mean exactly what they say? Or is the surface language of prophecy a coded message which means something else entirely?

It is very easy to go astray when man starts imposing his own meaning on God's own words. The process of allegorizing essentially gives the interpreter of prophetic scripture a free hand in deciding what God meant at the time the passage was written and what it means to us today. This type of interpreter seems to know God's thoughts better than God Himself. The allegorical interpreter is essentially correcting God for His misuse of our written language. The interpreter who allegorizes scripture places himself in a position of power over others, holding people hostage to an interpretation that they cannot understand without the assistance of the interpreter. This perspective dominates the prophetic understanding of many Christian denominations today.

The first and primary consideration in the study of prophecy is whether to take a literal approach to understanding the prophetic scriptures or whether to view them in an allegorical or spiritualized sense. I believe God is a literalist and God means what He says. There are passages of scripture which we will examine that only make sense if taken literally. For example, the rapture of the church does not make sense unless it is a very real event on God's prophetic timeline. It is often observed that a consistent literal interpretation of the relevant prophetic passages of scripture naturally leads the reader to a premillennial perspective.

## Imminence

Jesus promised to return and gather His believers to Himself in heaven (Jn 14:2-3). When will this event take place? Must other prophetic events take place first? What is the next event that will take place on the prophetic timeline for the church? Upon what event did Jesus teach His followers to place their expectation?

These questions are important to consider when dealing with the concept and the timing of the rapture. Many people's understanding of the rapture is influenced by how they apply the doctrine of imminency to this event. Imminence implies an anticipation that something is going to happen at any time. There is no expectation that a different event will take place first; otherwise, there would be no imminency. However, imminency does not require that the expected event be immediately fulfilled or that no other event can take place before it.

In the context of Bible prophecy, the relevance of imminency is important. Is the dividing of the old Roman Empire or the entire world into ten kingdoms imminent? Is the rise of the Antichrist and the False Prophet to power on the global stage imminent? Is the mark of the beast (666) imminent? Is the War of Armageddon imminent? When we consider these questions, we should observe that the mark of the beast and the War of Armageddon cannot take place until sometime after the Antichrist and the False Prophet come into their positions of global power. Thus, we should realize that neither of these events is imminent. When an event is known or expected to take place before another event, there is no anticipation of imminency applied to the second event.

Some people discount the concept of imminency regarding Christ's coming for His church as being important or relevant. They view the long history of the church, sometimes struggling with persecution and at other times growing in influence, over the past almost two thousand years as an argument against looking for an imminent return of Christ. We could argue that since Peter was told by Jesus that he would be led by others against his will in his old age, Peter did not have any expectancy of the imminent return of Christ (Jn 21:18). We could also argue that since important prophetic events have been fulfilled at times later than the birth of the church, during the Church Age, these prophetic events erase the relevance of imminency. Examples of these prophetic events include:

- Jesus prophesied "I will build my church" (Mt 16:18). The process of Jesus building His church would take a period of time.

- The future destruction of the Jewish Temple in Jerusalem which Jesus predicted (Lk 13:35; 21:5-6; Mt 24:2). This was fulfilled in 70 A.D.
- The future persecution of the Jewish Christians by the authorities which Jesus predicted (Lk 21:12-17);
- The future dispersion of the Jewish people from the land into all nations by the Romans which Jesus prophesied (Lk 21:20-24). This process began with the downfall of Jerusalem in 70 A.D. and lasted several decades.
- The prophesied widespread immorality in society and the apostasy within the Christian church that would take place "in the latter times" and in "the last days" which Paul taught Timothy under the influence of the Holy Spirit (1 Tim 4:1; 2 Tim 3:1).
- The return of Israel to the land and to Jerusalem and the rebirth of the nation of Israel in the Promised Land (Ezek 36:24; 37:21; Amos 9:14; Zech 8:8).
- The land of Israel would change from being desolate to becoming fruitful for the returned people (Ezek 34:13; 36:6-12).

It would seem that during the first few decades after the crucifixion of Christ, an imminent view of His return was not very practical. However, while Jesus and the Holy Spirit had much work to do in building the early church and in bringing judgment upon the generation of Jews who rejected Him as God's Messiah, how does that affect the expectation of an imminent rapture of the church today? While prophetic events have taken place during the Church Age and more prophetic events can possibly occur before the rapture, such as a regional war in the Middle East pertaining to Psalm 83, or the destruction of the city of Damascus in Isaiah 17, or the rise of ten prominent kings (Dan 7:24; Rev 17:12), there is no biblical prophetic event that I am aware of that absolutely must be fulfilled before Jesus can return for His church.

Is the rapture of the church imminent? Jesus taught His disciples the importance of keeping watch – being watchful for His return (Mt 24:42-43; 25:13; Mk 13:33-35, 37; Lk 12:38; 21:36; Rev 3:3). While we are to be observant and recognize the general signs of the end of the age: increasing apostasy, hypocrisy, immorality, violence, greed, injustice, self-centeredness (1 Tim 4:1-3; 2 Tim 3:1-5), or even wars, rumors of war, earthquakes, famines, and pestilence around the world (Mt 24:6-7), it is the promised return of Jesus that is our great expectation. The more characteristics of the end-times that we witness the greater our anticipation for an imminent rapture should be.

We all know the common lesson that is applied in many sports, "Keep your eyes on the ball!" An athlete cannot be an effective team player if he does not know where the baseball, tennis ball, volley ball, basketball, football, or soccer ball is on the court or playing field. For Christians, Jesus is the ball. We are to keep our eyes on Him. He is the center of our action. We are to be watchful, looking for Him. It is the return of Jesus that is the next great event for the collective Christian team.

The apostle Paul and other church fathers taught believers to have a character of expectant watchfulness regarding the return of Christ. They warned about the evil characteristics of the Day of the LORD and the coming judgments of God against unbelievers; however, their focus was on the imminent return of Christ and that it could happen at any time. It is not the coming of the Antichrist that is an immediate concern for the watchfulness of the church. The church is looking for the coming of Christ, and the overwhelming emphasis in the New Testament is that it is imminent. This is particularly true for us, from both our historical and prophetic perspectives, as we are already in the latter times and last days of the Church Age. At this point in the history of the church, Jesus can come at any moment.

## The Sudden Coming

The return of Jesus Christ and the Day of the LORD are both strongly characterized as coming suddenly, unexpectedly, and catching the unbelieving world by surprise. Both of these supernatural interventions by God are described as a thief coming in the middle of the night (Mt 24:42-44; 1 Thes 5:2-6; 2 Pet 3:10; Rev 3:3).

**1 Thessalonians 5:2-6**

> For yourselves know perfectly that the day of the LORD so cometh as a thief in the night. For when they shall say, Peace and safety; then sudden destruction cometh upon them, as travail upon a woman with child; and they shall not escape. But ye, brethren, are not in darkness, that that day should overtake you as a thief. Ye are all the children of light, and the children of the day: we are not of the night, nor of darkness. Therefore let us not sleep, as *do* others; but let us watch and be sober.

Not only will the timing of the rapture catch the church and the world by surprise, it will catch Satan by surprise. The timing of the rapture has not been explicitly revealed in scripture. Therefore, Satan does not know the timing of the rapture.

During His prophetic Olivet Discourse, Jesus emphasized the point that no one knows the timing of a specific day or hour. Matthew renders this teaching:

> Mt 24:29 Immediately after the tribulation of those days ….
> Mt 24:34 Verily I say unto you, This generation shall not pass, till all these things be fulfilled.
> Mt 24:36 But of that day and hour knoweth no *man*, no, not the angels of heaven, but my Father only. [Mark's version: But of that day and *that* hour knoweth no man, no, not the angels which are in heaven, neither the Son, but the Father (Mk 13:32)].
> Mt 24:42 Watch therefore: for ye know not what hour your Lord doth come.
> Mt 24:44 Therefore be ye also ready: for in such an hour as ye think not the Son of man cometh.

What day and hour is Jesus referring to? Jesus ties this day and hour to the time of His coming, and yet His coming at the time of Armageddon at the end of the Tribulation will hardly be a surprise. Jesus is not referring to the events of a single twenty-four hour day. In the context of the day, He is referring to the entirety of the days of the end-time tribulation, which is the prophetic "Day of the LORD" (1 Thes 5:2). In the context of the hour, He is referring to the exact same period of time as He used it in Revelation 3:10: "the hour of temptation, which shall come upon all the world, to try them that dwell upon the earth." The hour and the day both represent the Day of the LORD, and it is the beginning of this particular period of time that comes as a surprise.

## Tribulation and Wrath

Is the church told that it will undergo the period known as the Tribulation or Great Tribulation? Will the church face the wrath of God that is promised to the nations of the world? Some people argue that the concept of the rapture is unjustified escapism and that the Bible teaches tribulation for the church. Since the church has experienced tribulation in the historical past with much persecution and martyrdom, why should the future Tribulation be any different? Passages such as John 16:1-2, 33; Acts 14:22; and Romans 12:12 are used to support the idea that the church must go through the time of the Tribulation. However, these and other passages speak of tribulation as a normal, everyday occurrence that a believer faces in his faithful walk with Christ. They are not referring to the specific time of Tribulation referred to as "the time of Jacob's trouble" (Jer 30:7), or great tribulation (Mt 24:21; Rev 7:14), or to the hour of temptation or testing that will come upon the entire world (Rev 3:10), or to the time of God's wrath (Rev 6:17; 14:10, 19; 15:1,7; 16:1,19; 19:15). Instead, passages such as Lk 21:36; Jn 3:36; Rom 5:9; 1 Thes 1:10; 1 Thes 5:9-10; and Rev 3:10 clearly teach that believers are not destined to endure the wrath of God, but will be protected from it by being kept out of it entirely.

**Luke 21:36** Watch ye therefore, and pray always, that ye may be accounted worthy to escape all these things that shall come to pass, and to stand before the Son of man.
**1 Thessalonians 1:10** And to wait for his Son from heaven, whom he raised from the dead, *even* Jesus, which delivered us from the wrath to come.
**1 Thessalonians 5:9-10** For God hath not appointed us to wrath, but to obtain salvation by our Lord Jesus Christ, Who died for us, that, whether we wake or sleep, we should live together with him.
**Revelation 3:10** Because thou hast kept the word of my patience, I also will keep thee from the hour of temptation, which shall come upon all the world, to try them that dwell upon the earth.

There is a strong focus on the persecution and martyrdom of saints during the Tribulation (Rev 6:9-11; 12:17; 13:7, 15; 14:13; 15:2; 16:6; 17:6; 18:24; 20:4). It is difficult to equate this mass martyrdom of believers with their supposedly being supernaturally protected by God during this time of Tribulation. The church has multiple promises from God that it will be delivered and kept from wrath. How is it that the church would then be supernaturally delivered into the hands of the Antichrist during the Tribulation?

The Antichrist will be supernaturally empowered for a period of 3 ½ years (Rev 13:5). "And it was given unto him to make war with the saints, and to overcome them: and power was given him over all kindreds, and tongues, and nations" (Rev 13:7). How can this apply to the church? While this does apply to believers during the time of the Tribulation, it cannot apply to the church. The only way that these promises from God to the church can be reconciled with the large scale martyrdom of believers during the Day of the LORD is for the church to be raptured before these tribulational events take place.

## The Church vs. Israel

Another relevant issue regarding the concept of and the timing of the rapture regards the extent of distinction that scripturally exists between the church and Israel. Some believe that when the leadership of Israel rejected Jesus as Israel's Messiah, Israel as a nation lost the covenant promises that God made to Israel. They teach that the church has replaced Israel in God's plan and now has sole access to the promises that were once Israel's. In their view the only Jews who are or will be saved do so by becoming part of the New Testament Church. This perspective is referred to as Replacement Theology or Supercessionism.

The advocates of Replacement Theology do not make any distinction between Israel and the church in the interpretation of end-time prophetic passages. They insert the church everyplace where Israel, saints, or the elect appear in prophecy without regard to the specific circumstances or the overall context of the prophetic passage. This approach is extremely problematic.

With the exception of the Mosaic Covenant, which was full of conditions and was completely fulfilled by Jesus Christ, the promises that God made to the nation of Israel are incorporated within unconditional covenants. The Abrahamic, Davidic, Palestinian, and New covenants are all unconditional promises that rely on God to fulfill rather than Israel. These covenant promises include Israel's everlasting national identity, Israel's future redemption, Israel's position of rulership during the Messianic Kingdom from the throne of David, as well as Israel's future inheritance of the Promised Land. Theses promises will be fulfilled by God in spite of Israel and its national failure. One of the primary reasons that God initiates His Day of the LORD judgments and wrath upon the earth is to refine the nation of Israel through fire during the time of Jacob's trouble (Jer 30:7), to bring Israel into its promised redemption. This is a matter of God's integrity and God's grace within the context of God magnifying His holy name. God will completely fulfill every unconditional promise He made to Israel because God is God – the God of Israel.

The mysterious creation of the New Testament Church has nothing to do with the fulfillment of these promises by God to Israel. The church does not and cannot prevent Israel from receiving these promises. The church is a mystery phase of God's overall plan for the salvation of mankind. Jews and Gentiles are drawn into the church through faith in Jesus as Christ by the grace of God during this phase. But this is an individual by individual process. It has nothing to do with national salvation – for any Gentile nation or for Israel. Israel is the only nation that is promised redemption and salvation at the national level (Is 59:20-21; Jer 31:31-37; 32:39-40; 50:4-5;

Ezek 11:19; 16:59-62; 34:25, 30; 36:25-27; 37:26; Rom 11:26; Heb 8:8-13). Israel is the firstborn son of God among the nations (Ex 4:22).

The church is Abraham's spiritual heir by faith. It is not an heir of Jacob (Israel) or any one of the specific tribes of Israel such as Judah or Levi. When prophetic passages refer to the promises of God to the descendants of Jacob, or to one or more of the specific tribes of Israel, there is no possibility that reference is being made to the New Testament Church.

In addition, Jesus proclaimed to Jerusalem (Israel) that it would not see Him until they are ready to say "Blessed *is* he that cometh in the name of the Lord" (Lk 13:34-35; cf. Ps 118:24-26; Zech 12:10-14). Jesus was looking far into the future to the time when Israel will finally be ready to repent and to call upon Him to come as God's promised Messiah. But Jesus will not come again as Israel's Messiah until Israel is ready to repent and receive Him as a nation. This has nothing to do with the church. In fact, the church has no control over the timing of Jesus' second coming in Revelation 19, or the timing of the beginning of the Millennial Kingdom. The Millennial Kingdom cannot begin until Israel is redeemed as a nation. The timing is completely dependent upon the nation of Israel and its response to God in national repentance.

The church has not replaced Israel on God's global prophetic stage. The church and Israel must be kept distinct. This distinction makes both the event of the rapture and the timing of the rapture highly significant. There are prophetic consequences that impact our understanding of the character and events of the Tribulation as a result of the rapture of the church.

## The Issue of a Partial Rapture

Some Christians do not believe that all believers will be caught up to heaven at the time of the rapture. It has been noted that the church is repeatedly commanded to watch and be ready for Christ's return for His church (Mt 24:42-44; 25:13; Mk 13:33-37; Lk 12:40; 21:36; 1 Cor 16:13; 1 Thes 5:6; Heb 9:28; 1 Pet 4:7; Rev 3:2-3; 19:7). Jesus placed a strong emphasis on watchfulness in His teachings. Some believers have proposed that only those believers who believe in the rapture and are watching for the rapture will be taken to heaven at the time of the rapture event, and other unwatchful, unready, or undeserving believers will be left behind to go through the Tribulation. This concept of a rapture that only takes those who are actively watching and ready for Christ's return for the church is referred to as a partial rapture.

It is true that many people will be left on earth at the time of the rapture. Those left behind will include:

- All people who deny Jesus Christ was a real person.
- All people who willingly and openly reject Jesus as the Christ, or the Messiah sent by God.
- All people who refuse to accept Jesus as the Son of God or God manifest in the flesh even though they believe in Jesus as a righteous teacher or some other historical person.
- All who have just not made the choice to believe in Jesus as their savior, including those who claim to be Christians, but who have not really trusted in Jesus.

But what about those people who do believe and have accepted Jesus into their hearts as their savior, yet otherwise are not ready or looking for His return? Is there truth to the concept of a partial rapture? Is it possible that people who truly have faith in Jesus Christ as the Son of God for salvation, but who do not believe in the concept of the rapture as the catching up of the church to heaven in a single event, or who are not looking expectantly for Christ's coming, can be left on earth when the rest of the believing church is caught up to meet Jesus in the air? Is it possible for saved Christians who believe in a posttribulational rapture to be left on earth at the time of a pretribulational, midtribulational, or pre-wrath rapture because they are not watchful at the right time?

We should note that while there is a strong emphasis on being watchful during the long absence of Jesus from the earth, there is no specific scripture which plainly states that only some of the church members will be caught up at the time of the rapture. The scriptural passages which deal specifically with the resurrection, bodily change, and catching up aspects of the rapture make no reference or illusion to a partial rapture. In fact, the exact opposite of a partial rapture is characterized. The event is portrayed as being inclusive of believers.

**1 Thessalonians 4:14-18**

1 Thes 4:14 "For if we believe that Jesus died and rose again, even so them also which sleep in Jesus will God bring with him." This clearly refers to the souls of dead believers which Jesus will bring back from heaven to be reunited with the resurrected bodies of those believers. Paul does not make any reference to "some" of those souls. Paul says Jesus will bring "them," meaning all of them.

1 Thes 4:16 "…the dead in Christ shall rise first" – not some of the dead, all of the dead who are in Christ.

1 Thes 4:17a "Then we which are alive *and* remain shall be caught up together with them in the clouds" – not some but all of those who are alive in Christ at the time of the event will be caught up along with the resurrected dead whose souls Christ brought with Him from heaven.

1 Thes 4:17b-18 "to meet the Lord in the air: and so shall we ever be with the Lord. Wherefore comfort one another with these words." – Paul emphatically states that "we" shall be with the Lord. The "we" is not exclusive of some, but inclusive of all who are in Christ. There is no expression of regret for the fate of any believers missing in action because there are no believers left behind. In fact, to emphasize the character of the event, Paul goes on to express the deep encouragement and hope this event holds for believers with his proclamation "comfort one another." This is not simply Paul telling the believers in Thessalonica to be comforted, but he is encouraging them to actually comfort each other as well as other believers with the powerful impact of his teaching.

**1 Corinthians 15:51-52**

1 Cor 15:51 "Behold, I show you a mystery; We shall not all sleep, but we shall all be changed," – Paul plainly states that "all" will be changed. While many Christians will have died, all believers who are not dead will be changed and caught up to meet Christ in the air.

1 Cor 15:52 "In a moment, in the twinkling of an eye, at the last trump: for the trumpet shall sound, and the dead shall be raised incorruptible. And we shall be changed." – Again, Paul plainly states that the dead, not some of the dead, shall be resurrected, and we, not some of us, shall be changed.

**1 Corinthians 15:54b-55**

1 Cor 15:54b "Death is swallowed up in victory." – Paul makes a blanket statement. He is not applying this to only some of the church.

1 Cor 15:55 "O Death, where *is* thy sting? O grave, where *is* thy victory?" – Could Paul really make this exclamation of triumph if some of his fellow believers and converts were being left behind?

**1 Corinthians 15:57**

1 Cor 15:57 "But thanks *be* to God, which giveth us the victory through our Lord Jesus Christ." – Paul is being thankful to God and proclaiming the thankfulness of all believers for this glorious truth. This great victory is being proclaimed because it applies to all believers. It does not just apply to a few, or a portion of the church.

All dead in Christ will be resurrected, and all living in Christ will be changed, and all believers will be caught up. No one will be resurrected or changed into immortal bodies and then left on earth. There is no focus on anyone being passed over and not resurrected or changed because they are not watchful or ready.

So, why is there an emphasis for the church to be watchful and ready for the appearance of Christ? The lack of watchfulness and readiness increases the risk and extent of complacency and apostasy which is predicted to influence the church towards the end (2 Thes 2:3; Rev 3:14-20). In addition, church believers are warned to be ready so that they are not ashamed at the time of Christ's appearing (1 Jn 2:28). This is a reference to the process of standing before the judgment seat of Christ for the purpose of being evaluated for rewards (Rom 14:10; 2 Cor 5:10).

This characterization of the judgment seat of Christ also points to a complete rapture of the church as opposed to a partial rapture. Different rewards (such as crowns) are promised for different types of accomplishments or perseverance as believing Christians. The inference is that not all believers will be awarded all of the possible crowns, and some believers may not be awarded any crowns (1 Cor 3:10-15; 9:25; 1 Thes 2:19; 2 Tim 4:8; Jas 1:12; 1 Pet 5:4; Rev 2:10; 3:11).

A crown is promised as a reward to those who long for and look forward to the coming of Jesus for His church, and thus look forward to the promise of the rapture. "Henceforth there is laid up for me a crown of righteousness, which the Lord, the righteous judge, shall give me at that day: and not to me only, but unto all them also that love his appearing" (2 Tim 4:8). In this teaching Paul is finally drawing a distinction within the ranks of believers. He leaves us with the strong implication that there will be some Christians who will not receive this crown. If some believers can come away from the judgment seat of Christ tried through fire with their works as believers burned up, yet saved with eternal life, then not all believers will receive this crown of righteousness for loving the appearing of the Lord (1 Cor 3:10-15). This condition substantiates the argument that not all of the Christians who are caught up at the time of the rapture will have been watchful, or ready, or even looking for the appearance of Jesus at all.

The rapture event distinguishes between believers and nonbelievers based upon faith, not between types or degrees of people's works. The judgment seat of Christ distinguishes between types and degrees of works that result from a person's salvation by faith. Thus, it follows that believers in Christ who reject the concept of the rapture, or who believe in a later timing of the rapture, or who are not looking for a literal second coming of Jesus to earth will be caught up to heaven in the rapture just the same.

What is God's measure of a believer? It is the indwelling of the Holy Spirit. When a person truly opens his heart to accept Christ as his savior, he is born again by the power of the Holy Spirit, and the Holy Spirit comes to dwell within the new believer. This is what is referred to as the New Birth.

A Christian believer is supernaturally indwelt by the Holy Spirit. This indwelling is automatically received the moment a person comes to Christ in faith. Following this indwelling of the Holy Spirit, a Christian is called by God to walk in fellowship with Christ and grow in the power of the Spirit. When a Christian does so, he is filled by the Holy Spirit and is said to be (Spirit-filled or in-filled). However, most Christians (if not all) will not always be walking in the power of the Spirit.

Unfortunately, when Christians walk contrary to Christ, and fall out of fellowship with God, they can grieve or quench the Holy Spirit (Eph 4:30; 1 Thes 5:19). Fortunately, this grieving or quenching of the Spirit does not result in the removal of the Spirit from the believer. The Christian retains his new birth and remains indwelt by the Spirit, while losing the infilling power of the Holy Spirit.

Every person who is indwelt by the power of the Holy Spirit will be caught up to heaven at the time of the rapture. No person who has been supernaturally baptized and indwelt by the Holy Spirit will be abandoned by the Spirit or left behind at the rapture.

It is like the natural power of magnetism. A strong magnet can quickly and accurately distinguish and separate different materials. A magnet can separate metal from wood or plastic based upon the internal composition of the metal and the affinity that the magnet has for the metal. It is the same with Christian believers. God can quickly distinguish and separate people based upon their internal composition of possessing or not possessing the Holy Spirit. When the time comes for the rapture, God's supernatural magnet will instantly attract all of those who are naturally drawn to Him by the indwelling power of His Holy Spirit.

Every believer is part of something much larger than himself, or herself. Every person who has accepted Christ by faith and been baptized by the Holy Spirit has entered a supernatural collective body of believers which has a unique spiritual relationship to God. This body has been referred to by several different names or descriptive titles, including: The Body of Christ, the Church (of God), One New Man, the House of God, and the Temple of God. Christians are members of the body of Christ (Rom 12:5; 1Cor 12:12, 27; Eph 1:22-23; 2:16; 3:6; 4:12; 5:23, 30; Col 1:18, 24), the Church (of God) (Mt 16:18; 1 Cor 1:2; 10:32; Eph 5:23; Col 1:18, 24; 1 Tim 3:5, 15), One New Man (Eph 2:15), , the House of God (1 Tim 3:15), and the Temple of God (1 Cor 3:16-17; 6:19; 2 Cor 6:16).

Paul has revealed that the rapture event will be initiated by the shout of Christ, the voice of the archangel, and the blowing of the trumpet of God (1 Thes 4:16). When Christ comes for His believers, He will come to claim His

Body, which is His Church, which is the Temple of God on earth during this Age of Grace. Do we visualize Jesus shouting out the individual names of all believers, dead and alive, to awaken them to His coming? I think not. More likely, Christ will give one great shouted collective command to all of His people. Christ could simply command, "Arise, My Body!" or "Come up here, My Church!" or "Christians, to Me!" Or Christ could simply call the Holy Spirit to Him. We are identified with Christ both individually and collectively. It is the collective call that we await. We will all go at one time.

Every person who has ever accepted Christ by faith and been baptized by the Holy Spirit into the body of Christ will be resurrected or changed and caught up at the time of the rapture. Every person who has outwardly professed belief, but has not inwardly accepted Christ by faith, will be left behind. This is not a partial rapture because these people were never indwelt by the Holy Spirit, nor were they baptized by the Holy Spirit into the supernatural body of Christ.

When Christ comes to claim His own – He will claim all of those who are His. No one who is "in Christ" will be left behind. There is no such thing as a partial rapture.

## The Symbolism of the Jewish Wedding

Several times in the Bible teachings regarding the church are presented in terms of the Jewish wedding customs with the church characterized as the bride of Christ. Several steps were involved in the Jewish wedding and they took place over a period of time:

1. A covenant or marriage contract was made.
2. The "bride price" was paid by the bridegroom (symbolizing the willingness of the bridegroom to make a sacrifice for his bride).
3. The bridegroom would return to his father's house to prepare a place (bridal chamber) for his bride.
4. When the bridegroom's father was satisfied with the preparations, often after a period of some time lasting up to a year, he would release his son to go claim his bride.
5. The bride, during this long period of waiting, was expected to be true to her future husband and to keep herself and her oil lamp ready for the sudden and unannounced arrival of the bridegroom, frequently during the middle of the night.
6. The bride's bridesmaids would also prepare for the approaching event and keep their oil lamps ready.
7. The Groom would approach the bride's house, often late at night, and would shout to give her warning that he was arriving to take her

to his father's house. The physical act of the groom of fetching the bride from her father's house and taking her to his father's house was a dynamic element of the marriage ceremony.

8. At the groom's father's house the bride and groom entered their "honeymoon" chamber where they remained secluded for a period of seven days. Afterwards they emerged to meet the assembled friends of the groom and the groom's father to celebrate the wedding reception which is specifically referred to as the marriage supper.

The church is the betrothed bride of Christ:

1. Under the "new covenant" promised in Jeremiah 31:31 where God's law is written in our hearts.
2. The "pure virgin" espoused to Christ (2 Cor 11:2; Eph 5:25-32).
3. For which Jesus willingly paid the bride price with His blood and His life on the cross (Eph 5:25-27).
4. For whom Jesus ascended to heaven to prepare a place in His father's house (Jn 14:1-3).
5. Waiting for Jesus while He sits at the right hand of God the father in heaven waiting for His enemies to be made His footstool (Ps 110; Heb 1:13; 10:13).
6. Waiting for Christ to return to claim her at any moment (1 Cor 1:7-8; 1 Thes 5:1-11; 2 Thes 3:5).
7. Expecting that heavenly shout from Christ accompanied by the voice of the archangel and the trumpet of God (1 Thes 4:16-17).
8. Looking for that "blessed hope and the glorious appearing of our Savior Jesus Christ" (Tit 2:13), "and so shall we ever be with the Lord" (1 Thes 4:17).
9. "Let us be glad and rejoice, and give honour to him: for the marriage of the Lamb is come, and his wife hath made herself ready" (Rev 19:7).
10. The future abode of the church as the "wife" of Christ will be in New Jerusalem (Rev 21:2, 9).

Sometimes Jesus used the wedding and the marriage supper (the feast which followed after the wedding ceremony) to characterize the distinction between the bride and the friends of the bridegroom. John the Baptist made this distinction between himself and Jesus with Jesus being the bridegroom who has a bride and John being a friend of the bridegroom (Jn 3:29). Luke 12:35-37 also makes the distinction that Christ will come from the wedding to a group (Israel) who are commanded to keep their lights burning and to open up to him immediately, and then He will sit them down to serve them meat (the marriage supper).

This emphasizes a distinction between the church and Israel as they relate to Christ in the concept of the Jewish wedding. The church is the virgin bride of Christ, dressed in white robes of righteousness (Rev 19:7-8), while Israel is the adulterous wife of God, who God divorced but will later reclaim and restore to her former position (Deut 7:6-11; Isa 54:1-8; 62:4-5; Jer 3:6-10, 20; 31:31-34; Ezek 16:35-43, 60-63; Hosea). It is possible that this second group is referred to in Revelation 19:9 as being “Blessed are they which are called to the marriage supper of the Lamb.”

## Major Rapture Views

With these issues and observations in mind we will consider the several major positions that have been put forth regarding the rapture. Since the postmillennial and amillennial camps do not generally include a rapture event in their theological perspectives, the rapture is an issue primarily focused on and grappled with by premillennialists. The concept of the rapture is very prominent within the premillennial perspective; however, there is not a uniform understanding by all premillennialists of when the rapture will take place.

Several major views are taught based upon the timing of the rapture in relation to the end-time period known as the Tribulation. These views differentiate between whether the rapture event takes place: before the Tribulation begins (pre-trib), during the Tribulation (mid-trib and pre-wrath), or immediately following the Tribulation (post-trib), or even whether the rapture occurs at all. These different perspectives for the timing of the rapture are largely influenced by how literally the scripture passages are interpreted as well as how the other issues that have been previously mentioned are approached. It is important to have a good foundational understanding of the rapture event. A person’s view regarding the rapture will have a serious influence towards his further understanding or misunderstanding of the sequence of events and God’s purposes within the bigger picture of the prophetic puzzle.

For the purpose of these arguments, the Tribulation is generally taken to be the last seven years (Daniel’s 70th Week) immediately preceding Christ’s second coming and His bringing in the Millennial Kingdom. This period specifically begins with the signing of a seven year covenant between Israel and the Antichrist (Dan 9:27). Nowhere does scripture indicate that the rapture is the specific event that begins the Tribulation.

## The Pretribulational Rapture View

The "pre-trib" perspective believes that the church will be removed from the earth to heaven sometime prior to the beginning of the Tribulation. Thus, the church will be absent from the earth during the entire time of the Tribulation, during which God's judgments are imposed upon a rebellious earth. While the church is in heaven as the "bride of Christ" it will experience the judgment seat of Christ and the wedding ceremony. The "pre-trib" perspective sees the rapture as the very next event in the sequence of prophetic events as they apply to the church. There is no prophetic event that must take place before the removal of the church from the earth. Thus, the event of the rapture can be seen as being imminent. There is no conflict between the church and Israel, as the church is removed from the earthly scene before God turns His focus to refining Israel during the time of Jacob's trouble.

Many students of prophecy interpret Daniel 12:11-12 as describing a separate 30 day period in verse eleven and another forty-five day period in verse twelve which are not included within the seven years of Daniel's 70th Week. These two periods are immediately added back to back as a period of seventy-five days sandwiched between the end of the Tribulation and the beginning of the Millennial Kingdom. For the sake of simplicity, these days are not depicted in the diagrams which accompany each of the major rapture views.

Pre-Trib View: Church Age → Rapture → Interim Period → Seven years of Tribulation → Christ's 2nd Coming

### Pretribulational Rapture

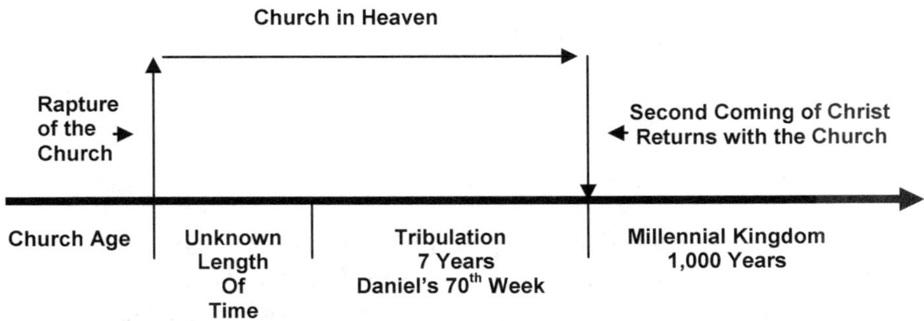

## The Midtribulational Rapture View

The "mid-trib" view places the rapture about half way through the seven year Tribulation. Thus, in the "mid-trib" perspective, the church is present on earth during the judgments of the seven seals and the first six trumpet judgments which are described in the book of Revelation. Since the church is promised to not experience the wrath of God, mid-tribbers claim that the wrath of God does not begin until the seventh trumpet judgment. Some proponents associate the rapture of the church with the resurrection and catching up to heaven of the two witnesses in Revelation 11. Others see the rapture in conjunction with the description of the 144,000 assembled on Mt. Zion in Revelation 14. The "mid-trib" perspective requires the fulfillment of prophetic events before the rapture, and thus there is no imminence for the church in looking forward to the rapture.

Mid-Trib View: Church Age → 3 ½ years Tribulation → Rapture → 3 ½ years Tribulation → Christ's 2nd Coming

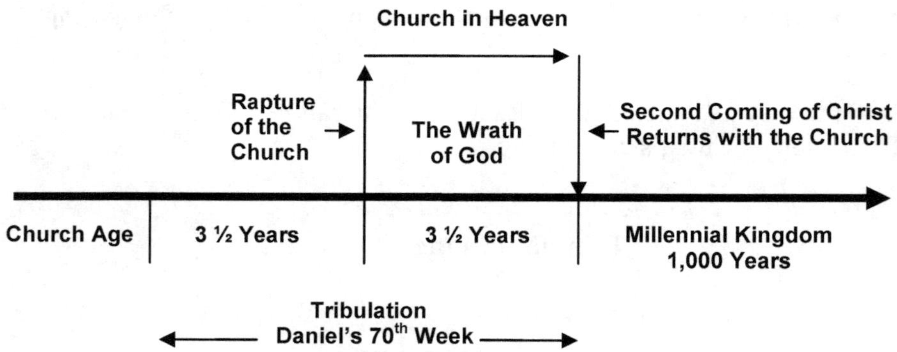


## The Pre-Wrath Rapture View

The "pre-wrath" advocates, Marvin Rosenthal and Robert Van Kampen, argue that the rapture takes place shortly before God's wrath begins to be unleashed upon the earth during the Tribulation. Thus, they identify their rapture position as prewrath. They conclude that the wrath of God begins with the seventh seal (Rev 8:1). Thus, the rapture takes place between the breaking of the sixth and seventh seals. However, they extend the first six seals into the middle of the second half of the Tribulation before the seventh seal is broken, initiating the Day of the LORD and the wrath of God.

In addition, from the perspective of the "pre-wrath" advocates, the opening of the seven seals on the heavenly scroll by Christ is broken into three divisions, each of which is characterized by a different form of wrath. The first four seals are broken during the first 3 ½ years of Daniel's 70$^{th}$ Week which they see as reflecting man's wrath. The fifth and sixth seals are then broken during the first portion of the second 3 ½ years of Daniel's 70$^{th}$ Week and mark the time of the Great Tribulation, which is characterized by Satan's wrath on earth. The seventh seal is finally broken near the middle of the second half of Daniel's 70$^{th}$ Week, unleashing God's wrath. Van Kampen states that "the Rapture will not occur until *after* the tribulation, at the point when the great tribulation of Antichrist is cut short sometime during the second half of the last "week" of Daniel."[1]

"The essence of the prewrath position is that Christ will rapture His church *immediately after* He cuts short the great tribulation by Antichrist and *immediately before* He unleashes His day-of-the-Lord judgment on the ungodly world."[2] Thus, in their view, the rapture takes place shortly before the breaking of the seventh seal which simultaneously initiates the prophetic Day of the LORD and the wrath of God. The time period of the Day of the LORD – Wrath of God is then argued to continue through the remainder of the second half of the Tribulation, plus an additional thirty days during which the seven bowl judgments are poured out upon the earth.

The effect of the "pre-wrath" position places the rapture event in the middle of the second half of the Tribulation. As with the midtribulational view, this timing places the rapture after a number of significant prophetic events and as a result it violates the concept of imminence regarding the sudden and unexpected timing of Christ's return for His body of believers. In addition, both of the mid-trib and pre-wrath views are dependent upon the denial of any of the first six seal judgments in Revelation 6 being considered the "wrath" of God. Van Kampen claims that, "after the sixth seal is broken we are told that 'the wrath of the Lamb [Christ]' is about to commence (Rev. 6:15-17)."[3] However, Revelation 6:17 clearly states, "For the great day of his wrath is come; and who shall be able to stand?" The events of the sixth seal clearly depict that the wrath of God has already begun, not that it is going to come shortly in the future. Most importantly, the people on earth are now aware that that God and Christ are intervening in wrath. They say "hide us from the wrath of the Lamb" because it is already falling upon them. It has been directed against them since Christ began opening the seals, but now they understand to some extent that they are facing judgment and wrath and who the judgment and wrath are coming from.

This issue regarding the timing of God's wrath in relation to the rapture is important. Many pre-trib rapture advocates argue that the wrath of God begins with the breaking of the first seal. They, along with myself, see God's wrath as clearly being evident in the content and context of all the seal judgments. With the fourth seal judgment God gives Death and Hades authority to destroy one-fourth of the earth by war, famine, pestilence, and wild beasts. Destruction on this scale is clearly wrath. The description of the sixth seal specifically mentions wrath in the context of God in two verses Revelation 6:16 and 6:17. In this passage, all of the people on earth are described as desiring to be hidden from the face of God and from the wrath of Jesus Christ (the Lamb) because they recognize that the great day of God's wrath has already come.

Pre-Wrath View: Church Age → 5 +/- years Tribulation (1st Six Seals) → Rapture → Day of the LORD → Christ's 2nd Coming

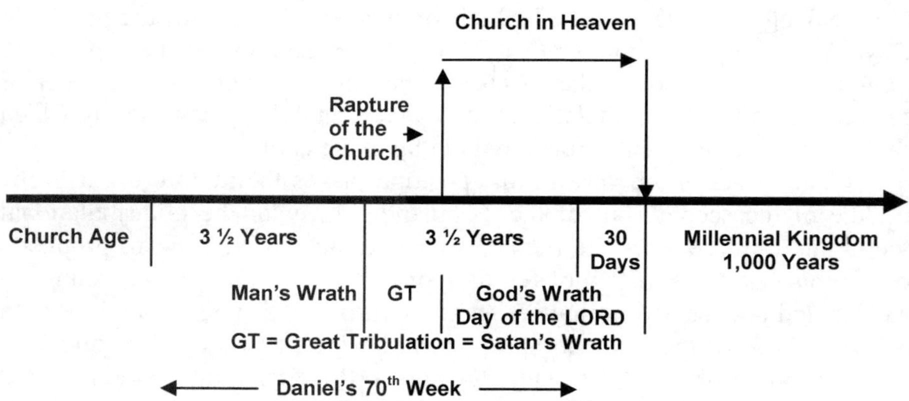


## The Posttribulational Rapture View

The "post-trib" scenario teaches that the church will not be raptured until the conclusion of the Tribulation. Thus, the church will experience and endure, but be saved through all of God's judgments and wrath that are directed at the earth during the final seven years. This view claims that the rapture and the second coming of Christ are immediate phases of the same event. In effect, the church would be resurrected and caught up to meet with the returning Christ in the air, only to immediately return to earth to fight the final battle of Armageddon.

From the post-trib perspective there is no unexpected suddenness or any concept of imminence regarding Christ's coming for the church. All of the events of the Tribulation must precede the rapture. The rapture is not a separate event but merely an afterthought or byproduct of Christ's second coming. This view fails to keep the distinct identities and roles of the church and Israel separate throughout the Tribulation. Also, there is an inherent conflict with the post-trib concept of the church being protected but enduring throughout the entire Tribulation versus the explicit statement of Revelation 13:7 that power is given to the Antichrist "to make war with the saints, and to overcome them." How are church saints protected by being persecuted, martyred, and overcome by the Antichrist? Under this view most of the church saints would be martyred for their faith and very few saints would be left to be raptured at the end of the Tribulation.

Post-Trib View: Church Age → 7 years of Tribulation → Rapture & Christ's 2nd Coming

**Posttribulational Rapture**

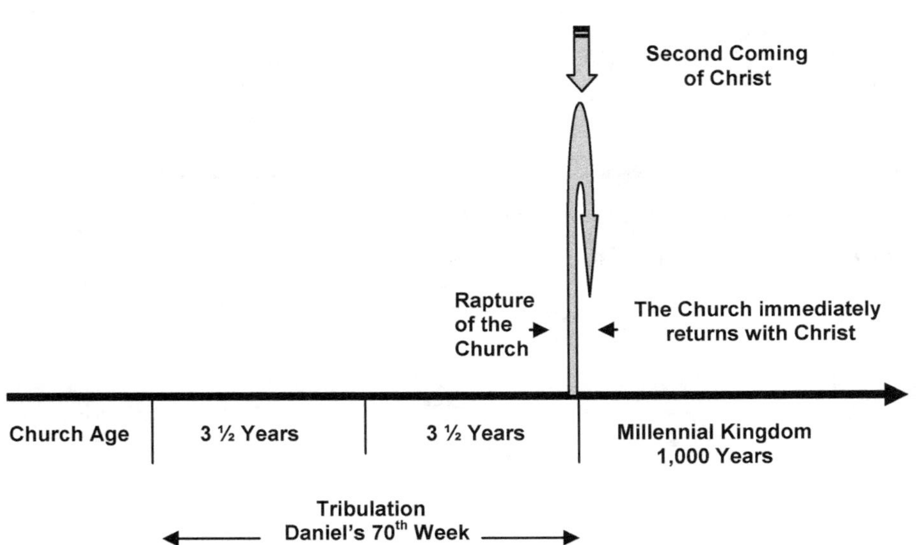

## The No Rapture View

The specific event known as the rapture of the church is not part of the inherent belief structure of either postmillennialism or amillennialism. According to these perspectives the second coming of Christ will follow the long Millennial Kingdom (not limited to 1,000 years) of the Church Age of Amillennialism, or follow the Golden Age phase of the Church Age of Postmillennialism. For those Amillennialists who do allow for a rapture of believers, it takes place in immediate conjunction with the second coming of Christ at the end of the Millennial Kingdom. Christ's second coming then results in a general resurrection of the dead and all people, believers and unbelievers, will face a final judgment and then enter into eternity in their respective places.

No Rapture View: Church Age (Millennial Kingdom / Golden Age) → Christ's 2nd Coming → General Resurrection & Judgment → Eternity

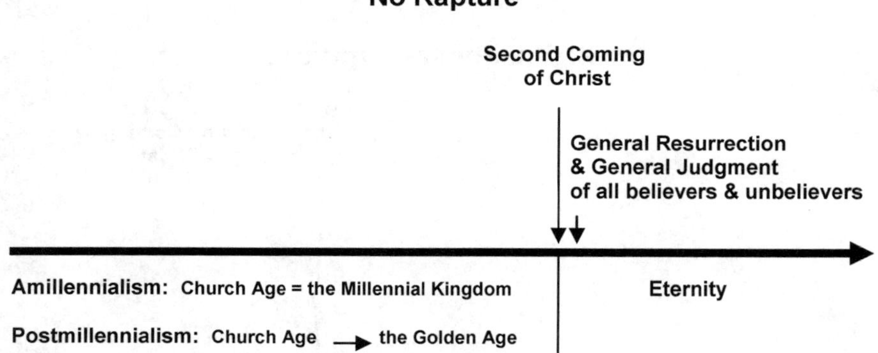

**A Comparison of Rapture Views**

| Rapture View | Sequence of Events |
|---|---|
| Pretribulational | Church Age → **Rapture** → Interim → 7 year Tribulation → 2nd Coming → Millennium |
| Midtribulational | Church Age → 3 ½ year Trib → **Rapture** → 3 ½ year Trib → 2nd Coming |
| Pre-wrath | Church Age → 5 +/- years Tribulation (1st Six Seals) → **Rapture** → Day of the LORD → 2nd Coming → Millennium |
| Posttribulational | Church Age → 7 years Tribulation → **Rapture** & 2nd Coming → Millennium |
| No Rapture | Church Age (Millennial Kingdom / Golden Age) → 2nd Coming → General Resurrection & Judgment → Eternity |

# The Rapture Timing Problem

Some Christians reject the pretribulational timing for the rapture because they cannot find a single clear statement in scripture that the rapture of the church is going to precede the Tribulation. Some believe that the faithful church is going to be kept through the terrible time of the Tribulation instead of being kept from it as insinuated in the message to the church in Philadelphia in Revelation 3:10. Some believe the concept of the rapture is merely unsubstantiated escapism and that the rapture is not sound teaching.

What is the scriptural basis for believing in the rapture of the church? What is the scriptural basis for the pretribulational timing of the rapture?

## Why the Rapture?

The rapture is a dynamic event that takes place when the dead in Christ will be resurrected and the living believers will be instantly changed into immortal bodies and all will be caught up to meet Jesus in the air. Why is there going to be a rapture event for the church? Why would God plant the promises of the church being caught up into the air within His scripture of the New Testament? What purpose does the rapture of the church serve God?

If the church is destined to go through the time of the Tribulation on earth, and be protected through it (as some believe), what purpose would the rapture serve? If God intends to supernaturally protect the church on earth through all of the terrible judgments and forms of wrath (man's wrath,

Satan's wrath, and especially God's wrath), why are there so many saints martyred during this same time? If God can protect the church through these preceding events, why would God not leave the church on earth and protect the church through the final wrath at the time of Christ's second coming?

If the church is to be on earth awaiting Christ at the time of Armageddon, then when and where would the church stand before the judgment seat of Christ? When and where would the marriage of the church to Jesus take place?

If God's purpose is for the church to endure the Tribulation and the Antichrist on earth, where are the passages of scripture which teach the church how to prepare for the Antichrist and to survive this ordeal? Would the church not know when to expect Christ's return if it is on earth at the time of Armageddon? Where is the scriptural passage depicting the church joyously welcoming Christ at the time of His second coming at the end of the Tribulation? Where in scripture is the church gathering in expectation of the long delayed fulfillment of its "blessed hope" – the long awaited return of Jesus? There is no such passage! Instead, prophetic scripture focuses on the second coming of Christ to the earth as a time of mourning (Zech 12:10-12; Mt 24:30; Rev 1:7). That is not characteristic of the church!

God has given the church the promise of the rapture as an imminent and sudden event that will come at a time that the church cannot know exactly in advance. The church will not have time to gather as a welcoming committee. One minute the church is on earth living life as usual. The next minute, in the twinkling of an eye, before it even knows it, the church will be caught up in the air in the presence of Jesus.

The rapture is a real event. It does serve a purpose, for both God and the church. From the pretribulational perspective, the purpose of the rapture is to fulfill the symbolism of the Jewish wedding – to unite the church to Jesus as His wife. The church, as the bride of Christ, must be taken to the Father's house in heaven where it will be joined to Jesus in marriage. Before the wedding ceremony the church must be completely purified. This will be accomplished by standing before Jesus at the judgment seat of Christ. White robes will be given to the bride to wear. The judgment seat and the marriage must take place in heaven. These events also must take place prior to the second coming of Christ at the time of Armageddon. Then the church, as the wife of Jesus, will return to earth with Christ at the time of His second coming.

## Observations

Passages of scripture regarding the church which have potential importance on the timing of the rapture include: (Jn 14:1-3; Rom 5:9; 1 Cor

15:51-55; Php 3:20-21; Col 3:4; 1 Thes 1:10; 2:19; 3:13; 4:13-18; 5:9-10; Tit 2:13; 2 Pet 2:9; 1 Jn 2:28; 3:2-3; Rev 3:10; 6:9-11; 7:9-17; 17:14; 19:1, 7-8, 14; 20:4-6). From these and other passages we can make a number of observations:

1. The church is the temple of God on earth during the Age of Grace (1 Cor 3:16-17; 6:19; 2 Cor 6:16).
2. The Age of Grace will end with the rapture of the church.
3. The Day of the LORD and the Tribulation are not part of the Age of Grace.
4. The Holy Spirit of God works within the church as a restraining force.
5. The "man of sin" (the Antichrist) cannot be revealed until God's restraining force is removed (taken out of the way) (2 Thes 2:1-8).
6. Christ can come for His church at any time. There is no prophetic event which must be fulfilled prior to the rapture of the church – the doctrine of imminence (Mt 24:36-42; 1 Thes 5:1-10).
7. The church is not destined for wrath (Lk 21:36; Rom 1:18; 2:5, 8; 5:9; Eph 5:6; Col 3:6; 1 Thes 1:10; 5:9; Rev 3:10).
8. Wrath is characteristic of the entire time of the Day of the LORD and the Tribulation, which includes the seven seal judgments, the seven trumpet judgments, and the seven bowl judgments of the book of Revelation.
9. The book of Revelation never depicts the church as being on the earth during the Tribulation.
10. There will be a series of resurrections which will make up the "first resurrection" (1 Cor 15:21-23; Rev 20:4-6).
11. There will be a series of judgments by Christ of the dead and the living (2 Tim 4:1).
12. Being united with Christ at the rapture is part of the "blessed hope" of the church which begins the Day of Christ (1 Thes 2:19; Tit 2:13; 1 Pet 1:13; 1 John 3:2-3).
13. The teaching of the rapture is to be a comfort to the church – which it would not be if the church is destined to experience and endure the time of the Tribulation (John 14:1; 1 Thes 4:18; 5:11, 14).
14. The church is never warned to prepare for the coming of the Antichrist or to prepare for the time of the Tribulation. Instead, the church is instructed to be watchful and ready for the return of Christ (Mt 24:42; 25:13; Mk 13:33-37; Lk 21:36; 1 Thes 5:6; 1 Pet 4:7; Rev 3:3).
15. Jesus will bring the souls of the dead believers in Christ with Him when He returns for the church (1 Thes 3:13; 4:14).

16. The church will be taken to heaven (Jn 14:1-3; Php 3:20-21; 1 Thes 4:17).
17. The church will stand before the judgment seat of Christ in heaven during the Day of Christ (Rom 14:10; 1 Cor 1:7-8; 4:5; 2 Cor 5:10; 2 Tim 4:8; 1 Pet 1:7).
18. The church is the bride of Christ and will be married to Christ in heaven during the Day of Christ (Jn 3:29; Eph 5:23-27; Rev 19:7-8).
19. The rapture will fulfill the symbolism of the Jewish wedding traditions.
20. The dead in Christ will be resurrected immediately preceding the catching up of the living believers at the time of the rapture (1 Thes 4:16-17).
21. The church will accompany Jesus, as His wife, and as an army from heaven, when He returns to the earth at the time of His second coming to do battle with the Antichrist (Zech 14:5; Col 3:4; Jude 1:14; Rev 17:14; 19:7-8, 14).
22. At the time of Christ's second coming there will be a worldwide harvest of the "elect" and a reaping of the "wicked" which will be accomplished by angels (Mt 13:39-42, 49-50; 24:31; Mk 13:27).
23. There will be a Kingdom of God on earth during the millennial reign of Christ which will be populated by mortal humans (who are not part of the church). There will be births and deaths on earth during the Millennium (Isa 65:20-23; Ezek 47:22).

## Pieces of the Rapture Puzzle

### The Fullness of the Gentiles

God has a master plan with a pre-determined time schedule. In His wisdom He supernaturally intervenes in the affairs of mankind at specific points when certain conditions on earth have fully developed. This can be compared to a master gardener waiting to pick his fruit or vegetables when they are perfectly ripe – not a moment too soon, or a moment too late.

This concept of ripeness or maturity is presented as "fullness" in scripture. The fullness of a time or an age, or the fullness of a people or nation reflects completed development towards an end from God's perspective – either for good or evil. Spiritual growth and maturity has been achieved and deserves God's reward or sinful iniquity has reached its putrid low and deserves God's judgment and wrath. God's plan has developed along its prophetic track to the point that the time is just right for His next major intervention.

The first coming of Jesus as Christ is characterized by the apostle Paul as God's intervention in the fullness of time. "But when the fulness of the time was come, God sent forth his Son" (Gal 4:4). Jesus appeared on Israel's prophetic stage right on time in fulfillment of Daniel 9:24-26.

God further develops the concept of the fullness of the times related to the fullness of Christ.

- "That in the dispensation of the fulness of times he might gather together in one all things in Christ, both which are in heaven, and which are on earth; even in him" (Eph 1:10).
- "And hath put all things under his feet (Christ), and gave him to be the head over all things to the church, Which is his body, the fulness of him that filleth in all." (Eph 1:22-23).
- "And he (Christ) is the head of the body, the church … For it pleased the Father that in him should all fulness dwell" (Col 1:18-19).
- "Till we all come in the unity of the faith, and of the knowledge of the Son of God, unto a perfect man, unto the measure of the stature of the fulness of Christ" (Eph 4:13).

We see that the church is directly related to the fullness of Christ. The church is in Christ and the fullness of the church is connected to the fullness of Christ. In the fullness of this dispensation, Christ gathers to Himself all of His fullness: the dead believers in heaven along with the living believers on earth (Eph 1:10). This dispensation relates to the time of the church – the Church Age, also known as the Age of Grace. When does the age of the church end?

Paul provides a clue. "For I would not, brethren, that ye should be ignorant of this mystery, lest ye should be wise in your own conceits; that blindness in part is happened to Israel, until the **fulness of the Gentiles** be come in" (Rom 11:25 bold added).

In Romans chapter 11, Paul deals with the issue of Israel's spiritual blindness and its relationship to Gentile believers. Paul utilizes the symbolism of an olive tree with natural branches being broken off (unbelieving Jews) and wild branches (believing Gentiles) being grafted in among the remaining believing natural branches. Paul refers to a mystery in terms of understanding the concept that while much of Israel has been subjected to a supernatural form of spiritual blindness from God, this blindness is just temporary. This supernaturally imposed spiritual blindness will come to an end after a specific condition or event is reached. That condition is what Paul refers to as the fullness of the Gentiles.

The mystery of the "fullness of the gentiles" is both an indication of a specific period of time – the Church Age, as well as a concept of completion by reaching a predetermined number. Paul alludes to a point in time when God's plan for the gospel of Jesus Christ to go out to the Gentiles for the purpose of building the church is complete. This is not the fulfillment of a universal church which began in the Old Testament. It is the Christian church which Jesus promised to build (Mt 16:18), which began at Pentecost in Acts 2, and which is completely formed when a pre-determined specific number of believers are saved through the gospel of grace by faith in Jesus as Christ.

Once the church is fulfilled to God's specifications there is no more Church Age to follow. This "fullness of the Gentiles" then triggers the next major event of God's intervention marking the end of the Age of Grace – the rapture of the church.

It should be noted that Paul's concept of the fullness of the Gentiles is to be contrasted with his inference to the future fullness of Israel in Romans 11:12. It is also in contrast to the reference to the fulfillment of the "times of the Gentiles" in Luke 21:24. The times of the Gentiles does not relate to the church, but to the times of Gentile domination over Israel. They are entirely different concepts and end at different times.

## Old Testament Support for the Rapture

The church, as a collective body of Jewish and Gentile believers with equal standing before God but having a separate identity from the nation of Israel, was a concept that was unknown to the writers of the Old Testament. Nevertheless, there is scripture in the Old Testament which supports the concept of the rapture of the church.

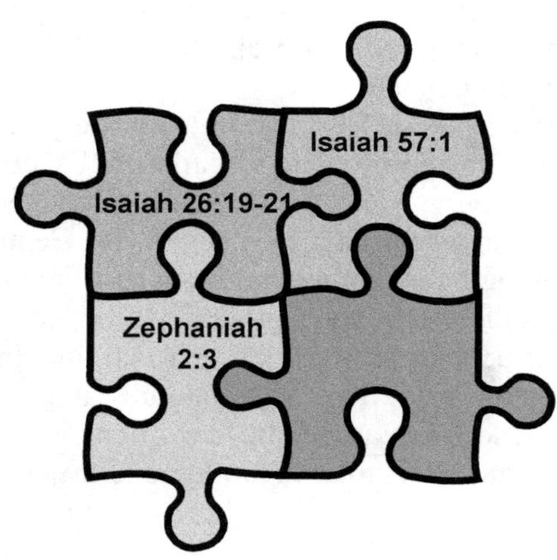

**Zephaniah 2:3** Seek ye the LORD, all ye meek of the earth, which have wrought his judgment; seek righteousness, seek meekness: it may be ye shall be **hid** in the day of the LORD'S anger.

It is interesting that Zephaniah would prophesy about the meek being hidden during the Day of the LORD, as the name Zephaniah means "whom Jehovah hid" or "God has secreted." Thus, there is an imbedded play on his own name in his plea to the meek of the earth to seek God, that they may be hidden by God when He manifests His anger upon the world.

**Isaiah 57:1** The righteous perisheth, [disappear] and no man layeth *it* to heart: and merciful men *are* **taken away**, none considering that the righteous is **taken away** from the evil *to come*. He shall enter into peace: they shall rest in their beds, *each one* walking *in* his uprightness.

**Isaiah 26:19-21**

> Thy dead *men* shall live, *together with* my dead body shall they arise. Awake and sing, ye that dwell in dust: for thy dew *is as* the dew of herbs, and the earth shall cast out the dead. Come, my people, enter thou into thy chambers, and shut thy doors about thee: **hide thyself** as it were for a little moment, until the indignation [God's fury or wrath] be overpast. For, behold, the LORD cometh out of his place to punish the inhabitants of the earth for their iniquity: the earth also shall disclose her blood, and shall no more cover her slain.

Zephaniah and Isaiah refer to a future time when a group of believers (the meek and righteous) will be hidden supernaturally from the manifestations of God's anger or fury which will be vented upon the inhabitants of the earth. Not only are they hidden, they are literally "taken away" from the evil events before they take place to another place entirely where they can "rest." They are described as entering a condition or state of peace. These people who are taken away and hidden are not merely being supernaturally protected in their own homes, or in the land of Israel, or anywhere else on the face of the earth. Isaiah places this in the sequential context of: first a resurrection of the dead, second God's people are taken away and hidden, third God unleashes His fury on the inhabitants of the earth, and fourth this is all characterized as God (Christ) coming out of heaven.

## New Testament Support for the Rapture

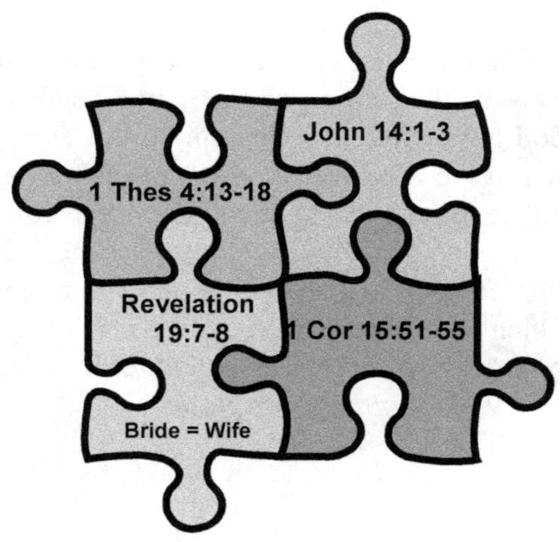


### John 14:1-3

> Let not your heart be troubled: ye believe in God, believe also in me. In my Father's house are many mansions: if *it were* not *so*, I would have told you. I go to prepare a place for you. And if I go and prepare a place for you, I will come again, and receive you unto myself; that where I am, *there* ye may be also.

Imbedded within this short passage are several important details in the form of promises from Jesus. Jesus was going to go away to His Father's house in heaven to prepare a place for His believers. Just as certainly that Jesus would go (ascend to heaven), He would eventually return. Why will Jesus return? Jesus will return to receive His believers unto Himself.

Jesus makes the point that where He is the believers will be also. Will this be on earth, or in heaven? In one sense this could simply be a way of stating that wherever Jesus is after His return His church will be also. But the inherent implication of the promise that Jesus made is that the location will be somewhere significantly different than where He was when He made the promise which was on earth and in the land of Israel.

Some believe that when Jesus returns the church will be caught up to meet Jesus in the air, like a group of city dignitaries going out to meet a king before he reaches the gate to the city, and then they will immediately return to earth to be with him on earth. However, Jesus is the one who placed this promise within the context of God's house in heaven. Why would Jesus go to prepare a place for His believers within God's house in heaven if Jesus was not then going to take His church to that place in heaven? The implied promise that Jesus made was that "I am going to My Father's house (heaven) to prepare a place for you, that where I am (in heaven), you may be also."

The context of this promise is not tied to the return of Jesus to judge the world as He does at the time of His second coming. This is a promise extended only to His followers. This promise implies that it has its own timing. This timing must allow for the church to be taken to heaven to be with Jesus. A pretribulational rapture allows for the church to be taken to heaven during the time of the Tribulation and then to return with Jesus at His second coming in judgment.

Some believe that Jesus will catch up all believers from the face of the earth at the time of His second coming and take them to heaven, thus leaving the earth in a destroyed and unpopulated condition. They believe that all believers will be in heaven in New Jerusalem during the Millennium. However, if this is true, it would create a situation where all people would be immortals, having been changed through resurrection or being translated at the time of the rapture.

How then could there ever be any more longevity issues or death for mankind? But Isaiah 65:20-23 reveals that there will be both longevity and death in the future kingdom, as a person who dies at a hundred years of age will be considered to be but a child. This passage in Isaiah 65 also emphasizes that the people at that time will build houses and dwell in them and plant vineyards and eat the fruit from them. This activity is on earth, albeit a renovated earth and a renovated Jerusalem, not in heaven. Contrast this with what Jesus states He will do during the absence of His ascension to heaven (Jn 14:3). Jesus went to heaven to prepare a place for His believers. There is no scriptural evidence that people will build their own houses in New Jerusalem.

Ezekiel 47:22 reveals that there will be births during the Messianic Kingdom. Scripture also teaches that death is the last enemy of man to be destroyed (1 Cor 15:26), and death is not destroyed until death is cast into the Lake of Fire at the great white throne judgment at the end of the Millennium (Rev 20:14). In addition, there are far too many passages of scripture regarding Israel's role on earth during the Messianic Kingdom for there to be any credibility to the concept of a completely unpopulated earth following the rapture of the church and Christ's second coming (Isa 4:2-6; Jer 33:4-18; Ezek 40–48; Hos 2:14-23).

**1 Thessalonians 4:13-18**

> 1 Thes 4:13 But I would not have you to be ignorant, brethren, concerning them which are asleep, that ye sorrow not, even as others which have no hope.
> 14 For if we believe that Jesus died and rose again, even so them also which sleep in Jesus will God bring with him.
> 15 For this we say unto you by the word of the Lord, that we which are alive *and* remain unto the coming of the Lord shall not prevent them which are asleep.
> 16 For the Lord himself shall descend from heaven with a shout, with the voice of the archangel, and with the trump of God: and the dead in Christ shall rise first:
> 17 Then we which are alive *and* remain shall be caught up together with them in the clouds, to meet the Lord in the air: and so shall we ever be with the Lord.
> 18 Wherefore comfort one another with these words.

In the passage of 1 Thessalonians 4:13-18, Paul outlines several important points and sequential steps regarding the event we know as the rapture of the church.

1. The event is delayed long enough from the time of Paul's writing for a number of church members to physically die, while other church members will be physically alive at the time of the event (1 Thes 4:13).
2. Believers are not to sorrow at the death of other believers (1 Thes 4:13). Those believers that die do not lose their place in the future gathering of the church to Christ (1 Thes 4:14-15).
3. The souls of the dead believers (those who sleep in Jesus) will be brought by Jesus (God) from heaven back to earth when He returns to claim His church (1 Thes 4:14).
4. The living believers will not precede the dead believers at the coming of Christ (1 Thes 4:15).
5. Christ shall descend from heaven with a shout (1 Thes 4:16).
6. The voice of the archangel will cry out (1 Thes 4:16).
7. The trumpet of God will sound (1 Thes 4:16).
8. The dead in Christ shall rise (be resurrected) (1 Thes 4:16).
9. The living believers shall be caught up, together with the dead believers, in the clouds to meet Christ in the air (1 Thes 4:17).
10. The church will be with Christ forever (1 Thes 4:17).

11. This teaching from Paul, which is by the word of the Lord, is to be used as a great comfort to believers (1 Thes 4:15, 18).

Does Paul teach that the souls of dead believers languish in the grave in a state of soul sleep until Christ awakens them? No. Paul is clear that when Jesus comes for His church, He will bring the souls of dead believers with Him.

Does Paul teach that Christ resurrects the dead believers and catches up the living believers after He returns to the earth and destroys the Antichrist and his armies? No. While Christ will come into the earth's atmosphere, He will not come down to the earth's surface during this event. The passage is specific by referring to both the air and the clouds. This family reunion of Christians with their Lord takes place in the earth's atmosphere.

Does Paul teach that the church must go through the time of the Tribulation? No. These words are to be a comfort to the church because the church will be removed before the Tribulation. Paul makes no mention that Christ comes riding a white horse, with armies from heaven, to do battle against the nations of the earth as Lord of Lords and King of Kings in connection to this rapture event (Rev 19:11-21).

Study the passage that immediately follows in 1 Thessalonians 5:1-11. Paul clearly states that the Day of the LORD will overtake the unbelieving world suddenly as a thief in the night. Paul distinguishes the "them" upon whom will come sudden destruction from the believing church (1 Thes 5:2-3). Paul also declares that the church is not appointed to wrath (God's wrath) (1 Thes 5:9). Believers are again encouraged to comfort other believers with this teaching (1 Thes 5:11). The dynamic of the church's removal at the rapture, before the Day of the LORD comes upon the world, is so important that it is a great comfort to believers. Study Paul's instructions to the church in 1 Thessalonians 5. These are not instructions in how to survive the coming time of the Tribulation, but how to hold fast until the time comes that Christ will come for the church.

**1 Corinthians 15:51-55**

> 1 Cor 15:51 Behold, I shew you a mystery; We shall not all sleep, but we shall all be changed,
> 52 In a moment, in the twinkling of an eye, at the last trump: for the trumpet shall sound, and the dead shall be raised incorruptible, and we shall be changed.
> 53 For this corruptible must put on incorruption, and this mortal *must* put on immortality.

> 54 So when this corruptible shall have put on incorruption, and this mortal shall have put on immortality, then shall be brought to pass the saying that is written, Death is swallowed up in victory.
> 55 O death, where *is* thy sting? O grave, where *is* thy victory?

In the passage of 1 Corinthians 15:51-55, Paul makes several important points regarding the resurrection of the dead and the rapture of the church.

1. Some of what will happen at the time of the rapture was unknown (a mystery) to the writers of the Old Testament (1 Cor 15:51).
2. Some believers will not physically die, but will be alive at the time of the rapture (1 Cor 15:51).
3. The rapture event causes a great change for all believers (1 Cor 15:51).
4. The rapture event will be very sudden and very fast (in the twinkling of an eye) (1 Cor 15:52).
5. The rapture will take place at the time the last trumpet sounds (1 Cor 15:52).
6. The dead believers will be resurrected to an incorruptible state (glorified bodies) (1 Cor 15:52).
7. The living believers will be changed (to glorified bodies) (1 Cor 15:52).
8. The changing of the dead and living believers brings incorruption and immortality (1 Cor 15:52-54).
9. For believers, death and the grave are swallowed up by victory (1 Cor 15:54-55).

One critical characteristic of this passage is the identification or misidentification of what Paul refers to as the “last trump.” 1 Corinthians 15:52 is the only scriptural reference to the last trump or last trumpet. Some believe that the last trumpet must be the seventh trumpet judgment that is mentioned in Revelation 8:2, and 8:6, and sounded in Revelation 11:15.

In 1 Thessalonians 4:16, Paul identifies the trumpet that is sounded at the time of the rapture as the “trump of God.” The seventh trumpet judgment of Revelation is never identified as the trumpet of God. None of the seven trumpet judgments in the book of Revelation are identified as being the trumpet of God. While all of the seven trumpets in Revelation are instruments of God’s wrath, they are all sounded by angels. The focus in 1 Thessalonians 4:16 is on Christ and the last trump in its relation to Him. The purpose for the sounding of the trump of God (the last trump) is specifically to call forth the believers in Christ: the dead in Christ to resurrection, and the living in Christ to supernatural transformation. The rapture of the church is a very short, fast, and dynamic event, as it takes place "in the twinkling of an eye."

In contrast, the characterization of the angel sounding the seventh trumpet is one of an extended nature. The passage in Revelation 10:7 gives us this description, "But in the days of the voice of the seventh angel, when he shall begin to sound, the mystery of God should be finished, as he hath declared to his servants the prophets." The "days of" indicates that the sounding of the seventh trumpet is an extended event. The "voice of the seventh angel" provides a focus on the angel with the trumpet, not a focus on Christ calling forth the rapture of the church, or a focus on the voice of God.

The seventh trumpet sounds (Rev 11:15) and the sequential story line of Revelation is interrupted until chapter 15, where seven angels are introduced with the seven last plagues of God's wrath. These are the bowl judgments. There is no description of Christ coming for His church between the sounding of the seventh trumpet and the beginning of the seven bowl judgments. Christ's second coming does not take place until the end of the seven bowl judgments when He returns to do battle with the Antichrist and the False Prophet in Revelation chapter 19. No one knows exactly how long a period of time will take place during which the seven bowls of God's final wrath are poured upon the earth, but they play out over a period of time. Thus, there is an inherent delay between the sounding of the seventh trumpet and the return of Christ. The sounding of the seventh trumpet judgment neither characterizes nor symbolizes the return of Christ for His church nor the immediacy of His second coming at the time of Armageddon.

The book of Revelation never describes or identifies the angel with the seventh trumpet as having or sounding the last trumpet. In actuality, even though the seventh trumpet is the last of the seven trumpet judgments, it is not the last prophetic trumpet sounded in scripture.

When Jesus taught His parables, He characterized the end of the world (age) as a time when He will send His angels as reapers of the harvest. Christ will return in glory with His angels (Mt 16:27; 25:31; Mk 8:38; Lk 9:26), the angels will gather the elect (Mt 24:31; Mk 13:27), and the angels will also gather the wicked out of the world (Mt 13:39, 41, 49). Matthew 24:31 describes this event: "And he shall send his angels with a great sound of a trumpet, and they shall gather together his elect from the four winds, from one end of heaven to the other." This event takes place "Immediately after the tribulation of those days" (Mt 24:29), as part of the second coming of Christ (Mt 24:30). The seventh trumpet is inherently part of the Tribulation. It ushers in God's most intensive time of wrath which lasts throughout the bowl judgments. It does not come after the Tribulation of those days. Some time following the blowing of the seventh trumpet by the angel and the pouring out of the seven bowls of the seven "last" plagues of God's wrath (Rev 15:1; 16:1), Christ will return with the sound of a great trumpet and send His angels to gather His elect. Thus, contrary to the thinking of some, the seventh trumpet is not the last prophetic trumpet blast.

Is the scene of Matthew 24:31 a description of the rapture of the church? Many people believe it is. If it is, it takes place at the sound of a trumpet which is not identical to the seventh trumpet of Revelation.

Who are the people identified as Christ's "elect" in Matthew 24:31 and Mark 13:27? Are they the body of believers who make up the church? Or are they the people who will become believers during the Tribulation, including the nation of Israel? I believe that the "elect" in Matthew 24:31 are primarily the people of Israel who are redeemed at the end of the Tribulation. The portrayal of this gathering of the elect by angels is different from Paul's descriptions of the rapture of the church. There is no description of any resurrection of dead believers or the supernatural translation of the bodies of the elect to incorruptible, immortal bodies, or their being caught up into the air to be taken to heaven. There is no indication that the elect at the time of the second coming are removed from the environment of the earth at all after they are gathered by the angels. On the other hand, there is evidence that the wicked who are gathered are judged and removed from the earth so that they cannot enter into the Millennial Kingdom (Mt 13:39-42, 49-50).

If these elect represent all believers on earth at the time of Christ's second coming, and they are all changed (immortalized) as Paul plainly states (1 Cor 15:51-52), then there will be no mortal humans to enter a Kingdom of God on earth during the millennial reign of Christ. However, if these elect are not the church which will be all changed and raptured, and if these elect are not raptured at all, but are supernaturally gathered on earth as part of Christ's judgments of Israel and the Gentile nations, then there is no conflict with mortals entering the Kingdom to populate a renovated earth.

The need for scriptural consistency and continuity regarding the time of God's wrath during the Tribulation and the earthly character of the Messianic Kingdom require that the trumpet focused on by Paul as the last trump is different from both the seventh trumpet in Revelation and the great trumpet mentioned in Matthew 24:31.

## Saints in Heaven – Clothed in White

If the rapture takes place at the time of Christ's coming at the end of the Tribulation, then there should be no evidence that the church is in heaven prior to that second coming. If the rapture takes place at an earlier point in time, then there should be evidence that there is a large group of redeemed saints in heaven earlier than the end of the Tribulation. Theoretically, the earlier the rapture the earlier the evidence should appear in the book of Revelation. What can we deduce from the content of Revelation?

The point has been made by many scholars that there is an obvious focus on the church in chapters one through three of Revelation while the church is seemingly ignored from chapter four until chapter nineteen where it appears as the wife of Christ (the Lamb). Where is the church during the events of chapters four through eighteen, on earth or in heaven? Why are the church saints never named or identified in any of these chapters of Revelation, or are they?

**Revelation 6:9-11**

> Rev 6:9 And when he had opened the fifth seal, I saw under the altar the souls of them that were slain for the word of God, and for the testimony which they held:
> 10 And they cried with a loud voice, saying, How long, O Lord, holy and true, dost thou not judge and avenge our blood on them that dwell on the earth?
> 11 And **white robes** were given unto every one of them; and it was said unto them, that they should rest yet for a little season, until their fellowservants also and their brethren, that should be killed as they *were*, should be fulfilled.

In chapter six of Revelation Jesus breaks six of the seven seals on a scroll, which He has taken from the right hand of God. At the opening of the fifth seal (Rev 6:9-11), John saw the souls of martyrs under the altar in heaven who I believe had already been slain during the Church Age. Many scholars believe that these souls do not represent martyrs of the Church Age, but represent martyrs from the early part of the Tribulation. This passage describing the souls under the altar makes it clear that there will be other people killed as martyrs during the Tribulation.

The souls are given white robes and told to rest for a little season. This is the first and only description of disembodied souls being given white robes in the Bible. What is the significance of the white robes and the little season? White robes symbolize the righteousness of all saints who overcome through faith in Christ, not just martyrs (Rev 3:4-5, 18; 19:8).

The problem with the concept that these souls were martyred only during the Tribulation is that souls do not need robes. Only bodies need robes. White robes are not pacifiers for souls while they wait under the altar in heaven. The giving of the white robes is not passive; it is a very dynamic action. The souls are told they will rest, but when they are given the white robes they are not told they will remain under the altar. Our examination of Old Testament passages which support the concept of the rapture revealed that the meek or righteous will be hidden or secreted away by God and that they will enter their chambers and shut their doors and "rest" in their beds during the time of God's indignation. This time of "rest" is also consistent with the symbolism of the Jewish Wedding.

The white robes represent the resurrection of the martyred saints and the little season is the time of the Day of the LORD during which God's vengeance will play out on earth. The only souls which qualify for this granting of the white robes are the martyrs of the Church Age, and possibly martyrs of the Old Testament era, as they are the only ones ready to be resurrected during the time frame of the breaking of the seven seals. The souls of those who come to faith after the event of the rapture of the church and are later martyred during the events of the Day of the LORD are not resurrected until after the second coming of Christ (Rev 20:4-6).

The souls of the martyred Church Age saints cannot rest as souls under the altar in heaven throughout the Tribulation while they are joined by the martyrs of the Tribulation because that would create a situation where the Church Age martyrs would not be resurrected until after Christ's second coming (Rev 20:4-6). The Church Age martyrs must be resurrected immediately prior to the catching up of the living believers of the church. Therefore, the giving of the white robes must point to the resurrection of the martyrs as a special group to God. Martyrs will receive a special reward at the judgment seat of Christ (Rev 2:10). Since the resurrection of Church Age martyrs must take place at the same time as the other dead in Christ of the Church Age – at the time of the rapture of the church, the breaking of the fifth seal is a subtle revealing of the event of the rapture. The martyrs will rest for a little season as part of the resurrected and raptured bride of Christ in heaven, while other saints are slain as martyrs during the Tribulation.

The apostle John has an interesting contrasting vision in Revelation 15. He gets his first view of the seven angels who have the seven last plagues (bowl judgments) which have not yet been poured out upon the earth (Rev 15:1). Then John immediately describes another group in heaven. "And I saw as it were a sea of glass mingled with fire: and them that had gotten victory over the beast, and over his image, and over his mark, and over the number of his name, stand on the sea of glass, having the harps of God" (Rev 15:2).

The only people who have gotten victory at this point in the Tribulation over the beast (Rev 13), his image (Rev 13:15), his mark (Rev 13:16-17), and the number of his name (Rev 13:17-18) are those Tribulational believers who have been true to their faith in Jesus and been martyred during the Tribulation. These martyrs are the only believers who fit this description. These are some of the very martyrs that were predicted in Revelation 6:11.

However, it is interesting that there is no mention of these martyrs being given white robes. Nor are these martyrs located under the altar in heaven as were the martyred souls revealed in the fifth seal. Why is there a difference? What John sees in Revelation 15:2 is a vision of the souls of these martyrs. They have not yet been resurrected as we are specifically given the timing of their resurrection as taking place after the Tribulation is over (Rev 20:4). It is possible that they do not have white robes because they are still waiting to be resurrected. It is also obvious that they do not represent the same group of martyrs that are revealed in the fifth seal.

**Revelation 7:9-17**

> Rev 7:9 After this I beheld, and, lo, a great multitude, which no man could number, of all nations, and kindreds, and people, and tongues, stood before the throne, and before the Lamb, clothed with white robes, and palms in their hands; ....
> Rev 7:13 And one of the elders answered, saying unto me, What are these which are arrayed in white robes? and whence came they?
> Rev 7:14 And I said unto him, Sir, thou knowest. And he said to me, These are they which came out of great tribulation, and have washed their robes, and made them white in the blood of the Lamb.

Between the breaking of the sixth and seventh seals, there is an interruption in the flow of events while John is shown two groups of people. The first is comprised of 144,000 Jews who are supernaturally sealed as servants of God. This group is on earth during the Tribulation; otherwise, there would be no need to seal them supernaturally. The second group appears in Revelation 7:9. This group of redeemed people is revealed as standing before the throne of God and in the presence of the Lamb (Jesus Christ).

I believe that this great multitude is a depiction of the resurrected and raptured church very soon after it is taken to heaven. This great multitude is not under the altar, but is standing before the throne. This is a perfect representation of the Church Age saints, and it happens to come at just the right time for the church to be in heaven. The souls of the Church Age martyrs have been given their white robes (pointing to the resurrection of the dead in Christ) following the breaking of the fifth seal. The unredeemed people who inhabit the earth begin to realize that they are experiencing the Day-of-the-LORD judgments and wrath imposed by God and Christ with the catastrophic events that accompany the breaking of the sixth seal (Rev 6:15-17). A great multitude of redeemed believers suddenly appears in heaven as a collective group which has come out of all of the nations on earth. All of these saints are clothed in white robes, and thus have experienced the translation of the earthly bodies to incorruptible, immortal bodies which is what takes place at the resurrection and rapture of the church. The passage of Revelation 7:16-17 describes the characteristics of their "peace and rest" while they serve God in heaven.

Many commentators of Revelation interpret this great multitude to be people who come to be believers only during the Tribulation as a direct result of the work of the 144,000 sealed servants of God. They take the statement from the fifth seal which predicts more martyrs to come and conclude that this great multitude of Revelation 7:9 looks forward to the end of the Tribulation and represents that group. However, the description of this multitude makes no reference to the end of the Tribulation or to martyrdom. This vision is not looking forward to a group who will be converted and martyred during the Tribulation and then resurrected and caught up to heaven to stand before God's throne at or after the end of the seven-year Tribulation. Instead, it is revealing a group who is already resurrected and in heaven before the breaking of the seventh seal. Compare this multitude in Revelation 7:9 to the group that is revealed in Revelation 15:2. That group does represent the believers and martyrs of the Tribulation, but they are not described as having white robes because they have not yet been resurrected. There is a distinct difference between these two groups. They do not represent the same people.

Why are the 144,000 servants mentioned before the great multitude? Are the 144,000 servants not responsible for the conversion of the great multitude? Actually, that is an assumption that is made by many commentators. There is no support for it at all. There is no statement made in the passage regarding any cause and effect relationship between the 144,000 and the great multitude. In my view, the structure of the chapter makes it more logical to see these as two groups who are simultaneously or almost simultaneously situated, one on earth and one in heaven. God never leaves the earth without a faithful remnant of believers to represent Him. When God decides it is time to remove the Church from the earth, what group will become the faithful remnant on earth at that time?

Without God's direct and immediate intervention, there would be no faithful remnant of believers on earth immediately following the rapture of the church. The supernatural effect of the rapture will result in the removal of all born again Christians from the earth. There will be Jews and other people who believe in God, but none of them will have accepted Jesus Christ as God's Messiah or as their personal and necessary savior. With the supernatural removal of the church, God's attention is marked by a sudden and dynamic shift in focus from the church to the nation of Israel regarding earthly events. It makes sense that God would have prepared a group of believers in God for immediate conversion to accept Jesus as the Messiah at this very point in time. It also makes sense that this group would be entirely comprised of Israelites from the bloodline of Abraham, Isaac, and Jacob for the purpose of representing God and the nation of Israel on the world stage.

The 144,000 Jewish servants sealed to God immediately preceding or simultaneous with the rapture of the church is the only possible group revealed in Revelation to become that remnant. The 144,000 Jewish servants are sealed to God to directly replace the departing church believers as they are taken to heaven at the time of the rapture.

Some scholars make an issue out of the statement that this great multitude "came out of great tribulation," concluding that this requires an ongoing coming out of the Tribulation over that period of time. However, the entire believing church throughout the Church Age has been coming out of great tribulation, one at a time, since the birth of the church and will ultimately be delivered out of the Great Tribulation as a collective group simultaneously by being kept out of it entirely. All Christian believers, from the beginning of the Church Age, whether they are martyred or not, have obtained salvation because they "washed their robes, and made them white in the blood of the Lamb" (Rev 7:14).

Revelation chapter seven reveals that the church is standing before the throne of God in heaven before the seventh seal is broken. The events of the seven trumpets and the seven bowl judgments are yet to play out during the course of the Tribulation. The church is a great multitude from every nation which comes out of the Great Tribulation by being kept "from the hour of temptation, which shall come upon all the world, to try them that dwell upon the earth" (Rev 3:10).

During the Tribulation there is a distinction between two groups: those who dwell on earth and who are subject to God's wrath, and those who dwell in heaven and who are reviled by Satan and the Antichrist (Rev 13:6). In Revelation 18:20, those in heaven, including the apostles and prophets, are enjoined to rejoice at the destruction of Babylon. In Revelation 19:1, John hears "a great voice of much people in heaven." John is referring to a multitude of people not angels. Who are these people who dwell in heaven if they do not include the Christian believers of the Church Age who have been previously caught up to heaven?

**Revelation 19:7-8** Let us be glad and rejoice, and give honour to him: for the marriage of the Lamb is come, and his wife hath made herself ready. And to her was granted that she should be arrayed in fine linen, clean and white: for the fine linen is the righteousness of saints.

Then, in Revelation 19:7-8, we are finally introduced to the wife of the Lamb. The church is the bride of Christ. By the time of Revelation 19:7, the church as the bride of Jesus has been taken to heaven, made ready (appeared before the judgment seat of Christ), arrayed in white robes, and become the wife of the Lamb. The church as the wife of Jesus is now ready to accompany Him to the earth.

## Christ Returns with His Saints

**Zechariah 14:5** And ye shall flee *to* the valley of the mountains; for the valley of the mountains shall reach unto Azal: yea, ye shall flee, like as ye fled from before the earthquake in the days of Uzziah king of Judah: and the LORD my God shall come, *and* all the saints with thee.

**Jude 1:14** And Enoch also, the seventh from Adam, prophesied of these, saying, Behold, the Lord cometh with ten thousands of his saints …

**Revelation 17:14** These shall make war with the Lamb, and the Lamb shall overcome them: for he is Lord of lords, and King of kings: and they that are with him *are* called, and chosen, and faithful.

**Revelation 19:14** And the armies *which were* in heaven followed him upon white horses, clothed in fine linen, white and clean.

When Jesus returns to earth at the time of the event known as His second coming, He will be accompanied by the saints and armies from heaven. This is not one army but multiple armies. These armies originate in heaven. They are in heaven when Jesus begins His return to earth. This passage does not describe Christ picking up these armies on the way to earth. None of these armies are resurrected and raptured during the process of Christ's second coming.

These saints and armies located in heaven include both redeemed humans and angels. These human saints and armies have been glorified and purified. They are wearing fine, white, and clean linen, which is a characteristic of the righteousness of the church as the bride (wife) of Christ just prior to the return of Jesus in His full glory (Rev 19:7-8). Jesus describes overcomers as being clothed in white raiment (Rev 3:4-5, 18). The twenty-four Elders wear white raiment (Rev 4:4). White robes are given to the souls of Christian martyrs symbolizing their resurrection (Rev 6:11). The great multitude of Christians (the resurrected and raptured church) which suddenly appear before the throne in heaven in Revelation 7:9 are dressed in white robes (Rev 7:9, 13-14). Several references to angels describe them as wearing white (Mk 16:5; Jn 20:12; Act 1:10), and at least some of the angels in heaven, if not all, are dressed in white linen (Rev 15:6).

When Christ returns from heaven for His church to initiate the rapture, He will bring with Him the souls of those Christian believers who had died in faith over the centuries since the birth of the church at Pentecost ten days after His ascension to heaven (1 Thes 4:14). Is Christ's act of bringing the souls of dead believers with Him what is being described by the saints and armies who accompany the return of Jesus from heaven to do battle against the Antichrist and the False Prophet and their earthly armies in the war we know as Armageddon?

### Characteristics of Christ's Second Coming

| **Characteristics** | **Old Testament Support** | **New Testament Support** |
|---|---|---|
| Tribulation | Dan 7:7-8, 11-12, 19-21, 23-25<br>Zech 14:1-5 | Mt 24:29<br>Mk 13:24-25<br>Lk 21:25-26 |
| Christ comes in glory with clouds and/or His Angels | Dan 7:13-14 | Mt 16:27; 24:30; 25:31<br>Mk 8:38; 13:26<br>Lk 9:26; 21:27<br>Rev 1:7; 14:14 |
| Christ comes with His Saints | Dan 7:22<br>Zech 14:5 | Jude 1:14<br>Rev 17:14; 19:14 |
| Angels gather the Elect | | Mt 24:31<br>Mk 13:27 |
| Angels sever out the Wicked | Dan 7:26 | Mt 13:39-42, 49-50<br>Mt 25:32-33, 41, 46<br>Rev 14:15-19 |
| Righteous (Saints) inherit the Kingdom | Dan 7:18, 22, 27<br>Zech 14:9, 11 | Mt 13:43; 25:34, 46<br>Lk 21:31 |

The souls that Christ brings with Him to the resurrection/rapture event have yet to be reunited with their bodies and changed into their incorruptible glorified state. They have not yet stood before the judgment seat of Christ in heaven (Rom 14:10; 2 Cor 5:10), and had their works as believers tested by the consuming fire of God (1 Cor 3:10-15), and received their rewards (1 Cor 3:8, 14; 2 Tim 4:8; Jas 1:12; 1 Pet 5:4; Rev 3:11). These souls will not be dressed in the white robes of fine linen until after their resurrection.

The distinctive characterizations of these groups, the souls coming from heaven to be reunited with their bodies in resurrection versus the glorified saints already wearing white robes, reveals the incompatibility that these are one and the same body of believers at the same point in prophetic time. The coming of Jesus for His church at the rapture and the second coming of Jesus with His saints and armies from heaven are two completely different events with different purposes and they take place at different times.

## Sequence of Resurrections

### Revelation 20:4-6

> Rev 20:4 And I saw thrones, and they sat upon them, and judgment was given unto them: and *I saw* the souls of them that were beheaded for the witness of Jesus, and for the word of God, and which had not worshipped the beast, neither his image, neither had received *his* mark upon their foreheads, or in their hands; and they lived and reigned with Christ a thousand years.
> 5 But the rest of the dead lived not again until the thousand years were finished. This *is* the first resurrection.
> 6 Blessed and holy *is* he that hath part in the first resurrection: on such the second death hath no power, but they shall be priests of God and of Christ, and shall reign with him a thousand years.

There are several important observations that we can make or deduce from the information that is provided in the passage of Revelation 20:1-6, which follows the description of Christ's second coming in Revelation 19.

1. Christ returns with His saints and armies from heaven to defeat Satan, the Antichrist, the False Prophet, the kings of the earth and their armies (Rev 19:11-21).
2. The Antichrist (beast) and the False Prophet are cast into the lake of fire (Rev 19:20).
3. Satan is imprisoned in the bottomless pit (abyss) for one thousand years (Rev 20:1-3).

4. There is a judgment scene where thrones are set up, and those believers who were martyred for their faith during the Tribulation are resurrected from the dead (Rev 20:4). Revelation 15:2 depicts the souls of these martyrs (or at least some of them), prior to being resurrected, as standing on the sea of glass mingled with fire in heaven. The martyrs of the Tribulation first appear as souls and then they live and reign with Christ. This is describing a resurrection sequence. Interestingly, there is no mention of these martyrs wearing white robes in either passage (Rev 15:2; 20:4). These are not the souls of believers who die and sleep in Christ throughout the Church Age which Paul mentions in 1 Thessalonians 4:14. Nor are they part of the glorified saints who return with Christ as the wife of Christ at His second coming (Rev 19:7-8, 14). This resurrection takes place on earth after the second coming and the events of Armageddon are completed. Therefore, there must have been a previous resurrection and rapture of Christians who comprise the body of believers wearing white robes mentioned in Revelation 7:9-17 and 19:7-8, 14.
5. This resurrection is identified as the "first resurrection" (Rev 20:5). However, since there had to be a previous resurrection of believers before Christ's return at the time of Armageddon, this must mean that this resurrection of the martyrs of the Tribulation is the end of the first resurrection. This resurrection completes a series of several resurrections which all comprise the "first resurrection." There was the resurrection of Jesus Christ, the firstfruits of resurrection (1 Cor 15:20-23). There was the resurrection of some Old Testament saints immediately following the resurrection of Christ (Mt 27:52-53). There will be the resurrection of Church Age believers at the time of the rapture. There will be the resurrection of God's two witnesses after their 1,260 day ministry (Rev 11:3-12). There will be the resurrection of the Old Testament believers (Job 19:25-27; Ps 49:15; Isa 26:19; Dan 12:2, 13; Hos 13:14; Jn 5:28-29; 11:23-26). While some scholars believe that the Old Testament saints will be resurrected at the same time as the rapture of the church, others believe their resurrection takes place following the second coming. The prophet Daniel was informed that he would die (rest) and then he would be resurrected to stand in his lot at the end. This insinuates that there are multiple lots, multiple divisions of people at the time of the end. Whether the Old Testament and New Testament believers are resurrected simultaneously, all believers are not resurrected at the same time (1 Cor 15:20-23). Then, there will be the resurrection of the martyrs of the Tribulation whose awakening concludes this "first

resurrection" series of events. "Blessed and holy is the one who has a part in the first resurrection" (Rev 20:6a NASB).

6. The "first resurrection," which is completed by the beginning of the Millennium, is distinguished from the resurrection which takes place at the end of the Millennium (Rev 20:11-15). This final resurrection and judgment takes place before the great white throne of God and results in the "second death" of the Lake of Fire for all unrighteous people not found in God's book of life.

## Sequence of Judgments

**2 Timothy 4:1** I charge *thee* therefore before God, and the Lord Jesus Christ, who shall judge the quick and the dead at his appearing and his kingdom …

Paul teaches that there will be multiple judgments. Two judgments are indicated in 2 Timothy 4:1. One judgment takes place at the time of Christ's appearing, and another judgment takes place at the time of Christ's kingdom. In each case, Christ will judge the quick (the living) and the dead. Why does Paul distinguish between Christ's appearing and Christ's kingdom? Could it be that Christ's appearing is not a reference to Christ's second coming to do battle to reclaim the earth as His inheritance, which would be connected to the beginning of Christ's kingdom, but a reference to Christ's appearing for His church at an earlier point in time?

When Christ returns at the time of His second coming to reclaim the earth from Satan and to initiate His Millennial Kingdom, He will conduct a judgment of the quick (living) and the dead. Christ will return with His angels who will serve as the reapers of the harvest of wickedness. The angels will remove all wicked people from the face of the earth. The wicked will be removed (killed) so that none of the wicked shall enter the Millennial Kingdom of Christ (Mt 13:39, 41, 49; 16:27; 24:31; Mk 8:38; 13:27; Lk 9:26). Christ will slay many by His intervention at the time of Armageddon (Rev 19:21). Following Christ's defeat of Satan and his forces:

- Christ will judge the Jewish survivors of Israel (Ezek 20:33-38);
- Christ will resurrect the Old Testament saints (Dan 12:2) if they have not been previously resurrected;
- Christ will judge the surviving nations regarding their relationship to Christ and His brethren (nation of Israel and Tribulation saints) (Joel 3:2; Mt 16:27; 25:31-46); and
- Christ will resurrect the martyrs of the Tribulation and make judgment for them (Rev 20:4).

At the time of the end of the Millennial Kingdom, there will be another series of judgments.

- Satan will be released from his confinement in the abyss and will initiate his final revolt (Rev 20:7-10).
- Some of the living will be deceived by Satan and will revolt against God. God will judge them by fire from heaven.
- Satan will be judged and cast into the lake of fire.
- The unrighteous dead of all time are then resurrected to stand before God at what is referred to as the great white throne judgment (Rev 20:11-15). This is the last of God's judgments against fallen men as death and hell are cast into the Lake of Fire. From this point on there will be no more sin and no more death.

Paul's teachings are instructive. Paul focuses on the hope that his words have for the Christian believer. That hope is not directed towards looking for the revealing of the Antichrist or the False Prophet, or the abomination of desolation or desecration of the temple (Mt 24:15), or God protecting the church through the terrible time of the Tribulation, or the War of Armageddon and Christ's conquering of the Antichrist. That great, comforting hope is directed to the promise of Christ's appearing for the church to gather the body of saints to Him. That is why Paul distinguishes between different judgments and what Paul means by Christ's appearing. That is what Paul is pointing to in his epistle to Titus.

**Titus 2:11-14**

> For the grace of God that bringeth salvation hath appeared to all men, Teaching us that, denying ungodliness and worldly lusts, we should live soberly, righteously, and godly, in this present world; **Looking for that blessed hope, and the glorious appearing of the great God and our Saviour Jesus Christ;** Who gave himself for us, that he might redeem us from all iniquity, and purify unto himself a peculiar people, zealous of good works.

Instead of being watchful for any of the specific dynamic and terrible events that will take place during the Day of the LORD, Paul instructs believers to be looking expectantly for the appearance of Jesus. However,

Paul also emphasizes that there is a different judgment at Christ's appearing, a judgment which involves the believing church.

**Romans 14:10** But why dost thou judge thy brother? or why dost thou set at nought thy brother? for we shall all stand before the judgment seat of Christ.

**2 Corinthians 5:10** For we must all appear before the judgment seat of Christ; that every one may receive the things *done* in *his* body, according to that he hath done, whether *it be* good or bad.

**1 Corinthians 3:10-15**

> 1 Cor 3:10 According to the grace of God which is given unto me, as a wise masterbuilder, I have laid the foundation, and another buildeth thereon. But let every man take heed how he buildeth thereupon.
> 11 For other foundation can no man lay than that is laid, which is Jesus Christ.
> 12 Now if any man build upon this foundation gold, silver, precious stones, wood, hay, stubble;
> 13 Every man's work shall be made manifest: for the day shall declare it, because it shall be revealed by fire; and the fire shall try every man's work of what sort it is.
> 14 If any man's work abide which he hath built thereupon, he shall receive a reward.
> 15 If any man's work shall be burned, he shall suffer loss: but he himself shall be saved; yet so as by fire.

Judgment starts with the house of God (1 Pet 4:17). The church must appear before the judgment seat of Christ (Rom 14:10; 2 Cor 5:10). This judgment takes place in heaven and judges a Christian's works of faith, not his life of sin before faith. One of the objectives of a Christian should be to earn rewards in heaven (1 Cor 3:8, 14; 2 Tim 4:8; Jas 1:12; 1 Pet 5:4; Rev 3:11). Thus, Christ has a glorious appearing for His church. Christ comes to gather His believers, the dead of the Church Age are resurrected, the living (the quick) are raptured, and the church is taken to heaven to stand before the judgment seat of Christ. There is a judgment of both the quick and the dead at the time of Christ's appearing, which is the time that Christ comes for His church and initiates the Day of Christ. This is not associated with the event known as the second coming to conquer the Antichrist at the time of Armageddon.

## The Removal of the Restraining Force

### 2 Thessalonians 2:1-13

> 2 Thes 2:1 Now we beseech you, brethren, by the coming of our Lord Jesus Christ, and *by* our gathering together unto him,
> 2 That ye be not soon shaken in mind, or be troubled, neither by spirit, nor by word, nor by letter as from us, as that the day of Christ is at hand.
> 3 Let no man deceive you by any means: for *that day shall not come*, except there come a falling away first, and that man of sin be revealed, the son of perdition;
> 4 Who opposeth and exalteth himself above all that is called God, or that is worshipped; so that he as God sitteth in the temple of God, shewing himself that he is God.
> 5 Remember ye not, that, when I was yet with you, I told you these things?
> 6 And now ye know what withholdeth that he might be revealed in his time.
> 7 For the mystery of iniquity doth already work: only he who now letteth *will let*, until he be taken out of the way.
> 8 And then shall that Wicked be revealed, whom the Lord shall consume with the spirit of his mouth, and shall destroy with the brightness of his coming:
> 9 *Even him*, whose coming is after the working of Satan with all power and signs and lying wonders,
> 10 And with all deceivableness of unrighteousness in them that perish; because they received not the love of the truth, that they might be saved.
> 11 And for this cause God shall send them strong delusion, that they should believe a lie:
> 12 That they all might be damned who believed not the truth, but had pleasure in unrighteousness.
> 13 But we are bound to give thanks always to God for you, brethren beloved of the Lord, because God hath from the beginning chosen you to salvation through sanctification of the Spirit and belief of the truth:

Paul emphasizes a distinction between the believers in the church who are characterized by "salvation through sanctification of the Spirit and belief in the truth" (2 Thes 2:13), versus those people who do not receive the love of the truth of God (2 Thes 2:10-12). This distinction applied to Paul's day during the first century and will especially apply at the time when Christ returns to initiate the Day of Christ for the church, which will be taken to heaven, and the judgments of the Day of the LORD for those on earth.

Paul gives an overview perspective. The Day of Christ/Day of the LORD cannot come, or be recognized on earth, until there first is a falling away (*apostasia* in Greek) and then the man of sin is revealed (2 Thes 2:3). Some believe that this reference to *apostasia* indicates the rapture of the church, as the church is taken away from the earth. However, that is not a clear teaching. The greater weight of this statement seems to be that there will be a falling away into apostasy from the believing church which accepts the truth to greater numbers of people who claim to be the "church" but who do not love the truth.

Some, like the Seventh Day Adventists, use this passage to teach that the Antichrist must be revealed while the church is present on earth and that the church must go through the Tribulation. However, is that what Paul is saying? Is Paul stating that the church must be present to witness the revealing of the man of sin?

Paul focuses in from his overview point, the Day of Christ had not yet started because the falling away had not yet happened and the man of sin had not yet been revealed, to a specific critical detail. A detail which Paul reminds the Thessalonians he had previously instructed them about. Paul teaches that there is a restraining force present in the world which supernaturally prevents the revealing of the wicked man of sin until that restraining force is taken out of the way (2 Thes 2:5-7). The restraining force will not be removed prematurely, as the man of sin will only be "revealed in his time" (2 Thes 2:6).

This is a specific time set by God. God has a time for the Day of Christ/Day of the LORD, and God has a time for the revealing of the Antichrist. God has a specific time period of 3 ½ years allotted for the supernatural empowerment of the Antichrist (Rev 13:5). God also has a restraining force which prevents the premature arrival of the Antichrist. While there have been several proposals for the identity of this restraining force, such as the power of Rome, or the power of human government, the most credible identification is that of the Holy Spirit and His indwelling presence in the body of church believers. This force must be supernatural and more powerful than the power of Satan. Otherwise, Satan would have already brought forth his ultimate man of sin. Since the only entity more powerful than Satan is God, it is the power of God that restrains the revealing of the Antichrist. Thus, the restraining force can only be removed as a direct act of God.

If Paul was teaching that the church must be present to witness the revealing of the man of sin, how could his words be a comfort to the Thessalonians? They could not. Thus, we can see that Paul is not emphasizing to the Thessalonians to not be troubled because they have not yet seen the revealing of the man of sin, but exactly the opposite, to not be alarmed because the restraining force has not yet been removed by God. Since the man of sin cannot be revealed until the restraining force (about which Paul had already taught them) is removed, and since they (the church) were still present on earth, they need not have any concern about having missed entering the Day of Christ or about having entered the Day of the LORD.

How and when is the man of sin revealed to the world? In one sense he is revealed when he enters the temple in Jerusalem and declares to the world that he is god (2 Thes 2:4). That is the ultimate form of the revealing of the Antichrist. We see that Paul makes reference to that event in this passage. That is the event which fully defines the character of the man of sin. Note, however, that Paul does not actually state that the desecration of the temple and the Antichrist's public declaration of being God is the event by which he is revealed.

The first revealing of the man of sin is likely to be the event which will mark the initiation of the Tribulation (Daniel's 70$^{th}$ Week). That will be the signing of the seven year covenant between Israel and the Antichrist (Dan 9:27). That will be the first event by which the man of sin can be truly identified.

Since the focus of this age (the Age of Grace) is the calling out of a body of believers in Christ (the church) to God, it is the presence of God in the church in the form of the Holy Spirit that serves as the restrainer until God has completed building the body of Christ in the church (Eph 5:27). God's restraining force, the power of the Holy Spirit indwelling the Christian church, must be removed by God before the man of sin can be revealed. The church cannot be present on earth without the indwelling presence of the Holy Spirit. A person only enters the body of the church through baptism by the Holy Spirit and being indwelt by the Holy Spirit (Jn 16:7-15; Rom 8:9, 11; 1 Cor 12:13). The Holy Spirit will not be taken away from the church; therefore, the Holy Spirit will not be removed from the earth while the church is on earth. The church must be taken out of the way, when the restraining force is removed. The indwelling presence of the Holy Spirit will be removed from the earth at the exact moment the church is caught up to heaven by Jesus Christ at the rapture.

In addition, God's unique relationship to Israel in the Old Testament often focused on His indwelling presence in the Tabernacle in the wilderness and later in the Temple in Jerusalem. Since the birth of the church at

Pentecost, the true temple of God on earth is the body of believers who make up the church and are indwelt by the Holy Spirit (1 Cor 3:16-17; 6:19; 2 Cor 6:16; Eph 2:19-22; Rev 3:12).

Consider the implications of Malachi 3:1-5 regarding the Messiah coming suddenly to His temple (Mal 3:1), followed immediately by a description of God's judgment during the Day of the LORD (Mal 3:2-5).

**Malachi 3:1-2**

> Mal 3:1 Behold, I will send my messenger, and he shall prepare the way before me: and the Lord, whom ye seek, shall suddenly come to his temple, even the messenger of the covenant, whom ye delight in: behold, he shall come, saith the LORD of hosts.
> 2 But who may abide the day of his coming? and who shall stand when he appeareth? for he *is* like a refiner's fire, and like fullers' soap:
> 3 And he shall sit *as* a refiner and purifier of silver: and he shall purify the sons of Levi, and purge them as gold and silver, that they may offer unto the LORD an offering in righteousness.

Malachi 3:1 is generally attributed to the first coming of Jesus as the Messiah. John the Baptist was sent as a prophet heralding the coming of Christ; however, that was merely a partial fulfillment. Jesus did not really "suddenly come to his temple." Nor did Jesus initiate God's Day of the LORD judgments against Israel for the purpose of refining Israel. That is a depiction of what will take place during the "time of Jacob's trouble" (Jer 30:7). Compare the question posed by Malachi 3:2 with the question raised in Revelation 6:17, at the time of the breaking of the sixth seal. "For the great day of his wrath is come and who shall be able to stand?" Immediately after the description of the events of the sixth seal, Revelation 7:9 reveals the great multitude of the raptured saints standing before the throne in heaven. That is one group who will be able to stand in the day that God shakes the earth at the beginning of the Day of the LORD.

Malachi reveals that the Messiah will suddenly come to His temple, just as Jesus Christ will come suddenly to and for His church – the present temple of God. Both sudden comings are immediately followed by a period of God's judgments.

Since the Antichrist's ultimate revealing will be his entering the temple of God to proclaim his own deity (2 Thes 2:4), and since the Antichrist cannot actually enter into the body of Christ (which is the believing church) and true temple of this age (which the man of sin will not enter because he is not a believer in Jesus as Christ), it makes sense that God will remove His temple from the earth before the revealing of the man of sin. The removal of the believing church from the earth will end the Age of Grace. The removal of the church as the temple of God would also allow for Israel to rebuild its temple in Jerusalem to function as the temple of God during the Tribulation.

According to this interpretation, the removal of the church at the rapture and the removal of the restraining force by the Holy Spirit simultaneously allow for the rise of Satan's man of sin to the point where he is subsequently revealed to the world. The pretribulational timing of the rapture is the only timing that completely fits the teaching of the removal of the restraining force prior to the revealing of the Antichrist.

## The Rapture Logic Problem

We have introduced several pieces of the prophetic puzzle which impact our understanding of the resurrection of believers and the event known as the rapture. We have identified several important characteristics and a few individual steps in the sequence of events of which the rapture is a part. How do these pieces of the puzzle fit together? Can we draw further conclusions from the evidence of scripture regarding the timing of the rapture? Let's examine the evidence.

1. Jesus has gone to His Father's house in heaven to prepare a place for His church. Jesus will return to receive the church to Himself and take the church to heaven (Jn 14:1-3).
2. The rapture is an event that involves the resurrection of dead Church Age believers and those believers who are living at the moment when Christ returns for His church (1 Cor 15:51-52).
3. Christ brings the souls of the dead believers with Him when He comes (1 Thes 4:14).
4. Christ shouts His command; the archangel's voice rings out; the trumpet of God sounds (1 Thes 4:16).
5. The dead believers rise first (1 Thes 4:16). This means that the souls of the dead believers are brought back from heaven. The souls reunite with the dead bodies. The bodies are then immediately resurrected in an incorruptible, immortal state (1 Cor 15:52-54).
6. The living believers are then changed into incorruptible, immortal bodies (1 Cor 15:52-54).

7. The resurrected dead and the living believers are caught up (raptured) into the clouds to meet the Lord in the air above the earth (1 Thes 4:17).
8. This is a global event. It takes place everywhere dead or living believers are located.
9. This is an almost instantaneous and simultaneous event. It takes place in a span of time described as "the twinkling of an eye" (1 Cor 15:52). This would be much faster than the blink of an eye.
10. The resurrected dead and the raptured living believers will be with the Lord forever (1 Thes 4:17).
11. The Day of Christ begins with Christ's appearing and the rapture of the church to heaven (1 Cor 1:8; 5:5; 2 Cor 1:14; Php 1:6, 10; 2:16; Eph 1:13-14; 4:30).
12. The Day of the LORD begins on earth and the nations are left to go through the time of the Tribulation (Is 2:12; 13:6, 9; 34:8; Jer 46:10; Ezek 13:5; 30:3; Joel 1:15; 2:1, 11, 31; 3:14; Amos 5:18-20; Obad 1:15; Zeph 1:7-8, 14; 2:2-3; Zech 14:1; Mal 4:5; 1 Thes 5:2; 2 Thes 2:2-3; 2 Pet 3:10).
13. A posttribulational rapture is out of the question. The rapture must take place prior to the second coming of Christ.
14. The church appears before the judgment seat of Christ in heaven (Rom 14:10; 1 Cor 3:10-15; 2 Cor 5:10).
15. The church is prepared as the bride of Christ for its marriage to Jesus as the Lamb of God (Rev 19:7-8). The marriage of the church to Christ takes place in heaven.
16. The marriage supper takes place following the marriage (Rev 19:9). Some scholars believe the marriage supper will take place in heaven. Others believe it will take place on earth following Christ's second coming. I believe it will take place on earth. There are guests invited to the marriage supper who are not part of the church as the bride of Christ, but are friends of the bridegroom (Lk 12:36-37; Jn 3:29).
17. Christ returns to earth in power and great glory with His angels and the clouds of heaven (Mt 16:27; 24:30; Mk 8:38; 13:26; Lk 9:26).
18. The church saints who are now the wife of Jesus are included in the armies of heaven who accompany Christ to earth at the time of His second coming (Zech 14:5; Jude 1:14; Rev 17:14; 19:14).
19. As part of His second coming, Jesus will send His angels to separate the elect from the wicked in preparation for judgment (Mt 13:39-42, 49-50; Mt 24:31; Mk 13:27).

20. Following Christ's second coming, thrones will be set up on earth for judgment and the martyred believers of the Tribulation will be resurrected to reign with Christ for one thousand years (Rev 20:4-6).
21. The nation of Israel is judged (Ezek 20:33-38). The Gentiles are judged (Mt 25:31-46). The righteous will enter the Millennial Kingdom while the unrighteous will be excluded from the Kingdom and set aside for eternal punishment.

This overview of events provides a beginning framework for understanding the dynamics of the rapture. It is very important to note the emphasis that Paul has placed on the sequence of events. The dead believers rise first. The dead believers are resurrected before the living believers are changed and caught up to meet with Jesus in the air. This specific sequence is devastating to the argument that the rapture takes place after the Tribulation (Posttribulational Rapture).

The rapture takes place before Christ actually returns to the surface of planet Earth. Some interpret the sequence of events and Mt 24:31 as the rapture being a part of Christ's second coming and that the church is caught up in the air, only to immediately return by accompanying Jesus to battle at the time of Armageddon. However, there must be both living and dead believers as well as living unbelievers on earth for Christ to judge when He returns at His second coming. If Christ resurrected all dead and living believers immediately after the Tribulation during His second coming, who would be left to resurrect afterwards? The rapture at this time would have to include the resurrection of all of the martyrs killed during the Tribulation. However, scripture describes those martyrs as unresurrected souls until Christ resurrects them as part of His judgments after taking His earthly throne following His victory over Satan and the Antichrist (Rev 20:4).

Also, if Christ raptured all living believers at the time of His second coming following the Tribulation, who would be left to populate the nation of Israel and the other nations of the world during the Millennium? All of the resurrected and raptured believers will be in glorified, immortal bodies. They cannot return and repopulate the nations with mortal people. Jesus implied as much when He stated that people once they are resurrected, "they neither marry, nor are given in marriage, but are as the angels of God in heaven (Mt 22:30). In other words, just as the angels do not procreate and make more angels in heaven – the resurrected and immortalized believers will no longer procreate and expand the human race. While the Millennial Kingdom will be a vibrant time of life and regeneration, the world must largely be populated by mortals as both sin and death will still exist. It will be from this group of mortals that Satan will draw his final rebellion against God at the end of his thousand year confinement.

Not only that, the rapture must take place early enough so that God can make a distinction between different groups in the series of resurrections and in the series of judgments. The description of the souls of the martyrs of the Tribulation in the judgment scene of Revelation 20:4 reveals that the rapture of the church must precede the time of the Great Tribulation (the second half of Daniel's 70th week). The rapture of the church does not include the resurrection of any of the believers who are killed resisting the worship of the Antichrist.

This observation is devastating to the proposed timing of the pre-wrath rapture well into the second half of the Tribulation. The martyrs resurrected in Revelation 20:4 include all of the believers killed, at the very least, during the last three and a half years of the Tribulation. This group is not necessarily limited only to those from that time frame, but it will include every one of them.

While some people believe that the resurrection and catching up of the two witnesses (Rev 11:3-13) represents the resurrection and rapture of the church in the middle of the Tribulation, scripture makes no such claim. The two witnesses are representatives of God much like some of the Old Testament prophets. They are endowed with some of the same supernatural powers exhibited by Moses and Elijah in the service of God.

The two witnesses are supernaturally empowered for 1,260 days (3 ½ years) (Rev 11:3). Throughout the entire 3 ½ year ministry of the two witnesses no one will be able to kill them (Rev 11:5). The Antichrist is supernaturally empowered for 42 months (3 ½ years) (Rev 13:5). Throughout the supernatural reign of the Antichrist the saints and the nations of the world are subjected to the power of the Antichrist (Rev 13:7).

As a result, the two witnesses and the Antichrist cannot be supernaturally empowered for the same 3 ½ years. The opposing supernatural characteristics and authorities of these two time periods of 3 ½ years places them in direct conflict with each other. Since the Antichrist will kill the two witnesses at the end of their time of empowerment (Rev 11:7), their time of service must come first. The death and resurrection of the two witnesses closes the second woe (the sixth trumpet judgment) (Rev 9:12-13; 11:14), prior to the blowing of the seventh trumpet judgment (which contains the final seven bowl judgments) (Rev 11:15; 15:6-16:1). Thus, the two witnesses dominate the first half of the Tribulation while the Antichrist and the False Prophet dominate the last half of the Tribulation.

The two witnesses neither symbolize nor represent the church in their actions. They are not God's agents during the Age of Grace, which is the time of the church. Instead, they are God's agents during a portion of the time of God's wrath unleashed during the Day of the LORD. The very character and prominence of the two witnesses argues that the church must not be present, but has already been taken from the earth by the time they step onto the world stage with their supernatural powers at the beginning of the final seven-years of the Tribulation.

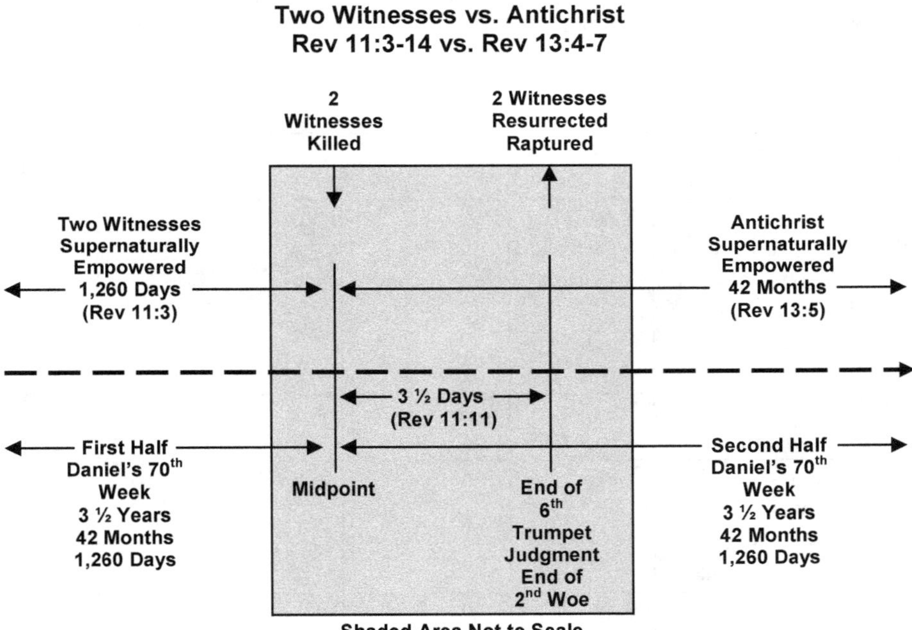


The depiction of the book of Revelation regarding many believers martyred during the entire period of the Tribulation, not just the last 3 ½ years, contrasts with the promises for the church to be delivered (kept from) the time of testing of the entire earth (Rev 3:10). God's judgments and wrath begin with Christ's breaking of the first seal on the scroll in heaven. God's wrath is very evident in the description of the sixth seal. If the church is going to experience these events and suffer so many martyrs, what purpose do these promises serve? For these promises to be true and effective the church cannot be present on earth during the time of these events. The martyrs described in Revelation must become believers and be killed after the church is removed from the earth. The church must be removed well before the middle of the Tribulation.

## Summary of Scriptural Support for the Timing of the Rapture

| **Concept / Scripture** | **Supports Pre-Trib Rapture** | **Supports Mid-Trib Rapture** | **Supports Pre-Wrath Rapture** | **Supports Post-Trib Rapture** |
|---|---|---|---|---|
| The teaching of the rapture is to be a comfort to the church | Yes | No | No | No |
| Doctrine of imminence | Yes | No | No | No |
| Sudden, unexpected return of Christ – at a time that is unknowable in advance | Yes | No | No | No |
| Church to escape God's wrath | Yes | No | No | No |
| A true distinction is maintained between the church and Israel | Yes | No | No | No |
| God's removal of the restraining force | Yes | No | No | No |
| Jewish wedding symbolism | Yes | No | No | No |
| Sequence of resurrections | Yes | Yes | No | No |
| Sequence of judgments | Yes | Yes | No | No |
| Saints in heaven | Yes | Yes | No | No |
| Christ returns with His saints | Yes | Yes | Yes | No |
| Messianic Kingdom on Earth | Yes | Yes | Yes | No |
| Isaiah 26:19-21 | Yes | No | No | No |
| Isaiah 57:1 | Yes | No | No | No |

| Concept / Scripture | Supports Pre-Trib Rapture | Supports Mid-Trib Rapture | Supports Pre-Wrath Rapture | Supports Post-Trib Rapture |
|---|---|---|---|---|
| Zephaniah 2:3 | Yes | No | No | No |
| Matthew 24:42-44 | Yes | No | No | No |
| Luke 21:36 | Yes | No | No | No |
| John 14:1-3 | Yes | No | No | No |
| 1 Corinthians 15:51-53 | Yes | Yes | Yes | No |
| 1 Thessalonians 1:10 | Yes | No | No | No |
| 1 Thessalonians 4:13-18 | Yes | Yes | No | No |
| 1 Thessalonians 5:2-9 | Yes | No | No | No |
| 2 Thessalonians 2:1-8 | Yes | No | No | No |
| Titus 2:13 | Yes | No | No | No |
| Revelation 3:3 | Yes | No | No | No |
| Revelation 3:10 | Yes | No | No | No |
| Revelation 17:14 | Yes | Yes | Yes | No |
| Revelation 19:7-9 | Yes | Yes | Yes | No |
| Revelation 19:14 | Yes | Yes | Yes | No |
| Revelation 20:4-6 | Yes | Yes | No | No |

Since the identity of the Antichrist can be known by his entering into the seven-year covenant of peace with Israel at the beginning of the Tribulation, the requirement that the supernatural restraining force be removed out of the way before his revealing also strongly argues against the midtribulational rapture position. This characteristic demands that the rapture take place before the covenant is confirmed at the beginning of the Tribulation.

The expectation of imminence, the characteristic of Christ's sudden coming at an unknown time, the removal of God's restraining force, the removal of the church as God's temple on earth, the deliverance of the believer from the time of wrath, the symbolism of the Jewish wedding, and the multiple sequences of resurrections and judgments, all point to an earlier timing of the rapture of the church than the beginning of the Tribulation. The perspective of the rapture that best accounts for all of the scriptural evidence and that most strongly distinguishes between Israel and the church is the pretribulational rapture view.

## Consequences of the Rapture

One consideration which sometimes is ignored in the argument of the timing of the rapture regards the natural or inevitable consequences of the rapture itself. What are the logical consequences of the rapture?

1. The rapture can actually be viewed as a form of judgment by God against the unbelieving world. By suddenly snatching all Christian believers from the earth at once, God is intervening in a form of divine wrath. The Age of Grace is over! The nations of the world are left to go through God's preordained series of judgments which are described by the seals, trumpets, and bowls in the book of Revelation. This is the beginning of the God's prophetic Day of the LORD.
2. God's restraining force is removed, which lifts the supernatural restraint against the rise of the Antichrist to world power and his being revealed for who he is.
3. The removal of the church and the indwelling power of the Holy Spirit take away God's restraint against immorality and lawlessness in general, which would unleash global chaos on an unprecedented scale. Rampant crime, political upheaval, and war are logical outcomes.
4. Millions of people suddenly missing from many nations of the world would result in an economic crisis in the best of times. What if the rapture occurred at a time when the global economy was already strained? Or at the same time as a major natural disaster like a large earthquake, or a major war? What happens when millions of relatives try to file police reports on the missing? Who investigates? Many law enforcement officers and emergency workers would also be missing. Some government workers and leaders could be missing. What happens when millions of people do not show up for work, are not paying taxes, and are not paying their mortgages and other debts? What happens to their property? How would the nations of the world deal with the inevitable identity crisis that would ensue? Who is missing? Who is dead? What happens when people steal the identity

and credit of someone who is missing but is no longer here to complain? What happens when an entire family is missing?

5. Some nations would be impacted more directly and more extensively than others. It is very likely that the United States would be severely affected by the loss of a larger percentage of its population compared to many other nations. Many of the nations of Europe will be much less impacted than the United States, as Christianity has weakened considerably throughout Europe. Russia, China, North Korea, all of the Muslim nations, and many Asian nations would be minimally affected by the direct loss of people. Several of these nations would immediately see opportunity in the global chaos to expand their territories and seize world resources by warfare.
6. With the United States and several nations of the West weakened, Israel would be left friendless on the world stage of nations. Israel's truest friends, Christian Zionists, would be gone. In spite of the Jewish population in the United States, the economic and military support of the United States for Israel would be a thing of the past. Israel would naturally be viewed as vulnerable prey by Russia and the Muslim nations. Israel would face a sudden invasion, most likely by the alliance of Gog and Magog (Ezekiel 38–39).
7. The rapture of the church ends the Church Age or Age of Grace. God now turns His full attention to fulfilling His prophetic program for Israel.

If the rapture occurred as a posttribulational event at the time of the second coming, all of these consequences would be minimal and ineffectual. All believers, dead and living, would be caught up in the air, leaving only unbelievers left on earth. We have already seen how this conflicts with God's program of a series of resurrections and judgments for both the living and the dead and how it would leave no mortal people on earth to populate the Messianic Kingdom. This timing does not allow for the removal of the indwelling power of the Holy Spirit in the church as God's restraining force to serve as a catalyst for the revealing of the Antichrist. The only chaos and divine wrath left in God's plan for the world are the events of the seventh bowl judgment.

If the rapture occurred as a midtribulational event, the consequences would also be somewhat limited. The power of the Holy Spirit in the church would be removed to allow for the Antichrist to enter the temple in Jerusalem and declare himself to be god. However, the Antichrist would have already been a major player in world events for at least 3 ½ years since his entering into a seven-year covenant of peace with Israel. The identity of the Antichrist can be known to discerning students of the Bible prior to the abomination of desolation event at the middle of the Tribulation. Many of God's forms of judgment and wrath (the seven seal judgments and the first six trumpet judgments) would have already been imposed upon the world.

If the rapture takes place prior to the seven-year covenant of peace, which actually begins the Tribulation, the consequences are the most impacting. The full effect of the rapture as a form of judgment and wrath from God is felt by the world. Chaos erupts causing international strife and warfare. The global chaos creates the ideal conditions for the man of sin to rise to international prominence and create his powerbase. It is very likely that this chaos would be seen as the opportunity to further the implementation of a global controlling government and a global controlled economy. Radically different economic, currency, and identity control measures would be adopted and imposed upon the nations. The seven-year covenant of peace between the Antichrist and Israel would eventually follow, beginning the Tribulation.

## Rapture Conclusion

The rapture will be a very real and very dynamic event that will not only impact the believers of the Christian church, but the entire world as well. The rapture will be a complete catching up of the church – all believers will be caught up to heaven. The rapture will take place suddenly, without warning or time for preparation. The rapture will remove the church as the bride of Christ and as the temple of God from the earth before God's wrath becomes manifest. The rapture of the church will result in the removal of the restraining force of the Holy Spirit who indwells the believers of the church so that the man of sin can rise to power and be revealed to the world. The rapture will take place before the time of the Tribulation begins.

**Notes: The Rapture of the Church**

1. Robert Van Kampen, *The Sign*, (Wheaton, IL: Crossway Books, 1992), p. 259.
2. Van Kampen, *The Sign*, p. 278.
3. Van Kampen, *The Sign*, p. 179.

# 3

# The Day of the LORD vs. The Day of Christ

## Day of the LORD

The "day of the LORD" is a specific title used by scripture to refer to an intense or dynamic period of God's intervention on earth. It is the key biblical title that denotes God's manifest intervention in judgment and overlaps both Old Testament and New Testament scripture. The Bible uses it as the primary designator for the time when God deems it necessary to rise up and remind Israel, the nations of the world, and all unrepentant sinners of His presence, His sovereignty, and His purpose for mankind. He is the God Almighty; His name will be magnified; He alone will be glorified. At the end of His Day of intervention all mankind "shall know that I am the LORD" (Ezek 36:23; 38:23; 39:6-7, 22, 28; Joel 2:27; 3:17). God not only purges the world of sin, He magnifies and sanctifies Himself in the process (Ezek 38:16, 23).

This phrase "the day of the LORD" appears in the Old Testament prophetic writings of: Isaiah, Jeremiah, Ezekiel, Joel, Amos, Obadiah, Zephaniah, Zechariah, and Malachi (Isa 2:12; 13:6, 9, 13; 34:8; Jer 46:10; Ezek 13:5; 30:3; Joel 1:15; 2:1, 11, 31; 3:14; Amos 5:18-20; Obad 1:15; Zeph 1:7-8, 14, 18; 2:2-3; Zech 14:1; Mal 4:5). In the New Testament "the day of the LORD" appears in: Act 2:20; 1 Thes 5:2; 2 Thes 2:2-3; and 2 Pet 3:10. There are many other passages which directly relate to the Day of the LORD such as those which allude to "that day" (Isa 2:17, 20; 24:21; Jer 30:7; Ezek 38:19; Zeph 1:15; Lk 21:34-36), "this is the day whereof I have spoken" (Ezek 39:8), "at the last day" (Jn 6:39-40, 44, 54), and "the great day of his wrath" (Rev 6:17).

Joel's Warning – The Day of the LORD

> Alas for the day! for the **day of the LORD** *is* at hand, and as a **destruction** from the Almighty shall it come. … Blow ye the trumpet in Zion, and sound an alarm in my holy mountain: let all the inhabitants of the land tremble: for the **day of the LORD** cometh, for *it is* nigh at hand; A day of **darkness** and of **gloominess**, a day of **clouds** and of **thick darkness**, as the morning spread upon the mountains: a great people and a strong; there hath not been ever the like, neither shall be any more after it, *even* to the years of many generations. … The earth shall quake before them; the heavens shall tremble: the sun and the moon shall be dark, and the stars shall withdraw their shining: And **the LORD shall utter his voice** before his army: for his camp *is* very great: for *he is* strong that executeth his word: for the **day of the LORD** *is* **great and very terrible**; and **who can abide it?** … And I will shew wonders in the heavens and in the earth, blood, and fire, and pillars of smoke. The sun shall be turned into darkness, and the moon into blood, before the **great and the terrible day of the LORD** come. … (Joel 1:15; 2:1-2, 10-11, 30-31; bold added)

> I will also gather all nations, and will bring them down into the valley of Jehoshaphat, and will plead with them there for my people and *for* my heritage Israel, whom they have scattered among the nations, and parted my land. … Proclaim ye this among the Gentiles; Prepare war, wake up the mighty men, let all the men of war draw near; let them come up: Beat your plowshares into swords, and your pruning hooks into spears: let the weak say, I *am* strong. Assemble yourselves, and come, all ye heathen, and gather yourselves together round about: thither cause thy mighty ones to come down, O LORD. Let the heathen be wakened, and come up to the valley of Jehoshaphat: for there will I sit to judge all the heathen round about. Put ye in the sickle, for the harvest is ripe: come, get you down; for the press is full, the fats overflow; for their wickedness *is* great. Multitudes, multitudes in the **valley of decision**: for the **day of the**

> **LORD** *is* near in the **valley of decision**. The sun and the moon shall be darkened, and the stars shall withdraw their shining. The LORD also shall roar out of Zion, and **utter his voice** from Jerusalem; and the **heavens and the earth shall shake**: but the LORD *will be* the hope of his people, and the strength of the children of Israel. (Joel 3:2, 9-16; bold added)

Zephaniah's Warning – The Day of the LORD

> Hold thy peace at the presence of the Lord GOD: for the **day of the LORD** *is* at hand: for the LORD hath prepared **a sacrifice**, he hath bid his guests. And it shall come to pass in the **day of the LORD'S sacrifice**, that I will punish the princes, and the king's children, and all such as are clothed with strange apparel. … The **great day of the LORD** *is* near, *it is* near, and hasteth greatly, *even* **the voice of the day of the LORD**: the mighty man shall cry there bitterly. **That day** *is* **a day of wrath**, a day of **trouble and distress**, a day of **wasteness and desolation**, a day of **darkness and gloominess**, a day of **clouds and thick darkness**, A **day of the trumpet and alarm** against the fenced cities, and against the high towers. And I will bring distress upon men, that they shall walk like blind men, because they have sinned against the LORD: and their blood shall be poured out as dust, and their flesh as the dung. Neither their silver nor their gold shall be able to deliver them in the **day of the LORD'S wrath**; but the whole land shall be devoured by the fire of his jealousy: for he shall make even a speedy riddance of all them that dwell in the land (Zeph 1:7-8, 14-18; bold added).

The focus of the day is on the LORD Himself – His actions and intent. Where the translators of the King James Version and other Bible translations render "LORD" in all capital letters, as they do with the references to "the day of the LORD," they are dealing with the actual name of God. LORD does not just mean God. LORD is rendered in place of the Tetragrammaton [יהוה], the four Hebrew letters (consonants) representing the name of God. These are often transliterated JHVH, IHVH, JHWH, YHVH, or YHWH, and are verbalized variously as Jehovah, Jahweh, Yahweh, or Yahveh. This is the supreme name of the supreme God. Interestingly, we first encounter this name of God in the Bible in connection to a day when He rose up in action –

His action of creation. Genesis 2:4 contains the first reference to this name of God in the context of "the day that the LORD God made the earth and the heavens."

The prophets Joel and Zephaniah reveal some of the primary characteristics of the Day of the LORD. It is a day of wrath – God's wrath! It is referred to as the great day, as well as the great and terrible day of the LORD. It is a day of trouble and distress (the time of Jacob's trouble mentioned in Jeremiah 30:7). It is also a time characterized by wasteness and desolation, darkness and gloominess, and clouds and thick darkness. It is a day when both the heavens and the earth shall shake. This is true physically, politically, and spiritually. Physically there will be great global earthquakes with islands and mountains being moved from their places as well as major effects to the atmosphere (Isa 2:19, 21; Ezek 38:19-20; Hag 2:6-7; Mt 24:7; Rev 6:12; 16:18). Politically, there will be a number of wars with nation turning against nation, kingdom against kingdom, some nations overthrown, the rise of ten kings, and the consolidation of world government under the rule of one dictator. Spiritually there will be war in heaven and on earth, with Satan and his angels finally cast completely out of heaven to the earth. The earth will be forced to endure the rise of Satan's theocratic dictator – the Antichrist, who will attempt to banish God and rule as the god of the earth.

This day has a voice – the voice of God (Joel 2:11; 3:16; Amos 1:2; Zeph 1:14). God's voice is often characterized in the Bible as the sounding of thunder or the sound of rushing waters. The day is marked as a day of thundering uproar reverberating across the landscape. It is the breaking of God's silence, the sounding of trumpets in the form of alarms, as well as the sound of weeping that follows. It is the sound of earthquake, of volcanic eruption, of violent storm. It is the sound of war and nuclear explosion accompanied by pillars of smoke (Joel 2:30). It is a time of verbal contrast. The day is dominated by the voice of God, the shouted commands of Christ before His armies – both to call His church to Him at the time of the rapture, and to lead them back from heaven at the end of the Tribulation to "the battle of that great day of God Almighty" (Rev 16:14). Out of the mouth of Christ thunders the word of God and flashes the sword with which He smites the armies of the Antichrist. Out of the mouths of the mighty men are flung shouts of blasphemy, cursing God for His judgments (Rev 16:9, 11, 21) and the cries of bitter weeping at the greatness of their destruction (Zeph 1:14).

The Day of the LORD is a day of sacrifice – a sacrifice prepared by God (Isa 34:6; Jer 46:10; Ezek 39:17-20; Zeph 1:7-8; Rev 19:17-18). God invites the nations to sacrifice themselves in war against Israel. God invites His birds and beasts to feast upon the sacrifice. The passages in Ezekiel 39 and Revelation 19 particularly illustrate God's preparation of great sacrifices or suppers for the carrion feeding birds or for the wild beasts. God invites them to feast upon the carnage of warfare amidst great battlefields in the immediate aftermath of both the Gog and Magog invasion of Israel and the War of Armageddon.

These and the other Day of the LORD passages portray the sense that this is not a normal day. There is nothing normal about this day. It is not even a twenty-four hour period of time, although some teach that it is. This "day" extends over a period of time – it has phases. There are warnings regarding the nearness of the Day of the LORD which apply to the very beginning phase when it comes upon the nations of the world very suddenly (Isa 13:6; Joel 1:15; 2:1-2, 30-31; Obad 1:15; Zeph 1:7-8, 14; 1 Thes 5:2-3). There are warnings that apply to the nearness of the day pointing to the very end of the Day of the LORD as in the multitudes of Gentiles in the valley of decision (Joel 3). The time that God gathers all nations against Jerusalem to face His judgment comes only at the very end of The Day of the LORD'S wrath.

Obadiah reveals that as the Day of the LORD approaches God will begin to levy the overdue debt of His curse for curse code of conduct (Gen 12:3) against the nations for their perpetual hatred of Israel and their repeated acts of violence against Israel. The Day of the LORD will be a time of judgment from God that will strongly enforce that ethical code of conduct – blessing for blessing and curse for curse. "For the Day of the LORD *is* near upon all the heathen [nations]: as thou hast done, it shall be done unto thee: thy reward shall return upon thine own head" (Obad 1:15).

Jeremiah referred to the Day of the LORD as that day. "Alas! for that day is great, so that none *is* like it: it *is* even the time of Jacob's trouble; but he shall be saved out of it" (Jer 30:7). Jeremiah 30:9 shows that this time of judgment, when Israel is saved through a period of terrible calamity, is immediately followed by God raising up King David over Israel (God restores the Davidic throne and kingdom), which is a reference to the Messianic Kingdom. God intentionally uses this time of the Day of the LORD as a period of refinement and purification of the nation of Israel to prepare it for its national redemption and its role in the Messianic Kingdom (Mal 3:2-4).

Psalm 110 employs a variant phrase "in the day of his wrath." "The LORD said unto my Lord, Sit thou at my right hand, until I make thine enemies thy footstool. ... The Lord at thy right hand shall strike through kings in **the day of his wrath"** (Ps 110:1, 5).

Jesus Christ ascended to heaven to sit at the right hand of God, the Father, until the time comes that God, the Father, declares His enemies to be fair game. Jesus will be the one who will conquer the enemies of God. In Revelation chapter 5, we see Jesus standing, taking a seven-sealed scroll from the right hand of God, the Father, seated on His throne in heaven. From a heavenly perspective, when Jesus begins breaking the seals on the scroll,

He initiates the Day-of-the-LORD judgments (the day of his wrath) against the enemies of God, on earth and in heaven. From the perspective of the church, when Christ comes suddenly to claim his own to Him at the rapture of the church, He will leave in His wake a world in the throes of chaos, war, and wrath that begins the Day of the LORD on earth and the Day of Christ in heaven.

## The Characteristics of the Day of the LORD

| Characteristics | Scripture References |
|---|---|
| The prophet Elijah to come before | Mal 4:5 |
| Sun turns dark & moon turns to blood (blood red moon) before | Joel 2:31; Act 2:20; Rev 6:12 |
| God begins to implement judgment upon nations based upon His code of conduct: blessing for blessing and curse for curse – as they do to Israel it will be done to them. Judgment begins before as the Day draws near. | Gen 12:3; 27:29; Obad 1:15 |
| Day of God's vengeance | Isa 34:8; Jer 46:10 |
| Destruction from the Almighty | Isa 13:6; Joel 1:15 |
| God's wrath and fierce anger | Ps 110:5; Isa 13:9, 13; Zeph 1:15; 2:2-3; Rev 6:17 |
| Great and very terrible | Joel 2:11, 31; Zeph 1:14; Mal 4:5; Act 2:20; Rev 6:17 |
| The day is great – none is like it | Jer 30:7; Joel 2:2; Mt 24:21 |
| Clouds and thick darkness | Ezek 30:3; Joel 2:2 |
| Darkness and gloom | Joel 2:2; Amos 5:18, 20; Zeph 1:15 |
| Sun dark, Moon dark, Stars dark | Isa 13:10; Joel 2:10; 3:15 |
| Trouble and distress | Zeph 1:15 |
| Wasteness and desolation | Zeph 1:15 |
| Trumpet and alarm | Joel 2:1; Zeph 1:16 |
| Heavens and earth shaken | Isa 2:19, 21; 13:13; Joel 3:16 |
| The voice of the day – The sound of God's voice vs. the sound of bitter weeping | Joel 2:11; Zeph 1:14 |
| God's presence | Zeph 1:7 |

| Characteristics | Scripture References |
|---|---|
| Who can abide it? | Joel 2:11; Mal 3:2; Rev 6:17 |
| Men hide in fear of God | Isa 2:10, 12, 19, 21; Rev 6:15-17 |
| Some can be hidden or escape during the time of earthly judgments | Zeph 2:2-3; Lk 21:34-36 |
| Comes upon all nations | Obad 1:15 |
| Prepared as a sacrifice | Zeph 1:7-8 |
| As a snare, or a trap | Lk 21:34-36 |
| Like a thief in the night | 1 Thes 5:2; 2 Pet 3:10 |
| Sudden destruction | 1 Thes 5:3 |
| As travail upon a woman with child | Isa 13:6-8; Jer 30:6; 1 Thes 5:3 |
| The Time of Jacob's Trouble | Jer 30:7 |
| A year of recompense for the controversy of Zion | Isa 34:8 |
| The proud and the lofty will be brought low | Isa 2:11-12, 17; 13:11 |
| Israel's hedge of protection is not made by Israel, its leaders, or its military forces | Ezek 13:5 |
| Multitudes in the valley of decision | Joel 3:14 |
| The last day – the resurrection of the righteous | Jn 6:39-40, 44, 54 |
| God will be exalted and glorified; God's name will be magnified | Isa 2:11, 17, 21; Zech 14:9 |
| God will deliver Israel | Jer 30:7; Joel 2:32; 3:16, 20 |

## The Timing of the Day of the LORD

There are several viewpoints regarding the timing and duration of the Day of the LORD. Some believe that it equates to the seven years of the Tribulation. Others identify it with the second half of Daniel's 70th Week, which many call the "Great Tribulation." The advocates of the "Pre-Wrath Rapture" begin it about half way through the second half of Daniel's 70th Week and then extend it for 30 days beyond the end of the seventh year. Yet others claim that it is limited to or only begins with the time of Christ's second coming at the very end of the Tribulation.

Many scholars note that although the Day begins as a time of God's judgment and wrath, it continues throughout the time of the Messianic Kingdom (the Millennium). The night of darkness is eclipsed by the daylight of God's glory. The kingdoms of man are replaced by the kingdom of God. Renald Showers makes an argument for this concept, with the following observation: "Just as each day of creation and the Jewish day were twofold in nature—a time of darkness ('night') followed by a time of light ('day'; Gen. 1:4-5)—so the future Day of the Lord will be twofold in nature—a period of darkness (divine judgment) followed by a period of light (divine blessing and rule)."[1]

While I believe that this characterization is true, this book is primarily focused on the characteristics and sequence of events relating to the beginning of the end. Thus, we are placing that portion of the day which transpires as a time of God's wrath under the lens of our microscope. In that context, the question of how and when the Day of the LORD begins is of primary concern.

## The Great Day View – The Day of the LORD

From this perspective the Day of the LORD is directly equated with the great day of the Second Coming or Revelation of Christ. This is taken in part because of the descriptive language of several references to the day as: "the day of the LORD *is* great and very terrible" (Joel 2:11), "the great and terrible day of the LORD" (Joel 2:31), "The great day of the LORD *is* near" (Zeph 1:14), "the great and dreadful day of the LORD" (Mal 4:5), "that great and notable day of the LORD" (Act 2:20), and "the battle of that great day of the God Almighty" (Rev 16:14). In this context, the day is often taken to be a literal single day incorporating a series of catastrophic events.

Richard L. Mayhue takes this position when he applies the phrase to God's judgment that "climaxes" the Tribulation. "Most significant in [Joel] 2:31 (NKJV) is the statement that the great cosmic signs will be a prelude 'before the coming of the great and awesome day of the Lord.' This seems to limit the day of the Lord to the very end of the Tribulation if Joel 3:15, Matthew 24:29, and Revelation 6:12 refer to the same event. The day of the Lord at the end of the Tribulation will contain unmistakable manifestations of God's greatness."[2]

Renald Showers supports this view, but he does it with the larger prophetic picture in mind. In his book *Maranatha Our Lord, Come!,* Showers argues that there is a dual character to the Day of the LORD, in the sense that there is both a broad day and a narrow day. In the broad sense he applies the Day to the entire seven years of Daniel's 70th Week as well as to the Millennium. We will further examine this broad view shortly.

**The Day of the LORD = The Great Day of Christ's Revelation**

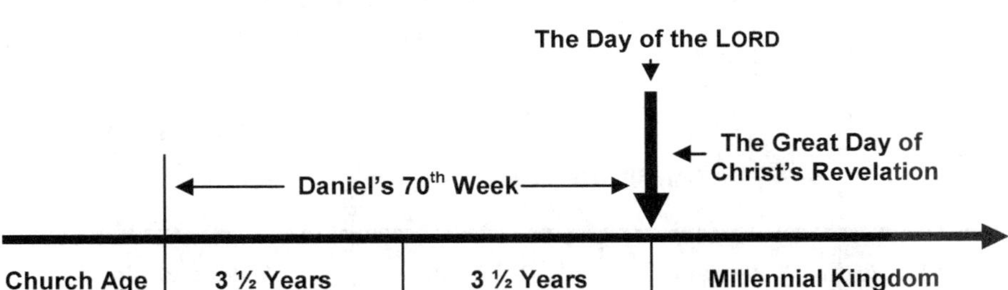


"The narrow sense refers to one specific day—the day on which Christ will return to the earth from heaven with His angels." Showers explains further,

> This other Day will be one part of the broad Day of the Lord, but there is a genuine sense in which it will be a complete Day of the Lord on its own, different from the broad Day of the Lord. … Thus, there will be two future Days of the Lord. … Thus, the narrow Day of Joel 3 and Zechariah 14 will be the day on which Christ comes to the earth. … Although the earlier part of the judgment phase of the broad Day will involve a great outpouring of divine wrath upon the domain of Satan and mankind, the narrow Day will be the grand climax of that judgment phase.[3]

Showers emphasizes, "we should note that the Scriptures apply the expression 'the great and terrible day of the LORD' to the narrow Day, not the broad Day." He insinuates that all of the references to "the great and terrible day" are to be applied only to the narrow day of Christ's revelation that climaxes the Tribulation. He specifically includes the passage of Joel 2:31, with its reference to the sun turning dark and the moon turning blood red "before the great and terrible day of the LORD come," in his focus on the narrow Day. Showers even quotes E. W. Bullinger who makes the same claim in his *Commentary on Revelation*.[4] I believe that this linkage is problematic. This is a key passage and its proper application is critical to understanding the sequence of events during the Day of the LORD. We will take a closer look at this issue shortly as a part of this examination regarding the timing of the Day of the LORD.

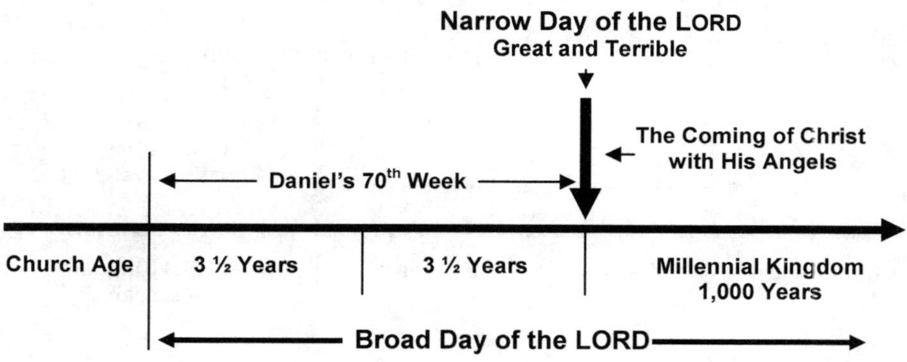


## Pre-Wrath Rapture View – The Day of the LORD

The perspective of the pre-wrath rapture is examined in the chapter regarding the rapture of the church. Where the pre-wrath advocates argue for a unique timing of the rapture, they also present a different concept regarding the timing and duration of the Day of the LORD. In his book *The Sign*, Robert Van Kampen teaches that the Day of the LORD begins with the seventh seal of the book of Revelation during the middle of the second half of Daniel's 70th Week. He envisions the Day of the LORD as extending through the remainder of Daniel's 70th Week, plus an additional thirty days beyond the end of the seventh year.

Van Kampen does characterize the Day of the LORD as the time of God's wrath, which immediately follows Christ's rapture of the church: "*The Rapture will, in effect, activate the wrath.*"[5] However, he envisions this period of God's intervention as beginning only after five or more years of the unleashing of man's wrath against man, as well as the Great Tribulation of Satan's wrath on the earth. "Christ will 'cut short' that time of great affliction by Antichrist and will gather His elect to Himself at the Rapture, on the same day that He unleashes His day-of-the-Lord destruction on the wicked world that remains, sometime during the second half of the seventieth week but before its completion."[6]

He argues that Christ's breaking of the first six seals on the heavenly scroll characterizes the first three-quarters of time of Daniel's 70th Week. Thus, in Van Kampen's view the first four seals characterized by false Christ's, wars, famine, along with plaque and death initiate the beginning of the birth pangs that play out during the first half of Daniel's 70th Week. With his late start to the Day of the LORD and its direct association to the wrath of

God, it is imperative for Van Kampen to emphasize his view that none of the first four seals involve any wrath of God. Accordingly he stresses, "it is essential to understand that the great calamities brought on by the four horsemen are not the beginning or any part of God's day-of-the-Lord wrath; the same is true even of the great tribulation which will follow during the second half of the last week. … it is essential to understand that these events do not correspond to the day-of-the-Lord wrath and that the church will not be raptured before these events occur."[7]

According to Van Kampen, the Great Tribulation of Satan's wrath begins at the midpoint of the 70th Week and is marked by the martyrdom of the fifth seal. The sixth seal, with its great earthquake, the sun being darkened and the moon turning blood red, then becomes the sign of the end of the age and the coming Day of the LORD.

**Pre-Wrath Rapture View of the Day of the LORD**

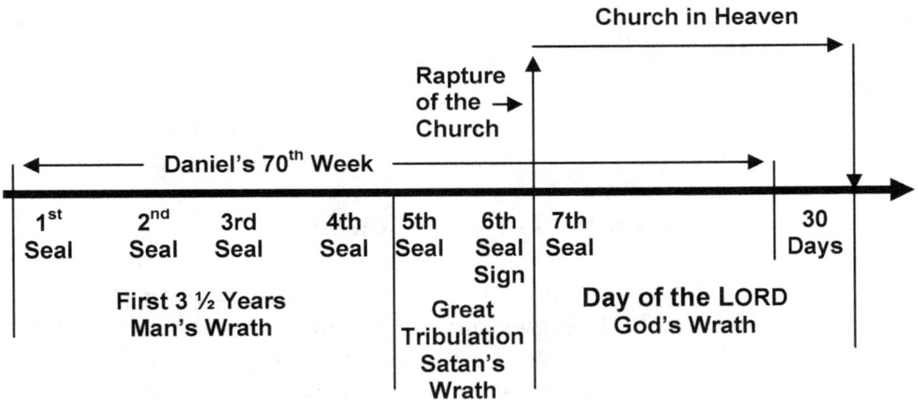


## Great Tribulation View – The Day of the LORD

The Day of the LORD is identified with the time of Great Tribulation that begins and ends with the 3 ½ years of the 2nd Half of Daniel's 70th Week. Clarence Larkin takes this view in his book *Dispensational Truth*. Larkin specifically equates the Great Tribulation with the second half of Daniel's 70th Week or the "Tribulation Period." He states the Day of the LORD "is the day of 'Vengeance of Our Lord,' and includes the period of the 'Great Tribulation' and the Millennium that follows."[8]

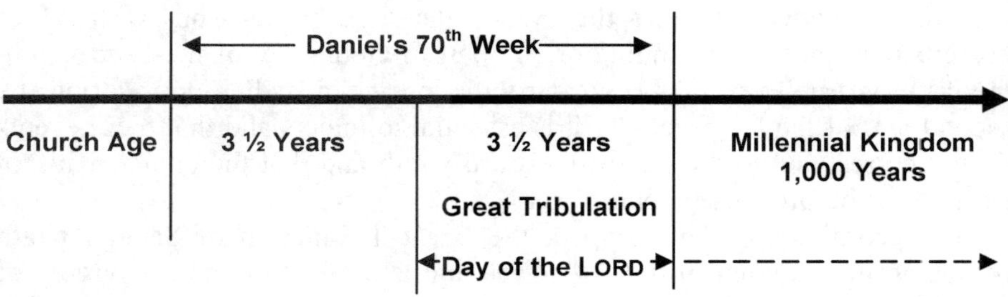


There are some students of prophecy who do not accept the premise of a future seven-year Tribulation. Some argue that Daniel's 70th Week has partially been fulfilled by the ministry of Jesus. They equate the first half of the week with the 3 ½ years of Jesus ministry so that Jesus was "cut off" in the middle of the 70th prophetic week. Thus, for some like David Dolan in his book *Israel in Crisis*, there only remains a tribulation period of 3 ½ years remaining to be fulfilled.[9] Although I am not aware of Dolan specifically equating the final half of Daniel's 70th Week with the Day of the LORD, it would be natural for people who limit the future Tribulation to 3 ½ years to adopt this position.

## Daniel's 70th Week View – The Day of the LORD

Many scholars teach that the Day of the LORD is the same time period as Daniel's 70th Week. It begins and ends with the seven years of the Tribulation of Daniel's 70th Week. We could easily refer to this as the Tribulation View. Some scholars who take this view also place the rapture at the beginning or immediately preceding the Tribulation (Daniel's 70th Week). Thus, they connect the Day of the LORD as beginning immediately, or after a gap in time, following the pretribulational rapture of the church coinciding it exactly with the time of Daniel's 70th Week.

Renald Showers describes the significance and timing of the Day of the LORD in *Maranatha Our Lord, Come!*

> In the Scriptures the expression 'the Day of the Lord' … is strongly related to God's rule of the earth, and therefore, to His sovereign purpose for world history and specific events within that history. The Day of the Lord refers to God's special interventions into the course of world

> events to judge His enemies, accomplish His purpose for history, and thereby demonstrate who He is—the sovereign God of the universe. … In addition, we should note that the biblical expression 'the Day of the Lord' has a double sense (broad and narrow) in relationship to the future. The broad sense refers to an extended period of time involving divine interventions related at least to the 70th week of Daniel and the thousand-year Millennium.[10]

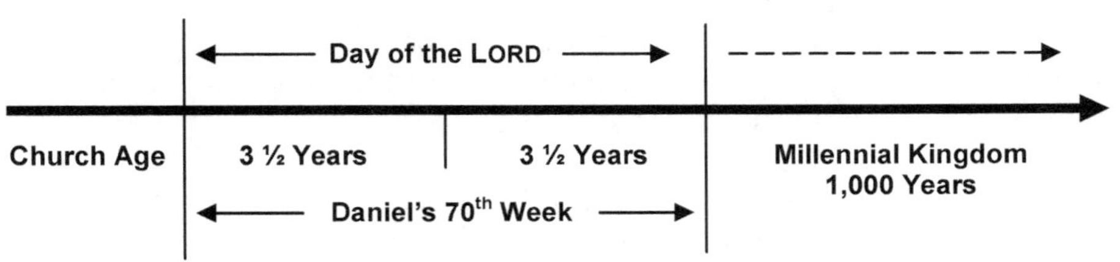


In regards to the relationship between the Day of the LORD and the rapture Showers observes, "the broad Day of the Lord is a different subject from the Rapture of the church. … since the Rapture will not be part of the Day of the Lord, there must be a period of time between the Rapture and the beginning of the broad Day. … since the Rapture will not be part of the Day of the Lord, it will not be the starting point of the broad Day."[11]

A number of scholars seem to take this position. It is not uncommon for scholars who advocate the pretribulational timing of the rapture to create an undefined gap or period of time between the rapture of the church and the beginning of the seven-year Tribulation as the Day of the LORD. In their book, *Charts of Bible Prophecy*, H. Wayne House and Randall Price include a chart titled: "Dispensational Time Chart of the Last Things." This chart identifies this period of time between the "catching up" or rapture of the church and the Day of the Lord as the "Interstitial Period."[12] The length and characteristics of this Interstitial Period are left undefined. An interstice is a small or narrow gap or space between things or between parts of a larger object. The implication of identifying this gap of time as an interstitial period is that it is perceived as somewhat short, somewhat insignificant, and somewhat unknowable. That there is a gap of time between the rapture and the beginning of Daniel's 70th Week is, or should be, inherent within the context of the pretribulational rapture position. However, is Showers correct in his assessment that there is an inherent gap between the rapture and the beginning of the Day of the LORD?

In his book *Things to Come*, J. Dwight Pentecost quotes Harry A. Ironside who says: "… when at last the day of grace is ended the day of the Lord will succeed it. … The day of the Lord follows [the rapture]."[13] Ironside's observation insinuates that logically the Day of the LORD cannot come before the end of the Age of Grace. Instead, it immediately follows the Church Age, which ends with the rapture of the church. Pentecost then insinuates that Ironside equated that beginning with the period of the Tribulation.

Pentecost then makes an observation and argument as to why the Day cannot be limited to the time of the second coming of Christ but must be an extended time in the sense of Showers' "broad Day." In the process of making that argument, Pentecost directly situates the rapture at the beginning of the seven-year Tribulation.

> If the Day of the Lord did not begin until the second advent, since that event is preceded by signs, the Day of the Lord could not come as a "thief in the night," unexpected, and unheralded, as it is said it will come in 1 Thessalonians 5:2. The only way this day could break unexpectedly upon the world is to have it begin immediately after the rapture of the church. It is thus concluded that the Day of the Lord is that extended period of time beginning with God's dealing with Israel after the rapture at the beginning of the tribulation period and extending through the second advent and the millennial age unto the creation of the new heavens and new earth after the millennium.[14]

Arnold Fruchtenbaum unequivocally takes this view in his book *The Footsteps of the Messiah*. Fruchtenbaum further distances the beginning of the Day of the LORD from the rapture of the church. He understands that the rapture is not the event which officially begins Daniel's 70th Week, as that distinction clearly belongs to the confirmation of a seven-year covenant with Israel. Fruchtenbaum intentionally chooses to attach the beginning of God's prophetic Day to the signing of the covenant at the beginning of Daniel's 70th Week.

> The term *the Day of Jehovah* is the most common term in the Old Testament for the Tribulation. It is a period of time that begins with the signing of the Seven-Year Covenant and ends with the Second Coming of Messiah

exactly seven years later. Some teach that the Day of the Jehovah starts with the Rapture itself, assuming that it is the Rapture that begins the Tribulation. But because there could easily be a period of time between the Rapture and the start of the Tribulation, it is better to view the Day of Jehovah as starting with the Seven-Year Covenant.[15]

## Issues Regarding the Timing of the Day of the LORD

We can see that there is disagreement as to how and when the Day of the LORD begins as well as how long it lasts. The proponents of each view attempt to align key pieces of the prophetic puzzle together to make their case. But which perspective of the Day of the LORD presents the best alignment of the key pieces of the puzzle? While Renald Showers' concept for a dual nature of the Day as a period of darkness followed by period of light, as well as having the dual sense of both a broad (extended period) as well as a different narrow period for the Great Day, makes sense, does it give us the full picture? Does the exclusive but limited Great Day of Christ's return have merit? Does the "great and terrible day" only apply to the return of Christ at the end of the Tribulation? Can the pre-wrath rapture view give a better picture of the puzzle? Can equating the 3 ½ years of the Great Tribulation of the final half of Daniel's 70$^{th}$ Week to the Day of the LORD provide the answer? Will extending the Day of the LORD to the full seven years of a future Tribulation (Daniel's 70$^{th}$ Week) resolve all the requirements for God's prophetic puzzle? Or are we still missing something that makes the picture of the puzzle come into a clearer focus?

There are several issues that need to be examined in an effort to answer these questions. In the numerous passages that describe the coming Day of the LORD, God's prophets have revealed several important clues that must be considered in solving the equation: The beginning of the Day of the LORD = ? How can we characterize the very beginning of God's Day of the LORD? What will the Day look like? Several key questions highlighting these characteristics include:

- "The great and terrible day of the LORD" – How does this key descriptive phrase relate to the beginning of the Day?
- Sixth Seal – How do the prophecies revealed in the passages of Joel 2:30-31 and Revelation 6:12-17 (6$^{th}$ Seal) relate to the beginning of the Day?

- Fear! – How does fear of God relate to the beginning of the Day of the LORD?
- Birth Pangs – How does the concept of "Birth Pangs" relate to the beginning of the Day? How does Jesus describe "the beginning of sorrows" or the beginning of birth pangs in Matthew 24?
- Sudden Destruction – How does the implication of "sudden destruction" impact the timing of the Day?
- Peace and Safety – How does the concept of "peace and safety" relate to the beginning of the Day?
- Acts 2 – How does Peter's quote in Acts 2 of a key passage from Joel 2 relate to the Day of the LORD?
- A Sign – How does the insinuation of a sign or pre-signs relate to or impact the beginning of the Day?
- The Rapture – What is the relationship of the rapture of the church to the beginning of the Day?

The issues pertaining to several of these questions are very much interconnected. The answers are going to intertwine to form a matrix that will give us a more comprehensive view of the prophetic puzzle.

One of the primary arguments for the Great Day View lies in the use of the descriptive phrase "the great and terrible day of the LORD" and it's several variations throughout the Bible. Some scholars, including the previous quote from Renald Showers, apply this phrase exclusively to the final day of the Tribulation when Christ returns to earth. After all, the classic concept of the War of Armageddon is specifically named "the battle of that great day of God Almighty" in Revelation 16:14. It seems natural to some prophecy teachers to conclude that the Day of the LORD begins at the beginning of Daniel's 70$^{th}$ Week, the Great Tribulation begins at the middle of the 70$^{th}$ Week, and the Great and Terrible Day equates to the day of Christ's Revelation at the end of the seven-year Tribulation. Is this an accurate interpretation of the particular phrase "great and terrible day," or can it have a broader application in the context of the Day of the LORD?

There is no question that both terms, the Day of the LORD as well as the Great and Terrible Day of the LORD have application to the time of Christ's Revelation. How are the descriptors "great" and "great and terrible" used in the passages relating to the Day?

- Joel 2:11 – the day of the LORD *is* **great** and very **terrible**; and who can abide it?
- Joel 2:31 – before the **great** and the **terrible** day of the LORD come.

- Jeremiah 30:7 – Alas! for that day *is* **great**, so that none *is* like it: it *is* even the time of Jacob's trouble.
- Ezekiel 38:19 – in the fire of my wrath have I spoken, Surely in **that day** there shall be a **great** shaking in the land of Israel (Global Earthquake).
- Zephaniah 1:14 – The **great** day of the LORD *is* near, *it is* near.
- Malachi 4:5 – before the coming of the **great** and **dreadful** day of the LORD. Note: The translators of the KJV rendered dreadful for terrible. However, Malachi and Joel use the same Hebrew word so the meaning is the same. Also, all of these uses of the word "great" in Joel, Jeremiah, Ezekiel, Zephaniah, and Malachi are translations of a different Hebrew word, but it is the same word in Hebrew in all of these passages.
- Acts 2:20 – before that **great** and **notable** day of the Lord come. Note: This is a significant quote by Peter from Joel 2:31.
- Revelation 6:17 – For the **great** day of wrath is come; and who shall be able to stand?
- Revelation 16:14 – the battle of that **great** day of God Almighty.

What is the context of these passages in which we find the word "great" used to describe aspects of the Day of the LORD? The passage of Revelation 16:14 clearly points only to the Great Day at the end of the Tribulation.

## The Time of Jacob's Trouble

"Alas! for that day *is* great, so that none *is* like it: it *is* even the time of Jacob's trouble; but he shall be saved out of it." Jeremiah 30:7 also refers to the day being great. In this case the day is so great that none is like it. That means that no other day, or corresponding time period, will exceed it in this type of greatness. Is Jeremiah referring to the day of Christ's glorious triumphant return? No, he is specifically referring to the time of Jacob's trouble. The time of Jacob's trouble is an extended period of time which lasts at least as long as the 3 ½ years of the second half of Daniel's 70th Week. Jacob's Trouble is often equated with the Great Tribulation of the final 3 ½ years.

In support of this we turn to the Olivet Discourse by Jesus in Matthew 24. Jesus predicts a future time marked by the Abomination of Desolation in the Temple in Jerusalem, in fulfillment of Daniel's prophecy, when the Jews must quickly flee to the wilderness for safety. "For then there shall be **great tribulation** such as was not since the beginning of the world to this time, no, nor ever shall be" (Mt 24:21). Jesus and Jeremiah both mention a time period that will be "great" in the context of "great tribulation" and one that will not be exceeded in its great impact. They must be referring to the same period of time. The time of Jacob's trouble must be the time of great tribulation.

So we can clearly conclude that there will be a period of "great day" time during the Day of the LORD that will not be excelled in its greatness before the "Great Day" of the second coming of Christ occurs. In the context of the Day of the LORD "great" does not only apply to the day of climax at the very end of the Tribulation.

## The Great and Terrible Day of the LORD

It has been noted that Renald Showers argues for the direct application of all of the expressions pertaining to the "great and terrible" Day exclusively to the Great Day or the Narrow Day at the end of the Tribulation. He specifically includes the passage of Joel 2:31 as well as Joel's description of the Day of the LORD and the valley of decision in Joel 3 to the Great Day. While God's gathering of all nations to the valley of Jehoshaphat (Joel 3:2) and His judgment of the multitudes when the Day of the LORD is near in the valley of decision (Joel 3:14) clearly take place at the time of the Campaign of Armageddon and the second coming of Christ, Joel 2 poses an interesting problem.

> The earth shall quake before them; the heavens shall tremble: the sun and the moon shall be dark, and the stars shall withdraw their shining: And the LORD shall utter his voice before his army: for his camp *is* very great: for *he is* strong that executeth his word: for the day of the LORD *is* **great** and **very terrible**; and who can abide it? (Joel 2:10-11 bold added)
>
> And I will show wonders in the heavens and in the earth, blood, and fire, and pillars of smoke. The **sun shall be turned into darkness**, and the **moon into blood**, before the **great** and the **terrible** day of the LORD come. (Joel 2:30-31 bold added)

How are we to know exactly what the passages of Joel 2:10-11 and 2:30-31 are referring to? The language could easily be that of the Great Day. Joel 3:15 even refers to seemingly parallel language with the sun and moon being darkened and the stars withdrawing their shining. Fortunately, the Bible does not leave the discriminating student of prophecy in the dark. There is a parallel passage to Joel 2 that provides more clues to the timing.

That passage is in Revelation 6 and describes the breaking or opening of the sixth seal.

> And I beheld when he had opened the sixth seal, and, lo, there was a **great earthquake**; and the **sun became black** as sackcloth of hair, and the **moon became as blood**; And the stars of heaven fell unto the earth, even as a fig tree casteth her untimely figs, when she is shaken of a mighty wind. And the heaven departed as a scroll when it is rolled together; and every mountain and island were moved out of their places. And the kings of the earth, and the great men, and the rich men, and the chief captains, and the mighty men, and every bondman, and every free man, hid themselves in the dens and in the rocks of the mountains; And said to the mountains and rocks, Fall on us, and hide us from the face of him that sitteth on the throne, and from the **wrath** of the Lamb: For the **great day of his wrath** is come; and who shall be able to stand? (Rev 6:12-17 bold added)

There are several parallel characteristics that Joel 2 and the sixth seal have in common. These specifically include:

- Sun turned into darkness – Sun becomes black
- Moon into blood – Moon becomes as blood = Blood Red Moon
- Wonders in the heavens – meteor shower of stars falling to the earth and heaven is split apart like a scroll being rolled up
- Wonders in the earth – Great Global Earthquake, every mountain and island moved out of place
- Great and terrible Day of the LORD – Great day of his wrath
- A key question: Who can abide it? – Who shall be able to stand?

We observe a very dynamic intersection of shared traits. Both prophecies ask a critical question. Joel asks "Who can abide it?" directly referring to the great and terribleness of the Day of the LORD. Who can survive this time of God's wrath? The apostle John raises the question "Who shall be able to stand?" for the great Day of God's wrath – Christ's wrath has come. This question essentially has the same meaning between both prophecies. It focuses on the dynamic change between the period of time before God's wrath begins and the very point that God's wrath is evident on earth. Who can stand before God when He shakes the earth? This question points to the very beginning of God's Day of the LORD. We examine this question in more detail along with its other parallel passages in the next chapter. Why is the Day of the LORD so great and terrible? It is the time of God's wrath. Who can abide God's wrath? Who can stand up to God – face to face – man to man?

The most unique parallel trait is the moon turning blood red. The only portrayals of a blood red moon in the Bible are in Joel 2:31, Revelation 6:12, and Acts 2:20, which is a direct quote by Peter of Joel's prophecy. This trait along with the other direct parallels specifically ties the timing of Joel 2:30-31 to the opening of the sixth seal. This is a critical linkage in the positioning of the pieces of the prophetic puzzle. Obviously, the timing of the interconnected pieces of Joel 2 and the sixth seal of Revelation 6 is important to determine. They are either both focused on the Great Day at the end of the Tribulation, or neither of them will be fulfilled at that specific point in time.

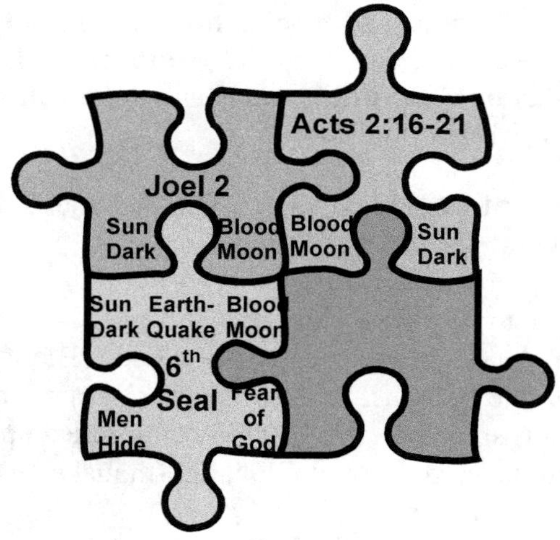


There are naturally occurring lunar eclipses of full moons which are called "blood moons." Will that be the case in this prophetic instance? A typical lunar eclipse cannot qualify as the prophetic fulfillment of this significant event. First, the significance of the intersection of Joel 2, Acts 2, and the sixth seal is tremendous, as a prophetic sign and as an event marker. The uniqueness of this prophetic conjunction is not going to be fulfilled by a fairly common phenomenon that occurs quite frequently.

Second the concurrent darkness of the sun must be accounted for. The sun will turn very dark, to black – black as sackcloth. It takes the light from the sun shining on the moon with the earth positioned directly in between the two heavenly bodies to produce a lunar eclipse. If the sun fails to shine, then there can be no lunar eclipse. The sun itself going dark and not giving out any light and the moon giving off a reddish glow are not compatible conditions. The prophecy directly associates the darkened sun and the blood red moon as simultaneous events, so some other mechanism must be at play. The sun must be shining and yet appear very dark from the surface of the earth. This must be a very widespread to global characteristic and yet temporary in its effects. The sun and moon will shine again during the Tribulation as they will both under go further cosmic disturbances as the Day of the LORD progresses.

The most likely cause-and-effect condition which could meet the criteria for this prophecy is for a massive amount of dust and debris to be violently thrown up into the atmosphere so that the light from the sun is obscured and the reflected light from the moon turns to a very dark red color. Several circumstances can contribute to this type of situation: earthquakes, volcanic activity, massive forest fires, and massive explosions from acts of war or terrorism, or nuclear warfare. Most likely there will be a combination of these causes. Note Joel's mention of fire and pillars of smoke (Joel 2:30). While volcanic activity is not specifically mentioned in either prophecy, it is very unlikely that a global earthquake associated with all mountains and islands being moved out of their normal locations will take place without accompanying volcanic eruptions.

Another possible cause or contributing factor to the sun becoming darkened while the moon turns blood red is for an astronomical body of some sort to pass between the earth and the sun. This body could be a comet, planet, large asteroid, or even a massive group of asteroids. This type of cosmic disturbance could help explain the simultaneous involvement of falling stars (meteors) as well as the heaven seemingly splitting apart like a scroll suddenly rolling itself up that is described in the sixth seal.

It is important, in the context of the Day of the LORD, to note that there is a significant difference between the moon becoming blood red and the moon being completely darkened so that it does not give any light. Both Joel 2 and Revelation 6 clearly refer to a blood red moon that does reflect light – just in a darkened blood red color. There are other Day of the LORD and Tribulation prophecies which speak of the moon not giving off any light at all. These include: Isaiah 13:10, Matthew 24:29, and Mark 13:24.

> For the stars of heaven and the constellations thereof shall not give their light: the sun shall be darkened in his going forth, and the moon shall not cause her light to shine. (Isa 13:10)
>
> Immediately after the tribulation of those days shall the sun be darkened, and the moon shall not give her light, and the

> stars shall fall from heaven, and the powers of the heavens shall be shaken: (Mt 24:29)
> But in those days, after that tribulation, the sun shall be darkened, and the moon shall not give her light, And the stars of heaven shall fall, and the powers that are in heaven shall be shaken. (Mk 13:24-25)

While these passages sound very similar to Joel 2 and the sixth seal, it is unlikely that Joel 2 and Revelation 6 are referring to the same event described in Isaiah 13:10, Matthew 24:29, and Mark 13:24. Regardless of the other similarities, a blood red moon and a moon which is so darkened that it gives no light are not the same. We note that both of the descriptions from Jesus in Matthew and Mark specifically indicate that the moon is completely dark following the Tribulation. In the very next verse in both gospels, Jesus is portrayed as visibly coming in the clouds at the time of His second coming. Therefore, the moon being completely dark is a characteristic of the Great Day portion of the Day of the LORD. The blood red moon must be a characteristic of a different part of the great and terrible Day of the LORD. Since Joel 2:31 states that these characteristics either come before or are in progress when the great and terrible Day of the LORD begins, Joel must be referring to the very beginning of the Day of the LORD, instead of the Great Day at the end of the Tribulation.

Showers quotes E. W. Bullinger in an effort to bolster his argument that Joel 2:31 is describing the narrow Day that climaxes the Tribulation. In his *Commentary on Revelation* Bullinger states, "See Joel ii. 28, 31, where it is called 'the great and terrible day of the LORD,' as though it were the climax of the whole period known as 'the day of the Lord')." Although Bullinger's comment supports Showers' narrow Day superficially, he does it by directly linking Joel 2 to the sixth seal and by associating the sixth seal with the very end of the Tribulation. Bullinger places the above quoted statement in context by immediately preceding it with: "The sixth seal evidently carries us forward to the time of the end ; for it speaks of the signs in the sun and moon and stars (vi. 12, 13), which the Lord associates with His personal appearance." Bullinger directly links this with Matthew 24:29, and subsequently adds, "The six seals present us with a preliminary summary of the judgments, which cover the whole period ; the sixth leading up to and ending in the actual coming of Christ."[16]

Thus, Bullinger takes all of these signs in the sun, moon, and stars, and lumps them all into one occurrence at the end of the Tribulation in conjunction with Christ's Revelation. Bullinger makes no distinction between the inherent differences that exist between some of these passages.

For him, Joel 2, the sixth seal in Revelation 6, and Matthew 24:29 all point to the same climactic event.

I, among many others including Showers, reject Bullinger's timing of the sixth seal at the very end of the Tribulation. The seven seal, seven trumpet, and seven bowl judgments comprise a telescoping series of God's wrath. The seventh seal must be opened before the first of seven trumpet judgments can be blown. The seventh trumpet must be blown before the first of seven bowl judgments can be poured out on the earth. Nothing in the text or the context of the book of Revelation supports the seals being opened throughout the entire period of either the Day of the LORD or the seven-year Tribulation.

Showers counters Bullinger's position when he rationalizes, "If the sixth seal were to follow the Great Tribulation and precede the beginning of the Day of the Lord, the Great Tribulation and the Day of the Lord would be totally separate from each other. … There are reasons for concluding that the cosmic disturbances related to the beginning of the Joel 3 Day of the Lord and the Second Coming of Christ immediately after the Great Tribulation are not the same as those of the sixth seal. … The fact that there will be further cosmic disturbances after the sixth seal indicates that the darkening of the heavenly luminous bodies of the sixth seal will be temporary."[17] I agree, as long as we keep a distinction in mind between Joel 2 and Joel 3. Joel 2 is directly related to the Great Day of wrath of the sixth seal, while Joel 3 is directly related to the Great Day of the Revelation of Christ. While Showers distinguishes between the sixth seal and the Great Day at the end, he directly associates Joel 2 with Joel 3, which confuses the inherent connection between Joel 2 and the sixth seal.

As a result of this, Showers draws an incomplete conclusion. "In light of this, we can further conclude that since the cosmic disturbances of Joel 3 are the ones that will come immediately before the Day of the Lord, those of the sixth seal will not immediately precede the Day of the Lord."[18] Let me clarify his position and then expand it to make it more compatible with how I perceive the fullness of the prophetic puzzle of the Day of the LORD. We can further conclude that since the cosmic disturbances of Joel 3 and Matthew 24:29 are the ones that will come immediately before the **Narrow** Day of the LORD, those of the sixth seal will not immediately precede the **Narrow** Day of the LORD. However, since the cosmic disturbances of Joel 2:31 and the sixth seal, including the Blood Red Moon, must precede the great and terrible Day of the LORD, they must immediately precede the very beginning of the **Broad** Day of the LORD.

Both prophecies, Joel 2 and Revelation 6:12-17, characterize the time of God's Great Day, which is the time of His wrath. Both ask a key question: Who can abide or stand, during the terrible time of God's Day of the LORD?

This question is very pertinent and appropriate at the very beginning of the Day of the LORD. Joel positions his prime characteristics as appearing "before" the great and terrible Day comes. The sixth seal positions the characteristics in the context that the great Day "has come" – the beginning has come. Both are referring to the very same catastrophic situation. That is the very beginning of God's Day of the LORD. The entire Day of the LORD is characterized by the description "great and terrible." The beginning is great and terrible. The Great Day at the end is great and terrible. Somewhere in between the two is the time of Jacob's Trouble – the Great Tribulation – which is a time unparalleled in its great affliction for the Jewish people.

### Scriptural References for the Day of the LORD

| Beginning Events of the Day of the LORD | General Events of the Day of the LORD | Ending Events of the Day of the LORD |
|---|---|---|
| Isa 2:10-21 | Isa 2:11-12, 17 | |
| Isa 13:6-8, 13 | Isa 13:9, 11-12 | Isa 13:10, 13 |
| Isa 24:17-20 | | Isa 24:21-23 |
| Isa 34:4 | | Isa 34:1-10 |
| Jer 46:10 | Jer 30:7 | |
| Ezek 13:5 | Ezek 30:3 | Ezek 13:5 |
| Ezek 39:8 (Ezek 38–39) | | |
| Joel 1:15 | | |
| Joel 2:1-2, 10-11 | Joel 2:1-9 | Joel 2:10-11 |
| Joel 2:30-31 | Joel 2:32 | Joel 3:1, 9-16 |
| | Amos 5:18-20 | |
| Obad 1:15 | | |
| Nahum 1:6-7 | Nahum 1:2-13 | |
| Zeph 1:7-8, 14-16 | Zeph 1:15-18 | Zeph 1:7-8 |
| Zeph 2:2-3 | | Zeph 2:8 |
| Zech 14:1 | Zech 14:1-2 | Zech 14:1-5 |
| | Mal 4:5 | |
| Luke 21:34-36 | | |
| Act 2:19-20 | | |
| 1 Thes 4:14-18 | | |
| 1 Thes 5:2-3 | | |
| 2 Thes 2:1, 6-7 | 2 Thes 2:2-4, 8-12 | 2 Thes 2:8 |
| 2 Pet 3:10 | 2 Pet 3:7 | |
| Rev 6:12-17 | | Rev 16:14 |

The problem is that in spite of some marked similarities, which I do not believe are the least bit coincidental, there are distinct differences that point to two separate major prophetic events related to the Day of the LORD, but which are fulfilled at different times. Similar phenomena can be repeated during different phases of the Day of the LORD. There can be warnings regarding the nearness of the very beginning of the great and terrible Day, as well as warnings of the nearness of the ending or climactic portion of the great and terrible Day. The "Broad Day" can be near, and the "Narrow Day" can be near. The "Broad Day" is great and terrible, and the "Narrow Day" is great and terrible.

The specific details and the contexts of the individual passages of prophetic scripture must decide the appropriate timing application for which portion of the Day of the LORD is intended. We need to keep in mind that God can easily provide a warning that incorporates both the Broad Day and the Narrow Day phases of the Day of the LORD. One of the ways He does that is by describing the entire Day of the LORD as "great and terrible." I believe that from God's perspective there is no part of the Day of the LORD that is not great and terrible in some manner.

## Hiding in Fear of God

What does fear of God have to do with the Day of the LORD? I believe that the revealed characteristic of fear on the part of the inhabitants of the earth in certain passages pertaining to the Day is indicative of a specific phase of the Day of the LORD. While we have demonstrated a close link between the sixth seal and Joel 2, there is also a close connection between the sixth seal and a Day of the LORD passage in Isaiah 2.

> Enter into the rock, and **hide** thee in the dust, for **fear** of the LORD, and for the glory of his majesty. The lofty looks of man shall be humbled, and the haughtiness of men shall be bowed down, and the LORD alone shall be exalted in that day. For the **day of the LORD** of hosts *shall be* upon every *one that is* proud and lofty, and upon every *one that is* lifted up; and he shall be brought low: ... And the loftiness of man shall be bowed down, and the haughtiness of men shall be made low: and the LORD alone shall be exalted in that day. ... And they shall go into the holes of the rocks, and into the caves of the earth, for **fear** of the LORD, and for the glory of his majesty, **when he ariseth to shake terribly the earth**. ... To go into the clefts of the rocks, and into the tops of the ragged rocks, for **fear** of the LORD, and for the glory of his

majesty, **when he ariseth to shake terribly the earth**. (Isa 2:10-12, 17, 19, 21 bold added)

When we compare the previous quote from the sixth seal in Revelation 6 to Isaiah 2, we see a few common denominators.

- Both take place during the Day of the LORD.
- Both describe a great earthquake – a Global Earthquake. Isaiah mentions twice that it is at the time that God arises to shake the earth in a terrible manner. This is not shaking a little part of the earth – God is shaking the entire earth. This is not the great earthquake that takes place at the very end of the Tribulation (which is marked by a series of earthquakes), but the first great earthquake. That is when God arises to shake the earth.
- The people react by hiding, in and under the earth, out of fear! Fear of God! Isaiah mentions the people's fear of God three times. Hide in the dust! Go into the holes of the rocks, and into the caves of the earth. Flee to the dens and the rocks of the mountains. These are certainly not believers. They have reason to fear. God is intervening in wrath.
- Isaiah refers to the proud, lofty, and haughty attitudes of men being brought low. The sixth seal depicts the great, rich, and mighty men being brought low into hiding along with the rest of humanity. Their riches and earthly power cannot hide them from God.
- Isaiah refers to man and men in general – all men – all mankind. He makes no national or regional focus or limitation. The sixth seal pointedly includes every person on the face of the earth in the scope of its warning. "And the kings of the earth, and the great men, and the rich men, and the chief captains, and the mighty men, and every bondman, and every free man, hid themselves in the dens and in the rocks of the mountains" (Rev 6:15). The all inclusive nature is indicated by the types of people descriptors as well as the specific mention of exactly seven categories of people:
  1) **Kings of the Earth** (JNT, KJV, NASB, NIV, RSV)
  2) **Great Men** (KJV, NASB, RSV), **Princes** (NIV), **Rulers** (JNT)
  3) **Rich Men** (JNT, KJV, NASB, NIV, RSV)
  4) **Chief Captains** (KJV), **Commanders** (NASB), **Generals** (JNT, NIV, RSV)
  5) **Mighty Men** (JNT, KJV, NIV), **Strong Men** (NASB, RSV)
  6) **Every Bondman** (KJV), **Every Slave** (NASB, NIV, RSV, JNT)
  7) **Every Free Man** (JNT, KJV, NASB, NIV, RSV).

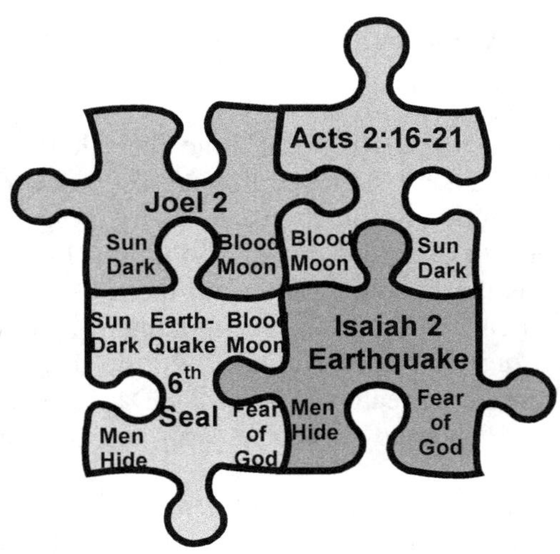


God intervenes by creating a great earthquake, or series of great earthquakes around the world which in their totality can be described as a global earthquake. Isaiah informs us that there comes a point in time when God arises to terribly shake the earth. This warning is specifically given in the context of the Day of the LORD (Isa 2:12). When does God arise to shake the earth? He arises at the very beginning of the Day of the LORD.

During the time of the end, there will be a series of earthquakes, just as there will be a series of instances when there are cosmic disturbances involving the sun, moon, and stars and the amount of light that they emit. There will be a great earthquake, in fact the greatest in the history of the world, at the time of the seventh bowl judgment during the Campaign of Armageddon (Rev 16:17-18). However, this comes at the very end of the telescoping series of God's judgments of wrath contained in the seven seals, seven trumpets, and seven bowls. This final global earthquake occurs years after God's Day of Wrath begins. God arises to shake the earth at the very point when His wrath begins to be manifested against the nations of the earth. God arises to shake the earth at the time of the very first great earthquake in the series of earthshaking events that take place during the time of the end.

A difference to note in comparing the global earthquakes in Isaiah 2 and the sixth seal versus the earthquake of the seventh bowl is that in the beginning the islands and mountains are simply moved, while in the end the islands flee away and the mountains disappear completely. The great shaking of the earth during the sixth seal results in every mountain and every island being moved out of their places, but they still exist (Rev 6:14). The greatest earthquake to ever shake the earth during the seventh bowl will actually wipe the islands and mountains away (Rev 16:20). Can we even begin to imagine the amount of force or the type of shaking that it will take to flatten mountain ranges?

The reaction of the people at the time that God arises to shake the earth is to hide in fear. They hide underground. They flee to the caves. They even call upon the mountains and the rocks to hide them from the face of God, and from the wrath of Jesus Christ – the Lamb (Rev 6:16). Isaiah both taunts and commands the people. "Enter into the rock, and hide thee in the dust, for fear of the LORD" (Isa 2:10). The mountains and the rocks might as well be nothing but dust, for all the good it will do trying to hide from the very face of the Almighty Creator. Why is the Day of the LORD great and terrible? Because God arises to shake the earth and no one shall be able to hide.

It should be noted that hiding underground during an earthquake is unnatural. Man's instinct is to run outside into the open during an earthquake. People have an inherent dread of being crushed by falling debris or being trapped by a collapsed structure. Thus, the fear of God is supernaturally overriding the people's common sense. Perhaps God is allowing nuclear warfare to simultaneously take place which forces the people to seek shelter underground at a time when the shaking of the earth should send them fleeing outdoors. Perhaps the falling meteors of the sixth seal are so terrible that they have the same effect.

In the context of the Day of the LORD, when would people be hiding out of fear of God? Would that reaction be consistent with what we know about the time of the Great Day of Christ's Revelation? Is that the prevailing characteristic during the Campaign of Armageddon? Absolutely not! At the time of the very end of the Tribulation, the armies of the nations of the world will be supernaturally gathered in the vicinity of Megiddo in northern Israel. They will be under the direct influence of the unified leadership of Satan, the Beast (Antichrist), the False Prophet, and the 10 Kings of the earth (Rev 16:13-14; Rev 19:19-20). The nations are aroused in defiance to attack Israel and to oppose the return of God's true Messiah. The character trait is one of blasphemy – blaspheming the name of God (Rev 16:9, 11, 21). At the time of the very end, the inhabitants of the earth who refuse to believe in God and Christ have been hardened by years of catastrophic judgment by God. They are not cowering in fear. They are openly fighting against God.

The most likely time for the people to react in fear is at the very beginning of the Day of the LORD. The world will be divided and disjointed. The nations will be competing with each other. There will be war with nation against nation and kingdom against kingdom (Mt 24:7). The Antichrist will not yet have risen to power. The nations of the world will not yet be under the influence of a unified leadership. A one world government and a one world economy will not yet be in place.

There is another Day of the LORD passage in Isaiah which relates to this subject. While it does not describe the people hiding from God, it does depict the fear that will prevail during the Day. It also introduces the concept of Birth Pangs as being directly related to the Day of the LORD.

> Howl ye; for the **day of the LORD** *is* at hand; it shall come as a destruction from the Almighty. Therefore shall **all hands be faint**, and **every man's heart shall melt**: And they shall be **afraid**: pangs and sorrows shall take hold of them; they shall be in pain as a woman that travaileth: they shall be amazed one at another; their faces *shall be as* flames. (Isa 13:6-8 bold added)
> Behold, the **day of the LORD** cometh, cruel both with wrath and fierce anger, to lay the land desolate: and he shall destroy the sinners thereof out of it. (Isa 13:9)
> For the stars of heaven and the constellations thereof shall not give their light: the sun shall be darkened in his going forth, and the moon shall not cause her light to shine. (Isa 13:10)
> And I will punish the world for *their* evil, and the wicked for their iniquity; and I will cause the arrogancy of the proud to cease, and will lay low the haughtiness of the terrible. (Isa 13:11)
> Therefore I will shake the heavens, and the earth shall remove out of her place, in the wrath of the LORD of hosts, and in the **day of his fierce anger**. (Isa 13:13 bold added)

Consistent with Isaiah 2 and the sixth seal of Revelation 6, Isaiah 13 depicts the Day coming as God's wrath and God's fierce anger which instills fear in the hearts of men. The arrogant, proud, and haughty will be brought low. The earth and the heavens will be shaken. The earth will be moved out of its place. This could be an increased tilt on its axis or a complete pole reversal. It can also include being moved closer to or further from the sun. Since the earth seems to get hotter under the sun during the Bowl Judgments, the earth may be moved out of its present orbit to be a bit closer to the sun.

This passage gives us an example of how God intermixes His messages regarding the Day of the LORD and its various phases. The focus of Isaiah 13:6-8 is on the beginning of the Day and the characteristic of fear. Verses nine and eleven relate to general characteristics which apply to the beginning but extend throughout the entirety of the Day. We have already connected Isaiah 13:10 to the very end of the Day as the cosmic disturbances include the moon being completely darkened. Isaiah 13:13 describes characteristics that are consistent with both the very beginning and the very ending of God's wrath during the Day of the LORD.

**Focused Characteristics:**
**Major Similarities and Major Differences**

| **The Beginning**<br>**Isaiah 2; Joel 2; 6th Seal** | **The Ending**<br>**Joel 3; Mt 24:29; Rev 16; Rev 19** |
|---|---|
| The Great and Terrible Day of the LORD; The Great Day of God's Wrath | The Battle of the Great Day of God Almighty |
| Global Earthquake | Global Earthquake |
| Mountains and Islands moved out of their places | Every Island fled away (Rev 16:20)<br>The mountains were not found |
| Cosmic Disturbances<br>Sun darkened<br>Blood Red Moon<br>Stars Fall - Meteors | Cosmic Disturbances<br>Sun darkened<br>Moon darkened – no light<br>Stars Fall – Meteors – no light |
| Fear and hiding from God | No fear, No hiding |
| No Blasphemy | Blasphemy and open defiance |
| No unified leadership | Antichrist and False Prophet |
| No Ten Kings | Ten Kings |
| A focus on the peoples of the earth | A focus on the nations of the earth |
| All nations are not assembled against Israel | All nations are assembled against Israel - Armageddon |

## Birth Pangs: The Beginning of Sorrows

Isaiah 13 introduced us to the concept of a time of sorrows and the birth pangs of a woman in labor in association with the Day of the LORD. "And they shall be afraid: **pangs and sorrows** shall take hold of them; they shall be in pain as a woman that **travaileth**" (Isa 13:8 bold added). In this passage Isaiah incorporates three characteristics which combined together paint a graphic picture. Birth pangs, sorrows, and a woman undergoing travail to give birth to a child all point to a period of intense pain and agony of forced labor that increases in intensity as it progresses until the climactic event of childbirth brings forth new life. It may not be insignificant that the term "travail" has also become associated with a specific instrument of torture incorporating three stakes.

The visual symbolism of birth pangs, sorrows, and travail is one that is used quite frequently throughout the Old Testament and even carries over into the New Testament. We encounter references to this symbolism in: Ps 48:6; Isa 13:8; 21:3; 26:17; 42:14; 66:7; Jer 4:31; 6:24; 13:21; 22:23; 30:6; 48:41; 49:22, 24; 50:43; Hos 13:13; Mic 4:9-10; 5:3; Mt 24:8; Mk 13:8; Jn 16:21; 1 Thes 5:3; and Rev 12:2. While most of these passages are not connected to the future Day of the LORD, a few of them are specifically given in that context. These include Isa 13:8, Jer 30:6 in connection to the time of Jacob's trouble, the references to it in the Olivet Discourse by Jesus (Mt 24:8; Mk 13:8), and Paul's application in 1 Thes 5:3.

We typically relate theses characteristics to a woman's pregnancy. The origin of this concept of pain and sorrow, connected to pregnancy and childbirth in the Bible, goes all the way back to Eve in the Garden of Eden. When God judged the sin of Adam and Eve for eating the fruit from the one forbidden tree, He prophesied to Eve, "I will greatly multiply thy sorrow and thy conception [pregnancy]; in sorrow thou shalt bring forth children" (Gen 3:16). The nine months of pregnancy include many signs that the woman is pregnant and that the birth of a child is to be expected. Towards the very end of the pregnancy a period begins that is marked by birth pangs. The arrival of this time is marked by the first birth pang. The first birth pang is different from all of the previous aches and pains that the woman endured throughout the months of her pregnancy. It comes as a sudden but short stabbing pain. It is then followed in intervals by more birth pangs that tend to become more intense and frequent as the time of delivery approaches until the final moment of delivery. The first birth pang is a sign that the time of delivery is very near.

Jesus gives us a context, "A woman when she is in travail hath sorrow, because her hour is come: but as soon as she is delivered of the child, she remembereth no more the anguish, for joy that a man is born into the world" (Jn 16:21). In applying this to our study, the Day of the LORD equates to the period of time denoted as "her hour is come." When the Day of the LORD comes, it brings birth pangs, sorrows, and travail along with it. God's Day of the LORD is directly associated with the final period of travail of a woman's pregnancy.

In the context of Bible prophecy, the woman is Israel. Israel must give birth to the remnant of Israel, who will be redeemed by Christ and enter into the Messianic Kingdom as the head of the nations. Israel's resurrection as a nation in 1948 marked a significant sign of the prophetic pregnancy. Although this event is often characterized as the re-birth of Israel and resulted through much tribulation, it was not the prophetic birth that is preceded by God's Day of the LORD and is characterized by the time of travail of Jacob's Trouble.

Interestingly, Jeremiah contorts the typical image of this picture in his application of it to the time of Jacob's trouble. Immediately preceding the verse that introduces Jacob's trouble, Jeremiah exclaims, "Ask ye now, and see whether a man doth travail with child? wherefore do I see every man with his hands on his loins, as a woman in travail, and all faces are turned into paleness?" (Jer 30:6). We are given the unnatural image of a man in travail, writhing in agony while trying to give birth to a child. Jeremiah is ultimately pointing God's finger at Israel, in the guise of the agonizing pregnant man. Yet in this unnaturally bizarre image, we can get a glimpse of the people of the world doubled over, hiding in fear from God as God's wrath is unleashed upon the nations.

There are many signs that the time of travail of the Day of the LORD is approaching. Israel is back in the land surrounded by enemies. There is civil war and unrest in the Middle East. Nations such as Iran and North Korea posture dangerously in their quest to show the world that they are powers to be reckoned with because of their possession of nuclear technology and weapons. The threat of war looms on the horizon. Earthquakes appear to be on the increase. Pestilence raises it ugly head. The danger of epidemic and pandemic disease increases as fast global travel by aircraft speeds up the transmission and spread of disease. The concern for an international outbreak of a disease such as bird flu plays out through the news. Famine in parts of the world and the increasing threat of famine in the more developed nations looms as natural disasters such as drought and flooding and changing weather patterns threaten the normal production of staple food crops in key parts of the world. The risk of a global economic crisis or collapse is also present. Is there a tipping point? We should ask, "When do signs become Birth Pangs?"

We should not be surprised that Jesus incorporated this very imagery into His prophetic Olivet Discourse.

> And as he sat upon the mount of Olives, the disciples came unto him privately, saying, Tell us, when shall these things be? and what *shall be* the sign of thy coming, and of the end of the world? And Jesus answered and said unto them, Take heed that no man deceive you. For many shall come in my name, saying, I am Christ; and shall deceive many. And ye shall hear of wars and rumours of wars: see that ye be not troubled: for all *these things* must come to pass, but the end is not yet. For nation shall rise against nation, and kingdom against kingdom: and there shall be famines, and pestilences,

> and earthquakes, in divers places. **All** these *are* the **beginning of sorrows**. (Mt 24:3-8 bold added)

Jesus introduces the concept "the beginning of sorrows" into His discussion of the time of the end. The Greek word translated by the KJV as *sorrows* is defined by Strong's Concordance as a pang especially as it is related to childbirth – pain, sorrow, travail. Vine's Complete Expository Dictionary indicates that it is "a birth pang," or "travail pain," and "is used illustratively in 1 Thess. 5:3 of the calamities that are to come upon men at the beginning of the Day of the Lord; the figure used suggests the inevitableness of the catastrophe."[19] Vine's makes the observation that the same word used by Jesus is also used by Paul in his Day of the LORD passage in 1 Thessalonians 5:2-3. There it is translated as travail – "as travail upon a woman with child; and they shall not escape." The time of sorrows is the time of birth pangs – the time of travail.

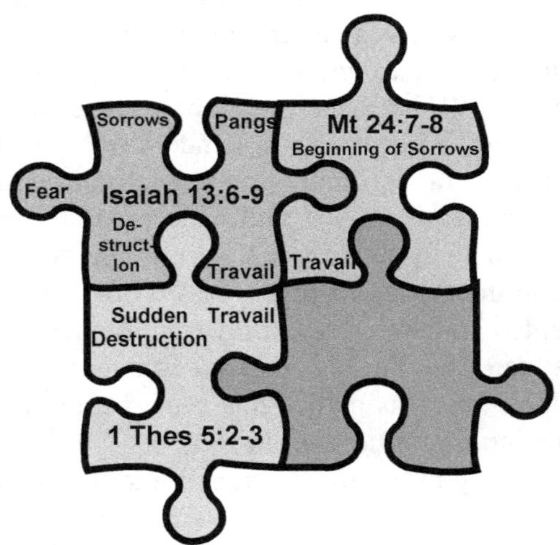


Note that in Matthew 24:8 Jesus just defined the singular "beginning" of sorrows as multiple conditions in the context of a singular time frame. He did not say the "beginnings" of sorrows. The KJV does render the parallel passage in Mark 13:8 as "beginnings of sorrows," but the Revised Standard, NASB, NIV, and the Jewish New Testament all translate both Mt 24:8 and Mk 13:8 in the singular as the "beginning" of sorrows or birth pangs. The significance of this is that Jesus just described multiple characteristics but only one beginning.

Each one of these criteria such as the war of nation against nation, and kingdom against kingdom, or earthquakes, or famine, or pestilence does not individually constitute a separate beginning in and of itself. Note that Jesus specifically stated, "All these" are "the beginning of sorrows." This is a collective, simultaneous, all-inclusive description. Jesus said that they will occur in diverse places. This is not going to take place in Israel alone, but around the entire world. It is not going to take place over an extended period of time, say months or years. These events and conditions will take place and prevail around many portions of the world simultaneously – at the same time they will be evident in Israel.

This total combination of events has never happened in the history of Israel or the world. This eliminates any consideration of past events, such as World War I or World War II, regardless of the perceived similarity, as constituting the beginning of sorrows. Israel had not been reborn as a nation. That condition is absolutely required before the Day of the LORD, or the Birth Pangs, or Sorrows can begin. There will be a short period of time, after Israel is back in the land as a nation, when there will be war against Israel simultaneous with wars between nations on a global scale (multiple wars between superpowers as well as smaller nations). This will simultaneously be accompanied by earthquakes around the entire planet (global earthquake). At the same time there will be widespread pestilence (contagious diseases spreading in the form of epidemics and pandemics) also on a global scale. Famine will be prevalent on a global scale as well, during and as a result of the major warfare, great earthquakes, and widespread disease, and any other resulting conditions such as massive effects to the weather patterns. The growing of crops and the raising of livestock are often severely hampered by these types of events. Epidemics resulting from something like bird flu or mad cow disease can require the massive slaughter of birds (such as chickens) or livestock (such as cattle) that have been exposed or even just suspected of being exposed to the disease.

This is just the beginning of the end. Where the KJV inserts "are" in italics, the NASB inserts "merely" in italics. "But all these things are *merely* the beginning of birth pangs" (Mt 24:8 NASB). The implication is that as bad as this global situation will be – it will get worse, much worse! Jesus is referring to the very first birth pang of the series of pangs that will be thrust upon the world throughout the Day of the LORD. The first birth pang is significant in that it marks the dynamic change between the present state of the world and the very beginning of the Day of Wrath. The signs we see today become birth pangs when all of these criteria listed by Jesus take place simultaneously around the world. That is the scale of calamity that will come upon the nations to cause the immediate reaction of people around the world to be one of hiding from God in fear.

The beginning is a singular event containing or comprising multiple simultaneous criteria. The Birth Pangs or sorrows are plural. The beginning of sorrows marks the very first birth pang. The phrase is specifically descriptive of the first birth pang. Showers agrees with this point. Regarding 1 Thessalonians 5:3, Showers notes, "Paul was referring to the very first birth pang. It is the woman's very first birth pang, not the later hard labor birth pangs, that comes suddenly at the start of the painful process of giving birth. … Paul was teaching that the beginning of the broad Day of the Lord will be characterized by the very first birth pang."[20] In this sense the Beginning of Sorrows can be called the birth pang of birth pangs. This is not because it is the most severe pang, but because it comes so intensively, so dramatically, so suddenly, and so catastrophically in "shock and awe" upon the world.

While the beginning of sorrows pointedly marks the very first birth pang, the larger concept of the beginning of sorrows, as a scene in a play, can also be applied to the initial phase of birth pangs that begin with the first pang and extend into the initial phase of the Day of the LORD. Thus, the period of the immediate aftermath of the series of conditions that make up the first birth pang can also be referred to as the "beginning of sorrows." As intensely as they start, the birth pangs will increase in intensity and severity as the Day progresses. The pangs at the end of the Day of the LORD that climax the time of God's wrath will be much worse. In this sense the final birth pang or pangs associated with the seventh bowl judgment and the Revelation of Christ comprise the Grand Finale of Sorrows. There will be no more birth pangs after the "Battle of that Great Day of God Almighty."

Another observation that we should make is to realize that Jesus did not make any mention of the event which begins Daniel's 70th Week in His Olivet Discourse. Daniel's last prophetic week specifically begins with a special seven-year covenant. Jesus ignored the covenant in His Olivet Discourse and in the prophecy given to John known as the book of Revelation, or the Revelation of Jesus Christ. Neither prophecy deals with that critically important covenant, and thus neither actually deals with the specific beginning of Daniel's 70th Week.

Jesus referenced the "abomination of desolation" which marks the midpoint of Daniel's 70th Week, yet He ignored the event which begins that specific seven years. Why? I believe that Jesus was focused on the more important and dominant prophetic time period of the End Times – The Day of the LORD. The time of Sorrows or Birth Pangs – the time of Travail – is the Day of the LORD. That period of time does not equal Daniel's final week of years, because it begins some time before the covenant is made that initiates the 70th Week. Thus, Daniel's 70th Week is a subset timeframe situated within the Day of the LORD.

The "beginning of sorrows," with its multi-faceted catastrophic dimensions, marks the beginning of the Day of the LORD when Christ rises up in wrath to bring judgment upon the world. It does not begin Daniel's 70th prophetic Week. That actually makes a lot of sense. Can you imagine the typical explanation for the conjunction of Daniel's 70th Week with the Day of the LORD? It assumes and suggests that God arises in wrath immediately with Israel's ratification of the seven-year covenant, which is supposed to give Israel a time of peace during the first half of the Tribulation.

Showers provides us with an example of this reasoning. He argues "that the Day of the Lord will start at the beginning of the 70th week."

> We should note a significant thing at this point. Ezekiel 34:23-30 says that when God establishes His covenant of peace with Israel, the covenant will result in safety, peace with nations, and the elimination of harmful beasts and famine. By contrast, when the Antichrist establishes his covenant of peace with Israel, God will inflict the world with conditions opposite of those His covenant of peace will bring. He will unleash war (the sword) [the second seal, Rev 6:3-4], famine (the third seal, Rev 6:5-6), and harmful beasts (the fourth seal, Rev 6:7-8) upon the earth to demonstrate that the Antichrist's covenant of peace is not the covenant of peace that will bring true peace and safety, as foretold in the Old Testament.[21]

Showers makes Israel's signing of the covenant with the person often identified as the Antichrist the focal point for the beginning of God's wrath. While I certainly do not discount the differences that Showers describes between God's covenant with Israel, which will be manifest during the Messianic Kingdom and the covenant that Israel will engage in at the beginning of Daniel's 70th Week, how does Showers know that the covenant of Daniel 9 is the direct reason that God unleashes His wrath through the seal judgments? That is his interpretation and is only speculation. Where is the scriptural evidence to support that teaching? Nowhere does scripture clearly state or even hint that Showers' reasoning has any similarity to God's motivation for initiating His Day of Wrath. Nor is there any specific scripture that clearly indicates that the Day of the LORD is initiated immediately with the ratification of the covenant.

If that were the case, then God's wrath should be primarily directed against Israel from the very beginning. Yet it is not directed against Israel. God rises up in Ezekiel 38 against Gog and Magog to intervene on Israel's behalf in spite of Israel's profaning God's holy name. This supernatural intervention incorporates a global earthquake that targets all men – all life on earth. Jesus' focus of the multiple conditions which make up the "beginning of sorrows" encompasses the diverse places of the entire world. The focus of

God's wrath in the seal judgments of Revelation is against the whole world. There is plenty of evidence that the Day of Wrath targets the entire world from its very beginning.

- For the day of the LORD *is* near "upon **all** the heathen" (Obad 1:15 KJV); "near on **all** the nations" (Obad 1:15 NASB);
- "For the day of the LORD of hosts *shall be* upon **every** *one that is* proud and lofty, and upon **every** *one that is* lifted up" (Isa 2:12);
- … "for the glory of his majesty, when he ariseth to shake terribly **the earth**" (Isa 2:19, and again in Isa 2:21);
- … "**every** man's heart shall melt" (Isa 13:7);
- "And I will punish **the world** for *their* evil" (Isa 13:11);
- … "**the earth** shall remove out of her place" (Isa 13:13;
- … "and **all the men** that *are* **upon the face of the earth**, shall shake at my presence" (Ezek 38:20);
- … "and **the earth** is burned at his presence, yea, **the world**, and **all** that dwell therein" (Nah 1:5);
- "And there shall be signs in the sun, and in the moon, and in the stars; and upon **the earth** distress of **nations**" (Lk 21:25);
- "For as a snare shall it come on **all** them that dwell on the face of the **whole earth**" (Lk 21:35);
- "the hour of temptation which shall come upon **all the world**, to try them that dwell upon **the earth**" (Rev 3:10);
- "to take peace from **the earth**" (Rev 6:4);
- "Authority was given to them" [Death and Hades] "over **a fourth of the earth**, to kill with sword and with famine and with pestilence and by the wild beasts of the earth" (Rev 6:8 NASB).

If Christ is going to rise up in wrath at that very point when Israel agrees to the covenant of Daniel 9, you would think that Jesus would have given a warning to that effect. But Jesus did no such thing. His warning focused on the larger global picture. The requirements for the beginning of sorrows in the Olivet Discourse do parallel the beginning seal judgments in Revelation. False Christ, War, Famine, Pestilence, Earthquakes – they are all there. Yet there is no focus on Israel as a nation, or as a people, or as a land, in the book of Revelation from the first through the sixth seals, until the sealing of the 144,000 servants of God from the tribes of the children of Israel (Rev 7:4), which is described in an interlude between the sixth and the seventh seals.

The traditional model that equates the beginning of the Day of the LORD with the beginning of Daniel's 70$^{th}$ Week at the signing of the prophetic seven-year covenant and associates that event with the breaking of the first seal is full of assumptions and short on facts. God's wrath (which is unleashed at the very beginning of His Day of the LORD) targets the nations of the world, not Israel. That time of sorrows (which begins with global calamity) has nothing to do with the covenant of Daniel 9 – other than it creates the conditions through which the person of the Antichrist and the nation of Israel both rise in stature and power and sets the stage for the covenant to follow some time later in the aftermath of – the Beginning of Sorrows.

## The Beginning of Sorrows and the War of Gog & Magog

Jesus combined large scale warfare, famines, pestilences, and large scale earthquakes into the Beginning of Sorrows. War plays a big part in the beginning phase of birth pangs. What prophetic war fits right into that scenario? It must share several of these same conditions. Since the Day of the LORD begins as a time of God's wrath, this war should also be directly associated with God's wrath. Ideally the prophecy would also be directly connected with God's Day of the LORD as well. Since we are looking for a war described in Bible prophecy, it is going to be focused directly on Israel. Since we are looking for a war connected to the beginning of the Day, it cannot be the War or Campaign of Armageddon as that comes at the very end. Since Armageddon involves all nations being gathered against Israel just before the time of the Great and Narrow Day of Christ's Revelation, we are looking for something that does not involve all nations. What war begins the Broad Day of the LORD?

There is one prophetic war in the Old Testament that perfectly fits the criteria for the Beginning of Sorrows – that is the War of Gog and Magog in Ezekiel 38–39. The timing of this war is completely controlled by God and comes specifically at the time that God says, "this is the day whereof I have spoken" (Ezek 39:8). Gog and Magog involves an alliance of nations that surrounds Israel from a distance, but not all nations. When the alliance attacks by invading Israel, God rises up in wrath and fury (Ezek 38:18-19). God reacts in the fire of His wrath. God also rises up to cause a great shaking of the earth. An earthquake begins in Israel and expands outward to encompass the entire planet. All life on the face of the earth, man and animal, shakes at the intervening presence of God (Ezek 38:19-20). God incorporates the sword of war along with pestilence, blood, overflowing rain, great hailstones, fire, and brimstone against the invaders (Ezek 38:21-22). God will rain fire down upon the land of Magog and other nations (Ezek 39:6). In addition, God introduces wild beasts into His judgment by calling upon the birds and the beasts of the field to feast upon His sacrifice (Ezek 39:4, 17-

20). Of the multiple conditions set by Jesus for the Beginning of Sorrows, the only one missing is famine. This combination intersects well with God rising to shake the earth in Isaiah 2, and with the wonders in the earth, and blood, and fire, and pillars of smoke in Joel 2:30.

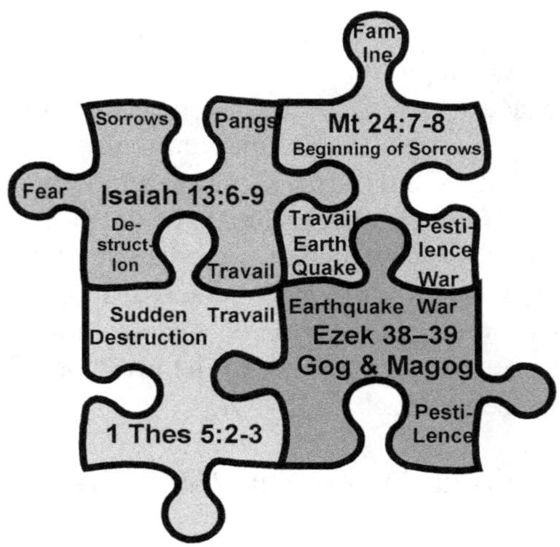


## The Beginning of Sorrows and the Seal Judgments

There is a direct parallel between the conditions that comprise the Beginning of Sorrows in the Olivet Discourse and the conditions which are released by the breaking of the seals in Revelation 6. Jesus gave the prophecy of the Olivet Discourse and revealed the multiple conditions of the Beginning of Sorrows that also begin the Day of the LORD. Jesus is the one who takes the book or scroll from the right hand of God the Father seated on His throne and breaks the seals. Jesus is the one who opens the seals because he is the only one who is worthy to initiate the judgment of the Day of the LORD.

Jesus breaks the seven seals. Jesus gives authority to the agents of catastrophe that are unleashed at the opening of each seal. Each seal involves judgment by God and Christ against the earth. There is no judgment stated or implied by any of the seals against Satan or his fallen angels. The seals do characterize God's wrath.

- **First Seal** – The rider on the white horse being given a crown symbolizes the release of God's supernatural restraining force holding back the Antichrist from the world. He now has authority to rise to power on the world stage by conquering – using war and false peace to accomplish his goal of global domination. He rises to power during the global chaos that is unleashed by Christ's breaking all of the seals.

- **Second Seal** – The rider on the red horse symbolizes War! This is great warfare. Many refer to it as WWIII. Peace is taken from the earth. This is not the breaking of the Antichrist's seven-year peace covenant with Israel as that has not yet been achieved. This is a focus on global peace which is suddenly replaced by global war. This will likely involve multiple wars – nation against nation, and kingdom against kingdom. China against Taiwan, or Japan, or India; North Korea against South Korea, or Japan, or the U.S.A.; Pakistan against India; and possibly Russia against the U.S.A. Bible prophecy, for the most part, ignores these as it is centered upon the nation of Israel. War against Israel at this point is guaranteed. Israel is the central prophetic target. This is the time of the invasion of Israel by Gog and Magog described in Ezekiel 38–39.

### 2nd Seal: Great War – The War of Gog and Magog

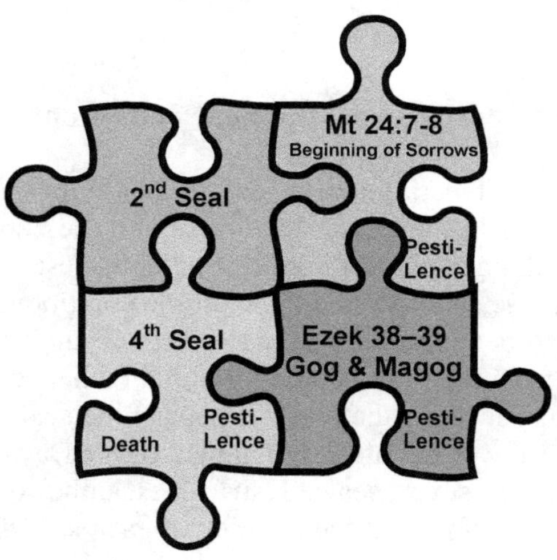


- **Third Seal** – The rider on the black horse symbolizes the unleashing of a global economic crisis accompanied by widespread inflation and famine. Food, while available in many places, will become significantly more expensive and harder to obtain. Food aid and relief programs will break down. Wealthy elitists and warlords will vie for the control of food resources.

- **Fourth Seal** – The rider on the pale horse (sickly pale green) symbolizes the authority given to Death and Hades (Sheol) to kill one-fourth of the world's population. They kill with the sword (war), hunger (famine), death (pestilence), and with beasts (wild animals). God refers to these as His four severe judgments in Ezekiel 14:21. This simultaneous combination of four judgments is a mark of God's wrath being unleashed. The specific mention of Hades directly following in the wake of Death is highly significant. Death has the power to kill the body and put a person in the ground (grave). Hades is given authority over all of those killed to swallow them up into its abode. Hades is the place of dead unbelievers. Hades is often referred to as Hell. Following Jesus' victory over death by the power of His resurrection, Hades or Sheol, as a place for the dead, has been strictly restricted to the confinement of only unsaved people. Hades has no authority over any Christian. The significance of this is that no Christian believers are included in this massive killing of one-fourth of the world's population. How is this possible? The Christian believers have just been snatched off the face of the earth at the rapture.
- **Fifth Seal** – The souls of martyred believers under the altar in heaven. These souls cry out to God. When will God break His silence and judge and avenge their spilled blood? These are not the souls of tribulational martyrs as so many proclaim. The Day of the LORD is just beginning. The bodies of these souls have been dead for awhile. They would not be crying out like this if they had just been killed. By the time the seven-year Tribulation begins, God will have already broken His silence and begun unleashing His wrath and vengeance – notably upon the forces and nations of Gog and Magog. How can any person's soul who is killed during the last seven years of the Tribulation cry out like this? Nor can these souls represent the same martyrs that will take place later during the Tribulation as those are directly prophesied as the fellow servants and brethren who will yet be killed. Thus, there is a distinction between the already martyred souls versus the Tribulational martyrs to come. These souls are martyrs of the Church Age. Sometimes people forget the multitude of believers who have been killed for their faith during the past two thousand years. These souls are given white robes. This is a direct symbol of their resurrection into glorified bodies. The only martyrs whose souls are eligible to be resurrected and receive white robes in the context of the timing of Jesus breaking the seals and initiating the Day of the LORD at the Beginning of Sorrows are the

multitude of martyred Christian believers who will be caught up to heaven during the event of the rapture of the church.

- **Sixth Seal** – Great cosmic and earthly disturbances. A great global earthquake which impacts all people on earth. If God has a fifth severe form of judgment, the global earthquake is it. A great sign appears in the sky as the sun turns completely dark and the moon turns blood red. Stars falling from heaven down to the earth depict a severe meteor shower with violent impacts to the planet. The atmosphere is violently shaken and torn apart. Heaven is described as splitting apart like a scroll suddenly rolling together. All mountains and islands are moved from their places. The combination of these characteristics indicate that the entire planetary globe has been jerked from its normal orientation on it axis and the poles have shifted (cf. Isa 13:13). All people on earth attempt to hide underground – in fear of God and Christ's wrath. "For the great day of his wrath is come." Their denial of God has been suddenly and violently shattered. They realize that God exists, God is angry, and God is judging the people on earth.

**6th Seal: Global Earthquake**

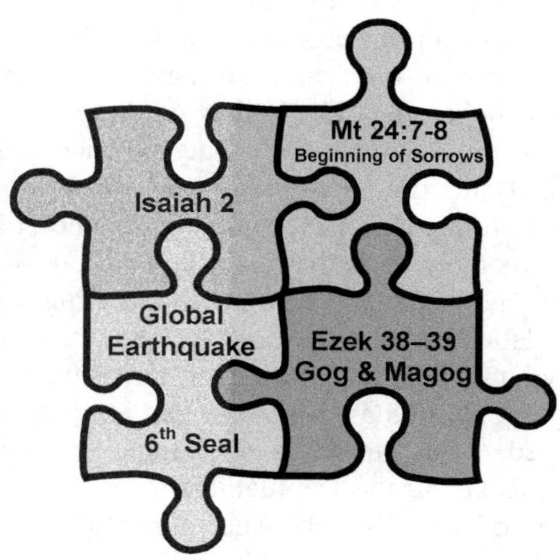


- **Seventh Seal** – Silence in heaven (about 1/2 hour). Seven angels are given seven trumpets. An angel presents the prayers of the saints to God with incense on the golden altar before God's throne. The angel fills a censer with fire from the altar and casts it onto the earth. This is accompanied by voices, thunder, lightning, and an earthquake on earth. This is God's official declaration of War against the sinners on earth. The time of God's wrath has begun.

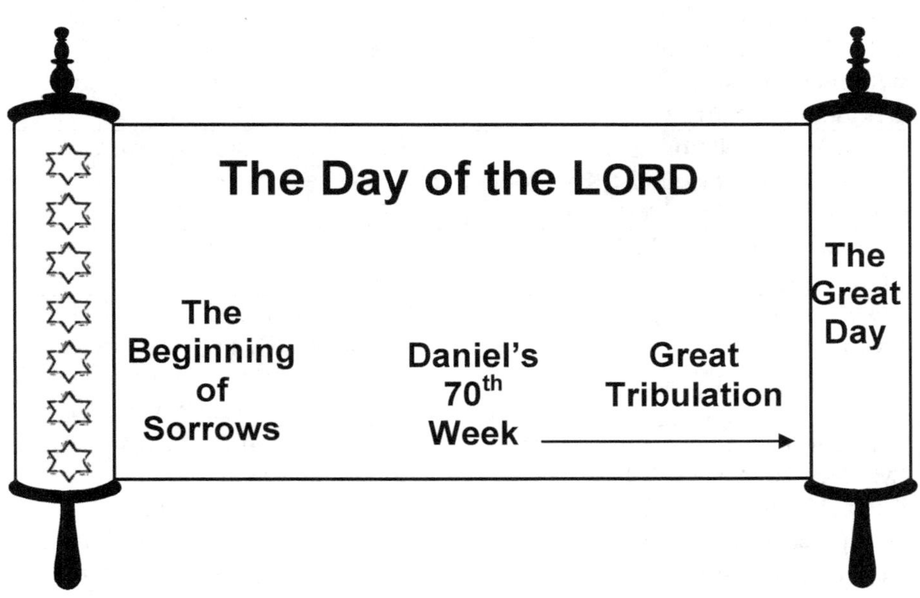


Specifically, the direct parallel between the Olivet Discourse and the opening of the scroll reveals the beginning phase of the Day of the LORD as a period of great global catastrophic change and judgment. The Beginning of Sorrows marks the beginning of the Day of the LORD when "nation shall rise against nation," when peace is taken from the earth (second seal). Great warfare erupts around the world, but Bible prophecy is focused around an invasion of Israel by the combined forces of Gog and Magog which will result in the supernatural destruction of the invading armies by the active intervention of God (Ezek 38–39). This catastrophic Beginning of Sorrows results in the death of one-fourth of the world's population from: war, famine, pestilence, and wild beasts (second seal, third seal, and fourth seal). These events are accompanied by earthquakes and global catastrophic change (global earthquake – sixth seal; Ezek 38, Isa 2), and cosmic disturbances (sixth seal; Joel 2; Lk 21:11). The destruction of this invasion of Israel will provide the mechanism for the emergence of the ultimate False Christ (first seal) who will later introduce his false peace.

## The Beginning of Sorrows vs. The Seal Judgments

| **The Olivet Discourse**<br>**The Beginning of Sorrows** | **Revelation 6**<br>**The Seal Judgments** |
|---|---|
| False Christs (Mt 24:4-5; Mk 13:5-6; Lk 21:8) – A condition which both precedes and follows the Beginning of Sorrows | 1st Seal – Antichrist (white horse) released to rise to power (Rev 6:2) |
| **Great War** – Nation against Nation; Kingdom against Kingdom (Mt 24:7; Mk 13:8; Lk 21:10) | 2nd Seal – War (A Great Sword) (red horse) (Rev 6:3-4)<br>Gog & Magog (Ezek 38–39) |
| **Famines** (Mt 24:7; Mk 13:8; Lk 21:11) | 3rd Seal – Famine (black horse) (Rev 6:5-6) |
| **Pestilences** (Mt 24:7; Mk 13:8; Lk 21:11) | 4th Seal – Death & Hades (pale green horse) – Death of ¼ earth's population by War, Famine, Pestilence, & Beasts (Rev 6:7-8) |
| Persecution & the Martyr of Saints (Mt 24:9-10; Mk 13:9, 11-13; Lk 21:12-19). A condition which both precedes and follows the Beginning of Sorrows | 5th Seal – Souls of Church Age Saints are under the Altar in Heaven. Given white robes = Resurrection. Prediction of Martyrs to come during Trib. (Rev 6:9-11) |
| **Earthquakes** (Mt 24:7; Mk 13:8; Lk 21:11) | 6th Seal – Global Catastrophe: great earthquake, sun darkened, blood red moon, stars fall, heaven departs as a scroll, all mountains & islands moved, men hide underground out of fear of God and from the wrath of Christ. (Rev 6:12-17; Joel 2:30-31; Ezek 38:19-20; Act 2:19-20; Isa 2:10-21)<br>7th Seal – Silence in heaven for ½ hour; the prayers of all saints at the altar before God's throne; fire from the altar cast to the earth; voices, thunder, lightning, earthquake (Rev 8:1-5) |

Observe how the fourth seal does not actually describe an entirely separate event. It adds to the information revealed by the previous seals.

Authority is given to Death and Hades over one-fourth of the population of the earth to kill them with sword (war – 2nd Seal), with hunger (famine – 3rd seal), with death (pestilence), and with the beasts of the earth. The fourth seal expands upon the previous seals. The Four Horsemen of the Apocalypse are commonly depicted as riding together, neck to neck – not chasing after one another with a long distance between each of them. These seal judgments form a continuous singularity in and of themselves.

We note that the conditions comprising the Beginning of Sorrows are very similar to the characteristics of the seal judgments. In addition, the sequence that is given for these events is all but identical in both passages. This correlation of characteristics between the Olivet Discourse and the seals is frequently recognized. J. Vernon McGee makes the association for us.

> We have seen the riding of the four horsemen, and this follows exactly the pattern that the Lord Jesus gave while He was on earth. In Matthew 24:5-8, in the Olivet Discourse, He said: "For many shall come in my name, saying, I am Christ; and shall deceive many [the white horse]. And ye shall hear of wars and rumors of wars [the red horse]: see that ye are not troubled: for all these must come to pass, but the end is not yet. For nation shall rise against nation, and kingdom against kingdom: and there shall be famines [the black horse], and pestilences [the pale horse], and earthquakes, in divers places. All these are the beginning of sorrows." This is the opening of the Great Tribulation.[22]

In setting the context for the opening of the seals, J. Vernon McGee states, "I do not think that the Great Tribulation breaks suddenly like a great tornado. The opening of the seals is gradual, logical, chronological. They are opened one at a time."[23] It is common for prophecy scholars to take the seal judgments and have them opened gradually. They typically spread them out over an extended period of time. We have seen the proponents of the pre-wrath rapture position extend the opening of the seals well into the middle of the second half of Daniel's 70th Week. Others, like Bullinger, extend the sixth seal through to the very end of the Tribulation to make it point to the Great Day of the Revelation of Christ. Most scholars extend the seals throughout either the first quarter or the first half of Daniel's 70th Week and refer to that time frame as the "beginning of sorrows." Showers sort of splits these last two perspectives. He directly equates the first four seals with the beginning of birth pangs and sees them opened over the first third of the Tribulation. By doing that he basically balances the timeframes for the seven seal judgments, the seven trumpet judgments, and the seven bowl judgments.[24]

Clarence Larkin and Tim LaHaye are two authors who depict the seals being opened over the course of the first quarter of the Tribulation. This perspective is also illustrated in a chart in *Charts of Bible Prophecy*.[25] Paul Benware gives us an example of how the first six seals are extended throughout the first half of Daniel's 70th Week in his book *Understanding End Times Prophecy*. "God's judgments begin when Christ breaks the seals on the scroll (Rev. 5:1-6:1). The first six seal judgments will take place probably during the first half of the tribulation. They are described by Christ as the 'beginning of birth pangs" … The term *birth pangs* is used to describe the judgments of God throughout the entire tribulation. … With months and months between each seal, people may see them as natural, though terrible, events." When referring to the sixth seal, Benware adds, "This seal is probably broken near the middle of the tribulation (and may introduce the final three and a half years—the great tribulation)."[26]

Benware illustrates the inherent flaw in the logic behind this methodology. He readily observes the linkage of Christ's description of the conditions marking the Beginning of Sorrows as relating to the first six seal judgments and notes that these are birth pangs. So on one hand he hints at the singular nature of the Beginning of Sorrows, yet on the other hand he treats each seal judgment as a separate birth pang separated by "month and months between each seal." Yet neither Jesus nor John said that there will be gaps of time extending into months between these catastrophic conditions.

In addition, placing the seals throughout either the first quarter or the first half of the Tribulation, inherently requires the rider on the white horse of the first seal to represent the Antichrist initiating his seven-year covenant with Israel at the very beginning of Daniel's 70th Week. That is a common interpretation of the first seal. Yet it is an interpretation of something that is not explicitly stated or even implied. "And I saw, and behold a white horse: and he that sat on him had a bow; and a crown was given unto him: and he went forth conquering, and to conquer" Rev 6:2). Where is a seven-year covenant of peace initiated with Israel either described or implied by this pictorial statement?

I agree that the rider on the white horse is a symbolic representation of the person who will become Antichrist. But as long as the church is on the face of the earth, he is restrained from rising to a position of global power by the supernatural power of the Holy Spirit indwelling the body of believers that comprise the church. The breaking of the first seal symbolizes the breaking of the bonds of restraint. Jesus is the one who breaks the seal, just as Jesus is the one who calls the church to heaven, removing the restraint of the Holy Spirit in the process. The rider on the white horse is given a stephanos crown, and thereby is granted authority by Christ to go out and conquer. The first thing that he does is just that – he goes out conquering. He must rise to power before he is in a position to be a party of the seven-year covenant with Israel.

While the first seal does represent the release of the Antichrist from his restraints to go out and rise to power by conquering through the use of war and false peace, I do not believe that it represents the signing of the seven-year covenant. In addition, in the previous section we examined the incompatible nature of God's unleashing His time of wrath as a result of and in conjunction with the covenant of Daniel 9. The signing of the covenant of peace and the Beginning of Sorrows is not the same event.

We have observed how Jesus combined the conditions of war, famines, pestilences, and earthquakes as coming together to mark the Beginning of Sorrows. While all or some of these conditions may last for an extended period, they are all present simultaneously to mark the beginning – the first birth pang of the Day of the LORD. How does this relate to the seal judgments in the book of Revelation? We have observed that several scholars equate the first four seals as the beginning of birth pangs spread out over time. It seems that they treat each seal as a separate birth pang. However, the group of seal judgments cannot be equated as comprising the Beginning of Birth Pangs if they are opened over an extended period of time, such as the first half of the seven-year Tribulation. The true singular nature of the multi-faceted catastrophic event, that comprises the Beginning of Sorrows with the first birth pang, requires that the seal judgments be interpreted in the same manner – as a singular multi-unsealing event which opens the scroll in the hands of Christ as the same first birth pang.

If you examine Revelation 6 closely, you will observe that there are absolutely no timing indicators regarding the seals. There is nothing which indicates how long each seal lasts, or how long an interval of time exists between the breaking of each seal. John records "And I saw when the Lamb [Christ] opened one of the seals, … And when he had opened the second seal, … And when he had opened the third seal, … And when he had opened the fourth seal, … And when he had opened the fifth seal, … And I beheld when he had opened the sixth seal, … And when he had opened the seventh seal" (Rev 6:1, 3, 5, 7, 9, 12; 8:1). The first and only direct reference to time comes with the seventh seal. "And when he had opened the seventh seal, there was silence in heaven about the space of half an hour." Does this sound like a process that is taking place over several years? Or are the seals being ripped open, one right after another without any delay between them?

The latter seems more logical and probable to me. Since there is concern enough to note a heavenly pause for "half an hour" following the catastrophic events associated with the opening of the seals, it must be because of the breathtaking speed at which these events take place. Why note a half hour pause to events which gradually unfold over two years or three and a half years? After all, none of the alleged pauses of "months and months" between the seals has been noted in any way. This is in spite of the fact that there are numerous references to specific time periods mentioned throughout the book of Revelation. While there are repeated references to a time period of 42 months or 1,260 days, Revelation is silent regarding any connection of the seals to such a period of time. Yet we are informed the fifth trumpet judgment lasts for at least five months (Rev 9:5), and the sounding of the seventh trumpet judgment, which introduces the bowl judgments, is said to last for some period of days (Rev 10:7).

**The Breaking of the Seven Seals = The Beginning of Sorrows**

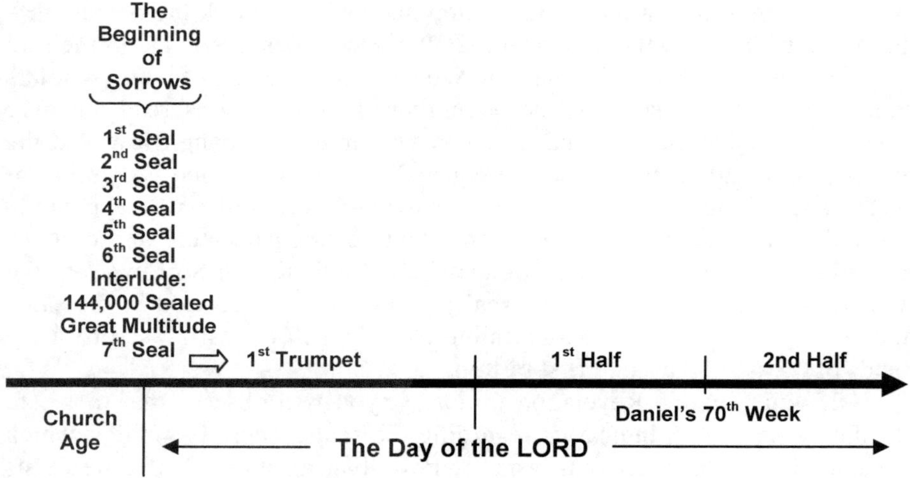


There is no reason to believe that Jesus delays the breaking of the individual seals to make the process of opening the scroll last for a period of years. The arguments that scholars make to claim that this occurs over years is based upon assumptions, not scriptural fact. Actually, when I think about it, that delayed process of revealing the contents of the scroll seems kind of counterproductive. The objective of Christ is to open the book and initiate judgment in the form of wrath which characterizes His Day of the LORD. Christ will do that quickly. It will not be a process of delayed, timed release as J. Vernon McGee insinuates, but a rapid outpouring of the initial phase of God's wrath which is intended to get the world's immediate attention. The ongoing effects and aftermath of this phase can then last for several years.

The difference, as I view the seals, is that while there are four horsemen of the Apocalypse associated with the beginning of birth pangs, the Beginning of Sorrows encompasses all seven seals. Jesus specifically incorporated earthquakes in diverse places into His first birth pang. That directly equates to the global earthquake of the sixth seal. The scroll that Jesus opens by breaking the seals is a single entity – a single birth pang – the first birth pang of the series that will extend throughout the Day of the LORD. The opening of the scroll by breaking all seven seals comprises the Beginning of Sorrows, and it is accomplished in a very short period of time. The contents of the scroll that follow, including the blowing of the seven trumpets and the pouring of the seven bowls, describe the subsequent birth pangs.

**The Beginning of Sorrows as a Mushroom Cloud of Cataclysmic Events**

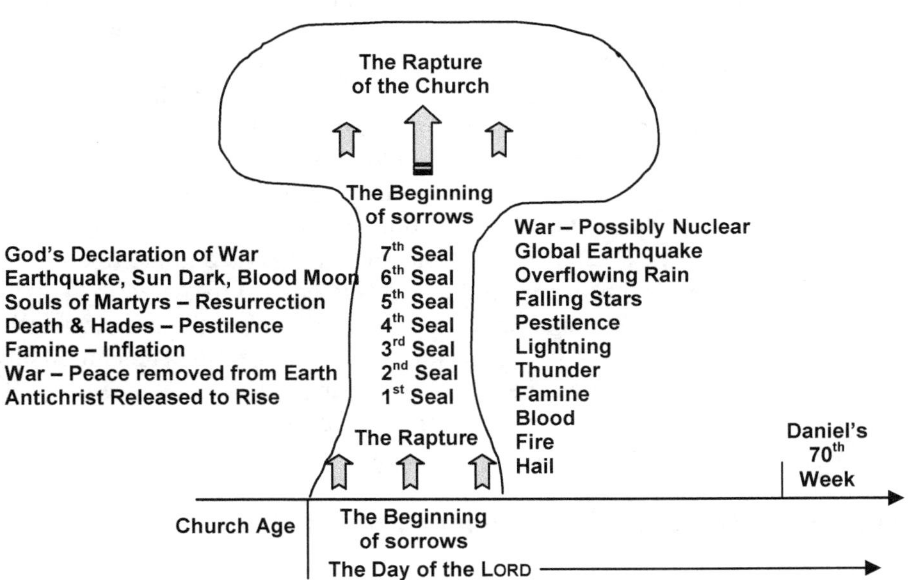


It is like Jesus is opening a door or a window. He is not simply cracking it open so that it is ajar and then leaving it in that condition for awhile; then coming back to slide it open just a little bit more; then returning again to nudge it open some more. Will Jesus stand in heaven with the scroll in His hands while He teasingly, very slowly, almost hauntingly breaks each seal over a long period of centuries, decades, or even two or three years of time on earth? Would that be a realistic picture of how Jesus is going to open the scroll after He receives it from God, the Father? Jesus is going to break the seals, releasing the restraints holding back God's wrath from the earth, and the earth will reel under the consequences. Contrary to J. Vernon McGee's denial, it will come like a great tornado, only it will be so intense it will make a great hurricane seem like a little waterspout. If ever there is a time that the concept of "shock and awe" will apply, the Beginning of Sorrows will be it.

If the correlation exists between the Beginning of Sorrows and the seal judgments, as appears to be the case, then there can be no delay between the breaking of each seal following the previous seal. They will be opened in rapid succession – almost like machine gun fire. God in His wrath – Christ in His judgment – Bang! Bang! Bang! Bang! Bang! Bang! Bang!

The seventh seal is often short changed in its relevance to the opening of the scroll. It is the final seal and it introduces the seven angels with the trumpet judgments, that much is commonly understood. However, there is much more said about this event. It reveals the first and only pause in the action of breaking the seals, a half hour of silence in heaven, and that comes when the scroll is opened because the last seal has been broken. An angel stands with a golden censer at the altar in heaven before God's throne. The angel is given incense to offer on the altar along with the prayers of all saints – the smoke of which wafts up before God. Jesus has broken the seals, opened the scroll, and God takes a short time out to reflect on the prayers of all saints. It seems like a very serious moment. What is God going to do? The angel fills the censer with fire from the altar and casts it to the earth. This is accompanied by voices, thundering, lightning, and an earthquake on earth. This is God's declaration of War against the sinners on earth. The church has been removed by the rapture. The 144,000 Jewish servants have been sealed. God's day of Wrath – The great and terrible Day of the LORD has begun. The Beginning of Sorrows has come with sudden destruction.

## As a Thief; Peace and Safety; Sudden Destruction

We have observed that Paul characterized the Day of the LORD with the time of travail or birth pangs. That time, the beginning of sorrows, starts with the first birth pang. In his characterization of this time, Paul focused on the suddenness of its appearance. "For yourselves know perfectly that the day of the Lord so cometh **as a thief in the night**. For when they shall say, Peace and safety; then **sudden destruction** cometh upon them, as travail upon a woman with child; and they shall not escape" (1 Thes 5:2-3 bold added).

Sudden destruction comes upon the world unexpectedly. It catches the unbelieving world by surprise, as a thief in the night. Peter uses the same analogy, "But the day of the Lord will come as a thief in the night" (2 Pet 3:10). But Paul does not say that it will catch all of the people in the world by surprise. In the very next verse Paul reminds his audience, "But ye, brethren, are not in darkness, that that day should overtake you as a thief" (1 Thes 5:4). "That day" in this context is the Day of the LORD - the beginning of the Day. The Christian brethren should be watchful for the return of Christ to call His church to Himself. The Day of Wrath will not blindside the watchful church because the church is not appointed to wrath (1 Thes 5:9). The church will escape God's wrath.

At the same time, Paul also focuses on the world's yearning for "peace and safety." Jesus stated that war and rumors of war will take place and be evident throughout the age (Mt 24:6). The threats of war, terrorism, violence, and crime seem to be never ending hazards which confront the peoples of the world. Are peace and safety issues of our times? Of course they are. The world will either face an event which will significantly threaten people's peace and safety to make it a grave concern, or something will happen to make peace and safety appear more secure. Many prophecy scholars associate this "peace and safety" with the signing of a seven-year peace covenant which marks the beginning of Daniel's 70$^{th}$ Week. However, as indicated in the previous section dealing with the beginning of sorrows, the initiation of that covenant is not compatible with God's initiation of His time of wrath against the entire world. In addition, the time of the signing of the covenant is one of the most significant prophetic time markers in scripture. How can the Day of the LORD come upon the world suddenly or unexpectedly at any point following that recognizable time marker? The Day of the LORD must begin before the covenant is agreed to.

As I wrote in The Silence is Broken! "I believe it must begin when the people of the world are in denial to the reality of God and are not expecting God's intervention in judgment. Once the prophesied events of the End Times actually begin to unfold, the occurrence of these events will reveal prophesied time periods, which will make the timing of the end a predictable event. So, once the era of the Tribulation begins, how can the Day of the Lord come unexpectedly, as a thief in the night, to bring sudden destruction?"[27]

It is more likely that there will be an event related to the circumstances in the Middle East and possibly associated with the threat of Islamic terrorism that gives the world a chance to catch its breath and sigh in relief. The relief will just be temporary, as the real series of explosive events marking the beginning of the great and terrible Day of the LORD will soon follow. It may be related to the civil war in Syria. It may be related to Iran and a setback to Iran's quest for nuclear weapons. It may be related to North Korea and its aggressive posturing and threats to use nuclear weapons against other nations such as South Korea, the U.S.A., and Japan. It may be a regional war in the Middle East, related to Psalm 83 and Isaiah 17, which Israel wins, and thus vents the explosive hot air in the balloons of Syria, Lebanon, Jordan, Egypt, Gaza, and the West Bank. It could easily be a combination of several of the above situations.

The Day of the LORD begins with sudden destruction. The first birth pang is associated with sudden destruction. The Day in its entirety is characterized with destruction from God. The end of the Day will be synonymous with destruction, yet the end of the Tribulation marked by the Revelation of Jesus Christ will not be sudden destruction. The destruction of the great Day of Christ's return will not come suddenly or unexpectedly. Peace and Safety is not the perception characterizing the time of the Campaign of Armageddon.

**Characteristics of the Beginning of the Day of the LORD**

| Beginning of Day of the LORD | Mt 24 Beginning of Sorrows | Revelation Opening of 7 Seals | Ezek 38–39 War of Gog & Magog |
|---|---|---|---|
| God Rises in Judgment | Implied | Christ Rises in Judgment | God Rises in Judgment |
| God's Wrath | | God's Wrath | God's Wrath |
| Birth Pang | Birth Pang | | |
| Sudden Destruction | Sudden Destruction | Sudden Destruction | Sudden Destruction |
| Great War | Great War | Great War | Great War |
| Global Earthquake | Global Earthquake | Global Earthquake | Global Earthquake |
| Famine | Famine | Famine | |
| Pestilence | Pestilence | Pestilence | Pestilence |
| Sun Dark | | Sun Dark | Implied |
| Blood Red Moon | | Blood Red Moon | |
| Men Hide | | Men Hide | |
| Heaven Shaken | | Heaven Shaken | Great Storm |
| | | Beasts | Beasts |

## Acts 2: The Apostle Peter Quotes Joel 2

Before Jesus ascended to heaven, He commanded His disciples to wait in Jerusalem for the promised baptism by the Holy Spirit from God. Ten days later, on the day of Pentecost, the Holy Spirit supernaturally descended upon the assembly of disciples. When some Jews accused the disciples of being drunk with wine, Peter rose and proclaimed:

> For these are not drunken, as ye suppose, seeing it is *but* the third hour of the day. But this is that which was spoken by the prophet Joel; And it shall come to pass in the last days, saith God, I will pour out of my Spirit upon all flesh: and your sons and your daughters shall prophesy, and your young men shall see visions, and your old men shall dream dreams: And on my servants and on my handmaidens I will pour out in those days of my Spirit; and they shall prophesy: **And I will shew wonders in heaven above, and signs in the earth beneath; blood, and fire, and vapour of smoke: The sun shall be turned into darkness, and the moon into blood, before that great and notable day of the Lord come**: And it shall come to pass, *that* whosoever shall call on the name of the Lord shall be saved. (Act 2:15-21 bold added)

Peter's response was to quote a prophetic passage from Joel incorporating Joel 2:28-32a. Peter denied the charge of drunkenness by pointing to the prophetic fulfillment of God's outpouring of His Holy Spirit upon the disciples as described by the prophet Joel. But Peter did a strange thing with his quotation. He incorporated Joel's passage regarding wonders in the heavens and signs in the earth and cosmic disturbances which come before or herald the beginning of God's great Day of the LORD. Why did Peter include that passage?

The people present witnessed wonders involving the Holy Spirit: "a sound from heaven as of a rushing mighty wind" which filled the house, "cloven tongues like as of fire" which hovered above or sat upon each disciple, the infilling of the Spirit, the gift of speaking in tongues declaring the wonderful works of God so that people from various nations could understand their speech as if it were their own native language (Act 2:2-11). However, the strange work of the Holy Spirit on that eventful day of Pentecost did not include turning the sun dark, the moon to a blood red color, fire (in the context of God's judgment, natural disaster, or warfare), blood, and pillars of smoke. The Holy Spirit was not initiating God's time of vengeance against Israel, or God's Day of the LORD, or God's Day of Wrath.

Instead what began was a Day of Grace. The birth of the church marked the beginning of an Age of Grace. This age is characterized by the grace of God extended to all the peoples of the earth. All peoples, Jews and Gentiles, can turn to God and have their sins forgiven by having faith in Jesus Christ as the Son of God, and as the Lord and Savior. Calling on the name of Jesus Christ in faith brings a person into a special supernatural relationship with God through the intervening power of the Holy Spirit. The Holy Spirit changes a new believer from within by baptizing the believer with the power of the Holy Spirit in what is often referred to as the new birth or being born again. The Holy Spirit then indwells or resides in the believer as a special link to God and Christ. What began on Pentecost with the gifting of the Holy Spirit continues to this day, albeit less dramatically.

God's Day of the LORD did not have anything to do with the birth of the church on Pentecost with the giving of the Holy Spirit. Yet the Holy Spirit was very much in charge of what was happening. It is evident that the Holy Spirit inspired Peter to utilize this very passage of prophetic scripture. In fact, that passage was likely given to Joel and recorded just waiting to be applied at this very moment. The inclusion of the portion of the passage applying to the giving of the Holy Spirit makes sense, but why include the portion containing the catastrophic warning?

I believe there is nothing accidental or coincidental about Peter's quotation of this passage from Joel. It was not a slip of the tongue. It seems that the Holy Spirit was using Joel's prophecy to create boundary lines for the Church Age. God was bracketing the Age of Grace with prophetic signs or bookends connected to the giving of and the work of the Holy Spirit. The Holy Spirit was given by God to the people of the world who will believe in Him through His Son Jesus Christ. This blanket offering of the Holy Spirit to supernaturally baptize new believers with the new birth marked a new relationship between God and mankind. The automatic indwelling of the Holy Spirit of all believers was not experienced by Israel or the nations during the Old Testament period.

The beginning of the church at Pentecost with the outpouring of the Holy Spirit is rather obvious. What does the rest of Joel's prophecy have to do with the church or the Holy Spirit? It seems that the Holy Spirit was using that prophecy to describe the conditions the world will experience at the time of the end of the Church Age – the end of the Age of Grace. The church began suddenly with an outpouring of the Holy Spirit, and the church will end suddenly with the calling out of the church by Christ at the time of the rapture. All of the Christian believers who have the indwelling of the Holy Spirit will suddenly be called out of this world. There will be an outpouring of the Holy Spirit, leaving this world accompanied by the church. This will allow God to release His supernatural restraining force through the Holy Spirit's presence in the church, which currently prevents the person of the Antichrist from rising to earthly power. Peter's quote points to Joel's prophetic relevance to the church and its mystery age – both its beginning and its ending. Thus, the Church Age, which ends with the rapture of the church, is marked in the end by the cosmic disturbances described in Joel's prophecy and its companion prophecy in Revelation 6 regarding the sixth seal. The timing of the Blood Red Moon, the global earthquake, along with the other wonders described as taking place simultaneously is highly significant in its relationship to the immediate ending of the Age of Grace and the removal of the church from the earth.

## A Sign – The Sign of the End of the Age

The prophetic Olivet Discourse, which was given by Jesus during the last few days before His crucifixion, was prompted by questions from some of His disciples. "And as he sat upon the mount of Olives, the disciples came unto him privately, saying, Tell us, when shall these things be? and what *shall be* the sign of thy coming, and of the end of the world?" (Mt 24:3). This rendering of the KJV "of the end of the world" is unfortunate and misleading. The disciples where not asking when the world will be destroyed or come to an end.

Vine's Complete Expository Dictionary indicates that "The phrase 'the end of the world' should be rendered 'the end of the age,' in most places." In examining the meaning of "End" Vine's elaborates that in regards to Matthew 24:3, "the rendering 'the end of the world' (KJV and RV, text) is misleading; the RV marg., 'the consummation of the age,' is correct. The word does not denote a termination, but the heading up of events to the appointed climax."[28] As such the translation of the NASB will better serve our purposes, "Tell us, when will these things happen, and what *will be* the sign of Your coming, and of the end of the age?"

The disciples asked a series of three questions which it seems they thought were inherently related.

- When will these things happen? – refers to the destruction of the Jewish Temple which Jesus had predicted (Mt 24:1-2).
- What will be the sign of Jesus' coming?
- What will be the sign of the end or consummation of the Age?

The answer to the first question is found in the passage of Luke 21:12-24, which gives a somewhat different relating of the material from the Olivet Discourse. Jesus answered the second question as to the sign of His coming specifically:

> For as the lightning cometh out of the east, and shineth even unto the west; so shall also the coming of the Son of man be. … Immediately after the tribulation of those days shall the sun be darkened, and the moon shall not give her light, and the stars shall fall from heaven, and the powers of the heavens shall be shaken: And then shall appear the sign of the Son of man in heaven: and then shall all the tribes of the earth mourn, and they shall see the Son of man coming in the clouds of heaven with power and great glory. (Mt 24:27, 29-30)

The answer Jesus gave points to the very visible form that His return will take. The people on the earth will have no trouble witnessing His coming from heaven. Jesus specifically identifies it as taking place "immediately after the tribulation of those days" in conjunction with cosmic disturbances including the moon being completely dark. With the sun and the moon not giving off any light, the brilliant spotlight of Christ's glory coming from heaven will be hard to miss. The tribulation of those days refers to the Day of the LORD and after the tribulation refers to the Great Day of Christ's return at the end of the Day of Wrath.

The third question that the disciples asked is of interest in the context of our current study. Were they consciously asking for multiple signs, one for the return of Jesus, and one for the end of the age? Did they ask a two part extended question, simply thinking that the sign of His return and the sign of the end of the age would be the same sign? It is difficult to completely understand their mindset. We know they expected the coming of the Kingdom sooner rather than later. Even after receiving the prophecy of the Olivet Discourse, experiencing the crucifixion and resurrection of Christ, and interacting with Jesus off and on over a period of forty days following His resurrection, they asked Jesus if He was going to restore the kingdom of Israel at that time just before He ascended into heaven (Act 2:6). They were so focused on a literal earthly kingdom of Israel led by its Messiah that they had difficulty comprehending the scope of His teachings and the length of His absence before the Holy Spirit came upon them on the day of Pentecost.

Regardless of their conscious awareness and intent, the form of their questioning points to there being two different signs of relevance to the time of the end, which is the Day of the LORD. The sign of the end of the age is not the same sign as the sign of the return of Jesus. Jesus actually gave His disciples four signs during the course of His Olivet Discourse, although He only directly referred to the last one as a sign in Matthew 24. That one was the "sign of the Son of man in heaven," which indicates His return in glory at the end of the Tribulation. The sign for their first question was to recognize that when they should see Jerusalem encompassed by armies, the time for the destruction of the Temple had come (Lk 21:20). This was fulfilled by the armies of Rome almost forty years later when Jerusalem was under a state of siege for a period of time and completely fell in 70 A.D. The two other signs provided by Jesus are the "beginning of sorrows" and the "abomination of desolation." The Abomination of Desolation is a sign for the Jews in Israel to immediately flee to the mountains of the wilderness. It takes place in the middle of Daniel's 70th Week and well into the time of the Day of the LORD.

The Beginning of Sorrows is the sign which becomes very relevant to us. It cannot be confused with the sign of Jesus' return. The Beginning of Sorrows marks the beginning of the Day of the LORD as the time of God's wrath, while the Revelation of Christ marks the end of the Day of the LORD'S outpouring of God's wrath. Each dynamic event has its own sign or signs. The parallel passage to Matthew 24:7 in Luke 21:11 includes "fearful sights and great signs shall there be from heaven." The sign of the end of the age is the sign for the Beginning of Sorrows.

This is where we fall back on the building blocks of our study of the Day of the LORD. We have observed the close association between the passage in Joel 2 and the passage of the sixth seal in Revelation 6, with their joint specific highlighting of the cosmic disturbances incorporating the Blood Red Moon. We examined the multiple conditions which Jesus gave: wars, earthquakes, famines, and pestilences which comprise the very first birth pang – the Beginning of Sorrows. We have noted how Peter quoted the passage of Joel 2 in his focused revelation of the work of the Holy Spirit in the birth of the church, again incorporating the cosmic disturbances surrounding the moon turning to blood. Peter's bracketing of the Church Age with the prophecy of Joel 2 gives the sign of the end of the Age of Grace. When we put all of these prophecies together: Joel 2; Isaiah 2; Matthew 24; Acts 2; Revelation 6:12-17 (sixth seal), we get a clearer picture of the sign of the sudden end of this age and the onset of the Day of the LORD which immediately replaces it.

- Blood Red Moon
- Sun is dark
- Cosmic disturbances in the heavens and stars
- Great Earthquakes – Global Earthquake

- Great Warfare – Nation against Nation; Kingdom against Kingdom
- People hiding underground in fear of God and His wrath
- Great Famine
- Great Pestilence

In practical terms, all of these conditions coming together simultaneously will create a great warning sign – The Day of the LORD has come! It will be undeniable. This is not a warning sign that the Day is coming in the near future as Renald Showers insinuated. It is the sign which marks the very end of one age and the beginning of the time that replaces it. The sign of the end of the Church Age will be so great even atheists will fear God at this point in time. What about believers? Where will believers be when the sign of the end of the Age of Grace suddenly appears in heaven and on earth?

**The Church Age and the Sign of the End of the Age**

**Peter Quotes Joel 2**
**Acts 2:16-21; Joel 2:28-32; Rev 6:12-17 Sixth Seal**

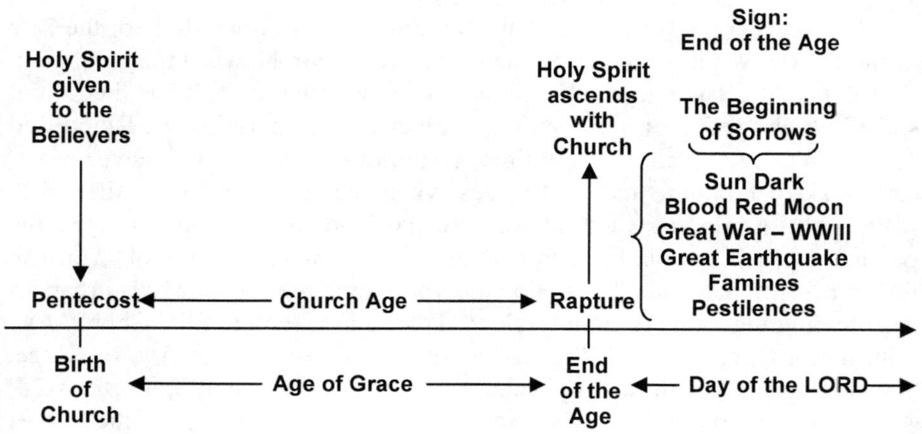


## The Rapture and the Day of the LORD

It is important to understand that the current Church Age does not extend into or overlap the Day of the LORD in any way. The birth pangs and the time of travail that are characterized by God's wrath have nothing to do with either the church or the Age of Grace. As Sir Robert Anderson emphasized in his book in *The Coming Prince*:

> If the day of wrath has come, the day of grace is past, and the Gospel of grace is no longer a Divine message to mankind. To suppose that the day of wrath can be an episode in the dispensation of grace is to betray ignorance of grace and to bring Divine wrath into contempt. The grace of God in this day of grace surpasses human thought ; His wrath in the day of wrath will be no less Divine. The breaking of the sixth seal heralds the dawning of that awful day ; the visions of the seventh seal unfold its unutterable terrors.[29]

The beginning of the Day of the LORD marked by the Beginning of Sorrows denotes a new dispensation in God's dealing with the human race. This is a dispensation of judgment and wrath, of eradicating unrepentant sinners from the face of the earth, of refining Israel as a nation for its Messiah and its Kingdom. The church is not destined to face or experience God's wrath. There is no sanctuary on earth for the church during this dispensation of the Day of the LORD. One of the problems with the mid-trib, pre-wrath, and post-trib rapture positions is that they all continue the Age of Grace into the time period of the seven-year Tribulation of Daniel's 70$^{th}$ Week.

If the Day of the LORD immediately follows the Age of Grace, what does that mean for the Christian church? The church is present on earth throughout the Church Age or the Age of Grace. The church must be removed from the earth before the Day of the LORD can begin. The removal of the church is actually the last event of the Church Age. The rapture of the church is that specific event that both ends the current age and unleashes the short age which immediately follows – the great and terrible Day of the LORD. While the rapture of the church is not actually part of the Day of the LORD, it is the last event that precedes it.

The rapture of the church is accompanied by the removal of the restraining force (the Holy Spirit) which holds back the rise to power of the Antichrist. Thus, the covenant of peace that begins Daniel's 70$^{th}$ Week could not be achieved before the rapture of the church. It will also most likely take a short period of time or even longer for the Antichrist to gain enough power or to be in a position to take advantage of a world crisis out of which he can emerge onto the world stage as the great problem solver. This removal of the church from the earth and of the Holy Spirit, who indwells the church, will unleash an immediate reign of chaos throughout the world. This is the perfect environment for the Antichrist to begin his rise.

Characteristics of the Rapture and the probable immediate effects of its aftermath:

- Sudden change
- The sudden presence of Christ coming for His church
- The voice of Christ
- The resurrection of dead Christians
- The sudden removal of all Christian believers from the earth
- The removal of the Holy Spirit's supernatural restraining force against the Antichrist
- The sudden end of the Age of Grace
- The wrath of God against the earth
- Possible global earthquake associated with the resurrection of millions of dead Christians
- Economic chaos
- Political and military chaos – War
- Full scale apostasy and rebellion against God
- The church must be removed from the face of the earth before God's wrath is unleashed.
- The rapture of the church is actually in itself an act of wrath, unleashed by God upon the world left in the wake of the church's sudden and violent removal. The collective body of the church is snatched away by Christ so quickly that it leaves a vacuum that must be filled. This vacuum involves spiritual, moral, political, economic, and military ramifications. It will be filled with a chaotic, violent, global implosion of sin.

How does the rapture of the church relate to the Beginning of Sorrows and the opening of the seven seals by Christ? Contrary to popular teachings I believe the rapture bears a central role in the mechanism of the opening each of the seven seal judgments.

- The first seal releases the supernatural restraint against the ultimate False Christ. The release of the rider on the white horse from the starting gate of his race to conquer the world is a form of wrath by God. It is one way that God curses the world. God and Christ literally sanction and empower the Antichrist. That is why he is given a "stephanos" crown. The Antichrist cannot go out to conquer and rise to power or be revealed to the world while God's restraining force, the indwelling presence of the Holy Spirit within the church (body of Christ), remains in the world. The removal of the Holy

Spirit, along with the body of Christ, by the rapture of the church must come first. While the church is on earth, the Antichrist is restrained.

**Relationship of the Rapture to the Opening of the Seven Seals**

- The second seal reveals that peace is taken from the earth and it is replaced by great warfare. This is another curse of God's wrath. Yet this is not the War of Armageddon involving God's wrath and judgment against all nations. War is a logical immediate aftermath of the removal of the church and the Holy Spirit. The prophetic war of Gog and Magog in Ezekiel 38–39 is described as taking place at a time of God's choosing; when God focuses on Israel as "My people," and "My land;" yet it is a time when Israel and all of the nations do not really know God. Israel is profaning God's holy name. All the nations are profaning God's holy name. So God rises up to magnify His own holy name and to unleash His wrath upon certain nations who invade Israel, and others who dwell carelessly, under a false sense of security in their sinful rebellion. These characteristics are true of the time immediately following the rapture of the church. With the church removed, God refocuses on Israel as His people, and His land. The world will be filled with unbelieving sinners – all the peoples of the world will be profaning God's name. The church does not face the wrath of God unleashed through this great level of warfare, even though the warfare does not yet involve all nations on earth.

- The third seal describes economic collapse, inflation, and widespread famine. This form of chaos is both logical and to be expected in the aftermath of the rapture. The simultaneous disappearance of millions of people will have immediate economic consequences. Any moral or ethical restraint that exists in the financial world of governments and business that can be attributed to the presence of the Christian church will have vanished. The loss of many people associated with food production and distribution will have a compounding impact as well.
- The fourth seal gives power to Death and Hades. It has already been observed that this authority given to Hades cannot apply to the believing church. The killing of one-fourth of the world's population does not involve the church. No Christians dies as a result of the events of the fourth seal. This is an argument that this massive scale of death caused by war, famine, pestilence, and beasts takes place in the aftermath of the rapture of the church. This truly is God's wrath poured out in fury.
- The fifth seal reveals the souls of martyrs under the altar in heaven. These souls are given white robes signifying the resurrection of their bodies. They are to rest for a little season. Other believers will be martyred during the time to come. This scene points to the resurrection and rapture of the church. The Church Age martyrs, along with all dead in Christ, are resurrected and taken to heaven to rest while God's wrath is unleashed on earth.
- The sixth seal depicts the Sign of the End of the Age. Cosmic disturbances are accompanied by a great earthquake which involves the entire planet. All people on earth are affected. It is possible that there is an association between this earthquake and the rapture of the church. It has been observed by several authors that the resurrection of people to spiritually glorified bodies in the Bible is accompanied by earthquakes. A great earthquake was unleashed when Jesus was resurrected. An earthquake will be associated with the resurrection of

the two witnesses during the Tribulation who will then be caught up to heaven (Rev 11). Peter Goodgame, David Lowe, and John Abent have all made observations regarding the association of earthquakes to this type of resurrection and its possible connection to the opening of the sixth seal. In his book *Red Moon Rising* Goodgame wonders, "Perhaps the global shaking of the earth signifies the global resurrection of dead believers *from every nation, tribe, people and language*."[30] Following Goodgame's lead, David Lowe began to research the direct association between resurrection to glorified immortal bodies and earthquakes, the study of which resulted in his book *Earthquake Resurrection*. David Lowe incorporates two elements into this future shaking of the earth. First, the reverberating power of the voice of Christ, shouting out His command in the form of a trumpet or accompanied by the trumpet of God, will directly cause intense vibrations to the surface of the earth when He calls His church to rise out of the dust. Secondly, the power inherently involved when the dead bodies are raised into the state of glorified immortality will contribute to the great earthshaking event. Lowe makes an observation regarding the effects of the rapture: "A worldwide resurrection of the dead in Christ, if accompanied by the same resurrection power described with the biblical accounts of resurrection to immortality, would cause sudden massive and catastrophic changes to the surface of the earth." Connecting this observation with the sixth seal, Lowe states, "If the pattern of earthquakes occurring at the resurrection of the dead to immortality continues, then the description of what will happen when the Lamb opens the sixth seal perfectly fits the presumed description of what will take place at the moment of the resurrection of the dead in Christ and transformation to immortality. It will occur within the blink of an eye, it will be accompanied by the voice of God shaking the earth, and it will leave in its wake a catastrophic change to the surface of the earth."[31]

- The splitting of the atmosphere as a rolling scroll in the sixth seal may also play a role in the rapture. John Abent suggests this possibility in his book *Signs in the Heavens*. "When the sixth seal is opened, global cataclysmic events will begin to unfold. The Church will be raptured when the sky rolls back like a scroll. … The heavens departing like a scroll (Rev 6:14) could be necessary for the Rapture to take place. This rolling back of the heavens will be like a door opening "in the heavens" like it did for John (Rev 4:1). It will be a kind of "gateway" to the heavenly presence of God. The earthquake associated with this event could very well indicate the resurrection of the dead in Christ (Mt 28:2, Rev 11:11-13)."[32]

- The sixth seal also depicts all types of people on earth hiding underground out of fear of God and as a result of the catastrophic disasters impacting the earth. The believing church has no reason to hide from God in fear. While Christians are subject to death, war, and natural disasters while they are alive on the earth, they are not subject to this supernatural onslaught of God's wrath or to the accompanying fearful hiding that will characterize this seal judgment. This is another strong argument for the absence of the church as a result of the rapture at the time the sixth seal is broken.
- The seventh seal depicts God's final pause to reflect on the prayers of all the saints before having an angel cast God's declaration of war against the earth. This includes the prayers of the Christian martyrs under the altar in the fifth seal. The prayers asking for God's judgment and vengeance will be acted upon. The casting of fire from the altar before God's throne, accompanied by thundering, lightning, and an earthquake denotes God's intervention in the affairs of men in wrath. The church, which does not face God's wrath, must be absent from the earth. Is it just a coincidence that a Great Multitude of believers from all nations wearing white robes, denoting righteousness and resurrection, suddenly appears out of nowhere into heaven, standing with Christ before God's throne immediately before this scene? God's timing is perfect. Praise God!
- Many Scholars argue that all or most of the seals will be opened before the rapture. Those arguments, whether in support of a mid-trib, pre-wrath, or post-trib rapture, completely collapse under the onslaught of God's wrath poured out upon the world during and as a result of the collective opening of these seals. There is not a single seal that does not relate to God's outpouring of wrath. Even the fifth seal reveals the souls of martyrs crying out to God asking when He will judge the earth and avenge their blood. They are pleading for God to intervene in wrath.
- The first four seals, the Four Horsemen of the Apocalypse, depict events and characteristics that are true conditions in the immediate aftermath of the removal of the church at the rapture. The fifth seal depicts the resurrection of Church Age martyrs, an event that takes place only at the time of the rapture. The sixth seal reveals the Sign of the End of the Age, which can only appear with the removal of the church. The sixth seal involves a global earthquake, which is quite possibly directly related to the resurrection phase of the rapture of

the church. The 144,000 Jewish servants of God are supernaturally sealed to God. The Great Multitude of Church Age believers suddenly appears in heaven wearing the white robes of resurrection. The seventh seal reveals God's declaration of wrath and war against the earth.

**The Relationship of the Rapture to the Seven Seals**

**Rapture of the Church**

**First Seal –**
**Restraining Force Removed**
**Empowerment of Antichrist to rise to power**

**Second Seal –**
**Peace Removed From Earth – Great War**
**Immediately in aftermath of Rapture**

**Third Seal –**
**Economic Collapse, Inflation, Famine**
**Immediately in aftermath of Rapture**

**Fourth Seal –**
**Death & Hades**
**Mass Death of 1/4 of Earth's Population**
**Hades has no authority over the Church**
**The Church is absent from the Earth**

**Fifth Seal –**
**Souls of Martyrs under the Altar in Heaven**
**Given White Robes = Resurrection of Church**
**Age Martyrs at time of the Rapture**

**Sixth Seal –**
**Sign of the End of the Age**
**Global Earthquake; Cosmic Disturbances**
**May be related to resurrection of Church**
**All men hiding underground in fear of God**
**The Church is not hiding – the Church is absent**

**Seventh Seal –**
**Silence in Heaven; Prayers of Saints Answered**
**God's Declaration of War against the Earth**
**The Church is absent from the Earth**

- Some of the seals point to what takes place immediately after the rapture, and some of the seals point to effects of the event itself. The entire process of Christ's breaking the seals is capped by God's declaration of war after the seventh is broken and the scroll is fully open. This combination of characteristics argues for the rapture of the church and the opening of the seals to be part of a dynamic but single collective phase that begins with Jesus taking the scroll and is not finished until God's fire is cast down to the earth. This phase is the Beginning of Sorrows.

If the rapture precedes Daniel's 70th Week, how do we identify this interim period of time? When God and Christ finally intervene in the affairs of mankind by snatching the collective body of Christian believers out of the ground and off of the face of the earth with the event we call the rapture, would they just sit and do nothing for a period of time waiting for Israel to enter into a covenant of peace with the Antichrist? What logically happens on earth during this time immediately following the removal of the church? I believe that the rapture of the church immediately initiates God's Day of the Lord judgments upon the earth, but Daniel's 70th Week does not begin until the covenant of peace is confirmed between the nation of Israel and the Antichrist some time later. The interim period between the pretribulational rapture and the covenant of peace is marked by chaos, war, global catastrophe, famine, and pestilence, and the ongoing aftermath of all of these. The rapture, in effect, initiates the Beginning of Sorrows.

## A Period Longer Than Seven Years

If the Day of the LORD is the period of time that immediately follows the Age of Grace and the rapture of the church, instead of the seven-year tribulation of Daniel's 70th Week, is there any support for God's Day of Wrath lasting longer than seven years? To answer that question we can draw upon four arguments.

First: **The War of Gog and Magog**. There is evidence within the prophecy of Ezekiel 38 and 39 that connects the War of Gog and Magog to the beginning of the Day of the LORD. Israel is invaded by an alliance of nations which surround Israel but primarily attacks from the north. This is the outer circle of nations. None of them actually border Israel. God rises up in wrath and shakes the entire planet with a global earthquake. Great warfare in conjunction with the time that God rises to shake the earth equates with the Beginning of Sorrows (Isa 2; Mt 24:7-8; sixth seal). To make it more clear, God declares in Ezekiel 39:8, "Behold, it is come, and it is done, saith the

Lord GOD; this *is* the day whereof I have spoken." In the aftermath of God's supernatural intervention, Israel is told that they will plunder the invaders' weapons and supplies and use them for fuel (energy) for a period of seven years. For Israel to accomplish this victorious plundering requires that Israel be living in its land unmolested for the entire time of seven years. That situation will be impossible at any point following the midpoint of Daniel's 70th Week, when the Antichrist betrays his covenant with Israel. Thus, for Israel to be able to freely fulfill the prophecy of Ezekiel 39, God's destruction of the armies of Gog and Magog must occur at least seven years prior to the midpoint of the Tribulation. This places the beginning of the Day of the LORD – as the Beginning of Sorrows at least 3 ½ years before the covenant is signed. That would require at least a period of 10 ½ years for the Day of the LORD.

Second: **The Ten Days of Awe**. Part of the significance of the fulfillment of future prophetic events will be the timing of each of the events and the relationship of each event to the Jewish calendar. God created a pattern of significant days to be observed by Israel during the time of the Exodus of the Israelites from Egypt. Israel's primary feast days are broken down into two groupings, one in the spring and one in the fall. The spring feasts include: the Feast of Passover; the Feast of Unleavened Bread; the Feast of Firstfruits; and the Feast of Weeks or Pentecost. The fall feasts include: The Feast of Trumpets; The Feast of Atonement; and the Feast of Tabernacles.

Jesus Christ served as the prophetic fulfillment of Israel's spring feasts during the last days of His ministry to Israel. Jesus was God's prophetic Passover Lamb sacrificed and crucified during the time of Israel's Feast of Passover. Jesus served as the symbolic "Bread of Life" of the Feast of Unleavened Bread. The resurrection of Jesus Christ from death fulfilled Israel's Feast of Firstfruits. Jesus ascended to heaven after forty days. Ten days later, fifty days after Firstfruits, was the Feast of Weeks (Pentecost). On this very day, the Holy Spirit descended upon the believers of Jesus Christ in Jerusalem to establish the Spirit-filled indwelling of the church. Pentecost has been followed by the long interval of summer, the present Church Age marked by the silence of God, which will soon come to an end.

The end of the long interval of summer is marked by the blowing of trumpets. The Feast of Trumpets or Rosh Hashanah falls on the first day of the Jewish month of Tishri. This day initiates a solemn period of ten days which culminates on the tenth of Tishri with the Day of Atonement (Yom Kippur), the holiest and most solemn day of the Jewish year. Yom Kippur symbolizes the day of God's judgment and is marked by mourning and atonement of sin. It is set aside as a day for Israel's cleansing of national sin. It marks the only day on the Jewish calendar that the High Priest entered the Holy of Holies in the Temple and presented himself before God to make atonement for Israel.

The Feast of Trumpets is characterized by a focus on God's judgments and points to the future Day of Judgment. It is a time that focuses on the reestablishment of the relationship between God and Israel and the regathering of Israel – the summoning of Israel back to the Promised Land. There is also a connection between the Feast of Trumpets and the theme of resurrection. Jewish tradition and teachings associate the resurrection of the dead to be announced by the blowing of God's trumpet (shofar). Due to its timing in the Jewish calendar and its various themes, the Feast of Trumpets bears a symbolic and prophetic connection to both the rapture of the church and the War of Gog and Magog. The beginning of the Feast of Trumpets is directly connected to the dawning of the new moon at the beginning of the month of Tishri. As such it was the one holy day in the series of Jewish holy days where the day or the hour could not be known exactly in advance. The presence of the new moon had to be confirmed by at least two witnesses before the day of the Feast of Trumpets could be officially declared.

The Feast of Trumpets begins a ten day period which ends with the Day of Atonement. These ten days are commonly referred to as the Days of Awe. They are also known as the Days of Repentance. This period is a solemn time when each Jew is expected to enter into serious introspection and repent of his sins before the Day of Atonement.

The Ten Days of Awe between Rosh Hashanah and Yom Kippur are obviously symbolic of the Tribulation period. But they also obviously represent a period of time longer than the seven years prophesied for Daniel's 70$^{th}$ Week. This time setting of ten days from Tishri 1 through Tishri 10 is indicative of the day for a year relationship consistent with the one that is portrayed within Daniel's prophecy of the seventy weeks, where one prophetic week of days equals seven years. But why did God interject the Days of Awe as a period of ten days instead of seven days? If there were only seven days on the Jewish calendar between the Feast of Trumpets and the Day of Atonement, prophecy scholars would be jumping at identifying that period as being a symbolic representation of Daniel's 70$^{th}$ Week, and thus the Tribulation. However, there are ten Days of Awe, and that throws a wrinkle into the prophetic tapestry. Since God created the exact schedule of Israel's feast days as a symbolic and prophetic timetable and since God does not create things without reason, God must have had a specific purpose for identifying this future period of time as ten symbolic days. It is clear that this period must be longer than Daniel's prophesied seven-year long 70$^{th}$ Week. The ten Days of Awe must represent a prophetic period of ten years.

The Ten Days of Awe could very well represent the time period of the Day of the LORD and demonstrate that the period of Daniel's 70$^{th}$ Week is a sub-category of time within the longer Day of the LORD. Thus, if the rapture of the church and the Gog and Magog invasion of Israel are events in God's opening act of the Day-of-the-LORD judgments, the Ten Days of Awe allow for a built in time of 3 to 3 ½ years following the invasion before the actual period of Daniel's 70$^{th}$ Week begins. This would allow for Israel to burn the weapons of Gog and Magog for a period of seven years before the midpoint of Daniel's 70$^{th}$ Week, when the Beast and the False Prophet under the complete domination of Satan initiate their full scale assault against the Jewish people. In this manner, the ten Days of Awe may be a representation of the Day-of-the-LORD judgments as a period of ten years, which begins with the dual events of the removal of the church by the rapture and the destruction of the invasion of Gog and Magog by God, and extends through the events of the Tribulation to the Revelation of Jesus Christ.

Third: **Christ's Ascension**. Christ ascended to heaven forty days after His resurrection. From Christ's ascension to heaven until the gifting of the Holy Spirit to the church on the day of Pentecost was a period of ten days. The Feast of Weeks (Pentecost) always follows the Feast of First Fruits by fifty days. The day of Pentecost on the Jewish calendar commemorates both the giving of the Law to Moses on Mt. Sinai and the giving of the Holy Spirit to the believers in Jerusalem which formed the birth of the church.

Why did Christ ascend to heaven ten days before the Holy Spirit was sent to indwell the church? Is there any prophetic significance to this ten day period of time?

God sent the Holy Spirit to indwell the church on Pentecost (Act 2). The parallel event in the future will be the time when the Holy Spirit is sent to all of the people of Israel who will survive the Great Tribulation to enter the Millennial Kingdom (Isa 32:15; Joel 2:28-29). Is there any connection between the ten day period between the ascension of Christ and the events of Pentecost and the length of time between the future ascension of the church and the future posttribulational sending of the Holy Spirit to the nation of Israel?

Since Christ ascended to heaven ten days prior to the arrival of the Holy Spirit for the church, will the ascension of the resurrected and raptured church precede the arrival of the Holy Spirit for Israel by a symbolic ten days? If so, these ten days could equate to a day for a year as in Daniel's prophecy of seventy weeks, and thus equal a period of ten years.

Fourth: **Ten Days of Tribulation**. In the letter dictated to the church in Smyrna, Christ had John write a somewhat cryptic verse. "Do not fear what you are about to suffer. Behold, the devil is about to cast some of you into prison, so that you will be tested, and you will have tribulation for ten days. Be faithful until death, and I will give you the crown of life" (Rev 2:10). Christ is telling some people that they will have "tribulation for ten days." Why does Christ mention a specific ten day period of tribulation? He also emphasizes the need for the believer to be faithful to the death. Christ is focused on a time when there will be much tribulation and many martyrs for their faith. This faith unto death earns them the crown of life. Is this part of the letter to Smyrna strictly past or does it still have prophetic significance?

This passage has been interpreted in various ways by different authors, but all of the interpretations that I have read seem strained in their treatment of this verse. What ten days could Christ be referring to? A simple ten days in the first century history involving only a few individuals of the church in Smyrna? Is it a reference to ten various waves of persecution against the church by the Emperors of Rome? That is the conclusion which Clarence Larkin applied to it. These arguments do not sound completely convincing.

In the context of Tribulation and the Day of the LORD, I believe the reference to the ten days is more likely symbolic of a prophetic period of ten years. Just as the ten days between Rosh Hashanah and Yom Kippur (the ten Days of Awe) may represent the Day of the LORD as a ten year period, these ten days of tribulation in the letter to Smyrna may also represent or symbolize the future and prophetic ten Days of Awe of the end-times Day of the LORD.

Israel will require at least seven years in order to have the prophesied amount of time to burn the weapons and equipment of the armies of Gog and Magog before the midpoint of Daniel's 70$^{th}$ Week. That places the invasion of Israel by Gog and Magog a least a little more than ten years before the end of the Tribulation. The Feast of Trumpets begins a ten day period known as the "Days of Awe" which ends on the Day of Atonement. Christ ascended to heaven ten days before the arrival of the Holy Spirit at Pentecost. Christ made reference to a specific period of ten days of tribulation in His message to the church at Smyrna. Is it all unrelated coincidence? Or does this pattern of God's intervention, resurrection and ascension, the giving of the Holy Spirit, and tribulation give us an indication that the Day of the LORD may be longer than the commonly held view of a final seven year period of Tribulation?

## Conclusions – The Timing of the Day of the LORD

There will be a Great Day at the end of the Tribulation involving the Revelation of Christ, but that day alone cannot account for all of the conditional requirements pertaining to the Day of the LORD. The phrase "great and terrible" does not exclusively apply to the Revelation. The single Great Day does not account for the characteristic of birth pangs and the Beginning of Sorrows. It does not allow for the Day to come with sudden destruction, or for it to come in the context of people saying "peace and safety" in any manner. It does not allow for the distinction between the blood moon giving off a blood red glow versus being completely darkened so that there is no light at all being reflected by the moon. Nor can it account for the incompatible conditions of people hiding underground because of what is being unleashed upon the world versus the massing of all armies against Israel at the time of Armageddon.

While the Pre-wrath View does focus on the Day coming immediately following the rapture of the church, and associates the first four seals with the Beginning of Sorrows, and sees the significance of the sixth seal as the sign of the end of the age, it presents serious issues in interpreting parallel prophetic passages. It cannot allow for any part of the wrath of God to begin before the middle of the second half of Daniel's 70$^{th}$ Week. Thus, the beginning of birth pangs and the first six seals involvement with God's wrath is denied. This completely separates the Beginning of Sorrows from the beginning of the Day of the LORD. The Day in this model does not come as sudden destruction because the great war, famine, and pestilence in which the death of one-fourth of the world's population (fourth seal) has already taken place. The concept of people saying "peace and safety" has no real relevance during the middle of the second half of the Tribulation, as the world has experienced numerous forms of catastrophic judgment from God and the Campaign of Armageddon is on the verge of being unleashed.

The Great Tribulation View also distances the beginning of birth pangs from the beginning of the Day. Jesus places the Beginning of Sorrows before the middle of Daniel's 70$^{th}$ Week by describing that beginning before He later describes the Abomination of Desolation. The birth pangs begin the Day of the LORD and that time must come before the Abomination of Desolation.

The Tribulation View of equating the seven years of Daniel's 70$^{th}$ Week with the Day does place the Beginning of Sorrows at the beginning of the Day. However, it also places both at the time of the signing of the covenant of peace, which is not consistent with God's motivation and characterization for the beginning of His Day of Wrath. It also stretches out the opening of the seals throughout a major portion of the first half of the Tribulation, which conflicts with the simultaneous nature of the picture that Jesus gave for the Beginning of Sorrows. The role of the rapture as the last event of the Church Age to be immediately followed by the Day is denied or minimized by the proponents of this view. The pretribulational rapture is often depicted as being followed by a vague, uneventful period of time before the Tribulation of Daniel's 70th Week begins. While Renald Showers enhances this view by incorporating into it the concept of both broad and narrow aspects of the Day, his model is still inhibited by these same drawbacks associated with establishing the beginning of the Broad Day of the LORD with the covenant which begins Daniel's 70th Week.

I believe that there is a different model that can better account for all of the various characteristics regarding the Day of the LORD and the Beginning of Sorrows coming with sudden destruction. This view sees the Day of the LORD being initiated immediately following the pretribulational rapture of the church, but it situates that point in time as occurring approximately three and one-half years before the beginning of Daniel's 70th Week. This allows for the beginning of birth pangs of war, famine, pestilence, and global earthquake to come as sudden destruction completely independent of Daniel's 70th Week and the covenant that marks its beginning. It equates Jesus' depiction of the Beginning of Sorrows with the immediate opening of all seven seals. Over the course of a very short period of time, Jesus breaks the seven seals; the church is raptured to heaven; the 144,000 Jewish servants are sealed to God; God declares war against the sinners left behind on earth; the birth pang of the Beginning of Sorrows is felt; Gog and Magog and other wars erupt on earth; the sun is dark and the moon is blood red – the sign of the end of the age is present in the heavens; a global earthquake shakes the planet; people hide in fear of God; the Day of the LORD has begun. The first evidence of this in heaven is when Christ takes the scroll from the hand of God. The first evidence on earth is the vanishing act of the church caused by the rapture. All of the other aspects of this sudden changing of the ages are sucked into the Maelstrom of violence and cataclysm which fills the vacuum created by the absence of the church and the indwelling presence of the Holy Spirit. This timing also allows for Israel to have the required seven years to burn the weapons of war from Gog and Magog before being betrayed by the Antichrist at the time of the Abomination of Desolation in the middle of the Tribulation. I refer to this perspective of the Day of the LORD as the Pre-Day of the LORD Rapture View.

## Pre-Day of the LORD Rapture View

The Pre-Day of the LORD Rapture View advocated in this book simply observes that the Day of the LORD immediately commences in the chaotic vacuum created by the rapture of the church. There is no "Interstitial Period" or undefined gap between the rapture and the beginning of the Day of the LORD. Thus, that Day, as the time of God's wrath, is longer than seven years. It begins with the pretribulational rapture of the church and extends until the Revelation of Christ at the end of Daniel's 70th Week. The Day of the LORD then continues as a new Day of light throughout the Millennial Kingdom reign of Christ on earth. The Pre-Day of the LORD Rapture View acknowledges the validity of the pretribulational rapture, but it is distinguished from the traditional pretribulational model in that it separates both the rapture and the beginning of the Day of the LORD from the beginning of Daniel's 70th Week and eliminates any gap of time between the rapture and the sudden onset of the Day of the LORD. The rapture in effect simultaneously initiates both the Day of the LORD and the Beginning of Sorrows.

The event of the rapture ends the Church Age or the Age of Grace. The Age of Grace is not compatible with any of the time concepts which characterize the End Times: the Beginning of Sorrows, the Tribulation, Great Tribulation, Daniel's 70th Week, the time of Jacob's trouble, or the Day of the LORD. The Age of Grace simply cannot extend into or overlap any of these time periods. The act of God which brings Christ to claim His church and take it to heaven is an act of love for the church – but it is also an act of wrath against the entire world that is left behind. That sudden act of wrath characterizes the snare or trap which is suddenly sprung upon the world by Christ so that it comes upon them unawares or unexpectedly (Lk 21:34-36).

For those who understand the truths supporting the teaching of the pretribulational rapture, where is the understanding of what period of prophetic time immediately follows? Too often in the standard pretribulational teachings this time period between the rapture and the Tribulation is a nebulous, poorly defined or ignored subject. Why? Perhaps one reason is that a number of scholars who advocate for a pretribulational rapture simply count down seven years from the rapture until the Revelation of Christ at the time of Armageddon. In effect, these teachers make the rapture as the event which initiates the seven year Tribulation, Daniel's 70th Week, and the Day of the LORD all at the same time. Where is the scriptural evidence to support that approach? There is none!

I have no problem with the convention of equating the seven years of Daniel's 70th Week as the time of the Tribulation, or with referring to the last half of the week as the Great Tribulation. However, as is acknowledged by many prophecy scholars, there is no scriptural support for linking the rapture to the beginning of Daniel's 70th Week. The beginning of that specific period of seven years is marked by the ratification of a covenant between Israel and some, as of now still unknown, world leader. This period is often thought of as a time of peace or false peace for Israel. The beginning of Daniel's 70th Week is not identified by either the rapture or any of the primary characteristics which note the Day of the LORD beginning unexpectedly with sudden destruction as a time of God's wrath.

God creates a powerful vacuum with the rapture of Christ's church. God will not waste that vacuum. God will utilize that time to His advantage and for His purpose. The Day of the LORD is that time which begins immediately after the rapture of the church. The wrath of God is the mechanism by which God will purge the world of sinners. Just as Peter Goodgame observed in *Red Moon Rising*, "The very purpose of the Rapture is to protect believers from the Day of the Lord's wrath, just as Paul said that '*God did not appoint us to suffer wrath but to receive salvation through our Lord Jesus Christ.*' Once the Rapture occurs and God's children are protected then there will be no reason for God to delay with the outpouring of His Wrath upon a world left only with unbelievers."[33]

God's wrath begins with the beginning of the Day of the LORD in that the very beginning of the Day of the LORD is marked by God's sudden intervention in wrath. God's wrath extends through the time of Christ's return at His Revelation. In the graphic for the Pre-Day of the LORD Rapture View, God's wrath is shown as ending at this point. It is recognized that God's and Christ's judgment continues through the next 30 to 75 days following the end of Daniel's 70th Week (Dan 12). However, that portion of the 75 Day Interval between the Tribulation and the Millennium, which includes judgment, is not characterized by wrath. After Christ's Revelation and the conclusion of the War of Armageddon, there will be a period of administrative judgment. This will likely occur during the first thirty days. These events will likely include: the judgment of Israel, the judgment of the sheep & goats (Gentiles, Mt 25), the resurrection of Old Testament saints, and the resurrection of tribulational martyrs. The judgment of Satan and his confinement to the Abyss is also possible during the beginning of this time, if he is not judged on the very day of Christ's return.

The Day of the LORD spans all of the traumatic and climatic end-time events that precede and include the second coming of Christ. The time of Jacob's trouble (Jer 30:7) is not limited to a single day but represents a period of time represented by great tribulation for the nation of Israel. The Day of the LORD also spans the era of the Millennial Kingdom, and thus incorporates the time of blessing that follows the time of God's wrath. The Day of the LORD will begin suddenly and devastatingly (as a thief in the night) sometime before the final seven years of the Tribulation, initiated by Christ with the rapture of the church. The necessary cause and effect of a pretribulational rapture is the pretribulational beginning of the Day of the LORD.

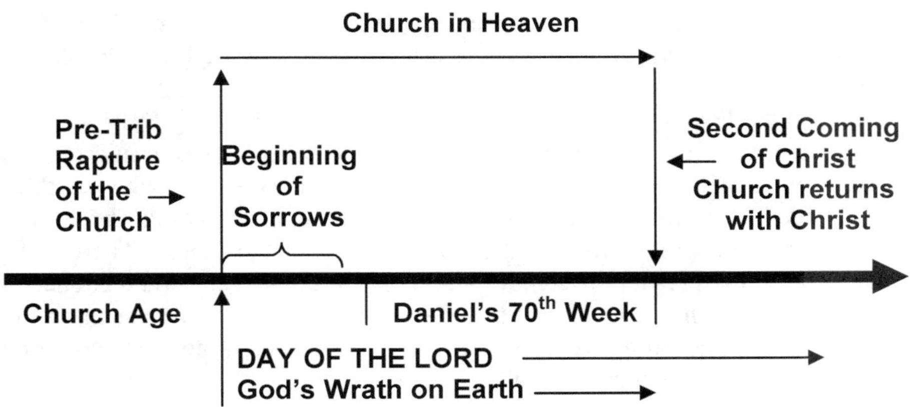


Israel and the nations are warned that a day is coming which will be characterized by the sudden presence of God in judgment, a heavenly voice, the sound of the trumpet (shofar), clouds and darkness, God's wrath, and a sacrifice by God. The church also awaits a day that is characterized by the sudden presence of Christ, the shouted command of Christ, the voice of the archangel, the trumpet of God, and being caught up into the clouds to be taken to heaven for judgment [judgment seat of Christ] (1 Thes 4:16-17). The prophets say, "Sound the alarm. The day is coming. It is near!" Jesus says, "Watch!" "Watch therefore: for ye know not what hour your Lord doth come" (Mt 24:42). "For as a snare shall it come on all them that dwell on the face of the whole earth. Watch ye therefore, and pray always, that ye may be accounted worthy to escape all these things that shall come to pass, and to stand before the Son of man" (Lk 21:35-36). The parallel between these two warnings and expectations is hardly a coincidence.

When all of the dominoes of worldly and heavenly conditions are stacked and exactly positioned, ready to fall in a precisely timed sequence of events; when the balloon of earthly iniquity is blown up to just the right capacity of explosive hot air; when all is in place for God's plan to proceed to the next level; in the fullness of Christ's body of church believers; in the fullness of God's timing – the Day of the LORD will be unleashed.

The Day of the LORD is a majestic tapestry of seemingly unrelated or haphazardly associated events woven by the hand of God. It is a horror story with both a tragic and glorious climax. It is science fiction of the most imaginative, the most alien, the most bizarre plot twists. It is drama unparalleled on the stage of human history. It is the ultimate divine comedy with the last laugh on Satan himself, when heaven rejoices – Hallelujah! It is a tragedy so deep and disturbing that once glorious angels in the service of God are cast out of heaven and are ultimately thrown into the Lake of Fire. It is the ultimate attempt of identity theft – the impersonation of Satan as a False God and Father; the Antichrist as a False Messiah; the False Prophet as a False Holy Spirit – the False Trinity attempting to dethrone the one true triune God the Father, Jesus the Son and Messiah, and the Holy Spirit.

The Day of the LORD marks a cataclysmic collision in the intersection between heaven and earth. One day, life as we know it on planet earth is busily speeding down the highway going from the past towards the future. The next second it violently collides with the Day of the LORD. There is no holding on to the present. The Church Age of Grace is over. God's silence is broken. The church is gone, up in a puff of cloud. It is too late to slam on the brakes. There is no going back. Reverse is not possible. Where are you, one second after? Do you know Christ?

## Day of Christ

Contrary to the period of judgment on earth that comprises the Day of the LORD, the "Day of Christ" points to the climax of the Age of Grace when the church finally meets its Lord, Jesus Christ, and is joined to Him in glory (1 Cor 1:8; 5:5; 2 Cor 1:14; Php 1:6, 10; 2:16; but **not** 2 Thes 2:2). The Day of Christ applies only to believers and is intimately associated with the "blessed hope" of the church (Tit 2:13). Not only will the church be physically united with Christ at the beginning of this Day, it will stand before Him, collectively as a body while each individual believer is evaluated for reward. The Day of Christ is also referred to as the "day of redemption" (Eph 1:13-14; 4:30). The reference to "the redemption of the purchased possession, unto the praise of his glory" in Ephesians 1:14, points to the resurrection and rapture of believers.

The Day of Christ is the light at the end of the dark tunnel of daily tribulation for church believers. It marks the end of the long time of patient endurance during the marathon race of life which the church runs while it occupies the earth waiting for the coming of Christ. It is a time to be hopeful about and to look longingly forward towards. It is the time the church will finally be united with its Lord. This is contrasted to the many warnings regarding the Day of the LORD directed towards the sinful nations. "Woe unto you who desire the day of the LORD! to what end *is* it to you? the day of the LORD *is* darkness, and not light (Amos 5:18).

Paul makes it clear that the Day of Christ is not the present Church Age. It is a future day which will have a specific beginning at the end of the age. "Being confident of this very thing, that he which hath begun a good work in you will perform *it* until the day of Jesus Christ: … That ye may approve things that are excellent; that ye may be sincere and without offence till the day of Christ" (Php 1:6, 10). When the Day of Christ begins the current work that is taking place within church believers ends. Why will the current work of Christ in His believers end? The church will no longer be on earth where it is tempted by sin and endures the trials of daily tribulation. The church will no longer be growing and expanding – the body of Christ will be complete.

Some sources teach that the term Day of Christ references a momentary event which only applies to the brief time when Christ returns to claim His church and the church meets Him face to face.[34] I do not believe that is an accurate understanding of either the character or the length of the Day of Christ. Others teach that the Day of Christ applies to events on earth during the Tribulation. Some think that the Day of Christ and the Day of the LORD must be two completely separate periods of time. J. Dwight Pentecost addresses this concept in his book, *Things to Come*.

> The word *day* as used in Scripture is not necessarily a time word, but may be used for the events which fall within any period. Paul so uses it in 2 Corinthians 6:2, when he speaks of the "day of salvation." Some, failing to see this, have felt that because Scripture mentions "the Day of the Lord" and the "Day of Christ" these two must come at two different periods of time, usually saying that the "Day of Christ" refers to events of the tribulation period and the "Day of the Lord" refers to events related to the second advent and the millennium to follow. Certainly two different programs are in view in these two days, but they may fall within the same time area. Thus the two days may have the same beginning, even though two different programs are in view. It may be that in 1 Corinthians 1:8 reference is made to "the day of the Lord Jesus Christ" to show that He is related to both of these days, being both "Lord and Christ" (Act 2:36).[35]

Pentecost articulates the realization that the Day of the LORD and the Day of Christ can be simultaneous parallel tracks of time without actually stating that one track takes place in heaven while the other track plays out on earth. He does state, "In each case in which Day of Christ is used it is used specifically in reference to the expectation of the Church, her translation, glorification, and examination for reward."[36]

Clarence Larkin defines the Day of Christ as, "That is the day when the Lord Jesus will come and take His Church out of the world, and includes the time between the "Rapture" and the "Revelation." On earth it is the "Day of Antichrist."[37] Larkin's distinction by implication is that the Day of Christ applies to the church in heaven as opposed to the events taking place on earth. The event of the rapture releases the supernatural restraint keeping the person of the Antichrist from rising to global power. Thus, an accurate understanding is needed for the timing of the rapture in order to understand the timing of the Day of Christ.

## Day of Christ vs. Day of the LORD

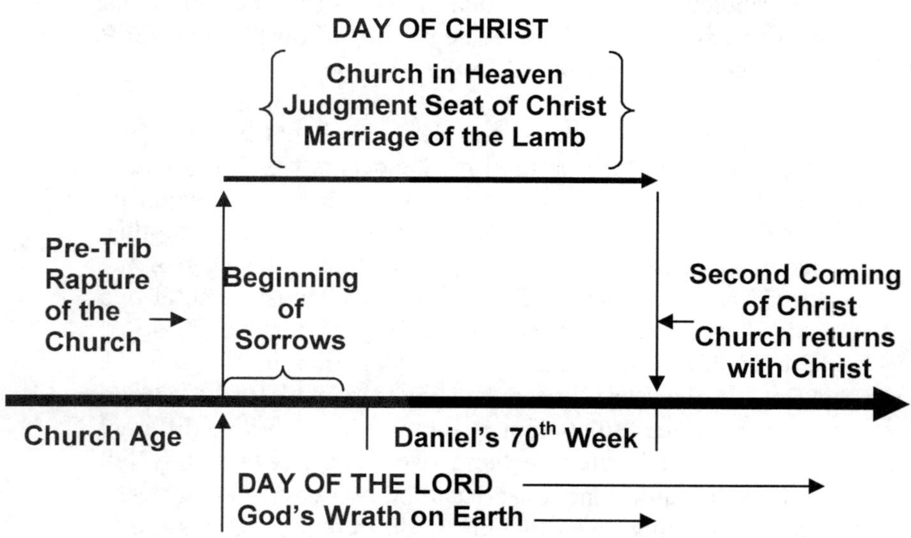


Gerald B. Stanton weighs in on this issue in his book *Kept From The Hour*: "While these two days under consideration do roughly parallel each other in point of time, one applies to the Church and finds its fulfillment in heaven, while the other applies to Israel and the nations in the Tribulation and finds its fulfillment upon the earth. Any premise which makes these two days synonymous, both applicable to the Church upon earth, must completely ignore the characteristics of each as displayed in Scripture."[38] The implication of Stanton's continued point is that anyone who teaches that the church must be on earth during God's judgments of wrath during the Day of the LORD has misplaced the rapture of the church and misunderstood the diverse characteristics of these two prophetic days.

While the Day of the LORD deals with events on earth involving God's judgments and wrath against the nations and His refinement and purification of the nation of Israel, the Day of Christ pertains to events which take place in heaven centered on the church. The Day of Christ does begin with Christ's coming for the church and His shouted command for the church to meet Him in the air above the earth (1 Thes 4:16-17). The Day of Christ continues to include: the rapture of the church, the judgment seat of Christ, the marriage of the church to Christ, and any other activities such as worshiping and praising God that the church will be involved in while it is in heaven prior to the second coming of Christ in all His glory at the end of the Tribulation.

The Day of Christ and the Day of the LORD will begin with the same event – the rapture of the church – which ends the Age of Grace. We can visualize the Day of Christ as a simultaneous partial parallel track in heaven to the track of the Day of the LORD on earth. While God's and Christ's judgment and wrath take place on earth, God's and Christ's judgment and reward take place in heaven. The Day of Christ ends at the triumphant Revelation of Christ when He returns to earth with His armies (including the church) from heaven. At this point the Day of Christ merges into the Day of the LORD with the event of the second coming. The church is then present with Christ on earth as He wraps up the climactic events of the Tribulation and prepares to usher in the Messianic Kingdom.

## Notes: The Day of the LORD vs. The Day of Christ

1. Renald Showers, *The Pre-Wrath Rapture View: An examination and Critique*, (Grand Rapids: Kregel Publications, 2001), p. 159. See also: Renald Showers, *Maranatha Our Lord, Come!*, (Bellmawr, NJ: The Friends of Israel Gospel Ministry, Inc., 1995), p. 33.
2. Richard L. Mayhue, "*Day of the Lord*," Tim Lahaye and Ed Hindson, General Editors, *The Popular Encyclopedia of Bible Prophecy*, (Eugene, OR: Harvest House Publishers, 2004), p. 74.
3. Renald Showers, *Maranatha Our Lord, Come!*, (Bellmawr, NJ: The Friends of Israel Gospel Ministry, Inc., 1995), pp. 35-37. See also: Showers, *The Pre-Wrath Rapture View*, pp. 163-164.

4. Showers, *Maranatha Our Lord, Come!*, pp. 36-37. See also: Showers, *The Pre-Wrath Rapture View*, pp. 163-164.
5. Robert Van Kampen, *The Sign*, (Wheaton, IL: Crossway Books, 1992), p. 279.
6. Van Kampen, *The Sign*, p. 34.
7. Van Kampen, *The Sign*, pp. 177-178.
8. Clarence Larkin, *Dispensational Truth or God's Plan and Purpose in the Ages*, (Glenside, PA: Rev. Clarence Larkin Est., 1918), p. 133.
9. David Dolan, *Israel in Crisis*, (Grand Rapids: Fleming H. Revell, 2001), p. 164.
10. Showers, *Maranatha Our Lord, Come!*, pp. 33, 35. See also: Showers, *The Pre-Wrath Rapture View*, pp. 152-153, 161-162.
11. Showers, *Maranatha Our Lord, Come!*, p. 59.
12. H. Wayne House and Randall Price, *Charts of Bible Prophecy*, (Grand Rapids, MI: Zondervan, 2003), p. 76.
13. J. Dwight Pentecost, *Things to Come*, (Grand Rapids: Zondervan, 1958), p. 229. Referenced from: Harry A. Ironside, *James and Peter*, pp. 98-99.
14. Pentecost, *Things to Come*, pp. 230-231.
15. Arnold G. Fruchtenbaum, *Footsteps of the Messiah: A Study in the Sequence of Prophetic Events*, (Tustin, CA: Ariel Ministries, 1982, revised 2003), p. 181.
16. E. W. Bullinger, *Commentary on Revelation*, (Grand Rapids, MI: Kregel Publications, 1984), p. 248. Originally published as *The Apocalypse*.
17. Showers, *Maranatha Our Lord, Come!*, pp. 66-67.
18. Showers, *Maranatha Our Lord, Come!*, p. 67.
19. W. E. Vine, Merrill F. Unger, William White, Jr., *Vine's Complete Expository Dictionary of Old and New Testament Words*, (Nashville, TN: Thomas Nelson Publishers, 1984, 1996), p. 640.
20. Showers, *Maranatha Our Lord, Come!*, p. 62.
21. Showers, *Maranatha Our Lord, Come!*, p. 62.
22. J. Vernon McGee, *Revelation Chapters 6-13*, Thru the Bible Commentary Series Volume 59, (Nashville: Thomas Nelson, Inc., 1991), p. 48.
23. McGee, *Revelation Chapters 6-13*, p. 37.
24. Showers, *Maranatha Our Lord, Come!*, p. 16, and chart on p. 68.
25. Larkin, *Dispensational Truth*, The Book of Revelation chart situated between pages 127 and 128 & Daniel's "Seventieth" Week chart situated between pages 133 and 134 and narrative p. 134. See also the Book of Revelation by Clarence Larkin. Tim LaHaye, *Revelation Unveiled*, (Grand Rapids, MI: Zondervan Publishing House, 1999), pp. 13, 18. See also House and Price, *Charts of Bible Prophecy*, Chart: "Major Events of the Tribulation," p. 118.
26. Paul N. Benware, *Understanding End Times Prophecy*, (Chicago: Moody Publishers, 1995, 2006), pp. 306, 308.
27. Douglas Berner, *The Silence is Broken! God Hooks Ezekiel's Gog & Magog*, (www.lulu.com and www.thesilenceisbroken.us, 2006), p. 321.
28. Vine, *Vine's Complete Expository Dictionary of Old and New Testament Words*, pp. 199, 685.
29. Sir Robert Anderson, *The Coming Prince*, (Grand Rapids, MI: Kregel Classics, reprinted 1957), p. 294.

30. Peter Goodgame, *Red Moon Rising – The Rapture and the Timeline of the Apocalypse*, (Xulon Press, 2005), p. 197. See also (www.redmoonrising.com).
31. David W. Lowe, *Earthquake Resurrection: Supernatural Catalyst for the Coming Global Catastrophe*, (www.earthquakeresurrection.com, and www.lulu.com, 2005), pp. 100-101.
32. John A. Abent, *Signs in the Heavens: Biblical Prophecy and Astronomy*, (Shippensburg, PA: Treasure House, Destiny Image Publishers, Inc., 1995), p. 266.
33. Goodgame, *Red Moon Rising*, p. 247.
34. *Wycliffe Bible Dictionary*, Hendrickson Publishers, Inc., pp. 429-430. Formerly published by Moody Press as, *The Wycliffe Bible Encyclopedia*, 1975.
35. Pentecost, *Things to Come*, p. 232.
36. Pentecost, *Things to Come*, p. 232.
37. Larkin, *Dispensational Truth*, p. 133.
38. Gerald B. Stanton, *Kept From The Hour*, (Miami Springs, FL: Schoettle Publishing Co. Inc., 1991) p. 73. Originally published by Zondervan Publishing House, 1956.

# 4

# Who Can Stand?

God literally throws a question at the world. This question takes several forms but essentially boils down to: Who can stand? It does not appear in scripture a single time out of the blue. Who can or who shall stand? It is hurled several times by several sources in the Old Testament and even appears in the New Testament. It emerges as a marker linking different pieces of the prophetic puzzle in the context of the Day of the LORD. This emphasis by repetition from God is important and alarming. This interrogation stands as a challenge, an accusation, and as an appeal by God to all mankind. God is going to arise and take a stand to mark iniquities. God directs this question to Israel, to the nations of the world, to you. Are you ready to answer God?

**Psalm 130:3** If thou, LORD, shouldest mark iniquities, O Lord, who shall **stand**?

*Stand* has a number of meanings. We stand on our feet. We can stand something up like a pillar. We can take a stand for a belief. A person can stand up in an official position like a prophet, or a priest, or a king. Some can stand in service to God, such as the tribe of Levi before the congregation of Israel (Num 16:8-9), or before God and the Ark of the Covenant (Deut 10:8), or as an angel who stands in the presence of God (Lk 1:19). Others stand as evangelists, pastors, or teachers of God's Word (Eph 4:11). In the context of warfare, "to stand" relates to being successful in defending against an invading or attacking force, or gaining a military victory (Deut 11:25; Judg 2:14; 2 Ki 10:4; Esth 8:11).

The concept of "to stand" also bears on our relationship to God. We are told to stand in awe of God (Ps 33:8). We learn that our faith should not stand in the wisdom of men, but in the power of God (1 Cor 2:5). The believer is to put on the whole armor of God so that he may "be able to stand against the wiles of the devil" (Eph 6:11). Ultimately, people will stand before God in judgment (Rom 14:10; Rev 20:12).

There are several Hebrew and Greek words which are used throughout scripture to translate this concept of "to stand." These include Strong's Hebrew words 3320, 3557, 5975, and 6965, and Strong's Greek words 2476 and 3306. When it comes to God's question, "Who can stand?" these words carry a range of meanings, primarily centered within the context of standing fast or withstanding. The words also carry the meaning of: to abide, remain, continue, dwell, or endure. Of these additional meanings, "to abide" bears significant relevance. At least two times the writers of scripture combined the meanings of both stand and abide within the same verse in the context of this important question.

In the context of our study, to stand or to abide points to location – a person's physical and spiritual proximity to God, as well as to the process of continuance – a person's relationship with God. A person takes a stand on faith, faith in God, or faith in something else, something of this world. From God's perspective people are justified by faith and are to stand by faith (Rom 3:28; 5:1-2; 2 Cor 1:24; Gal 3:24). The only solid foundation upon which a person can stand is faith in God through His Son, Jesus Christ (1 Cor 3:11; Gal 3:13-14, 22). Faith in Jesus Christ brings closeness in proximity – Christian believers are "in Christ" (Rom 8:1; 12:5; 1 Cor 1:30; 2 Cor 5:17). Christians are instructed to abide in Jesus. The apostle John encourages and warns: "And now, little children, **abide** in him; that, when he shall appear, we may have confidence, and not be ashamed before him at his coming" (1 Jn 2:28 bold added). In this sense "abide" points to the believer's process of continuance in Christ: remaining, enduring, lasting, standing fast, withstanding, and persevering.

Faith brings a believer into a passive sense of abiding in Christ. The believer receives salvation and is "in Christ" by the gift of the Holy Spirit. The believer does not earn salvation, the new birth, or the indwelling of the Holy Spirit – they are a gift from God. This gift brings a believer into a relationship which requires growth, maturity, and maintenance. This is a process which is an active sense of abiding in Christ. This active sense of abiding in their daily lives and walk with Christ is what the apostle John is encouraging in 1 John 2:28. This walk with Christ of abiding in Him not only leads to an increased fellowship in the present day but also leads to an even closer relationship in heaven and reward during the Day of Christ.

## Who Can Stand? Who Can Abide?

From the perspective of God, this is not a casual question. Nor are the implications of the question to be taken lightly. Through His prophets God proclaims that the time is coming when He is going to begin to judge the nations of the world. This time is known in prophetic scripture as the Day of the LORD. One of the primary characteristics of the Day of the LORD is the manner by which it will impact every person on earth – in Shock and Awe!

Who can stand or abide in God's wrath or God's presence when God arises in judgment? In the book of Job, God casts a form of this question by using the leviathan, a symbol of Satan the great dragon, as a challenge.

**Job 41:10** None *is so* fierce that dare stir him [Leviathan] up: who then is able to **stand** before me [God]?

Directing attention to God, the Psalms ask this question in different forms. The focus is on the time when God rises up in anger, when God judges the iniquity of sinners. One of God's instruments in venting His wrath upon unrepentant sinners is hail – great hailstones.

In the book of Job God reveals to Job that He has reserved great storehouses of hail for a future time of judgment as one of His weapons of war. "Hast thou entered into the treasures of the snow? or hast thou seen the treasures of the hail, Which I have reserved against the time of trouble, against the day of battle and war?" (Job 38:22-23). God utilizes a great hailstorm in His supernatural intervention to destroy the armies of Gog and Magog when they invade Israel (Ezek 38:22). Revelation 16:21 depicts a great hailstorm with hail the size of boulders. Each hailstone is said to have the weight of about a talent – the heaviest weight in the Hebrew system of measuring weights. This analogy puts these hailstones in the range of seventy to one hundred pounds each. Who can stand against that kind of armory?

**Psalm 76:7** Thou, *even* thou, *art* to be feared: and who may **stand** in thy sight when once thou art angry?

**Psalm 130:3** If thou, LORD, shouldest mark iniquities, O Lord, who shall **stand**?

**Psalm 147:17** He casteth forth his ice like morsels: who can **stand** before his cold?

The minor prophets weigh in with versions of this pointed question. Both Nahum and Malachi pose it in a doubled up, reinforced format which incorporates both stand and abide. These questions are asked in the context of God rising up in judgment and wrath in the form of the Day of the LORD.

**Joel 2:11** And the LORD shall utter his voice before his army: for his camp *is* very great: for *he is* strong that executeth his word: for the day of the LORD *is* great and very terrible; and who can **abide** it?

**Nahum 1:5-6** The mountains quake at him, and the hills melt, and the earth is burned at his presence, yea, the world, and all that dwell therein. Who can **stand** before his indignation? and who can **abide** in the fierceness of his anger? his fury is poured out like fire, and the rocks are thrown down by him.

**Malachi 3:2** But who may **abide** the day of his coming? and who shall **stand** when he appeareth? for he *is* like a refiner's fire, and like fullers' soap:

Even the New Testament includes a version of this question. The question is asked in conjunction with the breaking of the sixth seal in the book of Revelation. Again, it is raised specifically in the context of the Day of the LORD.

**Revelation 6:17** For the great day of his wrath is come; and who shall be able to **stand**?

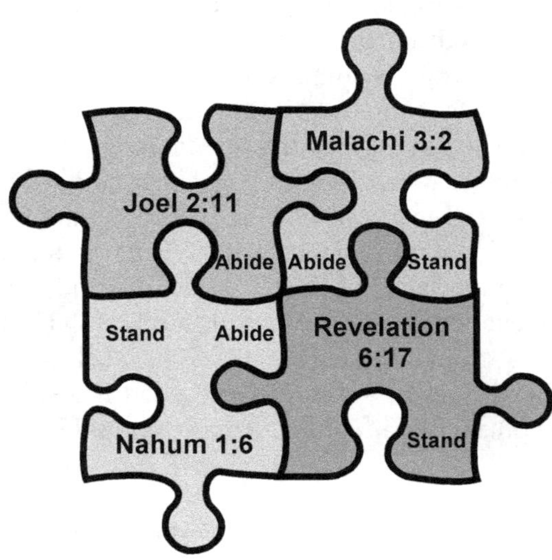

The common query posed by these four prophetic passages in Joel 2:11; Nahum 1:6; Malachi 3:2; and Revelation 6:17 form a key intersection in the linkage of the pieces of the prophetic puzzle related to the Day of the LORD. This question forms a thread linking these passages together in the larger picture of the puzzle. They mark a dividing line: on one side life and death in this world as we know it – | – on the other side life or death in the face of God standing in judgment.

## When God Intervenes (Stands)

Upon His ascension to heaven, Jesus Christ took His rightful place, sharing God's throne seated at the right hand of God the Father (Mk 16:19; Lk 22:69; Act 2:33; Col 3:1; Heb 10:12; 12:2; 1 Pet 3:22). Psalm 110:1 informs us that God the Father instructed Jesus the Son: "Sit thou at my right hand, until I make thine enemies thy footstool." Jesus is to share God's throne until such time as God sees fit to send Jesus forth as the rod of God's strength, judgment, and wrath (Ps 2; 110:2, 5-6; Act 3:20-21).

The scene in chapters 4 and 5 of the book of Revelation reveals God sitting on His heavenly throne surrounded by His heavenly court. A search is made for the one worthy to open the seven sealed scroll. Jesus, the Lamb of God, is found standing in the midst of God's throne. He takes the scroll from the right hand of God and begins the process of breaking (opening) the seven seals. The breaking of the sixth seal, Revelation 6:12-17, reveals the unrighteous people of the world attempting to hide from God – "hide us from the face of him that sitteth on the throne, and from the wrath of the Lamb: For the great day of his wrath is come; and who shall be able to **stand**?"

The time has finally come for God to tell Jesus to rise up and take His long awaited stand in judgment against the enemies of God. By taking the sealed scroll from God and breaking the seals, Jesus initiates God's Day of the LORD judgments and the wrath of God. Jesus is not initiating the final seven years of the Tribulation (Daniel's 70$^{th}$ Week), as this time period does not begin until sometime later when the Antichrist and the nation of Israel enter into a seven-year covenant. The Day of the LORD begins suddenly and catastrophically on a global scale. Daniel's 70$^{th}$ Week does not begin with sudden destruction. The seven years of Tribulation is a subset of the Day of the LORD - not the other way around as so many would have us believe.

**Revelation 6:17** For the great day of his wrath is come; and who shall be able to **stand**?

This question implies both a physical standing and a righteous standing before God. What is the context of this question in relation to God's sudden intervention? The prophets Joel, Nahum, and Malachi and the apostle John paint an interesting picture of God's intervention.

Joel asks his key question in 2:11 after literally shouting a warning, "Alas for the day! for the day of the LORD *is* at hand, and as a destruction from the Almighty it shall come. … Blow ye the trumpet in Zion, and sound an alarm in my holy mountain: let the inhabitants of the land tremble: for the day of the LORD cometh, for it is nigh at hand" (Joel 1:15; 2:1). While Joel goes on to present conditions and events characterizing both the beginning and the ending stages of God's intervention during the Day of the LORD, it is the beginning phase we are primarily interested in. "And I will show wonders in the heavens and in the earth, blood, and fire, and pillars of smoke. The sun shall be turned into darkness, and the moon into blood, before the great and the terrible day of the LORD come" (Joel 2:30-31).

The immediacy of Nahum's prophecy, including his pointed questions, was targeted at the Assyrian city of Nineveh. However, the intensity of his description in 1:5-6 did not take place at the time that God took His revenge against Nineveh. The descriptive language points to the future Day of the LORD. The prophetic passage will literally be fulfilled when God rises in judgment against "the world, and all that dwell therein." Nahum points us to God's global focus.

Malachi raises his questions in the context of the coming of the Lord. But he frames it with a double reference to the day of His coming and the time of His appearing. Interestingly, this reference immediately follows the context of Christ suddenly coming to His temple. Jesus will come suddenly to His temple, the church, when He calls the church out from the earth at the time of the rapture. That is the day of Christ's coming which initiates the Day of the LORD. However, the time of Christ's appearing, both to Israel and the nations, will be in conjunction with the end of the Day of the LORD. God's intervention in wrath is evident on earth at both times, as well as throughout the intervening Day of the LORD.

Malachi provides an immediate and continued illustration of Christ acting "like a refiner's fire, and like fullers' soap: And he shall sit *as* a refiner and purifier of silver: and he shall purify the sons of Levi, and purge them as gold and silver, that they may offer unto the LORD an offering in righteousness" (Mal 3:2-3). This refining and purification process of Israel takes place during the Day of the LORD, not after Christ's second coming. The day of Christ's coming in Malachi 3:2 must point to the event that begins that final refining process at the beginning of the Day of the LORD. This process of Israel's purification begins immediately in the vacuum of chaos left on earth in the aftermath of the rapture of the church.

This brings us to the context in which our key question is raised in Revelation 6, at the time of a great global earthquake when all the people of the world are suddenly and massively shaken. The violence of the shaking is so terrible that every mountain and every island are moved out of their previous locations to new locations. The earth's atmosphere splits as if, in ancient imagery, a scroll was released to suddenly roll itself up, or as in present times, a large rubber band or bungee cord breaks suddenly while under extreme tension. The sun turns very dark. The moon turns blood red. Stars fall from heaven. Compare this prophetic warning to the catastrophic violence of the single meteor that streaked across the sky over Russia without warning and explosively broke up into pieces in February 2013. Imagine an onslaught of dozens or hundreds of similar, or even larger, meteors simultaneously falling from the sky – exploding in the atmosphere and violently impacting the surface of the earth.

Revelation 5 depicts Jesus Christ as He prophetically stands up to initiate judgment against the earth. He is going to begin the refining process of Israel to purify it for the purpose of bringing about Israel's national redemption. Jesus breaks the seals on the scroll.

- Seal # 1 – God's supernatural restraining force is removed so that the Antichrist is released to begin his rise to power.
- Seal # 2 – War is unleashed upon the earth on a global scale.
- Seal # 3 – Economic collapse and famine become widespread.
- Seal # 4 – Death and Hades are granted authority to kill one-fourth of the population of the world. The mechanisms for this destruction are war, famine, pestilence, and wild beasts. This overlaps the previous seals making them simultaneous judgments of God's wrath. No Christian believers are involved or affected by this as Hades has no power over the church.
- Seal # 5 – The souls of martyred Church Age believers cry out to God. They ask when God will avenge their deaths. These believers have been dead for some time – long enough for them to wonder why God has delayed His vengeance for their shed blood. These souls were not martyred as a result of these seal judgments.
- Seal # 6 – A global earthquake; the sun turns dark; the moon turns blood red; stars fall from heaven; the earth's atmosphere is violently torn apart; every mountain and island are moved out of their places; all people on earth try to hide underground. They are ultimately hiding from the wrath of God and Christ. They realize that God's Day of the LORD has finally come.

A worldwide earthquake shakes all people and life on earth (Rev 6:12-16; Ezek 38:19-20; Isa 2:10-21). This shaking is caused by God rising up in judgment of the nations of the earth. God arises "to shake terribly the earth" (Isa 2:19, 21). Many terrible and catastrophic things happen simultaneously around the world: war, famine, economic collapse, pestilence, and earthquakes (Mt 24:6-8; Rev 6). People are hiding underground out of fear of what is happening in the world and out of fear of God (Isa 2:10, 19, 21; Rev 6:15-16). The people are terrified and admit that it is the judgment of both God and Christ (Rev 6:17). Who is abiding safely and confidently on earth? Who is left standing at the time immediately after God arises "to shake terribly the earth" and begins the judgments of the Day of the LORD?

There are seven (God's number for totality) categories of people who are described in Revelation 6:15 as being affected by these events. This description literally includes every person on the face of the earth. Isaiah 2:10-21 provides a parallel description of these events: God arising in terrible judgment, a global shaking of the earth, and men hiding underground in fear. In the prophecy of the Gog and Magog invasion of Israel, Ezekiel also describes a global earthquake, in the context of God arising in supernatural intervention and wrath, where "all the men that *are* on the face of the earth, shall shake at my [God's] presence" (Ezek 38:19-20).

This is not the second coming of Christ to the earth at the time of the War of Armageddon at the end of the Tribulation. The format of the book of Revelation and the sequence of events which it reveals makes it clear that the first of seven trumpet judgments has not yet sounded and the first of seven bowl judgments ("the seven last plagues" Rev 15:1) has not yet been poured upon the earth. None of these passages in Isaiah, Ezekiel, or in Revelation, depict God or Christ actually coming to the surface of the earth.

God's Day of the LORD begins with a catastrophic series of events, and it will end with an even greater catastrophic series of events. Revelation 6 describes the beginning series of events. Jesus referred to these events as "the beginning of sorrows" in His Olivet Discourse (Mt 24:6-8).

The final series of catastrophic events, which includes the War of Armageddon and the second coming of Christ, does not take place until all of the seven trumpet judgments and most of the seven bowl judgments have been implemented by God's angels. When the sixth bowl judgment containing the wrath of God is poured out upon the Euphrates River (Rev 16:12), the final series of events is underway leading to the climax of Christ's second coming and the great global earth-shaking event of the seventh bowl judgment (Rev 16:18-21).

The context of when and how this question is asked at the time of the opening of the sixth seal, as well as in the related prophets, points to the very beginning of the Day of the LORD as the dividing line for the time that Jesus

Christ stands up in judgment to impose God's wrath upon the world. It is at the very beginning of the time of travail when the first birth pang of the Beginning of Sorrows is felt that this question posed by God is most relevant.

## The Foolish Shall Not Stand

**Jeremiah 10:10** But the LORD *is* the true God, he *is* the living God, and an everlasting king: at his wrath the earth shall tremble, and the nations shall not be able to **abide** his indignation.

**Psalm 1:5** Therefore the ungodly shall not **stand** in the judgment, nor sinners in the congregation of the righteous.

**Psalm 5:5** The foolish shall not **stand** in thy sight: thou hatest all workers of iniquity.

**John 15:4-6 Abide** in me, and I in you. As the branch cannot bear fruit of itself, except it **abide** in the vine; no more can ye, except ye **abide** in me.
I am the vine, ye *are* the branches: He that **abideth** in me, and I in him, the same bringeth forth much fruit: for without me ye can do nothing. If a man **abide** not in me, he is cast forth as a branch, and is withered; and men gather them, and cast *them* into the fire, and they are burned.

**Revelation 20:12, 15** And I saw the dead, small and great, **stand** before God; and the books were opened: and another book was opened, which is *the book* of life: and the dead were judged out of those things which were written in the books, according to their works. … And whosoever was not found written in the book of life was cast into the lake of fire.

Jesus states: "I am come a light into the world, that whosoever believeth on me should not **abide** in darkness" (Jn 12:46). What does it mean to abide in Christ and not to abide in darkness? There is a dual nature to the use and meaning of the word abide. It can indicate a permanent condition of abiding based upon faith. It can also indicate a process of remaining in a certain relationship with Christ by persevering. Marty Cauley addresses this dual nature of abide that appears in the gospel of John in his two volume work *The Outer Darkness*.

> All believers *abide* (*meno*) in the light (Jn 12:46). All believers remain (abide) in the light permanently and completely. The fact that all believers abide in Christ can also be seen in Jn 6:56. However, not all believers abide in

> Christ in Jn 15:1-6. *Abide* (*meno*) is used in different ways, determined by its various contexts. Most of the time, it refers to the experience of eternal life in fellowship with Christ. On the other hand, it is also used to refer to the present possession of eternal life independent of experience, which is the case in Jn 6:56. *Abide* in Jn 6:56 contextually refers to a **promise** concerning an eternal relationship: "He who eats My flesh and drinks My blood abides in Me, and I in him." Here *abide* means to remain in eternal union with Christ, to eternally have life (cf. Jn 6:27, 56-58). In contrast, in Jn 15:4 *abide* is a **command** concerning temporal communion: "Abide in Me, and I in you." Therefore, Christ's abiding in us and us in Him is used in the Johannine writings both experientially and non-experientially.[1]

Shock and Awe! This will be a fortunate or unfortunate reality for both believers and unbelievers. *Unbelievers in shock* – The unrighteous people and nations of the world will not be able to stand or abide physically or spiritually during the Day of the LORD. Nor, will the unrighteous be able to withstand the accusations cast before them at the time they are resurrected and are forced to stand before God in judgment. *Believers in Awe* – Paul reveals that believers cannot even imagine the wonders that God has prepared for those who love Him (1 Cor 2:9). Christians will stand before Christ and be judged during the Day of Christ in heaven at the Judgment Seat of Christ. Many will be awed with the rewards that they receive and the splendor of their new abode. *Believers in shock* – The unfaithful righteous (foolish believers) will face rebuke much to their surprise (but not loss of salvation) when they stand in judgment and their walks of faith are evaluated by the LORD. Loss of reward will be an unfortunate experience for many Christians who have been negligent in their daily lives as believers "in Christ."

## God's Alternative: His Call to Stand and Abide

God has a different message for anyone who will listen to Him. God wants people to abide in Him through a persevering faith in Jesus Christ, and thus to be able to stand before Him with confidence. Faith in God through a personal *saving* relationship with Jesus is the only way any of us can be counted righteous by God. Having an *intimate* relationship with God through an active abiding faith and fellowship with Jesus Christ is the only way that anyone can stand in God's presence and be counted righteous and worthy of reward. Jesus wants people to be not only worthy to escape God's judgments during the Day of the LORD, but to be worthy of reward when they stand before Him. God's desire is not to judge in wrath, but to judge with reward. Unrepentant sinners (nonbelievers) will face God's wrath. Believers will face reward, or loss of reward depending upon the nature of their abiding relationship with God through Christ.

**1 Corinthians 7:24** Brethren, let every man, wherein he is called, therein **abide** with God.

**Ephesians 6:13** Wherefore take unto you the whole armour of God, that ye may be able to **withstand** in the evil day, and having done all, to **stand**.

**Luke 21:34-36**

> And take heed to yourselves, lest at any time your hearts be overcharged with surfeiting, and drunkenness, and cares of this life, and *so* that day come upon you unawares. For as a snare shall it come on all them that dwell on the face of the whole earth. Watch ye therefore, and pray always, that ye may be accounted worthy to escape all these things that shall come to pass, and to **stand** before the Son of man.

**1 John 2:28** And now, little children, **abide** in him; that, when he shall appear, we may have confidence, and not be ashamed before him at his coming.

**1 Corinthians 3:14** If any man's work **abide** which he hath built thereupon, he shall receive a reward.

**Micah 5:4** And he shall **stand** and feed in the strength of the LORD, in the majesty of the name of the LORD his God; and they shall **abide**: for now shall he be great unto the ends of the earth.

In the passage from Luke's gospel, Jesus extends the opportunity to escape "all these things," which are the prophesied events and forms of God's wrath. The only possible mechanism for escaping the wrath of God on earth is the rapture of the church. All of the believers in Christ will be included in the catching up event of the rapture. Faith in Christ makes believers worthy to be taken to heaven. Abiding faith makes them worthy for reward when they stand and face Christ at the Judgment Seat of Christ.

Even the death of an individual before the Day of the LORD begins does not provide a means of avoidance from facing God's judgment. At the very least everyone faces the certain prospect of being resurrected to stand before God's throne of judgment.

We can abide in Christ and escape the wrath of God when it comes upon this world, or we can abide in this world and face the wrath of God when it suddenly shakes the earth. People have a choice. They can come to Christ in faith before the Day of the LORD begins, and thus can stand and face Jesus Christ at the judgment seat of Christ and be evaluated for reward. Or they can remain unrepentant sinners and stagger, and reel, and fall before God's wrath. For when the Day of the LORD finally comes, who can abide in that day? As John Phillips wrote, "The day is coming when this world will see such a demonstration of God's power as will leave nothing standing at all, except what is founded on His grace."[2]

## Last Man Standing

God has presented the world with a critical question. The world which denies God is going to face a time of terrible judgment. When the Day of the LORD begins, who shall be able to stand physically and endure before the earthshaking and heaven shaking judgments of God's wrath? When the Day of the LORD begins, who shall be able to stand spiritually and abide before the presence of God and Christ? Who is left standing at the end of the Tribulation when God's wrath has finally run its course?

Shortly after this question "Who shall be able to stand?" is raised in Revelation 6:17, it is revealed that 144,000 Jewish servants of God are supernaturally sealed for identification and protection in Revelation 7:1-8. They are specifically identified as coming from the tribes of the children of Israel, and twelve tribes are named for emphasis. There can be no doubt that God is clearly emphasizing His relationship with the physical descendants of Old Testament Israel in this passage. This sealing of Jewish servants to God demonstrates that God's face is fully returned to Israel as His prophetic focus at this point in time. These 144,000 Jewish servants are sealed as the firstfruits to God and Christ of Israel's promised national redemption (Rev 14:4). These servants will be standing up in special spiritual service to God, and that service will be on earth. These 144,000 servants sealed to God will replace God's remnant of Jewish believers within the church (Rom 11:5), who are presently sealed by the Holy Spirit, when Jesus snatches the church away at the time of the rapture.

> And after these things I saw four angels standing on the four corners of the earth, holding the four winds of the earth, that the wind should not blow on the earth, nor on the sea, nor on any tree. And I saw another angel ascending from the east,

> having the seal of the living God: and he cried with a loud voice to the four angels, to whom it was given to hurt the earth and the sea, Saying, **Hurt not the earth**, neither the sea, nor the trees, till we have sealed the servants of our God in their foreheads. And I heard the number of them which were sealed: *and there were* sealed an hundred *and* forty *and* four thousand of all the tribes of the children of Israel. (Rev 7:1-4 bold added)

This description of the sealing of the 144,000 Jewish servants to God is revealed in an interlude to the sequence of events that has been taking place in Revelation 5 and 6. John does not see this sealing until after the first six seals are opened by Christ. When does this sealing take place? Since this chapter begins with "And after these things" being the first six seals it can be interpreted that the sealing of the 144,000 takes place at that point in time between the breaking of the sixth seal and the seventh seal. In this perspective God's servants are being sealed for their protection against the effects of the seven trumpet judgments, which will be released after the seventh seal is opened.

However, the four angels are commanded to not hurt the earth until after the 144,000 Jewish servants are supernaturally sealed. Since the great war of the second seal and the global earthquake and falling stars of the sixth seal will entail considerable destruction or "hurting" to the earth by the explicit authority of Christ, I believe **this interlude is looking backwards**. The 144,000 Jewish servants are sealed for their identification to God and their supernatural protection from all of the forms of God's wrath during the Day of the LORD. This includes all of the seven seal judgments as well as the trumpet and bowl judgments.

I believe this sealing takes place in conjunction with the rapture of the church or immediately following the rapture. This makes sense in that God would not be leaving the earth without a group of special witnesses to represent Him. If God delayed His sealing of the 144,000 Jewish servants for a period of some time after the pretribulational rapture, who would be God's witnesses during that time? It could not be the "Two Witnesses" of Revelation 11, as they will not be on the scene yet. Since they are only supernaturally empowered for a period of 1,260 days (3 ½ years), which will be the same time as the first half of Daniel's 70th Week, a pretribulational rapture will occur before they are empowered to take their stand for God. The 144,000 Jewish servants are the only viable group who can take their stand and replace the church as God's special witnesses at the time of the Beginning of Sorrows.

Immediately after the revelation of the sealing of the 144,000, John witnesses a great multitude of believers standing before the throne in heaven in Revelation 7:9. As this interlude in Revelation chapter 7 is looking backwards to the sealing of the 144,000 it is also looking backwards to the assembling of this great multitude. This great multitude of believers has come out of the many ethnic groups and nations on earth and is wearing the white robes of righteousness which denote resurrection and glorification. In a song sung in Revelation 5:9 it is acknowledged that Jesus is worthy to break the seals on the heavenly scroll because He redeemed or purchased for God, at the cost of His blood, a number of people "out of every kindred, and tongue, and people, and nation." All of those who came to faith in Jesus as Christ, the Son of God, and trusted the redeeming work that Jesus accomplished through His death on the cross as the "Lamb of God," and through the power of His resurrection, have been rescued from the great tribulation that comes to the earth in the form of God's Day of the LORD judgments.

> After this I beheld, and, lo, a great multitude, which no man could number, of all nations, and kindreds, and people, and tongues, **stood before the throne**, and before the Lamb, clothed with white robes, and palms in their hands; And cried with a loud voice, saying, Salvation to our God which sitteth upon the throne, and unto the Lamb. .... And one of the elders answered, saying unto me, What are these which are arrayed in white robes? and whence came they? And I said unto him, Sir, thou knowest. And he said to me, These are they which came out of great tribulation, and have washed their robes, and made them white in the blood of the Lamb. Therefore are they before the throne of God, and serve him day and night in his temple: and he that sitteth on the throne shall dwell among them. They shall hunger no more, neither thirst any more; neither shall the sun light on them, nor any heat. For the Lamb which is in the midst of the throne shall feed them, and shall lead them unto living fountains of waters: and God shall wipe away all tears from their eyes. (Rev 7:9-10, 13-17 bold added)

I believe this great multitude of believers depicts the raptured church that has been removed from the earth and taken to heaven. All of the believers "in Christ" during the Church Age stand before God as part of this great multitude. This group includes the ones "kept from the hour of temptation which shall come upon all the world to try them that dwell upon the earth" (Rev 3:10). It also includes the ones "worthy to escape all these things that shall come to pass, and to stand before the Son of man" (Lk 21:36). These are the ones revealed standing before the throne during the time that God's wrath is being unleashed upon the earth. These are the ones who can stand and abide in heaven during the time of God's Day of the LORD. These are the ones who have entered the Day of Christ.

This scene is depicted in the same interlude as the sealing of the 144,000 Jewish servants. The great multitude is standing before God's throne and they are standing before or with the Lamb (Christ). Christ is not specifically depicted as having the scroll in His hands or to be breaking any seals on the scroll. Yet in the linear sequence of events the seventh seal has not yet been broken or opened. The opening of the seven seals deals with the time of the Beginning of Sorrows. The only group of believers who can possible be represented in heaven at this point in time standing before God's throne and wearing white robes is the raptured church.

The prophet Nahum immediately follows up his double barbed version of the question "who can stand – who can abide?" in verse 6 with a partial answer in verse 7. "The LORD *is* good, a strong hold in the day of trouble; and he knoweth them that trust in him."

Revelation 7 contains the immediate answer to the question which closes chapter six – "Who shall be able to stand?" There will be only two groups left standing as the beginning of the Day of the LORD gets underway.

- God's remnant of 144,000 Jewish servants, who will be supernaturally sealed and protected by divine intervention, will be standing on earth.
- The great multitude of the church or body of Christ, which will have been resurrected and raptured to heaven, will be standing before Christ and before God's throne.

Who is able to stand at the end of the Tribulation?

- The larger remnant of the nation of Israel which is refined and purified in the forge of affliction and which turns in repentance to Jesus Christ as its long awaited Messiah during the time of Jacob's trouble will be left standing to enter the Messianic Kingdom (Isa 1:9; 4:2; 10:20-23; 37:31-32; Joel 2:32; Mic 5:3-4; 7:18; Zeph 3:13; Zech 8:12; Rom 9:27; Rev 11:13).
- The Gentile tribulational believers who survive the Great Tribulation will stand before Christ and be rewarded to inherit the Kingdom (Mt 25:31-40).

- The martyrs of those Jews and Gentiles who turn to Christ in abiding faith during the Day of the LORD will stand in resurrection and be rewarded to reign with Christ during the Millennial Kingdom (Rev 20:4).
- The Old Testament saints who will be resurrected to everlasting life and to enter the Messianic Kingdom (Dan 12:2). As Daniel was told, "But go thou thy way till the end *be*: for thou shalt rest, and stand in thy lot at the end of the days" (Dan 12:13).

But all of these believers who live through the Day of the LORD and who are left standing at the end of the Great Tribulation will have gone through terrible hardship, endured much persecution, and been refined and purified the hard way through the fires of God's forge (Isa 48:10; Ezek 22:20-22; Zech 13:8-9; Mal 3:2-3). Faith during the time of the Day of the LORD is literally a trial of endurance. As Jesus characterized the plight of people who come to faith during the End Times: "But he that shall endure unto the end, the same shall be saved" (Mt 24:13).

God has used His prophets Joel, Nahum, and Malachi, and the apostle John to literally throw a question at the world. Who can stand? Who can abide? This dual natured question stands as a plea and as a warning. It serves as a flag linking pieces of the prophetic puzzle together. The Day of the LORD is coming upon the nations of the world. God is going to take His stand against the unrepentant sinners on earth. Jesus is going to take the heavenly scroll from the hand of God the Father and break the seals. Jesus will unleash God's wrath. Are you ready?

**Notes: Who Can Stand?**

1. Marty Cauley, *The Outer Darkness, Volume Two*, (Misthological Press, www.UnconditionalSecurity.org, 2012), p. 770.
2. John Phillips, *Exploring Hebrews: An Expository Commentary*, (Grand Rapids, MI: Kregel Publications, 1977, 1988 Revised ed.), p. 187.

# 5

# The Beginning of the End vs. The End of the End

The Day of the LORD, from its dynamic beginning through to its climatic ending, will be characterized by supernatural occurrences from God that will set the entire period of the time of "The End" apart from any other time in the history of man. The Day of the LORD will begin with a bang; the global earthshaking, catastrophic intervention of God in partial judgment. It will end with a bigger bang; the planet wrenching, cataclysmic, demonstration of the wrath of God's full judgment at the Revelation of Jesus Christ. By design God has created many similarities between the events which come together to initiate His time of wrath at the beginning of the great and terrible Day of the LORD and the events which converge in His Grand Finale at the climax of the great Day of God Almighty.

For the purpose of this analogy I am referring to the time of "The End" as the time period of God's wrath during the Day of the LORD which begins with the Beginning of Sorrows and extends through the Revelation of Christ. I am excluding the subsequent time of the Millennial Kingdom from this comparison. It is a major premise of this book that the significant similarity between how the Day of the LORD begins and ends is expressly intentional on the part of God. There is no accident or coincidence between this pattern of conditions and events. It is the very nature of how God treats this period of time as a single unit that makes it – The Great and Terrible Day of the LORD.

## Characteristics of the Beginning of the Day of the LORD

| Beginning: Characteristic or Event | Scripture Reference |
|---|---|
| Sun turns dark | Joel 2:31: Act 2:20; Rev 6:12 |
| Blood Red Moon | Joel 2:31; Act 2:20; Rev 6:12 |
| Wonders in the heavens<br>Wonders in the earth<br>Blood, fire, pillars of smoke | Isa 13:13; Joel 2:30; Act 2:19 |
| Suddenly – as a Thief in the night | 1 Thes 5:2-3 |
| God rises to terribly shake the earth | Isa 2:19, 21 |
| Global Earthquake | Isa 2:19, 21; Ezek 38:19-20;<br>Mt 24:7; Mk 13:8; Rev 6:12, 14 |
| Islands & Mountains moved out of place – Earth moved out of place | Rev 6:14<br>Isa 13:13 |
| Stars fall – Meteor shower | Rev 6:13 |
| Atmosphere violently split apart – as a scroll rolled together | Rev 6:14 |
| People are afraid | Isa 13:7-8; Zeph 1:14 |
| Men hide underground out of fear – Fear of God | Isa 2:10-21; Rev 6:15-16 |
| Clouds & thick darkness | Ezek 30:3; Joel 2:2; Zeph 1:15 |
| Birth Pangs of Travail<br>The Beginning of Sorrows | Isa 13:8; 1 Thes 5:3<br>Mt 24:8; Mk 13:8 |
| War – Nation against Nation<br>Kingdom against Kingdom | Mt 24:7; Mk 13:8; Rev 6:4;<br>Ezek 38–39 Gog & Magog |
| Famine | Mt 24:7; Mk 13:8; Rev 6:5-6 |
| Pestilence | Mt 24:7; Mk 13:8; Rev 6:7-8 |
| The LORD utters His voice | Joel 2:11; Zeph 1:14; 1 Thes 4:16 |
| God / Christ initiates His wrath | Isa 13:9; Zeph 1:15; Rev 6:16-17 |
| Destruction from God | Isa 13:6; Joel 1:15 |
| Great & Terrible Day of the LORD<br>Great Day of God's Wrath has come | Joel 2:11, 2:31; Zeph 1:14<br>Rev 6:17 |
| Who can abide it?<br>Who shall be able to stand? | Joel 2:11<br>Rev 6:17 |

## Characteristics of the End of the Day of the LORD

| End: Characteristic or Event | Scripture Reference |
|---|---|
| Sun is dark | Isa 13:10; Joel 2:10; 3:15 |
| Moon is completely dark – no light | Isa 13:10; Joel 2:10; 3:15 |
| Stars are dark - give no light | Isa 13:10; Joel 2:10; 3:15 |
| Prepare for War | Joel 3:9-10 |
| The nations of the whole world gathered to Armageddon | Rev 16:14 |
| All nations gathered to Valley of Jehoshaphat – Valley of Decision | Joel 3:2, 11-12, 14 |
| The Harvest is ripe – The winepress is full – Vats overflow | Joel 3:13; Isa 63:3 Rev 14:9, 20; 19:15 |
| Euphrates River dried up | Rev 16:12 |
| Kings of the East cross Euphrates towards Israel | Rev 16:12 |
| 7th Bowl Judgment of God's Wrath | Rev 16:17 |
| Earthquake Greatest Global Earthquake ever | Joel 2:10; 3:16 Rev 16:18 |
| Every Island flees away; Every Mountain disappears | Rev 16:20 |
| The Cities of the nations fall Babylon the great falls | Rev 16:19 |
| Great Hail Storm | Rev 16:21 |
| The heavens tremble, shake | Isa 13:13; Joel 2:10; 3:16 |
| Heaven opened – Atmosphere violently split apart – as a scroll rolled together | Rev 19:11 Isa 34:4 |
| Men blaspheme God | Rev 16:21 |
| The LORD utters His voice from Jerusalem | Joel 3:16 |
| God will judge all nations | Joel 3:2, 12 |
| The Battle of the Great Day of God Almighty | Rev 16:14 |

A misunderstanding of this very nature of God's design has been a major source of confusion and conflict in the interpretation of the timing and sequence of these events on the part of many scholars and students of prophecy. Some authors, like E. W. Bullinger and Hilton Sutton, extend Christ's opening of the seven seals to the end of the Tribulation. They miss the parallel aspects of the beginning and the ending of the Day of the LORD. Several times I have encountered authors who have taken similarity and automatically equated it with equality. They take a number of similar prophecies and link them together without distinguishing the major differences or the differential pattern within the indicated prophecies which alludes to multiple occurrences. They tend to support their conclusions by making a statement to the effect, "Certainly there cannot be more than one of these events during the Tribulation," etc. But is this an accurate conclusion?

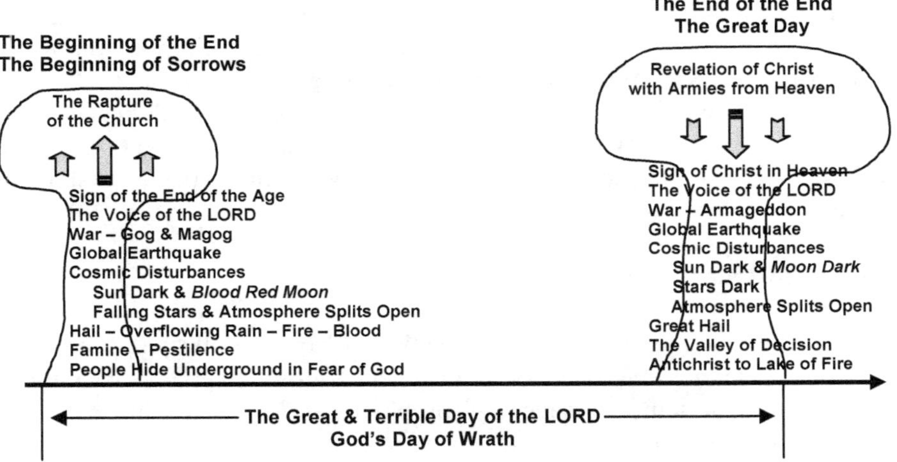


The failure to discern this parallel pattern between the beginning and the ending of the prophetic time of judgment that God has planned as the Day of the LORD promotes the variety of conflicting interpretations that the student of prophecy is faced with today. In the absence of noting the repeated pattern and drawing upon the important distinctions between passages, the focus on partial similarity leads many to make unnecessary associations and to arrive at false conclusions. These include:

- Misinterpreting the timing of the beginning of God's wrath.
- Misinterpreting the timing of the rapture.

- Misinterpreting the telescopic nature of the Seal, Trumpet, and Bowl judgments, and thus extending the sixth seal to the end of the Great Tribulation.
- Associating anything described as "great" or "great and terrible" in connection to the Day of the LORD as directly applying to the end of the Day at the Revelation of Christ.
- Confusing the War of Gog and Magog with the War of Armageddon.
- Associating Gog, the leader of Gog and Magog, with the Antichrist.
- Associating the intervening presence of God in Ezekiel 38–39 with the second coming of Christ.

Can there be more than one almost identical event during the Day of the LORD? What about more than one major war during the End Times? What about the major feasting of birds on the fallen armies following a war in the Middle East? What about more than one global earthquake? What about multiple major signs in the heavens? What about multiple instances of cosmic disturbances? What about multiple great hailstorms? The design of the Day of the LORD and the intersection of key prophetic passages shouts a resounding – Yes!

## Prophetic Telescoping

There is a concept in the interpretation of Bible prophecy referred to as *The Law of Double Reference*, or as *Prophetic Telescoping*. This is simply a recognition that some passages of prophetic scripture, while seemingly dealing with the same subject matter within a passage, skip over an interval of time, so that the passage continues the prophetic message with no observance by that particular scripture that the time interval exists. The prophecy presents a near view of fulfillment and a far view of fulfillment, while the intervening time is jumped over as if looking through a telescope. Thus, the description of a person or an event, which would eventually become two completely different events in history, is presented by the prophet as a single, continuous flowing event, or the same leader in action. In this manner, God can use a prophet to present an important message to his own generation, while, at the same time, reveal a message for or about a future generation.

Clarence Larkin referred to this condition as "The Mountain Peaks of Prophecy." The Old Testament prophets were led by the Holy Spirit to predict the coming of the Messiah. However, they did not fully understand the prophecies they were given by God. Larkin characterized these prophets as looking at a series of mountain peaks in the distance, so that individual peaks that were actually separated by a valley between them, simply appeared to the prophets as though they were peaks on the same mountain or the same ridge.[1] Thus, in the recording of prophetic scripture, the timing of certain prophetic events seemed to run together when in the reality of fulfillment they would be separated by gaps of time. Sometimes these gaps were short and at other times they were very long.

The timing and accomplishments of a suffering Messiah can become confused with the timing and accomplishments of a victorious Messiah. An ambitious leader, as a type of antichrist, can become merged into the coming of the Antichrist. The characteristics of one expulsion from the land or one return from exile can be linked to the conditions of a later expulsion or return. The prophetic significance of the building or destruction of one Temple can merge into the events of another, later Temple. The events of the end of an age can blend with the events of the beginning of that age. The giving of God's covenant promises can leap to the fulfillment of the promises, without noting the long wait between.

In his book *Israel's Destiny*, S. Maxwell Coder outlines an example of prophetic telescoping from the Old Testament which Jesus revealed and is dramatically recorded in the New Testament.

> Perhaps the best-known of such passages is Isaiah's Messianic prophecy in which he spoke of 'the acceptable year of the LORD, and the day of vengeance or our God' (Isa. 61:1-2; see also Lk 4:16-21). Jesus began his ministry in Nazareth by reading this part of Isaiah, but He stopped reading at the comma between the two phrases. The reason was that He had come to proclaim 'the acceptable year of the Lord,' during which God was going to accept all who came to Him, Gentiles as well as Jews. He had not come to proclaim the day of vengeance. That must await the latter days and His return to the earth, ...The fact that He stopped reading where He did is an illustration of the importance of noticing the exact words, and even the punctuation, of prophecy. It is also a good example of the way in which prophecy was written to permit the unsuspected introduction of a new age and a new purpose, here indicated only by the comma in the English text.[2]

The concept of prophetic telescoping recognizes that God is in control of time, history, and prophecy. God is the "I AM" of the eternal present. God is outside of our time; God uses time; God ignores time; God hides events in time. God blends the past and future within the ever-present reality of the Bible. This creates a situation where it is important to recognize God's progressive revelation of His plan for man as laid out in the Bible, to use scripture to interpret scripture, and to understand scripture in the context of history. There must be a complete fulfillment of every prophetic passage of scripture. A partial, historical fulfillment does not end the prophecy – it points to and assures the complete prophetic fulfillment at a later time in history, or even at a time yet to come.

The prophet's view of God's Day of the LORD was no different. The prophet was applying shorter-term warnings to the Kingdoms of Israel and Judah and the nations surrounding them while looking far into the future at the mountain peaks of God's looming Day of Wrath. It is not surprising that the mountain peaks of the Day of the LORD are treated as one great peak or range. A prophet like Joel was given the burden of a prophetic vision by God and compelled to give God's ominous warning. Joel and the other prophets could not distinguish multiple mountain peaks out of the huge mountain menacing in the distance. They did not know exactly how far off the mountain was, nor could they see the valley between the beginning of the Day of the LORD and the end of the Day of the LORD.

**Prophetic Telescoping**

**The Day of the LORD**
**As two mountain peaks viewed from a distance**

In the illustration the first mountain marks a short but intense period of events, a "range of events," which comprise the Beginning of Sorrows. The second, larger mountain marks another short but intense "range of events," coinciding with the War of Armageddon and the Great Day of the Revelation of Christ. This last mountain peak can be referred to as the Mount Everest of prophetic mountain peaks. The great and terrible Day of the LORD incorporates everything from the first mountain to the second larger mountain, including the valley hidden between them.

## The Beginning vs. The End

God does not change. His character does not change. His righteousness and holiness do not change. His moral and ethical standards do not change. It is not surprising that God would use the same forms of intervention and judgment multiple times throughout history and throughout His Day of the LORD. It is not surprising that many scholars remark on the similarity between the judgments in Revelation to the judgments which God used to plague Egypt at the time of Israel's Exodus from that land. God claims war, pestilence, famine, and wild beasts as His four severe judgments. To those we can add great earthquakes, storms, fire, blood, hail, signs in the heavens, unusual darkness, and falling stars. We should not be surprised that these conditions are repeated multiple times throughout the time of the end.

The beginning and the ending of the Day of the LORD are two windows in prophetic time which are inherently connected together, and yet each is characterized by its own specific set of conditions and series of events. Each window presents us with a unique individual picture or scene. There are dramatic similarities between these two windows. There are also significant differences. The distinctions between them are critical in understanding the bigger picture of the Day of the LORD.

This picture can be likened to bookends on a shelf of related books. Or it is similar to the front and rear covers of a book. Two bookends are often very similar with each other, or they are mirror images of each other. There is often great similarity between the front cover and the rear cover of a book. They are tied together by the binding or the spine. Even though they usually have different information printed on them, they contain or promote different information regarding the same book. They are designed to compliment each other in order to promote the distinct identification of that particular book. The title of the book applies to both front and rear covers, as well as everything in between. The bookends with an enclosed set of special books, or the front and rear covers enveloping the chapters of a single book, contain a story as a continuum.

We encounter a pair of bookends within the Jewish calendar. The Feast of Trumpets (Rosh Hashanah) and the Day of Atonement (Yom Kippur) form bookends that bracket the period of time known as the ten "Days of Awe." We are also introduced to a period of God's judgments revealed as a book. Jesus Christ opens the book by breaking the seven seals that secure its contents. This book is the title deed to the earth, but it is also the revealed judgments of God's wrath during the Day of the LORD.

In the space of the blink of an eye, the entire story rests, beckoning, waiting to unfold, written in the past but bound in the eternal present. The story of the Day of the LORD unfolds from its dramatic beginning to its climactic ending: knowable yet illusive, symbolic yet real, supernatural yet tangible, one moment frozen in time, yet timeless. The beginning of the end and the end of the end: two prophetic bookends – so different, yet the same in so many ways.

The Day of the LORD both initiates the Time of the End and concludes the Time of the End. It will have a definite beginning point marked by a special series of events and a definite ending point marked by another special series of events.

The Day of the LORD does not begin peacefully as many believe. It begins as sudden and unexpected destruction and ends with great destruction that is anything but sudden and unexpected. It begins with the unleashing of God's wrath in the breaking of the seven seal judgments and ends with a great outpouring of God's wrath with the sixth and seventh bowl judgments. It begins with war and ends with war. It begins with the great sword of war taking peace from the earth (second seal) and ends with the great sword from the mouth of Christ slaying the enemies of God and returning peace to the earth.

It begins with nation against nation and kingdom against kingdom and ends with all nations targeting one nation – Israel, and one kingdom – the Kingdom of God. It begins with the invasion of Israel by the alliance of Gog and Magog and ends with the Campaign of Armageddon, when the armies of all nations are gathered against Israel. It begins with God's supernatural but invisible intervention from heaven and ends with the supernatural but visible intervention of Christ on earth. It begins with Christ coming as a thief in the night, suddenly and unexpectedly upon the world, and ends with Christ explicitly riding as the commanding general at the head of His armies from heaven.

It begins with Christ standing as the worthy Lamb to claim the scroll from God seated on His throne in heaven and ends with Christ seated on His white horse, as the Word of God, returning to claim His rightful throne. It begins with the shouted command of Christ for His church to assemble in the atmosphere for the rapture and ends with the voice of the LORD roaring out of Jerusalem (Joel 3:16). It begins with Christ coming for His church and ends with Christ returning with His church. It begins with heaven being split open, as a scroll suddenly rolled together (Rev 6:14), and ends with heaven being split open as a scroll rolled together when "all the host of heaven shall be dissolved" (Isa 34:4; Rev 19:11).

It begins and ends with a major difference in global leadership. It begins with no unified global government and ends with the world being unified under the leadership of Satan, the Antichrist, the False Prophet, and ten Kings. It begins with the release from supernatural restraint for the Antichrist to rise to power, a supernatural world leader who will become the Global Theocratic Dictator of the earth, and ends with the reign of Jesus Christ as the Faithful and True, KING of Kings, and LORD of Lords.

It begins with the very first birth pang of travail – the Beginning of Sorrows and ends with the last birth pang and the final delivery of Israel from its great tribulation during the Time of Jacob's Trouble. Israel as a spiritual nation separate to God will truly be born again.

It begins with cosmic disturbances and ends with cosmic disturbances. It begins with the sun turning dark and the moon turning blood red and ends with the sun being dark and the moon being dark – completely dark – giving off no light at all.

It begins with a sign in the heavens and ends with a sign in the heavens. It begins with the sign of the End of the Age and ends with the sign of the Revelation of Christ. It begins with the heavens being shaken and stars falling to the earth and ends with the great Shekinah Glory of God Almighty flashing across the supernaturally darkened heavens visible to all on earth.

It begins with God humbling the arrogance, pride, loftiness, and haughtiness of men and ends with the elimination of sinners from the earth. It begins with men hiding underground in fear of God and ends with Satan's, the Antichrist's, and mankind's open, blatant, and blasphemous rebellion against God and Christ.

It begins with God arising in wrath to shake the earth with a global earthquake and ends with an earth shaken to the core. It begins with islands and mountains moved out of their places and ends with islands and mountains completely erased from the surface of the earth.

It begins with the nation of Israel in spiritual rebellion against God and Jesus Christ and ends with Israel's national recognition of Jesus as God's Messiah. It begins with Israel and all the nations polluting the holy name of God and ends with Israel and the nations knowing that Jesus is the great "I Am," the LORD, the Holy One in Israel. It begins with Israel and the world, fallen, broken, in need of a savior and redemption and ends with the redemption of Israel and the restoration of the earth through the work of Jesus as the Kinsman Redeemer.

## Conclusions and False Conclusions

There are predictable consequences to this uncanny similarity that God has designed into the pattern of the Day of the LORD. As the world pauses to catch its breath, following the sudden onslaught of catastrophes on a global scale, the similarities are going to captivate the survivors of the Beginning of

Sorrows. Of course, they will not understand the cataclysmic conditions, that the world has just experienced and that they have just endured, are just the beginning of the End Times. Everything will be reported as being compared to Biblical destruction. The supernatural intervention by God will be undeniable. Israel and the nations will conclude that the Bible's prophecies of war and destruction and of Jerusalem being the source of trouble for the world have all been fulfilled. Israel will know that the prophecy of Gog and Magog has happened and will believe the Time of Jacob's Trouble is also over. The New Testament War of Armageddon will seem, to the world at the time, to have been realized by the War of Gog and Magog against Israel along with whatever associated wars occur in other parts of the world.

The destruction will be terribly horrendous in magnitude. It will seem that the earth has been turned inside out and upside down. It is probable that a significant pole shift has taken place. All islands and mountains are out of their places. Nuclear war has likely been unleashed with devastating effects. Pestilence is rampant. Famine is widespread. One-fourth of the world's population is either dead or dying. What more destruction can possibly take place?

What will the reaction of Israel and the global community of nations be to this cluster of events? What major changes will likely take place in the aftermath of the Beginning of Sorrows?

- The War of Armageddon (War to end all Wars) is over.
- The Time of Jacob's Trouble is over.
- God has intervened to save Israel from Gog & Magog.
- Israel and the Jews are validated on the world stage.
- Israel is empowered – Who can prevail against Israel?
- Islam has been handed a major setback – The world need not fear Islamic terrorism any longer.
- It is time to pick up the pieces – Time for Restoration.
- It is time for Israel's (and the world's) Messiah.
- It is time for Israel's Golden Age – the Messianic Kingdom.
- It is time to rebuild the Jewish Temple in Jerusalem.
- Jews will flock to the Promised Land from all over the world, but particularly from the United States. They will take all of the wealth with them that they can.
- It is time for global disarmament – but some nations will resist.
- There will be a push for greater "identity control" over the survivors.
- There will be an increased push for a global government.
- The world will be divided into ten kingdoms led by ten kings.

- There will be an increased push for global religious tolerance and the unification of a one-world religion intermixed with commercialism.

The lack of true Biblical discernment will lead the world to struggle with attempting to gain a sense of normalcy on its own terms without truly turning to God in repentance. Destruction and catastrophe continue to plague the world as God's judgments are an ongoing process throughout the Day of the LORD.

The beginning and the ending of the Time of the End have many similarities that are designed by God to confuse Israel into accepting the beginning of the end as the fulfillment of prophecies which really apply to the end of the end. Israel must be conned into thinking its troubles are all over. Israel must be brought back to the God of its fathers. Israel must be set up and forced to make a national decision regarding its Messiah. Israel failed to recognize Jesus as God's Messiah when He came, exactly as scheduled, in fulfillment of the prophecy of Daniel 9. Israel will be presented with another Messiah. Will Israel recognize the falseness of his claim?

The seven-year covenant of peace of Daniel 9 confirmed with Israel by this emerging world leader will result from a short period of extreme global chaos that is initiated at the beginning of the Day of the LORD as the Beginning of Sorrows. Israel will emerge victorious in the beginning of the Day by the supernatural intervention of God. Israel will proclaim its Messiah. Israel will rebuild its Temple in Jerusalem. It is only after Israel's troubles are seemingly a memory and Israel believes it has entered its long awaited Golden Age that the time of Jacob's trouble actually begins. Israel will be betrayed by its False Messiah. God will use this time to refine Israel in the fires of His supernatural forge until Israel awakens to the truth of God and His true Messiah – Jesus Christ.

## The Beginning vs. The End

| Beginning of the End | End of the End |
|---|---|
| Signs in the heavens:<br>dark sun; blood red moon; stars fall (Joel 2:31; Rev 6:12-13) | Signs in the heavens:<br>dark sun; completely darkened moon; stars fall; heavens shaken (Isa 13:10; Joel 2:10; 3:15-16; Mt 24:29; Mk 13:24-25) |
| Heaven split open as a scroll rolled together (Rev 6:14) | Heaven split open as a scroll rolled together (Isa 34:4; Rev 19:11) |
| Major event in the sky above Earth: | Major event in the sky above Earth: |

| Beginning of the End | End of the End |
|---|---|
| Rapture of the church – event in the sky most likely not observed by those on the earth (1 Cor 15:51-52; 1 Thes 4:13-17; 1 Thes 5:9-10) | Sign of the Son of Man (Shechinah Glory) in the sky – visible to all on the darkened earth (Mt 24:27, 30; Mk13:26; Lk 17:24; Lk 21:27) |
| Christ judges the raptured church – Bema Seat Judgment – grants rewards (Rom 14:10-12; 2 Cor 5:10; 2 Tim 4:8; Rev 2:7, 10, 17, 26-28; 3:5, 10, 12, 21) | Christ judges the nations for their treatment of Israel – Judgment of the sheep & the goats (Dan 7:22; Joel 3:2, 9-14; Mic 4:3; Mt 13:40-43; Mt 25:31-46; Rev 20:4) |
| Seven Seal Judgments initiated by Christ (Rev 6:12-17; Rev 8:1, 5-12) | 6$^{th}$ Bowl and 7$^{th}$ Bowl Judgments of the Wrath of God initiated by Angels (Rev 15:1; 16:12-18) |
| War of Gog and Magog (Ezek 38–39; Mt 24:7; Rev 6:4) | War of Armageddon (Isa 34:1-8; 63:1-6; Joel 3:2, 9-16; Zeph 3:8; Zech 12:1-9; 14:1-7, 12-13; Rev 16:14, 16; Rev 19:11-21) |
| God intervenes to deliver Israel from Gog & Magog. God supernaturally destroys the Gog & Magog alliance by Himself (Ezek 38:18-22; 39:2-6) | Jesus Christ intervenes to end the reigns of: Satan, Antichrist, False Prophet, and the 10 Kings. Christ supernaturally destroys the Antichrist and all his military forces (Rev 19:19-21; Rev 20:1-3) |
| Sacrificial feast for birds and beasts (Ezek 39:4, 17-20) | Great supper of God for the birds (Rev 19:17-18, 21) |
| Global earthquake and global catastrophe (Isa 2:10-21; Ezek 38:19-20; Mt 24:7; Rev 6:12-14) | Greatest global earthquake ever and global catastrophe (Isa 13:13; 24:17-21; Joel 2:10; 3:16; Mic 1:2-4; Nah 1:5-6; Hag 2:6-7; Zech 14:4-5; Heb 12:26-27; Rev 16:18-20) |
| The wrath of God's jealousy for Israel (Ezek 38:18-19) | God's wrath against the nations (Isa 34:2; Rev 15:1; Rev 16:1) |
| Partial spiritual revival of Israel to God (Ezek 39:7, 22, 25) | Full spiritual rebirth of Israel as a nation to God and Christ (Jer 31:31-34; Jer 32:37-42; Ezek 11:17-20; 36:24-28; Zech 12:10-14; Rev 1:7) |
| Rise of False Messiah (Jn 5:43; 2 Thes 2:3-9; Rev 6:1-2) | Revelation of Christ as King of Kings at his Second Coming (Rev 19:11-16) |

| Beginning of the End | End of the End |
|---|---|
| Partial re-gathering of Jews to Israel & Jerusalem in preparation for judgment – Israel is to be refined by fire (Ezek 22:18-22; Mal 3:2-3) | Final supernatural re-gathering of all Jews to Israel (Jer 32:37; Ezek 11:17; 36:24; 37:21, 25) |
| The Voice of the LORD –<br>Christ shouts for His church to assemble for the Rapture | The Voice of the LORD –<br>The Voice of Christ will roar before His army and from Jerusalem (Isa 30:27-28, 30; Joel 2:11; 3:16) |

## Similarities between the Beginning and the End

| Similarities<br>Beginning of the End | Similarities<br>End of the End |
|---|---|
| Unleashing of God's Wrath | Outpouring of God's Wrath |
| Great & Terrible Day of the LORD (Joel 2:31; Rev 6) | Great & Terrible Day of the LORD (Joel 3, Zech 14, Mal 4:5) |
| God's Supernatural Intervention | Christ's Supernatural Intervention |
| Antichrist symbolized as rider on white horse | Christ symbolized as rider on white horse |
| Cosmic Disturbances<br>Sun Darkened; Moon Darkened | Cosmic Disturbances<br>Sun Darkened; Moon Darkened |
| Heaven (Atmosphere) split open – departed as a scroll rolled together (Rev 6:14) | Heavens rolled together as a scroll (Isaiah 34:4)<br>Heaven is opened (Rev 19:11) |
| Global Earthquake | Global Earthquake |
| Major War – War of Gog & Magog | Major War – War of Armageddon |
| Worldwide Destruction | Worldwide Destruction |
| Great Hailstorm (Ezek 38:22) | Plague of Hail (Rev 16:21) |
| Fire and Brimstone (Ezek 38:22) | Fire and Brimstone (Rev 14:10)<br>Fire (Rev 16:8) |
| Blood (Ezek 38:22) | Blood to drink (Rev 16:4-6) |
| Voices, Thunders, and Lightnings (Rev 8:5) | Voices, Thunders, and Lightnings (Rev 16:18) |
| Feast of birds and beasts after defeat of Gog & Magog | Feast of birds after defeat of Antichrist & 10 Kings |
| Valley of Hamon-gog | Valley of Jehoshaphat / Decision |
| Introduces False Golden Age of Israel | Introduces Messianic Kingdom |

| Similarities<br>Beginning of the End | Similarities<br>End of the End |
|---|---|
| Temple in Jerusalem to be rebuilt (Dan 9:27; 12:11; Mt 24:15; 2 Thes 2:4; Rev 11:1-2) | Messianic Temple to be built (Ezek 37:26-28) |

## Distinctions between the Beginning and the End

| Distinctions<br>Beginning of the End | Distinctions<br>End of the End |
|---|---|
| No unified global government | Global government unified under Satan, Antichrist, False Prophet, and Ten Kings |
| God's Wrath unleashed | God's Wrath concluded |
| Christ opens the Seven Seals | Angels pour the Seven Bowls |
| God's supernatural but invisible intervention from heaven – As a thief in the night | Christ's supernatural and visible intervention – from heaven to earth – At the head of His armies |
| Rapture (Christ's parousia in the air)<br>Christ's coming for His church and His presence with His church – Day of Christ | Return (Christ's parousia on earth) Christ's coming (Revelation) to Israel and the entire world and His presence in Israel – Great Day of God Almighty |
| Immediately preceded by the resurrection of Church Age believers and martyrs | Immediately followed by the resurrection of Old Testament saints and Tribulational martyrs |
| Rapture of the church to heaven | Return of church with armies from heaven |
| Heaven (Atmosphere) split open – departed as a scroll rolled together (Rev 6:14) | Heavens rolled together as a scroll – But all the host of heaven shall be dissolved (Isa 34:4)<br>Heaven is opened (Rev 19:11) |
| Antichrist symbolized as rider on white horse – going out to conquer | Christ symbolized as rider on white horse – returning to conquer |
| Antichrist unrestrained – Release of Antichrist to rise to power | Antichrist restrained – Confinement of Antichrist to the Lake of Fire |
| Israel is polluting God's name | Israel is in belief and calling upon the name of the LORD |

| **Distinctions**<br>**Beginning of the End** | **Distinctions**<br>**End of the End** |
|---|---|
| Sign of the End of the Age | Sign of Christ in Heaven – The Shekinah Glory of God as lightning flashing across the sky |
| Blood Red Moon | Moon completely dark |
| Birth Pangs Begin – The Beginning of Sorrows | Birth Pangs End – Delivery<br>The Redemption of Israel |
| Global Earthquake | Greatest Earthquake ever |
| Islands and Mountains are moved from their places | Islands and Mountains cease to exist |
| Sudden Destruction | Destruction does not come suddenly |
| People hide underground | No hiding underground |
| War – Some nations invade Israel – Gog & Magog | War – All nations invade Israel – Armageddon |
| The great sword of war removes peace from the earth | The great sword from the mouth of Christ returns peace to the earth |
| No mention of the Winepress | Winepress is full – Christ treading the winepress (Isa 63:3; Rev 14:14-20; 19:15) |
| ¼ of world's population killed | All armies killed |
| Some soldiers spared – allowed to flee | None are allowed to flee away |
| Forces of Gog & Magog buried in mass grave | The slain of the LORD will not be buried (Jer 25:33). |
| Destruction of Gog – buried in mass grave with his troops | Destruction of Antichrist & False Prophet – not buried – cast into Lake of Fire |
| Valley of Hamon-gog<br>East of the Dead Sea<br>As place of mass burial for forces of Gog & Magog | Valley of Jehoshaphat;<br>Valley of Decision<br>Near Jerusalem<br>As place of God's Judgment |
| Israel buries the dead for 7 months | The slain are not buried (Jer 25:33) |
| Israel burns weapons of Gog & Magog for fuel for 7 years | No burning mentioned – Weapons are converted into agricultural tools |
| Does not end warfare – There will be more wars | The end of warfare – Nations will no longer train for war |
| Great Hailstorm & Overflowing Rain | Plague of Hail – Huge Hailstones – Each Hailstone is said to be about 70 to 100 pounds in weight (Rev 16:21) |

| Distinctions<br>Beginning of the End | Distinctions<br>End of the End |
|---|---|
| Jerusalem not destroyed | Jerusalem divided by earthquake<br>Mount of Olives split in two |
| 144,000 Jews sealed as First Fruits | Remnant of All Israel will be Saved |
| Israel returns to the God of Abraham, Isaac, and Jacob & the Law of Moses | Israel reconciled to Jesus the Messiah & the New Covenant |
| Many people will be awakened to the God of Israel and many to Jesus as Christ as a result of these events. Many will later become martyrs during the Tribulation (Ezek 38:23; 39:7; Rev 6:11; 15:2; 20:4) | This is not the time when people who do not believe in God and Christ come to faith. If they have not come to saving faith before Christ's Revelation, they will not be saved into the Messianic Kingdom |
| A time of comfort and joy at the coming of Christ for the church. Christ's coming for the church is taught as an encouragement and as a comforting expectation (1 Thes 4:18; 5:11) | A time of mourning at the Revelation of Christ – The Jews, the Tribes of Israel, will look upon the one who was pierced (Zech 12:10-14; Rev 1:7) |

Similarity does not necessarily equate to exactness or sameness. Distinctions are critical. The presence of significant differences should act as a red warning flag in our process of interpreting and assembling the pieces of the prophetic puzzle. Many pieces which at first glance seem to fit into the picture at the end of the end times actually belong to the beginning of the end.

**Notes: The Beginning of the End vs. The End of the End**

1. Clarence Larkin, *Dispensational Truth, or God's Plan and Purpose in the Ages*, (Rev. Clarence Larkin Estate, 1918), pp. 5 ½-7.
2. S. Maxwell Coder, *Israel's Destiny*, (Chicago: Moody Press, 1978), pp. 47-48.

# 6

# 24 Elders

**Revelation 4:2-4** Immediately I was in the Spirit; and behold, a throne was standing in heaven, and One sitting on the throne. And He who was sitting *was* like a jasper stone and a sardius in appearance; and *there was* a rainbow around the throne, like an emerald in appearance. Around the throne *were* twenty-four thrones; and upon the thrones *I saw* **twenty-four elders** sitting, clothed in white garments, and golden crowns on their heads. (NASB, bold added)

**Revelation 5:6-8** And I saw between the throne (with the four living creatures) and the **elders** a Lamb standing, as if slain, having seven horns and seven eyes, which are the seven Spirits of God, sent out into all the earth. And He came and took the book out of the right hand of Him who sat on the throne. When He had taken the book, the four living creatures and the **twenty-four elders** fell down before the Lamb, each one holding a harp and golden bowls full of incense, which are the prayers of the saints. (NASB, bold added)

## 24 Elders in Heaven

Revelation chapter four reveals a dramatic scene in heaven that confronted the apostle John as soon as he was called up into heaven as Christ's prophetic witness. The central focus in this scene is the throne of God and the glorious presence of God sitting on that throne. An emerald colored rainbow surrounds God and His throne. John's attention is next drawn to an array of twenty-four seats or thrones around or surrounding

God's throne upon which sat twenty-four elders. These twenty-four seats are actually thrones, as the Greek word used for these seats is the same word used for God's throne.

Closer than the twenty-four elders and also around God's throne are four living beings (beasts KJV). Before God's throne are seven burning lamps of fire representing the seven spirits of God (the Holy Spirit). Out from God's throne emanate thunder, lightning, and voices. This is God's heavenly courtroom.

This scene is not one where twenty-four thrones and twenty-four elders are isolated off to one side of a courtroom as is a modern jury, but one where they are "around" or "round about" the throne. A row of subordinate thrones lined up in either a straight line or an arc directly in front of God's throne does not even begin to give an adequate description of the scene. In order to be accurately considered "around" God's throne, the physical layout of the twenty-four thrones must actually surround the throne of God – a complete circle of thrones seems to be envisioned by John.

The picture of the emerald rainbow is a full circle in the vertical plane instead of an arc as well. In actuality, this rainbow is likely to radiate as a complete sphere. The green rainbow will be observed from whatever angle or perspective the viewer has to God and His throne.

In each of their own spheres, the rainbow, the four living beings, and the twenty-four thrones of the elders surround the central throne. The unique nature of God is that He can be enthroned in the midst (in the form of a circle or sphere) of a massive congregation of angelic and human servants and worshipers and yet never have His back turned towards any of them.

Looking down from above the scene might have the appearance of a glorious crown. The twenty-four elders, garbed in white robes, wearing their own golden crowns, and seated on their own thrones, surrounding God's emerald spherical rainbow and God Himself on His throne, would resemble gleaming gems set in God's own crown.

Who are these kingly characters so close to the throne of God? What merits their being mentioned next after God, even before the four living creatures or any of the other angels in God's court?

Scripture does not specifically identify these twenty-four elders, individually or collectively. It simply reveals them and their activity. All we have to go on is the few specific characteristics that are revealed by the twelve times they are mentioned as elders throughout the book of Revelation (Rev 4:4, 10-11; 5:5-6, 8-9, 11, 14; 7:11, 13-14; 11:16-18; 14:3, and 19:4). These passages reveal the presence and activity of the elders in heaven throughout the entire time of God's judgment against "all the world, to try them that dwell upon the earth" (Rev 3:10). They are present prior to the breaking of the seven-sealed scroll by Jesus and the releasing of God's sanctioned Day of the LORD judgments (chapters 4 and 5). They appear in chapter 11 in connection with events which take place around the middle of the Tribulation. The final appearance of the elders is noted immediately preceding the glorious second coming of Christ to do battle at the time of Armageddon (chapter 19).

Twice one of the elders is singled out as speaking individually to the apostle John, but both times he is simply identified as "one of the elders" (Rev 5:5; 7:13). This does not mean that he does not have an individual identity, but it does indicate that there is a strong focus on the identity of the twenty-four elders as a cohesive group. We should note that John gives us no indication that he has any recognition or knowledge of the identity of this elder or any of the other elders. He does not seem to recognize himself or any of the other apostles as being part of that group.

The very fact that an elder serves as a teacher for John is significant and reveals something important about the elder, and by extension about all of the elders. The elders must have seniority over John who, as an apostle and prophet of the church, occupied as high a position within the church as possible. The elder is instructing John. The elder is the senior – in both position and knowledge to John. The elder has been in heaven for a longer period of time. The elder is not John's contemporary or peer. Nor is the elder someone who comes onto the stage of history at a later time than John. The elder must have preceded John in the history of humanity and in the historical dealings of God with men.

The characteristics which give us clues to the identity and nature of the twenty-four elders include:

- Their position – sitting on thrones – surrounding the throne of God.
- Their title – elders.
- Their adornment – white garments and golden crowns.
- Their activities – worshiping God, falling down before God's throne, casting their crowns before God's throne, praising God, singing a new song, playing harps, handling golden bowls which represent the prayers of saints, and explaining some of the heavenly events to John.
- Their distinction – the elders are explicitly distinguished from the apostle John himself, the four living beings, the myriads of angels in heaven (Rev 5:11; 7:11), the great multitude of saints standing before the throne and before Jesus the Lamb (Rev 7:9-14), the 144,000 servants of God redeemed from the earth (Rev 14:3), the great multitude of people in heaven (Rev 19:1 vs. Rev 19:4), and the saints

who make up the wife of Jesus as the Lamb (Rev 19:4 vs. Rev 19:7-8). The elders comprise a separate distinct group from all of these.

## Thrones

The initial focus is on the twenty-four thrones – not the elders themselves. The thrones that the elders sit upon have an inherent importance of their own. Thrones speak of regality (kingship, royalty, sovereignty) and also judgment. These thrones bear kings, but not ordinary kings. There is no direct mention of a single kingdom, much less twenty-four kingdoms associated with these kings. This is God's heavenly realm. His throne reigns supreme, yet these twenty-four thrones play a key role in God's administration of His creation.

The overall scene points to a courtroom and judgment. God is the ultimate judge. However, the judgment of mankind has been relegated to Jesus Christ (Jn 5:22, 27). King David wrote about the LORD seated on His throne as a judge in heaven. "The LORD is in His holy temple; the LORD'S throne is in heaven; His eyes behold, His eyelids test the sons of men" (Ps 11:4 NASB). "But the LORD abides forever; He has established His throne for judgment, And He will judge the world in righteousness; He will execute judgment for the peoples with equity" (Ps 9:7-8 NASB).

Consider Daniel's prophetic vision of God's courtroom. "I kept looking Until thrones were set up, And the Ancient of Days took *His* seat; His vesture *was* like white snow And the hair of His head like pure wool. His throne *was* ablaze with flames, Its wheels *were* a burning fire. A river of fire was flowing And coming out from before Him; Thousands upon thousands were attending Him, And myriads upon myriads were standing before Him; The court sat, And the books were opened" (Dan 7:9-10 NASB).

The book of Revelation reveals that the inhabitants of the earth are about to be judged by Christ. The emerald rainbow represents God's mercy and grace and the permanence of His covenant promises to mankind and Israel in the midst of judgment. The twenty-four thrones represent God's ultimate witnesses against mankind and fallen angels – a combined Supreme Court and Grand Jury in heaven. They are the heavenly body who can immediately and unreservedly say "Amen" to the judgments of God and Christ.

The scene also points to worship and priestly service before God. These elders are not just kings. They are also priests. As priests they worship God, praise God, cast themselves down before God's throne, sing songs, play harps, and handle the golden bowls of incense which John specifically states are the prayers of the saints. Priests seated on thrones of royalty. The twenty-four elders are Priest-Kings or King-Priests. We encounter this specific concept of kings and priests embodied together in Revelation 1:6 and 5:10 (especially in the KJV). We also encounter this combined role in the mysterious person of Melchizedek, king of Salem and priest of the Most High God (Gen 14:18; Ps 110:4; Heb 7:1). Jesus Christ embodies the ultimate form of this double role as King of kings and High Priest of priests after the "order of Melchizedek" (Ps 110:4; Heb 5:6; 7:1-28).

## Elders

This group is a representative body. But who do they represent: angels in heaven, Israel, the church, Israel and the church combined, or mankind in general? The occupants of the twenty-four thrones are specifically identified as elders, collectively. Each of the twenty-four individuals is an "Elder" by his own right.

The Greek word for elders is *presbuteros*. This word occurs twelve times in the book of Revelation, where it always refers to this group of twenty-four individuals, or to one of the group individually, but only in the context of the elder as being a part of this particular group.

Throughout the scriptures of both the Old Testament and the New Testament, the title elder implies a positional ranking system based upon age, seniority, or experience. An elder has a certain position of authority over others based upon one or more of these conditions. An elder's seniority based upon age, being older in age, is especially emphasized in the Old Testament. As such the elder was often a forefather, or ancestor, or even the designation for the first-born or oldest child within a family.

The term elder has been applied to leaders of Gentile nations, leaders of the tribes and families of Israel, the Israelites selected to assist Moses, and later to the Jewish Sanhedrin. Elder is a title that was also applied to certain leaders within various church congregations in the New Testament. Regardless, these twenty-four elders have a certain form of seniority over everyone else in whatever group they represent.

## White Robes

The elders wear white robes. They are described as being clothed in white raiment (KJV) or having white garments. The meaning of the white clothing of the elders is not explained. However, the book of Revelation does explain the significance of white clothing.

Those who walk with God or Christ dressed in white are those who are considered worthy (Rev 3:4). Christ encourages His overcomers with the promise of being clothed in white (Rev 3:5). Christ exhorts people to obtain this white clothing from Him (Rev 3:18), as we cannot make them for ourselves or obtain them through our own merit. Clean, white linen is symbolic of the righteousness of the saints (Rev 19:8). Christian martyrs will be given white robes (Rev 6:11). The great multitude of human believers before the throne and Christ in heaven are dressed in white robes (Rev 7:9, 13-14). The wife of Christ will wear white (Rev 19:8). The armies of Christ in heaven wear white (Rev 19:14). Angels are also sometimes described as being in white (Mt 28:3; Mk 16:5; Jn 20:12; Act 1:10; Rev 15:6).

In the context regarding how white robes or white garments are portrayed throughout the book of Revelation, there is an inherent association with the glory of God. God's characteristics of holiness, righteousness, and glory are embodied by the color white. White stands out as a color associated with the deity of both God and Jesus Christ (Dan 7:9; Mt 17:2; Rev 1:14; 20:11). By extension white is imparted to those faithful followers of God and Christ, in the form of a white stone (Rev 2:17), and white robes or clothing (Rev 3:4-5, 18; 6:11; 7:9, 13-14; 19:8), which reflect the merit that the faithful have in standing before God and the high esteem that God places upon the relationship that He has with them.

## Crowns

The elders have golden crowns upon their heads. The elders do not merely have the appearance of wearing crowns. Nor are the crowns an integral part of their heads. The crowns are real crowns which the elders can remove from their heads. This activity is something they do as part of their worship as they are described in Revelation 4:10 as taking their crowns and casting them before God's throne. The elder's position and authority (thrones and crowns) comes directly from God, and they readily acknowledge and submit that authority before God in praise and worship.

The Greek word used for these crowns is *stephanos* as opposed to *diadem*. Where diadem denotes the crown of inherent royalty and kingship, stephanos points to a crown awarded as a prize. It is the crown of the victor. It is the crown given for athletic and physical triumph, military victory, and exemplary service in public recognition of the achievement. For God's believer the stephanos crown does not reflect his gift of salvation but rather marks the successful walk of the believer with God through faith and his victory over the obstacles of this world. It is possible for a believer to have salvation and yet not earn a crown (1 Cor 3:11-15; 2 Cor 5:10).

The presence of stephanos crowns and diadems is not always a mark of the righteous. The crown given to the rider on the white horse at the opening of the first seal (Rev 6:2) is a stephanos crown. This rider symbolizes the release from restraint of the person who will become the

Antichrist to begin his rise to power, and the stephanos crown marks the authority that God grants to that person to be victorious in advance of his conquests. The Antichrist is destined to be victorious over the inhabitants of the earth in an evil way (Dan 7:25; Rev 13:7), but his ultimate authority is limited in that it will only last for three and one-half years (Dan 12:7; Rev 13:5).

The demon locusts of the fifth trumpet judgment are described as having something like stephanos crowns on their heads (Rev 9:7). It should be noted that here again these locusts are released as a form of judgment and are destined to be victorious over unrepentant people within the limits of God's supernatural restraint for a specific period of five months (Rev 9:1-11). These stephanos crowns reflect that sanctioned authority.

Even Satan gets into the act with his crowning appearance. The great red dragon, which is revealed in Revelation 12:3, has seven heads, ten horns, and seven crowns upon his heads. These crowns are diadems. The beast that rises out of the sea in Revelation 13:1 (which has "seven heads and ten horns, and upon his horns ten crowns") is wearing diadems for crowns. Satan claims regal authority over the earth for himself and his ten kings; however, God has other plans.

The plaited crown of thorns placed upon Jesus before His crucifixion was a stephanos crown (Mt 27:29; Jn 19:2, 5). What was intended as an insult by fallen men became a crown of victory. It represented Christ's victory over sin and death. The crown worn by Jesus, the Son of man upon the white cloud in Revelation 14:14, as He prepares to reap the earth in wrathful judgment with the sickle in His hand, is a stephanos crown. However, the many crowns on the head of Jesus – as He makes His appearance from heaven to make war with Satan, the Antichrist, the False Prophet, the ten kings, and all unrepentant sinners on earth – are diadems (Rev 19:12).

The presence of crowns and the awarding of crowns is an important theme running throughout the prophetic story of the End Times. Men can walk with and abide in Christ by faith and share in His righteousness by separating their lives to Him and receive stephanos crowns as a valuable prize at the judgment seat of Christ. Where stephanos crowns are sometimes granted by God to mark authority for temporary triumph as part of His judgments, the Bible never depicts angels as wearing crowns.

God has granted the twenty-four elders the authority to wear golden crowns and to sit dressed in white robes upon thrones before Him – as His kings, His priests, His witnesses. Who are these twenty-four individuals who make up this unique representative body referred to as elders?

## Prominent Views – The Identity of the 24 Elders

There is no consensus among Bible scholars as to the identity of the twenty-four elders and the group whom they represent. The first question regarding their identity is whether they are angels or redeemed men. The second question is, "If they are redeemed men, what group of people from the earth do they represent?"

### The Church

The most prevalent view seems to be that the elders are redeemed men and they directly represent the body of the church in heaven. Hal Lindsey, Arnold Fruchtenbaum, J. Vernon McGee, Gerald Stanton, and David Jeremiah represent scholars who argue on the side of the church.

J. Vernon McGee states in his Thru the Bible commentary series (Revelation Chapters 1-5), "These twenty-four elders stand for the total church from Pentecost to the Rapture. Therefore, I can say categorically and dogmatically that here is the church in heaven."[1]

Gerald B. Stanton takes up this identity question in his book, *Kept From The Hour*, "They are not a symbolic group. …. These elders are individuals, although their title and their actions indicate that they function in a representative sense …. so although the elders of the Revelation cannot *symbolize* the Church in glory, they can be *representative* of the Church, …. There are five characteristics which seem adequate to identify the elders as representatives of the glorified Church: their *position*, their *worship*, their *raiment*, their *crowns*, and their *song*."[2]

It is claimed that the pretribulational rapture of the church is symbolized by the apostle John when he is taken to heaven at the beginning of Revelation 4. Since the church is promised to be kept from the hour of trial that is the Tribulation (Rev 3:10), these scholars believe the church must be in heaven prior to the opening of the seven seals in Revelation 6. Since the twenty-four elders are the only group in Revelation 4 and 5 that can possibly represent the church, they are taken to be the church in heaven.

As for the reason for the number twenty-four, it is pointed out that King David divided the Levitical priesthood into twenty-four courses (1 Chr 24:1-19). This division is said to be based upon a heavenly pattern revealed to David by God. Thus, the entirety of the church is taken to be directly represented by the twenty-four elders in heaven.

## Israel and the Church

Another strongly held view is that the twenty-four elders are human leaders representing the Old and New Testament saints (both Israel and the church). Victorinus, John Darby, Clarence Larkin, Tim LaHaye, and Grant Jeffrey take this stand.

This interpretation sees the twenty-four elders split between twelve Old Testament saints (usually denoting the patriarchs of the twelve tribes of Israel) and the twelve apostles of the church. For some it seems natural that Israel and the church would be represented by a universal body of believers in heaven. Others find this interpretation strained.

That this was an early view is evident by the writings of Victorinus, bishop of Petau, who wrote one of the earliest commentaries on the book of Revelation and who became a martyr in 304 A.D. In his *Commentary on the Apocalypse of the Blessed John*, Victorinus claims, "The four and twenty elders are the twenty-four books of the prophets and of the law, which give testimonies of the judgment. Moreover, also, they are the twenty-four fathers - twelve apostles and twelve patriarchs." What we have of Victorinus's commentary is recorded in *The Early Church Fathers: ANTE-NICENE FATHERS, Volume 7*. We encounter more than a little bit of human selectivity and allegorical approach in his interpretation. Victorinus seems to be conflicted in his own interpretation. Unless the elders are 24 prophets, how can the elders be the books of the prophets? How do the patriarchs of the twelve tribes of Israel and the twelve apostles of the church relate to 24 books (of the prophets and the law) in their roles as elders?

The Israel and the church perspective is enticingly articulated by David Haggith, in his, *End-time Prophecies of the Bible*, "The twenty-four elders seated on thrones around the throne of God probably represent the twelve patriarchs of the Jewish race and the twelve apostles of the Church. This is an amazing image because it perfectly unites (using the symbolism of a circle) the leaders of the Old Testament (Old Covenant) with the leaders of the New Testament (New Covenant). These once-divided people are pictured united around God and centered on his authority and apparently equal in stature."[3]

Advocates for this single body representing both Old and New Testament saints point to the depiction of New Jerusalem in Revelation 21:10-14. That passage, which describes the heavenly city coming down to earth, reveals that the city has twelve gates that are inscribed with the names of the twelve tribes of Israel and twelve foundations that are inscribed with the names of the twelve apostles of Christ. Thus, God is seen as further honoring the patriarchs of the twelve tribes and the twelve apostles in the enthronement of the twenty-four elders.

## Problems with the Church, and Israel + Church Views

These two perspectives are not without serious problems. Both are based upon assumptions made regarding group representation, which the passages of scripture never confirm. The book of Revelation could have clearly identified the elders as Israel, or the church, or a combination of both, but it did not. Why not?

The point has often been made when symbols are used in scripture, and in Revelation in particular, that they are also explained by scripture. Christ makes a specific point of identifying the symbolism of the seven stars in His hand and the seven lampstands (candlesticks) as the angels of the churches and the seven churches themselves, thus showing His divine presence in the midst of His churches (Rev 1:12-13, 20). If the elders and their thrones are symbolic of the church, why are they not explained?

Perhaps, the answer is that the very title "elders" was supposed to be enough to clearly identify them? In that case, Israel and the church would both be eliminated, as they are not the best candidates for consideration. Who are the oldest men in the Bible? The apostles of the church are mere youths and the patriarchs of the tribes of Israel are but young men compared to the true elders of the Bible. I will develop this train of thought shortly.

Gerald Stanton identified five specific characteristics (position, worship, raiment, crowns, and song) which he considered "adequate to identify the elders as representatives of the glorified church." While some of these characteristics differentiate the elders from celestial beings, such as the four living ones and angels, they do not distinguish the church from earlier redeemed men. Being a representative group does not make the elders the church.

When has the church ever been directly represented by twenty-four elders? Where does scripture treat Israel and the church as the same body of people united as one? Many Christians refer to a "universal church" down through time, overlapping the Old and New Testaments; however, that is a conception of man. God's promises to both groups are different. God's treatment of both groups is distinct. Israel and the church are redeemed at different times. Israel is still awaiting its national redemption and that will not come until the end of the Great Tribulation. Most scholars believe Israel will not be resurrected until after the second coming of Jesus. If Israel was being directly and specifically represented by either twelve or all twenty-four of the elders, it would be a very partial and incomplete representation.

The group of twenty-four elders also does not make a good representation of the nation of Israel because there is another body described in the book of Revelation which is identified exclusively with the tribes of Israel (Rev 7:3-8). The 144,000 Israelite servants of God are the firstfruits of

Israel's national redemption (Rev 14:1-4). The twenty-four elders are a completely distinct group from the group of 144,000 (Rev 14:3).

While there seems to be some logic to the argument that the twenty-four elders symbolize Israel and the church as representatives split between the twelve tribes of Israel and the twelve apostles of Christ, it is somewhat of an allegorical interpretation. This viewpoint is an imposed solution at best.

While there were twelve sons and twelve original tribes of Israel from Jacob; Jacob's son Joseph had two sons who were specifically adopted by Jacob and claimed as his own sons (Gen 48:1-6). This replaced the tribe of Joseph with two tribes: Ephraim and Manasseh. Thus, while Israel is scripturally referred to as twelve tribes – there were really thirteen tribes. In order to symbolically depict Israel as a group of twelve tribes, the recorders of scripture had to omit a tribe or two whenever a listing of twelve tribes was made. An example of this is seen in Revelation 7:4-8, which specifically states in verse four that the passage applies to "all the tribes of the children of Israel," and yet the tribes of Dan and Ephraim are omitted from those being sealed.

Also, while there were twelve primary named disciples of Jesus originally, one was lost. While Judas was replaced as an apostle by Mathias to bring the number back to twelve (Act 1:21-26), Jesus Himself chose Saul (Paul) to become His apostle to the Gentiles (Rom 11:13; 1 Cor 1:1). Thus, there were really a minimum of thirteen apostles. Some other early church leaders are also referred to as apostles (James), so it can be argued that there were actually more than thirteen apostles.

Thus, the twelve original sons of Jacob, plus the two sons of Joseph make up Israel as a representative group or body. The twelve apostles, plus Paul, plus others who personally knew Jesus during His earthly ministry make up the church as a representative group or body of apostles.

While the tribes of Israel are often referred to symbolically by the number twelve and where the church and the apostles are symbolized by the original twelve apostles of Christ, the twenty-four elders are not symbolic in any manner. These elders are real individuals with specific identities of their own who can represent a larger group, but who do not symbolize it. This characteristic was recognized by Gerald Stanton in his book, *Kept From The Hour*. Thus, limiting the elders to twelve persons of Israel and twelve apostles arbitrarily leaves out other very important individuals who equally represent these groups. Who is to be omitted from these key historical individuals? This observation diminishes the argument that the twenty-four elders represent a division of the twelve tribes of Israel and the original twelve apostles of Jesus in heaven.

While God will honor the tribes of Israel by naming the twelve gates of New Jerusalem after them and will honor the apostles by naming the twelve foundations of the city after them, that does not make Israel and the church a single cohesive group. There is still a distinction maintained between them in the heavenly city – gates vs. foundations. Revelation 21 does not provide any reference to the elders or any sound reason for associating these gates and foundations with the twenty-four elders.

If the twelve patriarchs of the tribes of Israel comprise the first half of the group of twenty-four elders, thus representing Old Testament Israel, and if the twelve apostles comprise the second half as representatives of the New Testament Church, then how do we reconcile the statement by Jesus in Matthew 19:28? Jesus specifically told the disciples that they will sit upon **twelve** thrones in judgment over the twelve tribes of Israel. Jesus did not mention twenty-four thrones in association with His twelve disciples. Nor did Jesus mention the twelve tribal patriarchs in this prophetic teaching.

Jesus did not point His disciples to thrones around God's throne in heaven. Jesus specifically pointed His disciples to positions on thrones on earth "in the regeneration" when Jesus Himself will sit upon His own throne of glory. This reference to the regeneration points specifically to the Millennial Kingdom on earth. The promise that Jesus made to overcomers in Revelation 3:21 is that they will sit with Him on His throne. Again, this looks forward to the Messianic Kingdom and the throne of glory that Jesus will have that is distinct from His present sharing of His Father's throne in heaven. John is destined to sit on a throne on earth over one of the tribes of Israel – not a throne in the throne room of God in heaven (Mt 19:28).

This point regarding the thrones and the timing of Christian co-rulership with Christ needs to be emphasized. All Christian believers must wait for Christ to take His own throne in the Millennial Kingdom before being enthroned as co-rulers with Christ. Since Christ is currently seated on His Father's throne, sitting at the right hand of the Father during this Church Age (Ps 110; Eph 1:20; Heb 8:1; 10:12), Christians are in a waiting mode looking for the coming of their Lord. Christians cannot and will not be seated on thrones during the Church Age, the Day of the LORD, or the Tribulation before Christ has obtained His own throne in the Messianic Kingdom following His glorious return to earth as revealed in Revelation 19.

However, the scene in Revelation 4 reveals twenty-four elders seated on twenty-four thrones long before Jesus Christ has returned in His glory to claim His throne on earth. In fact, Christ Himself is not in view in Revelation 4. In Revelation 5, Christ cannot be found anywhere – until He is revealed by God to be standing in the midst of God's throne. During this timeframe the twenty-four elders are already seated on thrones. Throughout the events of Revelation (including chapter 19), the elders occupy their own thrones around God's throne. The elders are not sharing God's throne, nor are they sharing Christ's throne as is promised to Christian overcomers (Rev 3:21).

How can we balance the facts that the elders are already enthroned at the time that John is taken to heaven to be a prophetic witness, as well as during the time that Jesus Christ is still sharing His Father's throne instead of having claimed His own throne, with the opposing fact that Christians do not have access to being seated on Christ's throne or any other heavenly thrones prior to the Millennial Kingdom reign of Christ? The necessary conclusion is that the elders and the church cannot be the same people.

Why does John show no sign of recognition of any of the elders if he himself, or any of the other apostles, whom he knew very well, are represented within that group? Would John have suppressed the emotion brought on by recognition if that were the case? Considering John's other displays of emotion and amazement during the experience of this revelation, I am doubtful that he would not mention it. Why would another elder or an angel not point that association out to John if he were in fact one of them. I must conclude that John is not one of the twenty-four elders.

There is a very strong difference between the twenty-four elders and the twenty-four courses of the Levitical priesthood. Each Levite served in one of the twenty-four divisions, and these courses rotated their service in the Temple throughout the calendar year. There is absolutely no indication in the book of Revelation, or any other reason to believe, that the twenty-four elders rotate their positions with anyone else. They are a very special group with a very special purpose. While we may see them as representative of humanity as a whole, we have no reason to envision any other humans (Israel, church, or otherwise) sharing or rotating the role of sitting on these twenty-four thrones.

There are problems with the direct association of John being caught up to heaven in Revelation 4 and the rapture of the church. John was taken to heaven in the spirit (not bodily) as Revelation 4:2 reveals, but the church will be taken bodily (glorified) to heaven when it is resurrected and raptured.

We should note again that the twenty-four elders are crowned and seated on thrones before John arrives in heaven. If the elders represent the raptured church and John represents the raptured church, they would all be arriving simultaneously. However, the elders have already been crowned before John arrives. The Elders must have already made their appearance before the judgment seat of Christ before John arrives in heaven. Therefore, it is impossible for both the elders and John to be direct representatives of the raptured church.

Why is it that the elders are extremely knowledgeable about things and events in heaven at a point when John is not and John cannot answer their questions – if they represent the church which has just been raptured and John himself is one of those same church members who have been taken to heaven? This difference in understanding points to the necessity that the elders have been in heaven for a longer time than the apostle John. They do not represent the same groups taken to heaven at the same point in time.

Either John represents the church and the elders do not, as they have been in heaven for awhile prior to the church's arrival, or the elders represent the church and John does not, as he appears in heaven at some point after the judgment seat of Christ when the elders (as the church) received their crowns and thrones. The twenty-four elders have obviously been in heaven for a longer period of time than John. Since John is obviously a representative of the church, in his roles as Christian believer, apostle, and prophet, under the direct instruction of Jesus, the elders, and angels, then the elders cannot be the direct representatives of the raptured church.

We should also note (again) that the twenty-four elders are crowned and seated on thrones before Jesus, as the Lamb of God, is even introduced in this scene. The elders are seated and serving before the scroll is opened. If John's being taken to heaven in the spirit is symbolically representative of the rapture of the church, as many believe, would the first appearance and depiction of the corporate body of church believers be twenty-four elders sitting on thrones at a point in time when Jesus is not characterized as sitting on a throne? If the elders represent the church in heaven, which has already appeared before the judgment seat of Christ, why are they not immediately mentioned in direct connection to Jesus Christ, as opposed to the elder's relative position to God, the Father?

The initial focus of the elders is upon God, the Father on His throne – they praise and worship God, the Father (Rev 4:10). Jesus is not evident (in sight or in focus) in the scene as we are brought into it. Jesus is obviously in the midst of God's throne (as He cannot be found anywhere else – Revelation 5), but He is not in focus. We can look right at Him but cannot see Him until God deems the time is right. John weeps because no man is found worthy to open the scroll which is in God's right hand. Then one of the elders consoles John and points out the presence of Jesus – "the Lion of the tribe of Judah, the Root of David." Only when Jesus is openly acknowledged and takes the sealed scroll from God do the twenty-four elders shift their focus to the praise and worship of Jesus the Lamb (Rev 5:8-12).

Does this scene really make sense if the elders are members of the church? The elders are too distinct from Christ to be the church! The church is explicitly "the body of Christ" and "the Bride of Christ." Why does the book of Revelation give the distinct impression that the twenty-four elders are closely associated with God the Father and His throne in heaven, as opposed to having the unique relationship to Jesus Christ that exclusively belongs to the church? The elders have a unique relationship with God the Father – while the church has a unique relationship with Jesus Christ!

Do the overcomers of the Church Age assume responsible positions on thrones around the throne of God prior to their marriage to Jesus Christ as the Lamb of God? That is the situation created by those who claim that the elders are either the church, or Israel and the church. In the book, *Europe After Democracy*, Arthur Brown states, "We conclude that the twelve from the Old Testament represent the wife of Jehovah, the nation of Israel, and the twelve from the New Testament represent the bride of Christ, the Church."[4] This creates a timing problem. At the time that the scene of Revelation 4 and 5 takes place in heaven, sometime before the Tribulation begins on earth, Israel has not yet been redeemed as a nation and God has not yet reclaimed Israel as His wife. Furthermore, while the church is the bride, it is not yet married to Christ. The marriage is not specifically mentioned until Revelation 19:7-9. This interpretation seems highly unlikely. In addition, the twenty-four elders (Rev 19:4) are distinct and separate from the wife of Christ who has made herself ready for the marriage (Rev 19:7-8). They cannot comprise the same group.

Where will the twenty-four elders be when the church (Bride of Christ) returns to Earth with Christ at His second coming? Will they still be in heaven? The fact that they sit on thrones in heaven argues that their positions are permanent. Will they abandon their thrones around God's throne in heaven to return to earth at the time of Christ's second coming and remain on earth during the Millennium? I believe that the twenty-four elders and their thrones are permanent fixtures in God's heavenly court, at least until after the judgment of the Great White Throne takes place at the end of the Millennium (Rev 20:11-15). The role of the twenty-four elders sitting upon thrones surrounding the throne of God in heaven will very likely be quite functional and relevant at the time of the Great White Throne judgment. It should be obvious that this final judgment will not take place on earth.

These overall observations tend to negate the views that the twenty-four elders are the church, or strictly represent the church, or comprise a combination of Israel and the church. Because of issues like these some scholars turn to another explanation for the identity of the twenty-four elders – the realm of angels – the messengers of God.

## Angelic Beings

The perspective that the elders are a special class of angels seems to be a minority view, but it is held by some. E. W. Bullinger, William Newell, John Phillips, and Robert L. Thomas take the angelic side of the argument.

Contrary to J. Vernon McGee's dogmatic vision of the elders as the church, E. W. Bullinger argues in his *Commentary on Revelation*, "So these four-and-twenty elders are the princely leaders, rulers, and governors of

Heaven's worship. They are kings and priests. They were not, and cannot be, the Church of God. They are seen already crowned when the throne is first set up. They are crowned now. They were not, and are not redeemed, for they distinguish between themselves and those who are redeemed. .... They are heavenly unfallen beings, and therefore they are 'arrayed in white robes.'"[5]

Proponents who conclude elders are angels identify problems with the previous views which proclaim the church, or Israel and the church combined. They do not see the elders as redeemed fallen beings. They also tend to discount the view that the twenty-four elders constitute a representative body for a larger group.

In part, the argument for an angelic identity of the elders is based upon the observation that the organization of the Levitical priesthood into twenty-four divisions was derived from a heavenly pattern. It is reasoned that the original pattern in heaven could not have been of humans but must have been composed of some type of angelic beings.

Another argument is derived from a variation of wording between different translations. In the passage of Revelation 5:9-10, the twenty-four elders sing a new song. The wording of this song takes a subtle but distinctive twist between the Authorized King James Version and the Revised Version.

> King James Version
> And they sung a new song, saying, Thou art worthy to take the book, and to open the seals thereof: for thou wast slain, and hast redeemed **us** to God by thy blood out of every kindred, and tongue, and people, and nation; And hast made **us** unto our God kings and priests: and **we** shall reign on the earth. (Rev 5:9-10 KJV bold added)

> Revised Version
> And they sing a new song, saying, Worthy art thou to take the book, and to open the seals thereof: for thou wast slain, and didst purchase unto God with thy blood ***men*** of every tribe, and tongue, and people, and nation, and madest **them** *to be* unto our God a kingdom and priests; and **they** reign upon the earth. (Rev 5:9-10 RV bold added)

> Jewish New Testament
> and they sang a new song, "You are worthy to take the scroll and break its seals; because you were slaughtered; at the cost of blood you ransomed for God **persons** from every tribe, language, people and nation. You made **them** into a

kingdom for God to rule, *cohanim* to serve him; and **they** will rule over the earth." (Rev 5:9-10 JNT bold added)

While the King James Version has the elders using the pronouns "us" and "we," and thereby directly including themselves within the context of redemption highlighted by the song, the Revised Version inserts "men" and utilizes the pronouns "them" and "they." The Jewish New Testament follows suit using "persons" and the pronouns "them" and "they." Thus, the translations of the Revised Version and the Jewish New Testament seemingly exclude the elders from being among those redeemed by the blood of Christ. The RSV, NASB, and NIV translations follow the wording of the Revised Version. Which translation is the most accurate is disputed among scholars.

Regardless of which translation of the Bible would be considered by God to be the most accurate to His intended meaning, the wording of the RV, JNT, RSV, NASB, and NIV translations in this passage does not definitively eliminate the elders from being redeemed humans. Compare this song in Revelation 5 with the song sung by Moses and the Israelites in Exodus 15. Portions of the song sung by the children of Israel when referring to themselves are recorded in the third person (Ex 15:13, 17). The issue of whether the elders are angels or redeemed humans must be decided in the larger context of all that is revealed regarding the elders. I do not believe that the issue regarding the correct wording of pronouns in this passage is the deciding factor.

We should note that the elders are distinguished from angels in Revelation 5:11 and 7:11. Where Revelation 5:11 mentions the voice of "many" (myriads of myriads, and thousands of thousands) angels in addition to the elders, Revelation 7:11 specifically states that "all" the angels were standing around the throne and that they were also standing around the twenty-four elders. If the elders are angels, why is there such a distinction? It seems that Revelation consistently goes out of its way to differentiate between the group of elders and angelic or celestial beings.

The angels who are fallen have no access to redemption and would not be sitting on thrones in God's courtroom. The angels who are not fallen have no need for redemption or the symbols which portray redemption among men. Thus, angelic beings are never portrayed as victors or overcomers, which would be symbolized by the wearing of stephanos crowns.

It has already been noted that the crowns that the elders wear are removable and that they do remove them and cast the crowns before God's throne as part of their worship (Rev 4:10). This activity makes sense for redeemed humans, as they have earned these crowns through their faithful service to God during their lives on earth.

One of Bullinger's arguments in the previous quote in favor of angels is: "They are seen already crowned when the throne is first set up. They are crowned now." However, what would crowns mean to angels who are created beings from the very beginning of God's creative activities? What significance would it have for a created being to cast a crown, which he had been given as an act of creation, before God's throne when the angel had not done anything to earn the crown? The true significance of the act of casting crowns before God's throne lies with the worship of redeemed men.

Throughout the scriptures of both the Old Testament and the New Testament leading up to the fourth chapter of Revelation, the title "elder" or "elders" is never applied to either an individual angel or a group of angels. Is this title now suddenly describing a group of angels in heaven?

While the account of creation in the book of Genesis does not describe the creation of angels, Psalms 104:1-5 and 148:1-6 do mention angels as created beings. Angels were created as spirits early in God's process of creation, prior to God's laying the foundations of the earth. While there seems to be a ranking system or hierarchy of authority or position between different types or classes of angels (four Living Ones, seven Archangels, and myriads of other angels), there is no indication of any distinction by age. All angels seemingly were created at the same time, and thus are the same age. The first and foremost application of the term elder is that of age or seniority by age or wisdom. Among the sphere of all angelic beings, the title elder seems to be misapplied.

How long have the twenty-four elders been seated upon their thrones in heaven? If they are a class of angels, they should have been there from the beginning when all angels were created. However, they are never specifically mentioned in scripture until Revelation 4.

Isaiah saw a vision of God on His throne and described the seraphim and their activity, but he made no mention of twenty-four elders or their thrones (Isa 6:1-7). Ezekiel also saw a vision of God on His throne and described the four living creatures (cherubim) and their activity, but again nothing about twenty-four elders or their thrones is revealed (Ezek 1:4-28; 10:1-22). All three prophets, Isaiah, Ezekiel, and later John, noted the characteristic wings of these beings. Yet there is no reference made to any of these beings having white robes, crowns, or thrones of their own.

The closest reference in the Old Testament may be the passage of Daniel 7:9. Daniel had a night vision (dream) where he witnessed thrones being cast down (set up) and God (Ancient of days) sitting on His throne. These thrones mentioned by Daniel could be the thrones of the twenty-four elders. However, this vision is set in the far future from Daniel's time and takes place sometime after the ascension of Jesus to heaven (Dan 7:13). It is interesting that the twenty-four elders are not mentioned in the heavenly court prior to the ascension of Jesus since redeemed men could not have gained their crowns and thrones before the crucifixion, resurrection, and ascension of Jesus.

## Redeemed Men vs. Angelic Beings

The title elder is one exclusively associated with humans. Scripture never applies the term elder to an angel. God sits on a throne and human kings sit on thrones, but with the possible exception of Satan, we are never informed in the Bible that angels sit on thrones. Christ wore a crown of thorns and will wear many diadems when He returns in glory. Human kings wear crowns, Christian martyrs are promised crowns (Rev 2:10), and many other saints will be awarded crowns, but scripture never says that angels wear or are awarded crowns. The twenty-four elders cannot be angels within the content and context of revealed scripture.

The twenty-four elders are men who have been redeemed from the earth. They have walked with God on earth and have either been resurrected from death or kept from death by being raptured to heaven. Enoch and Elijah are two men who were taken to heaven without experiencing death (Gen 5:24; Heb 11:5; 2 Ki 2:9-12). The elders have been judged by God and granted rewards which include: positions of extreme closeness around God's throne, thrones of their own, unique distinction in the ranks of heaven, white robes, and stephanos crowns.

Joseph Seiss, grappled with this issue regarding the identity of the twenty-four elders in his book, *The Apocalypse: An Exposition of the Book of Revelation*, originally published in 1900. Seiss observed, "They are not angels, but human beings. .... They are not the patriarchs, Jews, or apostles, only ; for they are from "every tribe, and tongue, and people, and nation." (Chap. 5 : 9.) .... They are "*Elders*," not only with reference to their official places ; for that term is expressive of *time*, rather than of office. The *elder*, is the older man ; and in the original order of human society, he was the ruling man because he was the older man. .... They are the first-born from the dead—the first glorified of all the company of the redeemed—the seniors of the celestial assembly .... They do not represent, by any means, the whole body of the redeemed, as some have supposed, but are exactly what their name imports—the seniors of them—the first-born of the household—the oldest of the family,—and hence the honored officials."[6]

Joseph Seiss recognized that the elders are redeemed men as opposed to angelic beings. He also distinguished them from merely being the patriarchs of the tribes of Israel or the apostles of the church. Seiss believed that the elders are the "first-born from the dead" and the "first glorified" of the family of man. If Seiss is correct in this observation, as I believe he is, then the church becomes disqualified in its claim to the position or identity of the twenty-four elders. It is impossible for the apostles or any other elders of the church to be the first-born of the dead, or the first glorified men before the throne of God.

Since it is highly problematic to identify the twenty-four elders as a class of angels, or as the apostles or direct representatives of the church, or as a combined group of Old Testament and New Testament saints representing Israel and the church, how can the elders be redeemed men from the earth and yet be distinct from both Israel and the church? Does the scripture of the Bible provide us with a possible or even better alternative for the identity of this group of elders and an explanation of when they could have obtained their thrones in heaven?

### 24 Elders: Redeemed Men vs. Angelic Beings

| Characteristics | Redeemed Men | Angelic Beings |
|---|---|---|
| Title – Elders | The title elder or elders is applied in scripture to individuals and groups of humans based upon seniority, age, rank, or position of responsibility regardless of whether they are Gentiles or Jews. It has been used to identify leaders of Gentile nations, leaders of Israel such as the heads of the tribes and families and the Jewish Sanhedrin, and later to leaders within Christian churches. | Outside of the question regarding the identity of these 24 Elders – the Bible does not apply the term elder or elders to any angel or group of angels. |
| Thrones | Human leaders (kings) sit on thrones. Christ's overcomers are promised to share His throne (Rev 3:21) and reign with Him (Rev 5:10; 20:6). | Do angels ever sit on thrones? There is no specific scripture which places an angel on a throne. |

| Characteristics | Redeemed Men | Angelic Beings |
|---|---|---|
| Crowns (stephanos crowns – the crowns of victors; not diadems – the crowns of rulers). | Human leaders receive crowns.<br>Victors receive crowns (1 Co 9:25; 2 Tim 4:8; Jas 1:12; 1 Pet 5:4).<br>Christ's martyrs and overcomers receive crowns (Rev 2:10; 3:11). | Do angels have crowns?<br>There is no specific scripture which states that any angels receive crowns or are crowned. |
| White Garments (symbols of salvation and righteousness, and most likely for humans symbols of resurrection). | White garments are given to believers.<br>Overcomers are promised white garments as a reward (Rev 3:5).<br>The martyred souls under the altar in heaven are given white robes (5th seal Rev 6:9-11).<br>The great multitude of saints in heaven are "clothed in white robes" Rev 7:9, 13-14).<br>The wife of Christ is arrayed in white (Rev 19:8).<br>White linen is described as the "righteousness of saints" (Rev 19:8).<br>The armies of Christ in heaven are "clothed in fine linen, white and clean" (Rev 19:14). | Do angels wear white garments? At least some angels do wear white (Mt 28:3; Mk 16:5; Jn 20:12; Act 1:10; Rev 15:6). |

## The Resurrection and Judgment of a Group of Men

When could this judgment of the elders and the granting of these gifts have taken place? What bearing can the timing of this judgment event have regarding the possible or probable identity of the twenty-four elders?

For those scholars who believe the twenty-four elders represent the church, or are comprised by at least twelve apostles of the church, the time of this judgment and award is the judgment seat of Christ following the resurrection and rapture of the church to heaven. However, is that the only possible timing of such an event? It should be observed that when Jesus was resurrected, many Old Testament saints were also resurrected.

> King James Version – Matthew 27:51-53
> And, behold, the veil of the temple was rent in twain from the top to the bottom; and the earth did quake, and the rocks rent; And the graves were opened; and many bodies of the saints which slept arose, And came out of the graves after his resurrection, and went into the holy city, and appeared unto many.

> Jewish New Testament – Matthew 27:51-53
> At that moment the *parokhet* in the Temple was ripped in two from top to bottom; and there was an earthquake, with rocks splitting apart. Also the graves were opened, and the bodies of many holy people who had died were raised to life; and after Yeshua rose, they came out of the graves and went into the holy city, where many people saw them.

At the time of the resurrection of Jesus, there were no New Testament saints to be raised from the dead. Technically, even though there were believers in Jesus as Christ, the church did not yet exist as it would not be born by the Holy Spirit until fifty days later at the time of Pentecost. The only saints or holy people who could have been resurrected from their graves were Old Testament believers.

Many Old Testament saints rose from the dead and appeared to people in Jerusalem as a witness to the resurrection of Jesus and His victory over death. This is the very first resurrection of a group of saints revealed in scripture. It points to the fulfillment or a partial fulfillment of a prophecy recorded by Isaiah. "Thy dead *men* shall live, *together with* my dead body shall they arise. Awake and sing, ye that dwell in dust: for thy dew *is as* the dew of herbs, and the earth shall cast out the dead" (Isa 26:19 KJV).

Unfortunately, the number and identity of these resurrected saints is not revealed. While the passage is vague, with few specific details, it can readily be understood that this resurrection was different than the resurrection of Lazarus. Jesus resurrected Lazarus from death, but that was only a temporary restoration of his life back into his mortal body. These Old Testament saints were resurrected as a demonstration of and part of the resurrection of Jesus, from physical death into eternal life. Some commentators like Matthew Henry have even characterized these saints as trophies of Jesus in the victory of His resurrection. These saints followed Jesus in resurrection, but they also have a share in the status of Jesus as the firstfruits of resurrection.

What happened to these resurrected saints? Since only "many" saints were resurrected, the implication is that some saints were left in their graves. When Jesus ascended to heaven, He took the resurrected saints to heaven, along with all the remaining souls of Old Testament saints. According to Ephesians 4:8, "When he ascended up on high, he led captivity captive, and gave gifts unto men." The souls of dead Old Testament saints were located in a compartment of the underworld referred to as "Abraham's bosom," awaiting Christ's victory over death through His resurrection. Jesus took these souls to heaven, but they are still waiting for their promised bodily resurrection which will not take place until the time of the end (Dan 12:1-2, 13).

Just as Christian believers are told that we must stand before the judgment seat of Christ following the resurrection–rapture event, it is logical to expect the same for these resurrected and ascended Old Testament saints. But instead of having to wait for the time of the end, they would have been judged by Christ for their individual walks with God by faith upon their arrival in heaven. This is a scene which is not revealed to us in scripture; however, the rewards they received could have included white robes and crowns. For twenty-four of theses Old Testament saints, the rewards could have included thrones in heaven. Christ makes similar promises to Christian overcomers (Rev 2:7, 11, 17, 26-28; 3:5, 12, 21).

## Just Men Made Perfect

The author of the book of Hebrews makes an interesting distinction which may have a direct relation to this group of individuals. "But ye are come unto mount Sion, and unto the city of the living God, the heavenly Jerusalem, and to an innumerable company of angels, To the general assembly and church of the firstborn, which are written in heaven, and to God the Judge of all, and to the spirits of just men made perfect, And to Jesus the mediator of the new covenant, and to the blood of sprinkling, that speaketh better things than *that of* Abel" (Heb 12:22-24).

In this passage we encounter several entities:

1. God, the Father – the Judge of all.
2. Jesus, the mediator.
3. A very large group of angels.
4. The general assembly of the church. Since Jesus Christ is the firstborn, the church of the firstborn is the same as the Church of Christ.
5. The spirits of just men made perfect.

There is no direct mention by name of the four living beings or the twenty-four elders. However, it is clear that the "just men" are a distinct group from the church. Merrill Unger regards this as "a reference to OT saints now made perfect by the cross of Christ."[7] Some scholars interpret the reference to spirits as indicating that these are the spirits of the Old Testament saints whom Christ took to heaven following His resurrection and that they are still awaiting their resurrection and rewards. However, the specific reference to the men being made perfect implies more than spirits awaiting future glorification. In the Jewish New Testament this is rendered as "spirits of righteous people who have been brought to the goal." Being made perfect implies the glorification and crowning which comes only by resurrection and being judged at the judgment seat of Christ. It is quite probable that these men made perfect include those who were resurrected at the time of Christ's resurrection. They could easily include the twenty-four elders.

The resurrection event recorded by Matthew only involved Old Testament saints. The church had not yet come into existence and would not until Pentecost, fifty days later. Only individuals who had lived and died in faith prior to the crucifixion and resurrection of Jesus could have participated. "Many," but not all, of the Old Testament saints were resurrected. Evidently, God made a choice as to whom from among His faithful followers deserved this special resurrection.

Who among the Old Testament saints, whom God could have chosen, were also perfect candidates for the twenty-four elders? While the patriarchs of the twelve tribes of Israel are possible for consideration, are there twenty-four better candidates?

## An Alternative Interpretation – The 24 Elders of Genesis

The appearance of the 24 Elders is something of a mystery. They appear like the mysterious Melchizedek in Genesis. All of a sudden there they are – center stage – no names, no beginning, no history, no genealogy, no individual personality. They simply are – God's associates – mature, wise, knowledgeable, redeemed, empowered, and enthroned. They serve as kings and priests of the Most High God.

Moses did not tell us about twenty-four elders in God's heavenly court. The prophets did not mention or describe the twenty-four elders. The four books of the Gospels are silent regarding them. Jesus did not reveal them in His teachings. The epistles of the New Testament draw a blank concerning a specific group of twenty-four elders.

Where do they come from? Perhaps we need to take a closer look at the book of Genesis. Genesis is the book of beginnings. Since it is often pointed out that what starts in Genesis ends in Revelation, it makes sense that what shows up suddenly in Revelation may have its origin in Genesis.

The twenty-four elders represent the realm of the earth and mankind, particularly redeemed humanity. The twenty-four elders are not Israel, nor are they the church. They are not and never were part of either Israel or the church. They precede and have a form of seniority over both groups. If redeemed humanity is represented in God's heavenly throne room by an entity other than Christ Himself, then all of humanity must be represented. By representing the totality of redeemed humanity, the twenty-four elders must begin their representation at the very beginning of mankind with the creation of Adam.

There was a lengthy history of mankind that needs to be represented prior to God's singling out Israel as His firstborn son among the nations of the world, and long before the church was born at Pentecost, ten days after Jesus ascended to heaven to sit at the right hand of God, the Father (Ps 110:1; Heb 10:12-13).

### Seven Days of Creation
### vs.
### Seven Thousand Years of Human History

There is a concept which tries to understand the prophetic puzzle through God's panoramic view of man's history. It is often pointed out that the Bible records four thousand years of human history followed by two thousand years since Christ. In the prophetic symbolism of the creation week, there were six days of creation immediately followed by a seventh day of

God's Sabbath rest. Since scripture records that a day is like a thousand years from God's perspective (Ps 90:4; 2 Pet 3:8), what we might refer to as a prophetic day, then six thousand years of human history precede the prophetic day of rest, the one thousand year reign of Christ during the Messianic Kingdom. This prophetic day of rest is referred to in Hebrews 4:9 as a time of rest ("Sabbath rest" NASB) that remains for the people of God.

**Seven Prophetic Days**

| **Day** | **Thousand Years** | **Historical Timeline** | **Human History** |
|---|---|---|---|
| First | Creation to 1,000 | 4,000 B.C. to 3,000 B.C. +/- | Adam to Enoch |
| Second | 1,000 to 2,000 | 3,000 B.C. to 2,000 B.C. +/- | Enoch to Abraham<br>Tower of Babel<br>Death of Noah |
| Third | 2,000 to 3,000 | 2,000 B.C. to 1,000 B.C. +/- | Abraham to Solomon (Temple) |
| Fourth | 3,000 to 4,000 | 1,000 B.C. to 1 A.D. +/- | Solomon (Temple) to Jesus Christ |
| Fifth | 4,000 to 5,000 | 1 A.D. to 1,000 A.D. +/- | Jesus Christ to Dark Ages |
| Sixth | 5,000 to 6,000 | 1,000 A.D. to 2,000 A.D. + | Dark Ages to Second Coming |
| Seventh | 6,000 to 7,000 | 2,000 A.D. + to 3,000 A.D. + | The Millennial Day of Rest (Sabbath) |

This is not a new concept. It was taught at least as far back as the early years of the church and is clearly articulated in the Epistle of Barnabas (a non-canonical writing that was well known to the early church fathers).

> And even in the beginning of the creation he makes mention of the sabbath. And God made in six days the works of his hands; and he finished them on the seventh day, and he rested the seventh day, and sanctified it.
>
> Consider, my children, what that signifies, he finished them in six days. The meaning of it is this; that in six thousand years the Lord God will bring all things to an end. For with him one day is a thousand years; as himself testifieth, saying, Behold this day shall be as a thousand

> years. Therefore, children, in six days, that is, in six thousand years, shall all things be accomplished.
>
> And what is that he saith, And he rested the seventh day: he meaneth this; that when his Son shall come, and abolish the season of the Wicked One, and judge the ungodly; and shall change the sun and the moon, and the stars; then he shall gloriously rest in that seventh day.[8]

Why is this important?

The last prophetic day, the seventh thousand years comprising the Kingdom of God, is directly represented by the Messiah (Jesus Christ) on the throne during the millennial day of rest. It is commonly recognized by both Jews and Christians that the prior six thousand years of human history can be broken down into three segments of roughly two thousand years each.

The present segment is the Age of Grace which is represented by the church. This period began with the birth of the church at Pentecost, following the crucifixion and resurrection of Jesus Christ, and His ascension to heaven almost two thousand years ago. The previous two thousand year span of history can be called the Age of Law and is represented by the nation of Israel. This time period spans the birth of the twelve sons of Jacob, which brought forth the tribes of Israel until the coming of Jesus as God's promised Messiah and the birth of the church. The first two thousand year segment of human history can be called the Age of Conscience and spans the time from the creation of Adam through the calling of Abraham and his descendants Isaac and Jacob.

The Jewish perspective of this concept is presented by David Stern in his book, *Jewish New Testament Commentary*. In his commentary of 2 Peter 3:3-9, Stern includes a quote from the Tractate Sanhedrin of the Jewish Talmud:

> "The school of Eliyahu teaches: 'The world exists for six thousand years — two thousand of them *tohu* ["void"]; two thousand, *Torah*; and two thousand, the era of the Messiah. But because of our numerous iniquities many of these years have been lost.'" (Sanhedrin 97a-97b). Stern comments, "According to Jewish tradition, there were 2,000 years without *Torah* — spiritual *tohu* — between the creation of Adam and the time when Abraham, aged 52, began convincing people to worship the one true God. .... Concerning the third 2,000 years, a footnote to this passage in the Soncino English edition of the Talmud says, 'Messiah

> will come within that period. He should have come at the beginning of [it]; the delay is due to our sins.'"[9]

Thus, Jewish tradition recognizes three symbolic eras of two thousand years. The first era preceded God's giving the Torah (the written word and law of God recorded in the first five books of the Bible by Moses) to Israel. The second era is symbolized by the Torah even though the Torah was not recorded at the very beginning of the Age of the Law. The third era is the Age of the Messiah – the time when the Messiah is supposed to come. The Messiah was supposed to come at the beginning of the third two thousand-year era, which is exactly when Jesus came. After Israel rejected Jesus as God's Messiah, the church was born and the Age of Grace has followed.

## The Prophetic Ages

| **Age** | **Historical Timeline** | **Representative Body** |
|---|---|---|
| Age of Conscience | First Two Thousand Years<br>4,000 B.C. to 2,000 B.C. +/-<br>Creation to 2,000 +/-<br>(Actually 2,108 +/- after Creation) | The 24 Elders |
| Age of Law | Second Two Thousand Years<br>2,000 B.C. +/- to 30 A.D. +/- | Israel |
| Age of Grace | Third Two Thousand Years<br>30 A.D. +/- to Present | The Church |
| The Millennial Kingdom | Seventh Thousand Years | Jesus Christ (Messiah & King) |

It should be readily evident that God is the one who is responsible for this overall pattern for the broad ages of human history. This pattern is by intentional design. It is no accident, nor is it a flight of fancy of human imagination. It carries a significant meaning to God, and we should pay attention to it.

In an overview sense, this broad pattern of seven prophetic days, broken down into three ages followed by the Kingdom Age of God, can be compared to the ancient concept of having sentries posted during three watches throughout the night, followed by the dawn of a new day. Each age serves as a watch during the long night of human history, which comes before the promised day of God's Messianic Kingdom. Jesus is characterized in scripture as the true morning star ushering in the day of God's Kingdom on earth (Rev 2:28; 22:16). This concept is even hinted at in Psalm 90:4. "For a thousand years in thy sight *are but* as yesterday when it is past, and *as* a **watch** in the night."

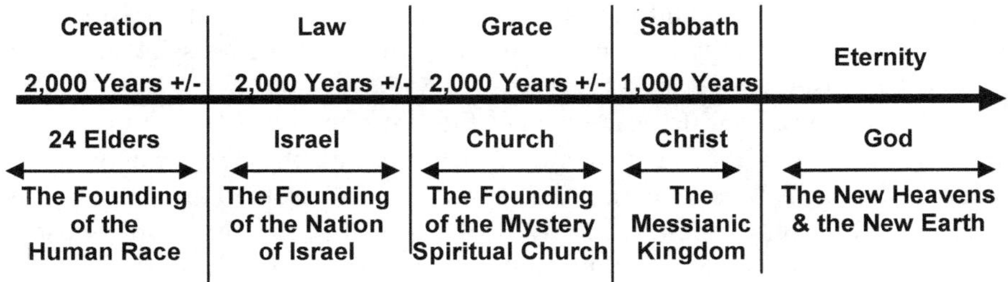


While the Romans later divided the nightly system of watches into four: evening, midnight, cockcrow, and morning, it was originally divided into three watches. Judges 7:19 mentions the middle watch, which points to there being three instead of four watches. Consider how Jesus utilized the pattern of the nightly watches as recorded in the passage of Luke 12:35-40.

> Let your loins be girded about, and *your* lights burning; And ye yourselves like unto men that wait for their lord, when he will return from the wedding; that when he cometh and knocketh, they may open unto him immediately. Blessed *are* those servants, whom the lord when he cometh shall find watching: verily I say unto you, that he shall gird himself, and make them to sit down to meat, and will come forth and serve them. And if he shall come in the **second watch**, or come in the **third watch**, and find *them* so, blessed are those servants. And this know, that if the goodman of the house had known what hour the thief would come, he would have watched, and not have suffered his house to be broken through. Be ye therefore ready also: for the Son of man cometh at an hour when ye think not.

Notice the emphasis that Jesus placed upon the second watch and the third watch. The Messiah came at the end of the second broad age (watch), but Israel did not accept Him. If Israel had accepted Jesus as the Messiah, He would have blessed it as a nation then and ushered Israel into the Kingdom. But Israel rejected Jesus as the Messiah sent by God, as God knew He would be rejected. As a result Israel's house was broken into and ransacked by the Romans (the thief), and Israel was cast out of the Land and dispersed among the nations. Now that Israel has been reborn as a nation in part of the Land the third age is coming to a close. Jesus will return at the end of the third watch and rapture the church to heaven for His wedding. When He returns following the wedding, and the time of great tribulation on earth, Israel will have another opportunity as a nation to accept Jesus as the Messiah and enter the long promised Kingdom Age.

If the church and Israel represent the last two ages of mankind over a span of about four thousand years, who represents the first two thousand years of history? I believe this earlier age is represented by twenty-four elders of the book of Genesis. Why do I claim that the first two thousand year span of human history is represented by twenty-four elders?

## 24 Elders on Earth

For our answer we have to turn back to the book of Genesis and examine what God reveals about the lineage of mankind. Genesis specifically presents this lineage as an unbroken line beginning with Adam and running through Noah and his three sons Shem, Japheth, and Ham. All of humanity is descended from Noah through these three sons. Genesis 10 provides a breakdown of their descendants and is often referred to as the "Table of Nations." God's chosen lineage runs from Noah through Shem onward through Abram (Abraham), Isaac, and Jacob (Israel). With Jacob, Genesis reaches another dividing point. Jacob becomes the natural ending point for the lineage that comprises the twenty-four elders.

Why would we stop at Jacob? At that point in human history, the Bible narrows its focus to the twelve sons of Jacob as the patriarchs of the twelve tribes or nation of Israel. The Bible picks up the story of Israel as the firstborn son of God from among the nations of the world, as well as the spiritual wife of God. The central tale of the next two thousand years deals with God's relationship to Israel and of Israel's relationship to God. This relationship reveals Israel as a people of promise. Israel was God's chosen vessel as the lineage of the promised seed – the Messiah – the Son of God – the Savior – Jesus Christ!

Genesis chapter 5 begins, "This is the book of the generations of Adam." Adam was created by God in God's own image and is even identified as the son of God (Lk 3:38). We could say that God begat Adam. Adam's descendants were then created in his own image (Gen 5:3). Adam begat Seth, who then begat Enos. The book of the generations of Adam delineates the genealogy of mankind from Adam to Noah; then it pauses with the mention of Noah's three sons Shem, Ham, and Japheth. The first book of Chronicles begins with this same genealogy: Adam, Seth, Enos, Cainan, Mahalaleel, Jared, Enoch, Methuselah, Lamech, Noah, Shem, Ham, and Japheth (1 Chr 1:1).

Genesis is somewhat vague at this point, so we have to solve a little logic problem. Noah was 500 years old when he had his first son (Gen 5:32). Genesis 5:32 simply mentions that Noah was 500 and he begat Shem, Ham, and Japheth. If we do not pay attention, we might think that these three sons were triplets, but they are not. They were each born in different years. How do we know who was the oldest? Shem is listed first. Does that mean he was the firstborn son?

As is often the case in God's dealings with man, the actual firstborn is not always the one to carry the promise. Among Abraham's sons, Ishmael did not take precedence with God over Isaac, nor did Esau over Jacob as sons of Isaac, nor Jacob's first son Rueben over a later son, Judah. The firstborn son tended to characterize the natural man or earthly man as opposed to the spiritual man. The earthly preceded the spiritual in time, but the spiritual had preeminence with God. This trend is also true with Noah's sons. Shem is listed first of the three sons in Gen 5:32 and Gen 6:10 because he is the one that God favored to carry the promised seed, but Shem was not the oldest son.

Genesis 7:6 and Genesis 7:11 inform us that Noah was 600 years old when the Flood event began. One of Noah's sons was 100 years old at the beginning of the Flood since Noah was 500 when he had his first son. Genesis 9:20-24 records an incident involving Ham, which resulted in Noah placing a curse on Ham's son Canaan. One significance of this is that Genesis 9:24 identifies Ham as Noah's "younger" son (youngest NASB). Genesis 11:10 picks up the genealogy with Shem and follows the lineage. Shem had his first son Arphaxad two years after the Flood when Shem was 100 years old. Therefore, Shem was not born when Noah was 500 years old and Shem was only 98 at the time of the Flood. Genesis 10:21 then refers to Japheth as the elder brother of Shem. Therefore, Japheth was the oldest son. Japheth was born when Noah was 500 years old. Shem was born two years later, and Ham was born at some point after Shem. The rest of the genealogy through Shem (Arphaxad, Salah, Eber, Peleg, Reu, Serug, Nahor, Terah, Abram, Isaac, and Jacob) is recorded throughout the book of Genesis as the narrative tale of events unfolds through the call of Abraham and the choice by God for Abraham's son Isaac and Isaac's son Jacob to be the vessels of God's covenant promises.

**The 24 Elders**

| Elders | Years From Creation<br>Birth | Begat Son At<br>Age | Lifespan | Years From Creation<br>Death |
|---|---|---|---|---|
| 1. Adam | 0 | 130 | 930 Years | 930 |
| 2. Seth | 130 | 105 | 912 Years | 1042 |
| 3. Enos | 235 | 90 | 905 Years | 1140 |
| 4. Cainan | 325 | 70 | 910 Years | 1235 |
| 5. Mahalaleel | 395 | 65 | 895 Years | 1290 |
| 6. Jared | 460 | 162 | 962 Years | 1422 |
| 7. Enoch | 622 | 65 | 365 Years | Raptured 987 |
| 8. Methuselah | 687 | 187 | 969 Years | 1656 |
| 9. Lamech | 874 | 182 | **777 Years** | 1651 |
| 10. Noah | 1056 | **500** | 950 Years | 2006 |
| 11. Shem | 1558 | 100 | 600 Years | **2158** |
| 12. Japheth | 1556 | Unknown | Unknown | Unknown |
| 13. Ham | 1560 (?) | Unknown | Unknown | Unknown |
| 14. Arphaxad | 1658 | 35 | 438 Years | 2096 |
| 15. Salah | 1693 | 30 | 433 Years | 2126 |
| 16. Eber | 1723 | 34 | 464 Years | 2187 |
| 17. Peleg | 1757 | 30 | 239 Years | 1996 |
| 18. Reu | 1787 | 32 | 239 Years | 2026 |
| 19. Serug | 1819 | 30 | 230 Years | 2049 |
| 20. Nahor | 1849 | 29 | 148 Years | 1997 |
| 21. Terah | 1878 | 70 | 205 Years | 2083 |
| 22. Abram | **1948** | 100 | 175 Years | 2123 |
| 23. Isaac | 2048 | 60 | 180 Years | 2228 |
| 24. Jacob | 2108 | Unknown | 147 Years | 2255 |

Surprisingly, when we list all of these elders, we discover that there are exactly twenty-two generations in a direct line from Adam through Jacob. When we add Noah's two other sons, Japheth and Ham to the list we arrive at exactly twenty-four elders presented in the narrative of Genesis, up to the point that God chose to bring forth Israel as a nation separate unto Him.

While some might argue against adding Japheth and Ham to the list, the overall recognition that this list of elders represents the foundational genealogy of all of mankind demands their inclusion.

For those who point out that Ham should not be considered redeemed or righteous because of the incident with Noah recorded in Genesis 9, we should note that both Ham and Japheth were greatly blessed by God by being saved at the time of the Flood. None of Noah's direct ancestors were killed in the judgment by God that took the form of a worldwide flood. God waited for the last of Noah's ancestors to die a natural death before sending the global deluge. Thus, the calling of Ham and Japheth into the safety of the ark and God's supernatural protection was a great blessing and a mark of their true character.

In addition, Noah did not directly curse Ham for whatever it was that Ham did. Noah prophetically looked into the future and singled out Ham's son Canaan as the object of his curse. There are a number of examples in the Bible of people who served God and who then erred, sinned, or failed in some significant way and yet retained their standing with God. Moses and King David are both excellent examples. After Moses struck the rock twice, instead of speaking to it as God had commanded, and was denied entry into the Promised Land by God (Num 20:11-12; Deut 32:48-52); nevertheless, we still see him actively playing a major prophetic role for God on the mount of transfiguration with Jesus and Elijah (Mt 17:3-4; Lk 9:30-33).

We should acknowledge an alternative interpretation for the identity of two of the twenty-four elders given by Henry M. Morris in his book, *The Revelation Record*. "They *do* represent all believers of all ages, but they are also individual men, the *elders* of all redeemed humanity. It is interesting, and possibly the answer to this question, that in the Book of Genesis there are twenty-four patriarchs listed in the line of the promised seed (Adam, Seth, Enos, Cainan, Mahalaleel, Jared, Enoch, Methuselah, Lamech, Noah, Shem, Arphaxad, Salah, Eber, Peleg, Reu. Serug, Nahor, Terah, Abraham, Isaac, Jacob, Judah, Pharez). These men could more properly be denoted the "elders" of God's elect than anyone else."[10]

Morris emphasizes the "line of the promised seed," which refers back to Genesis 3:15, the first Messianic prophecy in the Bible. Morris does not include Noah's sons Japheth and Ham, but includes the names of Judah and Pharez because they are in the direct bloodline of Jesus Christ (see the genealogy of Jesus in Mt 1:1-3; and in Lk 3:33). Morris's focus on the bloodline of Jesus is important and might be completely valid if the Messianic bloodline in Genesis stopped with Pharez. While Judah and Pharez are in the direct bloodline of Jesus and are introduced in Genesis, so is Hezron, the son of Pharez (Gen 46:12). Hezron is listed as Esrom in the genealogy of Jesus in the New Testament. Thus, Genesis introduces twenty-five individuals in the direct bloodline of Christ, and the ending of the line with Pharez (for the choice of the twenty-four elders) creates an incomplete picture.

I believe that the broad pattern of the ages that God has designed overrides this focus on the bloodline. Following Jacob, God focuses His attention on Israel as a particular people and as a nation set apart to Him. The chosen Messianic bloodline then flows through Judah and his descendants as a special part of Israel's storyline.

Another similar solution that has been proposed relies heavily on the genealogy that is outlined in Luke chapter 3:23-38. Luke delineates twenty-three individuals in the direct bloodline of Jesus from Adam to Jacob (two of them named Cainan). This proposal then adds Adam's first son Abel to the list to make twenty-four elders. Thus, Noah's sons, Japheth and Ham, are omitted from the list and replaced by Abel and a second Cainan.

This proposal is problematic. It misses the significance of the bloodline for all of humanity (not just Israel and Jesus). Abel is a dead end in the genealogy from Adam. Abel is not a forefather of Israel or Jesus. The Bible does not indicate that anyone is descended from Abel. Certainly, Abel has a special place in the heart of God as a worshiper of God and as the first martyr of God's human children. Nevertheless, Abel does not represent humanity within the genealogical bloodline from Adam to Jacob.

Luke lists two different individuals named Cainan, sometimes spelled Kenan, in the bloodline of Jesus. Luke identifies one Cainan as the son of Enos and the father of (Maleleel) Mahalaleel (Lk 3:37-38). This Cainan is readily identified in Genesis 5:9-14 and 1 Chronicles 1:2. The second Cainan is listed as the son of Arphaxad and the father of Sala (Salah or Shelah) in Luke 3:35-36. Thus, this second Cainan is inserted between Arphaxad (Arpachshad) and Salah. Supposedly, Luke's rendering of the genealogy follows information that is provided in the Septuagint (LXX) translation. However, this second Cainan is missing in the genealogy that is given in Genesis 10:22-24, Genesis 11:12-15, and 1 Chronicles 1:17-18, and in most translations of the Bible, including the KJV, NASB, NIV, and RSV. I believe the weight of scripture more strongly supports Japheth and Ham, as opposed to Abel and a poorly chronicled second Cainan, as two of the twenty-four elders of the Age of Conscience.

What makes these twenty-four individuals so special?

Literally, the twenty-four elders are God's human record of the history of mankind before the written word of the Bible was recorded. These are the ones who can attest to God's dealings with mankind from the very beginning of man at creation. In the manner that the book of Revelation utilizes a four-fold delineation for the people of the earth (Rev 4:9; 7:9; 11:9; 14:6), the twenty-four elders are the fathers of all nations, all people, all tongues, and every kindred throughout all time. John observes them (Rev 4:11) praise God for His creation and His act of creation – very characteristic of the twenty-four elders of Genesis!

They comprise a living genealogy, a unique family tree. Genealogies in the Old Testament were, and still are today, extremely important in establishing a person's right to inheritance and one's rightful ownership of land. Genealogies are also critical to establish the right for a relative to act as a kinsman-redeemer. The role of Jesus in redeeming the earth for Adam and the fallen human race is that of kinsman-redeemer (Heb 9:11-15; Rev 5:9).

The first book of Chronicles places a very strong emphasis on genealogy. The first eight chapters of the book lay out the genealogy of the nation of Israel (1 Chr 1:1–9:1). Notice how the first four verses of 1 Chronicles begins by simply listing the names of Adam through Noah and Noah's three sons: Shem, Ham, and Japheth. Verses seventeen through nineteen introduce the sons of Shem, Arphaxad, and Eber. The passage makes a special note regarding Peleg, son of Eber, revealing that the earth was divided in the days of Peleg. This refers to the event of the tower of Babel, when God confused the single language of the people into many tongues and scattered the people throughout the world (Gen 11:6-9).

Genesis 11:10 picks back up with the genealogy of Shem, and so does the 24$^{th}$ verse of 1 Chronicles. First Chronicles 1:24 continues the genealogy from verse four by repeating the name of Shem and then listing the direct line of ancestors from whom Abraham was descended. Verse thirty-four follows with Isaac as a son of Abraham and introduces Israel as a son of Isaac. It is interesting that the passage does not mention the name of Jacob but instead completely focuses on Israel, the national name. Chapter two then continues the genealogy with the twelve sons of Israel.

All twenty-four of these elders play an important role in the genealogy of Israel and its relationship to the nations around it. The twenty-four elders serve as a living genealogy, which establishes the early family tree and human bloodline of Jesus – the human witnesses to His claim to be the kinsman-redeemer for mankind against the claims of Satan.

Not only do these twenty-four elders represent the first two thousand years of human history, but they also represent all of mankind who are directly descended from them. Every human presently on earth and every human who has ever lived since the creation of Adam, whether redeemed or unredeemed, righteous or unrighteous, are represented by a direct ancestor or a line of ancestors within this sequence of twenty-four elders. Twenty-two of these elders (from Adam to Jacob through Noah's son Shem) comprise the direct bloodline of Jesus Christ as the seed promised by God. This line represents the bloodline of the nation of Israel as well. The remaining members of humanity, those who are not descendants of Shem, are descended from Adam to Noah and then through either of the other two sons of Noah, Japheth or Ham. These twenty-four elders literally comprise the most senior elders of the entire human race.

Isn't it curious that God placed exactly twenty-four elders in the book of Genesis spanning the time frame from the creation of Adam to Jacob, the founding father of the nation of Israel? Why would not this portion of the human historical record and the human bloodline of God's Son have a special position in heaven?

The argument made by some scholars that the church is the only complete body of redeemed men in heaven at the time of the scene of Revelation 4 cannot be scripturally proven. The twenty-four elders of Genesis do form a complete and distinct body in God's dealings with man. In all logical probability these twenty-four men of old are now in heaven and are the very same elders who are seated in positions of honor on thrones surrounding God's throne.

Many Bible scholars focus on the twenty-four elders before God's throne in Revelation 4 as reflecting the twenty-four divisions or courses of the Levitical priesthood, which rotated their service in the Temple. They see the twenty-four divisions of the Levites as being based upon a heavenly pattern. However, perhaps the numerical pattern goes deeper than that. Perhaps there are twenty-four thrones for elders in heaven because God created twenty-four elders in the early part of Genesis to specifically sit on those thrones. Perhaps the designation for the twenty-four courses of Levitical priests in Israel was merely a symbolic reflection and honoring of the positions of those twenty-four elders who preceded Israel in the history of God's relationship with man.

## The 24 Elders Conclusion

When we closely examine the book of Genesis, we encounter twenty-four men who hold positions of unique status, individually and collectively, in the relationship of God to mankind, in the history of man on earth, and in the direct human bloodline of Christ.

- Who has the most seniority of all redeemed people by reason of age or date of birth?
- Who among all of the people mentioned throughout the pages of the Bible, and all of the people who ever lived during the last six

thousand years of human history, could possibly be better suited to bear the title "elders" as representatives of mankind?

- Who could possibly be more eligible to sit on thrones in heaven, around the throne of God, and serve as kings, priests, judges, and jury?
- Who could be better qualified to be crowned and enthroned in heaven prior to the time that Jesus is presented to all creation as the one worthy to take the sealed scroll from the hand of God?
- What group of men could possibly be better differentiated, individually and collectively: from the four living beings, from the angels in heaven, from the patriarchs of the tribes of Israel and the nation of Israel itself, from the 144,000 Jewish servants of God, from the great multitude of redeemed believers from all nations (Rev 7), and from the church and bride (wife) of Christ (Rev 19)?

The books of Genesis and Revelation bracket the scripture of the Bible as bookends. Genesis provides the tale of the beginning – the foundation. Revelation provides the tale of the ending – the capstone. Since Revelation brings to completion the prophetic plan of God for humanity started in Genesis, it is only proper that the twenty-four elders of the human race are depicted as having positions of honor and responsibility in heaven.

I believe the best qualified representatives of mankind before the throne of God, individually and collectively, are the twenty-four elders of the human race: Adam, Seth, Enos, Cainan, Mahalaleel, Jared, Enoch, Methuselah, Lamech, Noah, Shem, Japheth, Ham, Arphaxad, Salah, Eber, Peleg, Reu, Serug, Nahor, Terah, Abram (Abraham), Isaac, and Jacob (Israel).

**Notes: 24 Elders**


1. J. Vernon McGee, *Revelation Chapters 1-5*, Thru the Bible Commentary Series Volume 58, (Nashville: Thomas Nelson, Inc., 1991), p. 134.
2. Gerald B. Stanton, *Kept From The Hour*, (Miami Springs, FL: Schoettle Publishing Co. Inc., 1991) pp. 200-202. Originally published by Zondervan Publishing House, 1956.
3. David Haggith, *End-Time Prophecies of the Bible*, (New York, NY: A Perigee Book, The Berkley Publishing Group , 1999), pp. 163-164.
4. Arthur H. Brown, *Europe After Democracy*, (South Plainfield, NJ: Bridge Publishing, Inc., 1993), p. 120.
5. E. W. Bullinger, *Commentary on Revelation*, (Grand Rapids, MI: Kregel Publications, 1984), pp. 219-220. Originally published as *The Apocalypse*.

6. Joseph A. Seiss, *The Apocalypse: An Exposition of the Book of Revelation*, (Grand Rapids, MI: Kregel Publications, 1987), pp. 103-104. Originally published in 1900.
7. Merrill F. Unger, *The New Unger's Bible Handbook*, (Chicago: Moody Press, 1966, Revised 1984 by Gary N. Larson), p. 603.
8. The General Epistle of Barnabas, *The Lost Books of the Bible*, (New York: Bell Publishing Company, 1979) p. 161. Originally published as the Apocryphal New Testament, by William Hone in 1820.
9. David H. Stern, *Jewish New Testament Commentary*, (Jewish New Testament Publications, Inc., 1992), p. 763.
10. Henry M. Morris, *The Revelation Record*, (Carol Stream, IL: Tyndale House Publishers, Inc., 1983), p. 88.

# 7

# Target Israel

## Israel the World's Target

Israel is the central focus of many prophecies that only make sense in the literal context of a specific tract of land in the Middle East. When Israel was to be recreated as a nation, there was only one place in the entire world that it could be reborn. Israel had to return to its ancient homeland – the very same geographical territory from which it was exiled many centuries ago (Deut 30:5; Jer 16:15; 23:3, 8; 24:6; 30:3; 32:37; Ezek 11:17; 34:13-14; 36:24, 28; 37:21-22; Amos 9:14-15).

The traumatic process of the rebirth of this nation brought it back to the land of its forefathers: Abraham, Isaac, and Jacob. Like the legendary Phoenix of myth, Israel rose from the ashes of exile, persecution, and holocaust to take root in the same place where its original fires of destruction began. It emerged from the flames as a national entity, taking its identity from the name that God gave their patriarch Jacob – Israel. The leaders of this newborn nation did not focus on the identity of a single tribe like Judah or Levi, but on the union of all of the twelve tribes descended from Israel.

The people did not return to the God of their forefathers to form a nation in full repentance and spiritual faith, however. Still, there was the realization that they were returning to their original homeland – the land of covenant promise. While the United Nations voted to authorize the establishment of a nation for the Jews on a small tract of land in the Middle East, Israel's claim to the land does not rest upon the goodwill of the United Nations. Israel's right to the land is not based upon military conquest, although it has had to fight several wars for its survival. Israel's claim rests upon God and the unique relationship that God had with its patriarchs.

God made specific covenant promises to Abraham, which were later confirmed to Isaac and subsequently bestowed to Jacob and his descendants. Genesis makes it clear that God chose Abraham to be the human mechanism through which God would move His divine plan to ultimately bless all the peoples of the world. It was by God's choice that Isaac became the son of promise instead of Ishmael and that Jacob inherited the covenant promises instead of Esau.

It was to Abraham that God declared, "And I will bless them that bless thee, and curse him that curseth thee: and in thee shall all families of the earth be blessed" (Gen 12:3). This promise was passed on from Isaac to Jacob in the context of Isaac blessing Jacob (Gen 27:29; 28:4). Through the descendants of Abraham, Isaac, and Jacob, the nations of the world would be blessed. However, the quality of the blessing would be based upon the relationship that the nations took with the chosen mechanism of God's promise. This principle is God's code of conduct for the nations. It is true for the world's relationship to the nation of Israel as God's chosen people. It is true regarding the world's recognition of Israel's relationship to the land promised by God to Israel. It is also true for each individual's relationship to God's ultimate promised seed through the lineage of Abraham, Isaac, and Jacob – God's Son, Jesus Christ.

It was to Abraham that God made a unique promise, "Unto thy seed have I given this land, from the river of Egypt unto the great river, the river Euphrates" (Gen 15:18). God chose Abraham and God selected a very specific tract of land for the homeland of Abraham's descendants (Gen 13:14-17; 17:7-8; 26:3; 28:4, 13-15; 35:10-12; 48:3-4; Ex 23:30-31; 32:13; 33:1; Num 34:1-12; Josh 1:4; Isa 60:21). "And I will establish my covenant between me and thee and thy seed after thee in their generations for an everlasting covenant, to be a God unto thee, and to thy seed after thee. And I will give unto thee, and to thy seed after thee, the land wherein thou art a stranger, all the land of Canaan, for an everlasting possession; and I will be their God" (Gen 17:7-8). God did not limit His promise to just a piece of geographical territory. God made an unconditional everlasting promise to the genealogical line of Abraham, Isaac, and Jacob throughout all of their generations. This is God's covenant, and it is dependent only upon God. God's promise of this land to Abraham, and ultimately to the descendants of Jacob, was so strong and repeated so many times in the Bible that Israel has become known as the "Promised Land."

However, Israel's birthright and title to the land by covenant promise is contested. Israel occupies only a fraction of the land promised to its fathers. The descendants of Ishmael and Esau, Israel's closest relatives, dispute the possession of what little land Israel does have. The descendants of the other sons of Abraham, by his last wife Keturah, also contend with

Israel. Israel even faces a constant tug-of-war to possession and control of Jerusalem and the land with the descendants of Noah's sons Japheth and Ham.

The world attempts to deny Israel's history and heritage. Few nations want Israel to have full control over Jerusalem and the Temple Mount. No nation wants Israel to expand its borders, much less expand any housing developments or settlements. It seems that many Arabs and Muslims want to wipe Israel off the map, while most of the rest of the world wants simply to strangle Israel to death. For the past twenty years or so, the United States and other nations have tried different ways to promote Israel's giving up land in the name of peace. The so-called land-for-peace process has been a complete failure from the beginning. It has not produced peace, nor will it ever be successful for Israel, for the Palestinians, for the Arab Muslim nations of the Middle East, or for the nations of the West. In fact the peace process will end badly for all.

The entire land-for-peace process is a violation of God's everlasting covenant promises to Israel. It violates Israel's right to the ownership and occupation of the land. It violates God's protection clause regarding Israel's blessings – those who bless Israel will be blessed by God, and those who curse Israel will be cursed by God. What leaders, in their right minds, would want to actively go out of their way to invoke God's curse upon themselves and their entire nations? Unfortunately, many have done exactly that. A close parallel between a number of economic downturns and natural disasters experienced by the United States in direct time correlation to pushing Israel into and through the Middle East peace process has been well documented by several authors such as John McTernan and Bill Koenig.

Where is the peace process in the Middle East headed? The Bible blatantly and adamantly predicts that the land of Israel is going to be the focal point of several future wars. The prophets repeatedly warn of the future Day of the LORD, when God intervenes in judgment and wrath and this period of time is accompanied by warfare. While some of their prophecies portray this future warfare and disaster in general albeit graphic terms, others are more specific and can be differentiated from each other. With concerted study of the key prophetic passages, we can distinguish between certain end-time wars such as:

- The final Campaign of Armageddon when all nations come against Israel and Jerusalem and Jesus Christ returns in triumphant revelation and victory (Isa 34:1-8; 63:1-6; Joel 3:1-2, 9-16; Zech 12:1-9; Rev 16:12-14; 19:11-21).

- The wars initiated by the king of the North and the king of the South against the Antichrist (Dan 11:40-45).
- The War of Gog and Magog when Israel is invaded by a large but limited alliance and God intervenes supernaturally (Ezek 38 and 39).
- The Confederacy of Psalm 83 (Psalm 83; Isa 17:1-14; Jer 49:2-6, 23-27, Amos 1:3-15; Obad 1-10, 15-20).

War is coming. Israel is the target. The enemies of Israel have her in the crosshairs of their scopes. Tens of thousands of rockets and missiles have been stockpiled for the sole purpose of being launched against Israel. Israel is surrounded by enemies everywhere she looks. To the:

- North – Lebanon, Syria, Turkey, and Russia
- East – West Bank, Jordan, Saudi Arabia, Iraq, Iran, Afghanistan, Pakistan, the other predominantly Muslim "Stans" of Central Asia, and China
- South – Sudan, Ethiopia, Eritrea, and Somalia
- West – Gaza Strip, Sinai Peninsula, Egypt, and Libya

In the immediate vicinity there is Lebanon to the north where a heavily armed Hezbollah, supplied and supported by Iran and Syria, has many missiles and fortified bunkers. Israel fought a short war with Hezbollah as recently as the summer of 2006. To the northeast is Syria, unstable in the midst of a civil war, yet heavily armed with missiles and chemical weapons, and supported by Iran and Russia. Hezbollah is heavily involved in Syria's civil war, supporting the Assad regime. Israel's possession of the Golan Heights, which was captured from Syria in the 1967 Six-Day War, has been a constant thorn of contention between Syria and Israel.

To the east, northeast, and southeast of Jerusalem is the contested West Bank, from Jerusalem to the Jordan River, which was captured from Jordan during the 1967 Six-Day War. It is referred to as the West Bank because it was considered to be the territory of the Kingdom of Jordan west of the Jordan River – the West Bank of Jordan. The West Bank comprises a mixture of Palestinian cities and villages including Jericho, Bethlehem, Nablus, and Hebron, and Jewish settlements and land controlled by Israel for security purposes.

To the east of the Jordan River is the Kingdom of Jordan, a semi-cooperative peace partner with Israel, yet heavily populated by Palestinians and refugees from Iraq, and now due to its civil war, refugees from Syria. The monarchy of Jordan is threatened by the increasing rise to power of the

Muslim Brotherhood in parts of the Middle East due to the momentum of the "Arab Spring."

To the south is Egypt, where the Muslim Brotherhood had risen to power and gained the Presidency. In July 2013, Egypt's military responded to civil unrest, ousted President Morsi from power, and arrested some of the Muslim Brotherhood leadership. The situation in Egypt is volatile. Egypt has a large military and air force supplied with advanced aircraft and weaponry by the United States. Egypt's peace accord with Israel is threatened. Egypt faces the serious threat of civil war (Isaiah 19). To the south is also the Sinai Peninsula, which to a large degree is essentially a no man's land, not effectively controlled by Egypt's military, but occupied by various enemies of Israel who are involved in terrorism and the smuggling of weapons.

To the west there are the Palestinians in Gaza, under the control of Hamas, and influenced by a number of other Islamic terrorist groups. Hamas has strong affiliations to the Muslim Brotherhood in Egypt and has been a proxy for Iran. The area of Gaza has been the source of many rockets and missiles fired against southern Israel and a constant thorn in the side of the Israeli Defense Forces. Israel has been goaded into military incursions against Hamas and other Islamic terrorist groups in Gaza in 2006, 2009, and again in 2012.

Further to the north is Turkey, which has turned from being pro-western to pro-Islamist, from being a military ally of Israel to being openly critical and hostile to Israel. Further to the east is Iraq and Iran. Iran is blatantly hostile to Israel and is seemingly pursuing a fast track course to obtain nuclear weapons. Iran is openly supported by Russia and China and more covertly by North Korea. Iran has repeatedly threatened to wipe Israel off the earth and claimed that Israel will soon cease to exist. Who will be the first to pull the proverbial trigger that starts the next Middle Eastern war?

For the purposes of examining Bible prophecy, we can consider Israel and Jerusalem to be the center of the geographic world. The Old Testament depicts Jerusalem and Israel as the spiritual center of the world in terms of God's relationship to the world. This pivotal theme is picked up again during the time of the end. Israel is certainly the center of God's prophetic events during the end-times. Any focus placed upon other nations in the Bible is there because it is relevant as to how it relates to the people and territory of Israel. According to Jewish tradition, Jerusalem and Israel are scripturally considered to be the center of the world or the navel of the earth (Ezek 5:5; 38:12; reflected in *Tanhuma* 106, and *Midrash Tanchumah K'doshim* 10).

There are several concentric circles – spheres of territory that surround Israel. Each sphere contains its own unique grouping of nations that will unite against Israel at a particular point on God's prophetic timeline. The predominant ethnic groups or nations within these various spheres will form alliances and confederations against Israel and attack or invade Israel at their appointed times. Each circle group reflects a different war on Israel's prophetic horizon.

**Israel the World's Target**

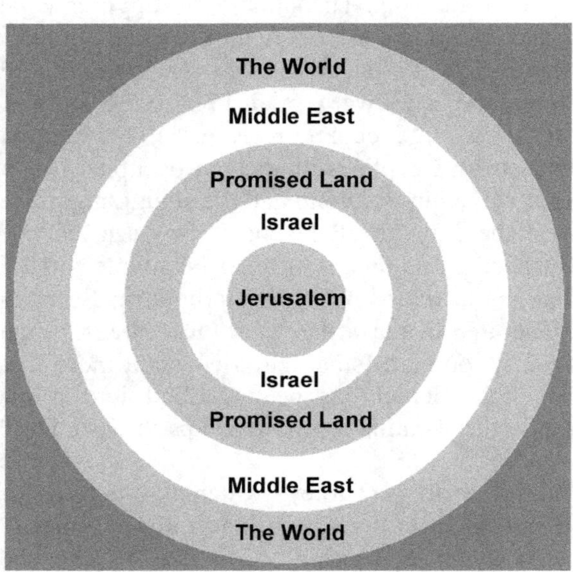


Israel sits in the center of the world as the bull's-eye of a target. Jerusalem is the ultimate prize.

An identifiable inner circle of Israel's enemies is predominantly situated within the geographical scope of the territory promised to Abraham, Isaac, and Jacob, and their descendants. This sphere is loosely surrounded by an outer circle of enemies comprising the greater Middle East, along with their primary military benefactor – Russia, and possibly portions of Central Asia. The outermost circle comprises all the nations of the world who will unite under ten kings. They will then be controlled by a one-world dictator and satanic theocrat who will rule the world as a god. All of the nations of the world will be brought against Israel during the Campaign of Armageddon.

Thus, if we imagine an archery target with the city of Jerusalem as the bull's-eye, we can view the concentric rings of the target as expanding circles of enemies surrounding Israel. Jerusalem is situated at the center of Israel and the West Bank. This is surrounded by a larger ring of territory comprising the remainder of the Promised Land (which Israel neither occupies nor controls) including: portions of the West Bank, Lebanon, Syria, the northern portion of Iraq, much of Jordan, Gaza, and the Sinai Peninsula up to what the Bible refers to as the "river of Egypt." This territory may also include land traveled by Israel during its wanderings at the time of its Exodus from Egypt including, portions of Egypt and portions of Saudi Arabia.

The area of the Promised Land is encompassed by the greater territory of the Middle East including: Cyprus, Turkey, Iran, Iraq, Kuwait, Saudi Arabia, Bahrain, Qatar, United Arab Emirates, Oman, and Yemen. For the purposes of this graphical image, the circle of the Middle East also includes: Egypt, Libya, Sudan, Eritrea, Ethiopia, and Somalia. The largest circle comprises the great expanse of the remainder of the entire world, particularly the three continents between which Israel and the Middle East form a central hub – Africa, Europe, and Asia. All the nations of the world will turn against Israel and will unite in coming against Jerusalem during the End Times.

## A Sequential Pattern

The attacks against Israel will come in successive waves. Each wave or war will be increasingly larger in scope, and the results of each war will be correspondingly greater in their effects. The smallest innermost circle will attack first, followed sometime later by the next larger circle, followed last by the outermost ring comprising all nations.

As a pebble is thrown into a pond and disturbs the water, the disturbance creates ripples that spread outward in expanding concentric circles. As the circles of Israel's enemies attack Israel one at a time, Israel's expansion of power and influence will ripple outward in increasing spheres of political, economic, and religious control. As the world increasingly turns against Israel and aggressively curses Israel by instigating warfare, God increasingly causes the curse to backlash upon the attackers. This results in a general corresponding principle – as Israel is attacked and subjected to multi-national invasion – Israel is rewarded with increasing amounts of territory and influence over the nations.

During the End Times, God's focus is on Israel with Jerusalem as the epicenter of the world's target. Israel is the anvil upon which God will progressively hammer the nations of the world. God will not pummel them all at once, but in phases over a period of several years. God will also use the nations as His hammer to progressively beat Israel into shape – to purify Israel in the forge of a cataclysmic conflict involving Heaven, the Abyss, and all of the nations.

There are two patterns that emerge throughout this study of God's prophetic drama. First, God's Day of the LORD will begin suddenly and catastrophically with a greatly intense series of events centered on Israel but impacting the entire world. This opening salvo is compared and contrasted to the even greater climactic series of events that will comprise Christ's Grand Finale. Second, the nations of the world attack Israel in waves or phases that increase in scope as the drama moves closer towards the end until all of the nations are simultaneously in view as coming against Jerusalem.

What I am dealing with in this chapter is the larger overview of that focus as it manifests in an identifiable sequential pattern. I am not trying to identify and incorporate every single war or military conflict that will take place in the prophetic future. There will be wars between nations that are not revealed in scripture because Israel is not the direct target. There will be some conflicts targeting Israel or directly affecting Israel or the central areas surrounding Israel that will take place between the primary phases of the overall pattern. These primary phases are like the acts of a play that God directs as He guides Israel and the nations of the world toward the crescendo of His Grand Finale.

We can deduce the repetition of a sequential pattern of nations coming against Israel during the End Times from scripture. God gives us a number of clues. These clues include: named alliances, territorial distinctions, behavioral characteristics of the attackers, how the conflict is won, and certain timing indicators. When we examine a future war involving Israel to determine when it will likely take place on the prophetic timeline, we should consider:

- Who is involved in the war? What nations or people groups are identified? Who initiates the conflict?
- What leaders are involved? Does the passage focus on a specific end-time leader or leaders? Is a leader identified for a nation or alliance of nations who unite to attack Israel?
- What geographical territory or territories are indicated as participating or being affected? What is the extent of the effects? Is territory gained for occupation? Is a city or area destroyed or abandoned? Is territory permanently desolated (like Sodom and Gomorrah)?
- Who wins the military conflict? Does Israel win because of the power of its military forces? Does God intervene supernaturally and win for His own purposes? Does the attacker or alliance against Israel gain a victory?
- What happens to the attacker's armed forces? Are the armies completely destroyed? Do some of the forces survive to escape or are they chased away? Are the dead soldiers buried or are they feasted upon by wild animals?

- What timing indicators or clues are present in the prophetic passage? Does it contain a reference to the Day of the LORD? Is there a reference to God's wrath? Is there a reference to the harvest being ripe or to the winepress? How does the conflict advance God's program toward the redemption of Israel?

**The Inner Circle – The Promised Land War**

At some point in the future, Israel must gain control over the land promised by God to its patriarchs. Most of this land is currently occupied and controlled by Arabs and Arab Palestinians. Israel cannot shrink any further and survive as a nation. Israel must expand its territory to allow for the immigration and settlement of additional Jews from the rest of the world, particularly from the United States. As a land and as a nation, Israel is the anvil upon which God is going to hammer the nations of the entire world. The process of the expansion of Israel's territory and sphere of control will start very early as a direct result of the military conflicts of the End Times.

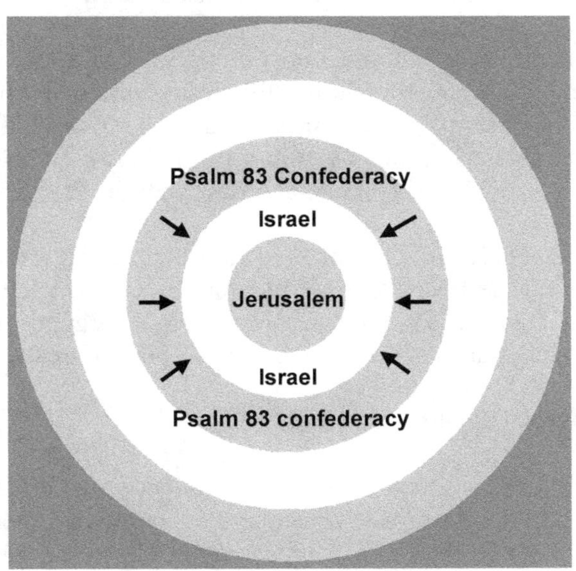


**The Curse:**
**The inner circle attacks Israel**

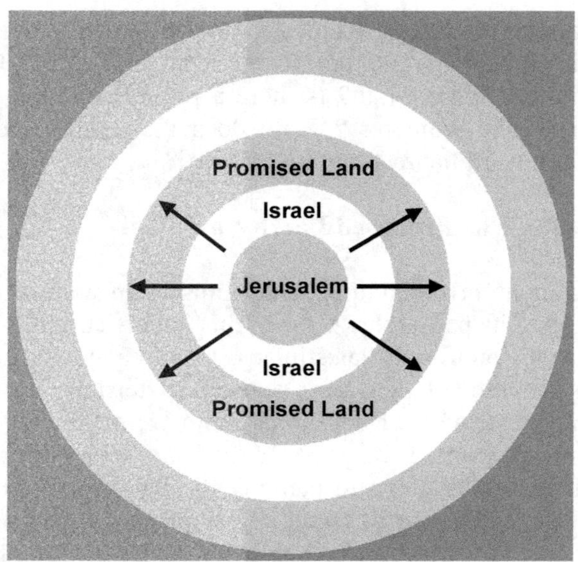


**God's Backlash:**
**Israel regains the Promised Land**

When the people of the innermost circle fully unite to curse Israel by instigating another Arab-Israeli war, the resulting curse from God will backlash upon them, resulting in their defeat and Israel's gaining control over all, or at least the majority, of the territory of the Promised Land. This inner circle is associated with the confederacy described in Psalm 83 and by the prophet Obadiah.

Israel will regain full control over Jerusalem and the Temple Mount. The territory of all the land promised to Israel by God (including: Lebanon, Syria, northern Iraq, Jordan, the Sinai portion of Egypt, Gaza, and the entirety of the West Bank) is destined to become part of greater Israel.

## Obadiah's Pattern – The Inner Circle

The Focus: The prophet Obadiah was given a vision by God against Edom. Edom (Esau) was a close relative and yet a perpetual enemy of Israel. Obadiah focuses on Edom and a confederacy of supposed friends of Edom who plan to rise up against Israel in warfare. At the time, Edom as a people has been made small among the nations and is identified as being "greatly despised" even by its so-called friends (Jer 49:15; Obad 1:2). It seems that the confederates act as though Edom is a pawn to be used in a strategic game against Israel. Obadiah's secondary focus is on the history of Edom's violence against Israel that just does not end. It seems to be the manifestation of a perpetual hatred.

The Timeframe: Just before the Day of the LORD. Obadiah specifically notes the timeframe as, "For the Day of the LORD draws near upon all of the nations" (Obad 1:15 NASB). When God and Jesus initiate their time of wrath as the Day of the LORD, it will be global in scope and impacting all nations, but not all at once. Edom's confederacy initiates warfare against Israel – just before the Day of the LORD (not that they know or acknowledge that it is coming – but God knows). Israel is targeted and attacked.

God's Backlash: God's "Code of Conduct" for the nations has been violated (Gen 12:3; 27:29). The curse directed at Israel by Edom and its confederates backlashes upon themselves. Obadiah emphatically makes this clear: "as thou hast done, it shall be done unto thee: thy reward shall return upon thine own head" (Obad 1:15).

The Aftermath: A united Israel becomes a fire that consumes its enemies. Israel defeats Edom and its confederates. Israel will occupy their lands. Israel "shall possess their possessions" (v. 17). Israel gains control over the Mount of Edom (Seir in Jordan), the plain of the Philistines (Gaza), Ephraim and Samaria (West Bank), and Gilead (part of Lebanon), the territory of the Canaanites even unto Zarephath (West Bank and areas of the Promised Land including the coastal area of Lebanon), and all of Jerusalem (which should include total control over the Temple Mount).

**Zephaniah's Pattern – The Inner Circle**

The Focus: Zephaniah opens with a warning regarding the approaching Day of the LORD. God has prepared a sacrifice. God has invited His guests – to bring them to punishment. The great day of the LORD is near, it is near! It comes quickly. It is a day of wrath (Zeph 1:7-8, 14-18). "Gather yourselves together, yea, gather together, O nation not desired; Before the decree bring forth, *before* the day pass as the chaff, before the fierce anger of the LORD come upon you, before the day of the LORD'S anger come upon you" (Zeph 2:1-2).

A contrasting focus is made in a call to the meek of the earth to seek God in repentance and righteousness as "it may be ye shall be hid in the day of the LORD'S anger" (Zeph 2:3). Who can be hid from God's anger just before or right at the beginning of the Day of the LORD? None of the Gentile nations can be hid from God. Neither can Israel be hid from God's anger at this time. They are all objects of God's judgment and intervention for the purpose of magnifying His own holy name. The only people who could qualify as the meek of the earth at this point in time, whose relationship to God's righteousness also qualifies them to receive God's judgment against the nations, is the believing body of Christians – the church. The church will be raptured and taken to heaven to be hid during the entire day of God's anger upon the earth. This is an argument for the rapture of the church to take place before or at the very beginning of the Day of the LORD.

There could be an interesting triple meaning in this passage. God is calling certain peoples to gather together for a certain purpose. Who is God calling and why?

- It could be Israel. Israel certainly could be referred to as the "nation not desired." The people of Israel need to gather together – be assembled out of the nations of their exile to return to the land. They need to gather in a spirit of repentance because God is going to bring judgment and wrath upon the nations. They need to do it before the Day of the LORD begins, as they are going to be the target.
- It could be Edom and its confederacy of nations bordering upon Israel. It could be a call to gather for war against Israel. They could be the first wave of invited guests to God's prepared sacrifice. As an enemy of Israel and an enemy of God, Edom has been made small among the nations and is greatly despised (Jer 49:15; Obad 1:2). Edom and her friends should come to God in a spirit of repentance because of their long history of violence against Israel.
- It could be the believers of the Christian church. They will be called by Christ to gather in the atmosphere for the "rapture" trip to heaven. The church is a nation not desired by the world system. The church is the most likely focus of the meek of the earth in verse 3.

Observe the parallel calls to gather together for war against Israel in Jeremiah 49, Obadiah, and Zephaniah 2, along with the parallel references to being despised or not desired.

- Jeremiah 49:14-15 – I have heard a rumour from the LORD, and an ambassador is sent unto the heathen, *saying*, Gather ye together, and come against her, and rise up to the battle. For, lo, I will make thee small among the heathen, *and* despised among men.
- Obadiah 1:1-2 – The vision of Obadiah. Thus saith the Lord GOD concerning Edom; We have heard a rumour from the LORD, and an ambassador is sent among the heathen, Arise ye, and let us rise up

against her in battle. Behold I have made thee small among the heathen: thou art greatly despised.

- Zephaniah 2:1 – Gather yourselves together, yea, gather together, O nation not desired;

An additional focus is placed upon the nations involved: Gaza, the coastal areas of the Philistines, Moab, Ammon, Cushites (Ethiopians or Sudanese), and Assyria. Except for Cush all of these peoples are included in Psalm 83. Cush is one of the allies mentioned in the Gog and Magog invasion of Israel (Ezek 38–39).

The Timeframe: Just before the Day of the LORD. The Day of the LORD is near – it is coming quickly!

God's Backlash: God brings judgment against certain nations and people groups. He does it because they reviled Israel and encroached upon its borders. "This they will have in return for their pride, because they have taunted and become arrogant against the people of the LORD of hosts" (Zeph 2:8, 10 NASB).

The Aftermath: Israel will possess the territories of these enemies. Gaza and the coastal areas will become habitations for Israel. Moab and Ammon will be made desolate as Sodom and Gomorrah, yet their territory shall be possessed by Israel. God will diminish the gods of the earth and people from different areas will begin to worship Him. The primary god of the Arab/Muslim nations involved in this judgment is Allah of Islam. Allah will begin to lose his enslavement of the Muslim peoples. The gods of the earth could also include: atheism, materialism, mammon, and other pagan gods.

## The Outer Circle – Gog & Magog

The second major war will see Russia and most of the remainder of the Middle Eastern nations uniting in an alliance and invading Israel. This is commonly known as the Invasion or War of Gog and Magog (Ezek 38–39). While the Israeli Defense Forces will be up to the task of defeating the confederacy of the inner circle, Israel will not be prepared to deal with the scope of this invasion by the outer ring. This aggression by the peoples of Gog and Magog cursing Israel will again backlash, this time with God intervening supernaturally to destroy the invading armies and bringing much destruction upon their homelands.

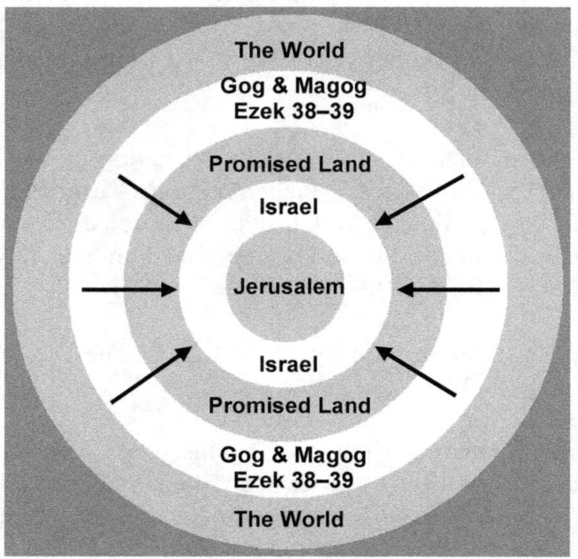


**The Alliance of Gog & Magog encompasses the Promised Land**

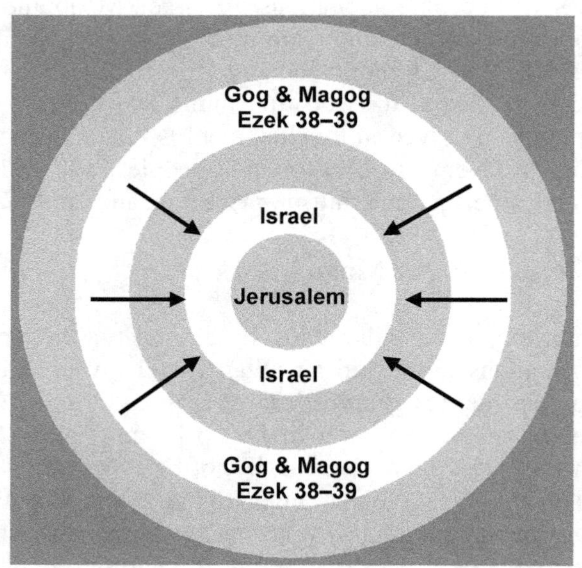


**The Curse:**
**The Alliance of Gog & Magog invades Israel**

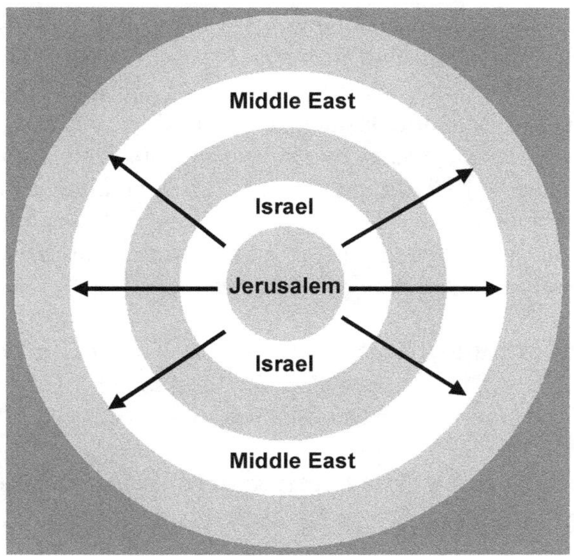


**God's Backlash:**
**Israel's sphere of influence expands over the Middle East**

Israel's sphere of influence will expand again to encompass the majority of the greater Middle East, North Africa, and Central Asia. Where the war involving the inner circle was an Arab-Israeli war for the territory of the Promised Land, Gog and Magog can be characterized as primarily a Muslim-Israeli war with an emphasis on the taking of spoils. God's wrathful intervention against Gog and Magog radically chastises and repudiates the religion of Islam. Allah is rendered incompetent.

In the realm of spiritual warfare, Satan loses his key power bases in Russia, Iran, and the religions of Atheism and Islam. Satan must now escalate his war against God by directly imitating God's Messiah. The Antichrist and the False Prophet must now rise to power. This will take some time during the aftermath of this war. This sets up the world for localized wars and false peace treaties in the power struggle for world domination. As George Martin titled one of his popular novels, the "Game of Thrones" is on.

The Aftermath: Israel will bury the dead and cleanse the land for a period of at least seven months. Gog and his armies will be buried in a mass grave on the east side of a sea – most likely the Dead Sea in the area of Jordan. Israel will spoil the defeated armies of the invaders by seizing the weapons and equipment of war and either burning them for fuel or converting them into fuel for energy for a period of seven years. God's supernatural intervention will have been so dynamic and Israel's survival and victory so great that Jews from around the world will rush to relocate to Israel. The world will be in complete shock. Jerusalem will become the "Mecca" of the world. There will be no Arab or Muslim obstacle to rebuilding the Jewish Temple in Jerusalem. The series of events encompassing Gog and Magog will be so global in effect and so devastating that it will be perceived as the fulfillment of the War of Armageddon. The time for the Messiah has come. Israel will seemingly be entering its "Golden Age" – for a time. But the storm clouds of war will eventually return. Israel will be betrayed.

Note: See the chapter titled *Ezekiel 38–39: The War of Gog and Magog* and my book *The Silence is Broken! God Hooks Ezekiel's Gog & Magog* for more detailed information regarding this war.

## The Outermost Circle – The Campaign of Armageddon

The Global Union, or the Global Confederacy of Ten Kingdoms represents the last and outermost circle to come against Israel. It comprises all the nations of the entire world existing at the time. The Bible makes no allowance for any exceptions (Isa 34:1-2; 43:9; Jer 25:29-33; Joel 3:2, 9-16; Zeph 3:8; Zech 12:1-9; 14:1-5; Rev 16:12-14; 19:11-21).

Zephaniah's Pattern – The Outermost Circle

> Therefore wait ye upon me, saith the LORD, until the day that I rise up to the prey: for my determination *is* to gather **the nations**, that I may assemble **the kingdoms**, to pour upon them mine indignation, *even* all my fierce anger: for **all the earth** shall be devoured with the fire of my jealousy. (Zeph 3:8 bold added)

Zephaniah mentions God's intent to gather the nations and the kingdoms to face His judgment. The focus is global – on all the earth. The combination of nations and kingdoms might seem strange at this point towards the end of the Tribulation when the world will be controlled by one theocratic dictator. However, it should be noted that scripture describes the world as being divided under the rulership of ten kings (kingdoms) who have subordinated their authority to the world dictator. The kings control the nations. Revelation 16:14 reveals that the evil spirits controlled by Satan, the Antichrist, and the False Prophet go out to "the kings of the earth" to gather them to the place called Armageddon. Satan is calling them to war against Israel and God, but God is gathering them for judgment.

Isaiah's Pattern – The Outermost Circle

> Come near, ye nations, to hear; and hearken, ye people: let the earth hear, and all that is therein; the world, and all things that come forth of it. For the indignation of the LORD *is* upon **all nations**, and *his* fury upon **all their armies**: he hath utterly destroyed them, he hath delivered them to the slaughter. (Isa 34:1-2 bold added)

Jeremiah's Pattern – The Outermost Circle

> For, lo, I begin to bring evil on the city which is called by my name, and should ye be utterly unpunished? Ye shall not be unpunished: for I will call for a sword upon **all the inhabitants of the earth**, saith the LORD of hosts. Therefore prophesy thou against them all these words, and say unto them, The LORD shall roar from on high, and utter his voice from his holy habitation; he shall mightily roar upon his habitation; he shall give a shout, as they that tread *the grapes*, against **all the inhabitants of the earth**. A noise shall come *even* to the ends of the earth; for the LORD hath a controversy with **the nations**, he will plead with **all flesh**; he will give them *that are* wicked to the sword, saith the LORD. Thus saith the LORD of hosts, Behold, evil shall go forth from nation to nation, and a great whirlwind shall be raised up from the coasts of the earth. And the slain of the LORD shall be at that day from *one* end of the earth even unto the *other* end of the earth: they shall not be lamented, neither gathered, **nor buried**; they shall be dung upon the ground. (Jer 25:29-33 bold added)

Jeremiah's focus is against all the nations in the context of all inhabitants of the earth and all of the territory of the earth. Jeremiah does not reference the nations being gathered against Israel in this passage, but is emphasizing the global scope of God's judgment.

Note that those slain by the LORD during this war are not going to be buried (Jer 25:33). This is to be contrasted with the very specific instructions in Ezekiel 39:11-16 for the burial of the dead soldiers and the cleansing of the land immediately following the War of Gog and Magog. Jeremiah is describing a different war and a different judgment from God, which must take place at a later time than Gog and Magog. Jeremiah's prophecy focused against all nations and all the inhabitants of the earth cannot be fulfilled before Ezekiel's prophecy against the few nations who participate in the alliance of Gog and Magog.

Joel's Pattern – The Outermost Circle

> I will gather **all nations** and bring them down to the valley of Jehoshaphat. Then will I enter into judgment with them there on behalf of My people and My inheritance, Israel, whom they have scattered among the nations; and they have divided up My land. …. Proclaim this among **the nations**: Prepare a war; rouse the mighty men! Let **all soldiers** draw near, let them come up! Beat your plowshares into swords and your pruning hooks into spears; Let the weak say, "I am a mighty man." Hasten and come, **all you surrounding nations**, and gather yourselves there. Bring down, O LORD, Your mighty ones. Let **the nations** be aroused and come up to the valley of Jehoshaphat, for there I will sit to judge **all the surrounding nations**. Put in the sickle, for the harvest is ripe. Come, tread, for the wine press is full; the vats overflow, for their wickedness is great. Multitudes, multitudes in the valley of decision! For the day of the LORD is near in the valley of decision. (Joel 3:2, 9-14 NASB, bold added)

Joel points to all the nations in the context of surrounding Israel. All the nations attack Israel. The wine press of iniquity is full! The Day of the LORD has been progressing for a number of years at this point, but now the end is in sight – it is near in the valley of decision. The mighty men assemble on earth and Christ returns with His mighty ones from heaven.

Zechariah's Pattern – The Outermost Circle

> Behold, I will make Jerusalem a cup of trembling unto all the people round about, when they shall be in the siege both against Judah *and* against Jerusalem. And in that day will I make Jerusalem a burdensome stone for all people: all that burden themselves with it shall be cut in pieces, though all the people of the earth be gathered together against it. …. And it shall come to pass in that day, *that* I will seek to destroy all the nations that come against Jerusalem. (Zech 12:2-3, 9)

In this passage Zechariah is focused on all who come against Jerusalem as opposed to specifically all nations. Although he is pointing towards the final phase of the Tribulation when all nations come against Israel, this passage applies to any and all attempts to attack Israel and Jerusalem.

> For I will gather **all nations** against Jerusalem to battle; and the city shall be taken, and the houses rifled, and the women ravished; and half of the city shall go forth into captivity, and the residue of the people shall not be cut off from the city. Then shall the LORD go forth, and fight against those nations, as when he fought in the day of battle. .... and the LORD my God shall come, *and* all the saints with thee. (Zech 14:2-3, 5 bold added)

Here Zechariah is focused on the end of the Tribulation when all nations are gathered against Jerusalem. This siege is interrupted by Jesus Christ when He returns with all of His saints and armies from heaven.

The Revelation Pattern – The Outermost Circle

> And I saw three unclean spirits like frogs *come* out of the mouth of the dragon, and out of the mouth of the beast, and out of the mouth of the false prophet. For they are the spirits of devils, working miracles, *which* go forth unto the **kings of the earth** and of **the whole world**, to gather them to the battle of that great day of God Almighty. ... And he gathered them together into a place called in the Hebrew tongue Armageddon. (Rev 16:13-14, 16 bold added)

Satan desires the nations to assemble to further his supernatural war against Israel and God; however, the "he" in Revelation 16:16 who gathers the armies is most likely God Himself. This is consistent with the Old Testament prophecies which clearly state that God will gather the nations against Israel and Jerusalem to face His judgment.

> And I saw heaven opened, and behold a white horse; and he that sat upon him *was* called Faithful and True, and in righteousness he doth judge and make war. His eyes *were* as a flame of fire, and on his head *were* many crowns; and he had a name written, that no man knew, but he himself. And he *was* clothed with a vesture dipped in blood: and his name

is called The Word of God. And the armies *which were* in heaven followed him upon white horses, clothed in fine linen, white and clean. And out of his mouth goeth a sharp sword, that with it he should smite **the nations**: and he shall rule them with a rod of iron: and he treadeth the winepress of the fierceness and wrath of Almighty God. And he hath on *his* vesture and on his thigh a name written, KING OF KINGS, AND LORD OF LORDS. .... And I saw the beast, and the **kings of the earth**, and **their armies**, gathered together to make war against him that sat on the horse, and against his army. And the beast was taken, and with him the false prophet that wrought miracles before him, with which he deceived them that had received the mark of the beast, and them that worshipped his image. These both were cast alive into a lake of fire burning with brimstone. And the remnant were slain with the sword of him that sat upon the horse, which *sword* proceeded out of his mouth: and all the fowls were filled with their flesh. (Rev 19:11-16, 19-21 bold added)

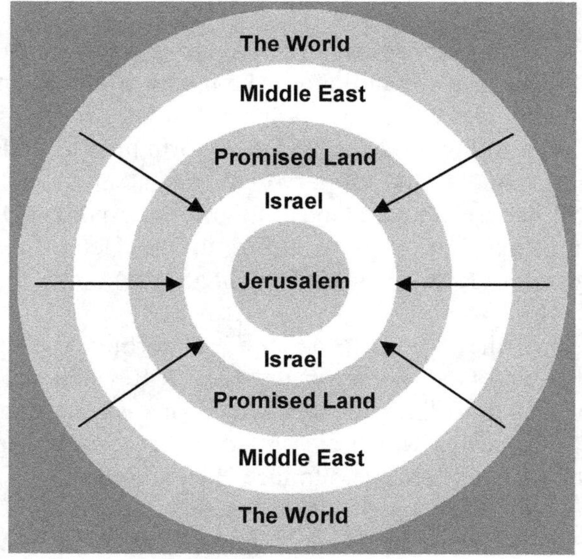


**The nations of the world assemble against Israel**

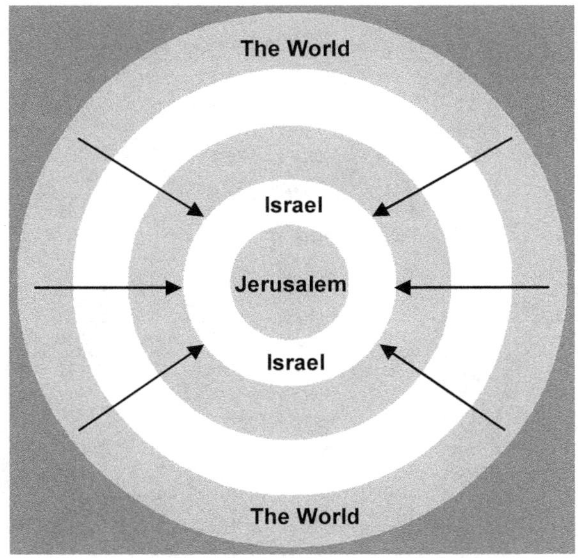


**The Curse:**
**The Campaign of Armageddon**

The Campaign of Armageddon will be the greatest war involving all nations, and it will come at the end of the Tribulation. This will be Satan's great assault against Israel and his stand against the return of Christ as the true Messiah. The nations will be under the control of Satan through his false-messiah the Antichrist, the False Prophet, and the ten kings of the world government.

This global attempt to curse Israel by bringing all the nations against her will result in the greatest backlash of all. Israel will finally awaken to the truth of Jesus Christ as God's Messiah and turn to Him for national redemption. Jesus will return when Israel calls for Him to come, and He will defeat the Antichrist and all of the world's armies assembled against Israel. Satan will be bound and cast into the Abyss for one thousand years. Israel's sphere of influence will then become global. Jerusalem will become the capital of the world. Jerusalem will be the seat of God's theocracy with Jesus Christ seated on His throne in glory. The theocratic dictatorship of Satan and the Antichrist will be swept away – to be replaced by the long promised Messianic Kingdom of God.

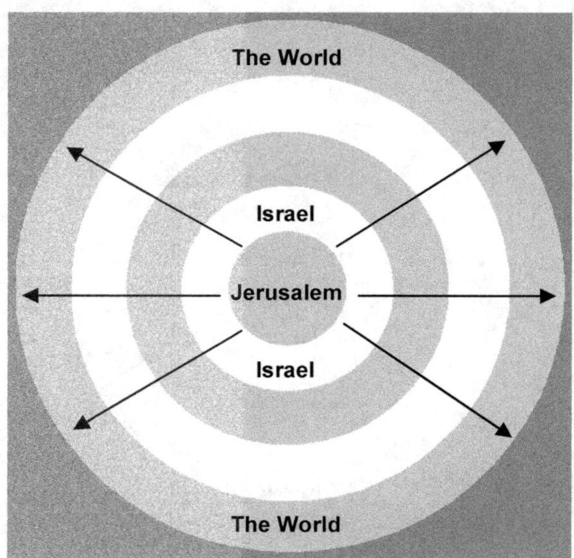


**God's Backlash:**
**Israel becomes the head of the nations**

Israel will completely occupy the full expanse of the Promised Land as its rightful possession. The nations will still exist within their allotted territories. However, since all nations will have oppressed Israel by coming against Jerusalem – all nations will have brought themselves under God's resulting curse instead of blessing – all nations shall lose their rights to individual and independent sovereignty. Israel will be the political, economic, and spiritual nucleus of the entire world. Israel will rule over the world, and the tail of the nations will finally become the head (Deut 15:6; 28:1, 13; Isa 14:1-2; 49:22-23; 60:1-7, 12; 61:6-7; 62:1-12; Ezek 45:1-8; 47:13-21; 48:1-29; Mic 4:1-5; Zech 14:16-21).

## Satan's Final Rebellion – The Four Quarters of the Earth

There is one final assault against Jerusalem that is global in scope, but it will not take place until the end of the Millennium. Following Christ's revelation and victory at the time of Armageddon, Satan will be imprisoned in the Abyss for a specific period of 1,000 years (Rev 20:2-3). Following his release he will instigate his final attempt to make war against God. Satan will go out to deceive the nations, Gog and Magog, and gather peoples from the four quarters (or corners) of the earth against God's holy city (Rev 20:7-10).

The passive reference to Gog and Magog is not a time indicator for Ezekiel's prophetic war, but a historical symbol for God's supernatural intervention and complete control over His enemies. Naturally, Satan fails again. God intervenes and defeats the rebellion by raining fire upon them from heaven. There is no actual mention of warfare. The rebels assemble and God simply wipes them out. Satan is then cast into the Lake of Fire.

God's backlash is simple. Satan is finished. Rebellion and sin against God is now a thing of the past. The time for universal cleansing has finally come. Scripture immediately enters into a description of God's final judgment – the Great White Throne Judgment. Following that judgment God creates a new heaven and a new earth. The Eternal State begins with the heavenly city of New Jerusalem coming down upon the new earth.

Note: See Appendix 1: *Satan's Little Season* for more detail regarding the timing of this rebellion.

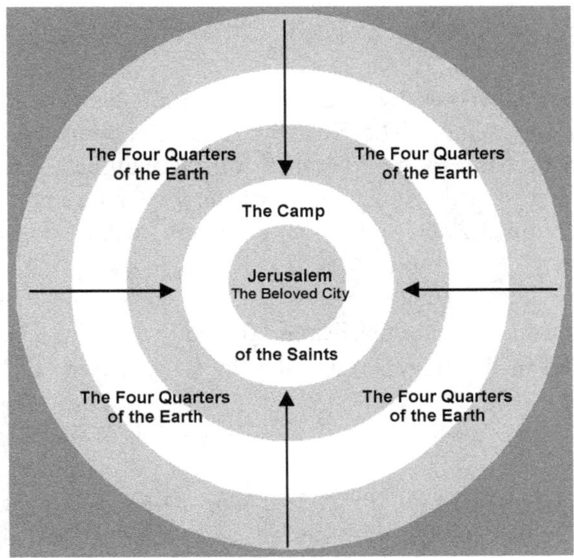


**Satan's Final Rebellion**

# 8

# The Psalm 83 Confederacy

## A Prayer for God's Intervention to Defend Israel

### The Author – the Prophet Asaph

Psalm 83 was written by a Kohathite of the tribe of Levi (1 Chr 6:33-39) by the name of Asaph. The Kohathites were descendants of Kohath, a son of Levi (Ex 6:16). Moses and Aaron were Kohathites (Ex 6:16-20). The Kohathites were responsible for the Ark of the Covenant and the furniture of the sanctuary (Num 3:27-31). The name Asaph means "collector." Asaph was:

- The author of 12 Psalms (Psalm 50, and Psalms 73-83).
- The chief of the singers appointed by King David (1 Chr 15:19; Neh 12:46).
- The chief Levite ministering before the Ark of the Covenant (1 Chr 16:4-5, 37).
- A seer (prophet) (1 Chr 25:2; 2 Chr 29:30). First Chronicles 25:2 indicates that Asaph prophesied according to the order of King David. Second Chronicles 29:30 reveals that at the time of King Hezekiah, the king and the leaders of Judah recognized Asaph as being a prophet during the time of King David and that they valued the written words of both King David and Asaph.

### Psalm 83 – A Song *or* Psalm of Asaph

- A prayer – A plea to God for God's intervention.

- A prophecy – The identification of a very specific future confederacy that will attempt to destroy the nation of Israel. The focus of this prophecy is not that these enemies will come against Israel individually, or one at a time over time, but that they will all join together against Israel simultaneously, in a coordinated and concerted effort, in an attempt to eliminate Israel as a nation.
- Written during the time of King David, prior to the division of the Kingdom of Israel into the northern and southern Kingdoms after the death of Solomon, this prophecy looks far into the future and focuses on Israel as a single nation at the time these enemies arise united as allies against Israel.

## The Plea (Psalm 83:1-4)

> Keep not thou silence, O God: hold not thy peace, and be not still, O God. For, lo, thine enemies make a tumult: and they that hate thee have lifted up the head. They have taken crafty counsel against thy people, and consulted against thy hidden ones. They have said, Come, and let us cut them off from *being* a nation; that the name of Israel may be no more in remembrance.

- The silence of God – A plea for God to break His silence. God has been silent to Israel for many centuries. When Israel's leaders rejected Jesus as God's Messiah sent to Israel in fulfillment of God's prophetic scriptures, God rejected the nation of Israel. God essentially told Israel, "You are not my people, and I will not be your God." This rejection by God placed Israel under all of the supernatural curses recorded in Deuteronomy 28. However, Israel's rejection by God would only be temporary. The day will come when a nation comprising all of the united tribes of Israel will be remembered by God, and God will reclaim Israel as His people (Hos 1:9-11; 2:19-23). The day will come when God will break His silence.
- The enemies of Israel are the enemies of God. Asaph argues that it is not only the nation of Israel that is threatened or targeted by these enemies. The peoples who make up this confederacy are God's enemies in that the God of Israel is their enemy. They hate the God of Israel (v. 2), and they have formed the confederacy against God as much as against Israel (v. 5). Without specifically saying it, Asaph is inferring that God's holy name as the God of Israel is at stake. The

Psalm 83 confederacy will raise its ugly head against Israel. If it is successful in eliminating Israel as a nation, or even pushing Israel out of the land, then God will have been proved a liar and impotent to protect Israel. Asaph views this as a double reason that God must intervene to defend Israel.

- Israel is referred to as thy people, God's "hidden ones" ("treasured ones" NASB, "protected ones" RSV, "those you cherish" NIV). When Israel came to Mt. Sinai following its Exodus out of Egypt, God informed Moses that Israel would be a "peculiar treasure" to Him (Ex 19:3-5). This claim of Israel being God's peculiar treasure is repeated in Psalm 134:4. "For the LORD hath chosen Jacob unto himself, *and* Israel for his peculiar treasure." Israel's relationship as a peculiar people to God is also mentioned in Deuteronomy 14:2 and 26:18. Psalm 91 poetically reveals that, "He that dwelleth in the secret place of the most High shall abide under the shadow of the Almighty. I will say of the LORD, *He is* my refuge and my fortress: my God; in him will I trust" (Ps 91:1-2).
- The conspiracy: Wipe Israel off the map! Let Israel cease as a nation! The objective is to accomplish this so completely that even the name of Israel will not be remembered. This has been the sentiment and characteristic behavior of the Arab nations surrounding Israel who fought unsuccessful wars against it in 1948, 1956, 1967, and 1973. Their desire was to push Israel into the sea and erase it from the land. While Iran is not one of the confederate enemies specifically identified in Psalm 83, it is a direct supporter and enabler of some of them. The world has repeatedly witnessed the blatant and flagrant expression of this exact anti-Israel sentiment from Mahmoud Ahmadinejad, while he was President of Iran. It remains the prevailing attitude of the Palestinian Authority in the West Bank and Islamic terrorist groups such as Hamas in Gaza, Hezbollah in Lebanon, as well as Islamic Jihad, and Al Qaeda.

## The Inner Circle – The Confederates (Psalm 83:5-8)

> For they have consulted together with one consent: they are confederate against thee: The tabernacles [tents] of Edom, and the Ishmaelites; of Moab, and the Hagarenes; Gebal, and Ammon, and Amalek; the Philistines with the inhabitants of Tyre; Assur also is joined with them: they have holpen the children of Lot. Selah.

- A confederacy of ten entities comes together for one common purpose – to destroy Israel. These ten enemies of God and Israel are: Edom, Ishmaelites, Moab, Hagarenes, Gebal, Ammon, Amalek, Philistines, Tyre, and Assur.
- Edom – descendants of Esau = Southern Jordan. While the territory of Edom was originally located and confined to the area of Mt. Seir southeast of the Dead Sea, the Edomites later expanded into southern Judah and were also known as the Idumeans (Greek for Edomites). Edom is the first enemy identified by Asaph. There is generally a primacy of importance placed upon the first entry in a list of enemies or adversaries in the Bible. That is probably the case with this list. They are the closest blood relatives of Israel on the list as Esau (Edom) was the brother of Jacob (Israel). Edom had a long tumultuous and vacillating history with Israel. There were periods of animosity and fighting against Israel, periods of being subjected to Israel, short periods of being allies with Israel, and periodical rebellions against Israel. Israel finally subdued the Edomites (Idumeans) during the time of the Maccabeans, and they were somewhat integrated into the Jewish society and religion by being circumcised. King Herod was an Idumean who gained rulership over Judea through his relationship to Rome.
- The Tents of Edom – Edom is the only enemy on the list to be described by the manner of their habitation as being that of tents or tabernacles. Bill Salus, in his books, *Isralestine* and *Psalm 83*, draws a connection between the Edomites and some of the modern Palestinians. He makes the observation that many of the Palestinians have been living in refugee camps (tents) ever since the unsuccessful war in 1948, when several Arab nations failed to keep Israel from becoming reborn as a nation. The surrounding Arab nations have, for the most part, refused to assimilate the Arab Palestinians into their societies and grant them citizenship. This refugee status of a Palestinian people without a nation has been the lit fuse on a Middle Eastern time-bomb that has been manipulated and kept smoldering as an ever present pretense for war against Israel. It is the convenient excuse through which the ancient hatred against Israel is kept burning in anger. All attempts to resolve this problem have failed because the Palestinians (pushing against Israel) and the Arab nations (who keep the Palestinians pushing against Israel) do not want any permanent resolution short of the complete elimination of Israel.

- Ishmaelites – 12 tribes of Arabs = Arabia. The descendants of Ishmael, the son of Abraham and Hagar (Sarah's Egyptian handmaid), who originated from Ishmael's twelve sons (Gen 25:12-16).
- Hagarenes – Hagarites (descendants of Hagar, the Egyptian mother of Ishmael), or possibly Arameans from the area of Damascus and Syria.
- Gebal – An area in the region of Edom between Petra and the Dead Sea; also an ancient Phoenician seaport in Lebanon (Ezek 27:9) sometimes referred to as Byblos.
- Amalek – Amalekites (descendants of Esau's grandson Amalek) = Sinai Peninsula. The territory of the Amalekites ranged from the Negev desert down through the Sinai Peninsula to Egypt and over to the northwest portion of Arabia.
- Philistines – the coastal area to the southwest of Israel = Gaza.
- Tyre – Ancient Phoenician seaport = Lebanon.
- Assur – Asshur the chief god of Assyria = Syria and northern Iraq.
- Children of Lot – Ammon and Moab = Northern and central Jordan.
- A confederate circle – the inner circle of Arab/Moslem nations surrounding Israel: The Palestinians (Gaza & West Bank), Egypt, Jordan, Syria, Lebanon and possibly portions of Iraq and Saudi Arabia. These groups that are specifically named in the confederacy against Israel will likely be supported by other Arab or Moslem nations which lie outside this inner circle of Israel's immediate neighbors. They may receive political, economic, logistical, or military support from nations such as Iran, Turkey, Libya, Qatar, and Saudi Arabia. They may be supported in some manner by non-Arabic or non-Moslem nations such as Russia, China, North Korea, or Venezuela. However, Asaph's prophetic prayer is focused on these named entities that form an immediate and adjoining presence in the midst and encircling the nation of Israel.
- This prophetic war can be thought of as the Promised Land War. This confederacy essentially represents various people groups located within the territorial boundaries of the Promised Land. They will attack Israel from within the scope of the territory that God promised to Jacob and his descendants. They will attack for the purpose of eliminating Israel as a nation and gaining the small portion of the Promised Land that Israel does possess.
- This specific confederacy of Israel's enemies never completely unified during ancient times. This unity began to emerge with the rebirth of Israel in 1948, and combinations of these enemies have

fought against Israel in several wars since. This confederacy is still in the process of unifying, in spite of Israel's peace accords with Egypt and Jordan, and will completely and simultaneously fight against Israel at some time in the future. With the uprising of the "Arab Spring" and the resulting ascendancy of the Muslim Brotherhood to power in Egypt (even if only temporary), there is ample evidence that the peace accord between Egypt and Israel is threatened. It is also evident that the Muslim Brotherhood has the monarchy of Jordan in its sights and desires to gain power over the Kingdom of Jordan. This threat to the stability of the monarchy of Jordan is also a threat to the peace treaty between Jordan and Israel. Regardless of the viability of the peace treaties between Israel and Egypt and Jordan, Israel is not surrounded by friends. While the Psalm 83 confederacy does not seem to be completely of one mind at the present time, conditions on the ground in the Middle East can change very quickly. An imminent coordinated attack may not be looming against Israel today, but it could easily come tomorrow.

- The Possible Territory of the Psalm 83 Confederacy

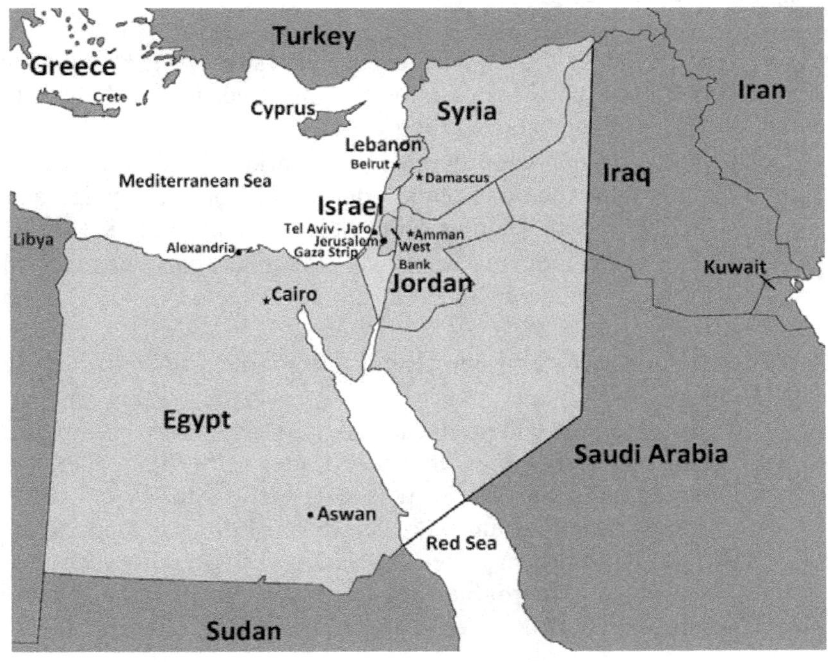


**The Possible Territory of the Psalm 83 Confederacy**

## A Comparison to History (Psalm 83:9-12)

> Do unto them as *unto* the Midianites; as *to* Sisera, as *to* Jabin, at the brook of Kison: *Which* perished at Endor: they became *as* dung for the earth. Make their nobles like Oreb, and like Zeeb: yea, all their princes as Zebah, and as Zalmunna: Who said, Let us take to ourselves the houses of God in possession.

Asaph points his finger at the Midianites as an example of an enemy of God and Israel. The Midianites were descendants of Midian, a son of Abraham by Keturah (Gen 25:1-2). The Midianites were distant relatives, yet constant enemies of Israel. During the time of Israel's judges, God raised up Gideon as a leader from among Israel to deliver Israel from the incursion of the Midianites (Judg 6–8). Under God's guidance Gideon's feats were mighty and miraculous. With God's help a small force can easily defeat a much larger army.

Asaph's specific examples include:

- The defeat of the Canaanite army of Jabin, king of the Canaanites, and Sisera, his general, at the Kishon River in the Valley of Jezreel, by Deborah and Barak (Judg 4:1-22).
- Oreb, and Zeeb were two Midianite princes who were defeated and killed by the men of Ephraim during Gideon's campaign against the Midianites (Judg chapter 7, but Judg 7:25; and Judg 8:3 specifically).
- Zebah, and Zalmunna were two Midianite kings decisively defeated and slain by Gideon (Judg 8:5-21).

## A Request for God's Supernatural Intervention (Psalm 83:13-17)

> O my God, make them like a wheel; as the stubble before the wind. As the fire burneth a wood, and as the flame setteth the mountains on fire; So persecute them with thy tempest, and make them afraid with thy storm. Fill their faces with shame; that they may seek thy name, O LORD. Let them be confounded and troubled for ever; yea, let them be put to shame, and perish:

Long before this attack is going to take place against Israel, Asaph pleads with God in intercessionary prayer asking for God's intervention. Asaph requests:

- That God make these enemies to be like a wheel, which is to say like dust caught in a whirlwind, or chaff blown away by the wind, or even blown around like tumble weed (Job 21:18; Ps 1:4; 35:5; Isa 5:24; 17:13; 29:5; 33:10-13; 41:13-16; Hos 13:3; Zeph 2:2).
- That these enemies become like a forest caught in a forest fire, unable to move to get away, as a roaring fire rushes across the ground, through the trees, and up the slopes of the mountains (Isa 5:24; 10:16-17; 29:6; 30:30; 47:14; Ezek 20:47-48; Joel 2:5; Obad 1:18).
- That God should pursue them with His tempest, and terrorize them with His storm. Asaph knew that God uses the elements of nature for His weapons: overflowing rain, hail, wind, fire from heaven, and earthquakes (Job 38:22-23; Ps 11:6; Isa 28:2; 29:6; 30:30; Amos 1:14; Ezek 38:22).
- That God should fill their faces with shame. Asaph desires that these enemies of Israel be judged for their hatred against God and Israel. They should be disgraced, dishonored, humiliated, and full of shame. Asaph is not asking for a temporary judgment from God or a temporary reversal of these enemies' attitude and behavior. Asaph desires a permanent solution and resolution to this hatred. The entities of this confederacy need to be confronted with the sovereignty of God, so that they may seek the name of the one true God (Ps 35:26; Isa 17:7; Ezek 36:7, 23; 38:23; 39:7). Otherwise, they deserve nothing less than to perish completely.

## The Ultimate Purpose (Psalm 83:18)

> That *men* may know that thou, whose name alone *is* JEHOVAH, *art* the most high over all the earth.

God's holy name is a dominant theme running throughout prophetic passages. God will magnify His name – in Israel, in the nations surrounding Israel, and throughout the entire world. Ultimately, God will rise up in supernatural intervention to defend Israel, not because Israel inherently deserves God's protection, or has earned God's favor, but because God will defend and magnify His own holy name (Isa 17:7; Ezek 20:44; 36:23; 38:23; 39:7, 21-22; Mal 1:11).

## Psalm 83 vs. Armageddon

There are some scholars who believe that Psalm 83 will be fulfilled during the War of Armageddon at the end of the Tribulation. A significant problem with this interpretation is that Psalm 83 describes a regional conspiracy against Israel focused on the close neighbors immediately surrounding it. At the time of the Campaign of Armageddon, all the nations of the world will assemble against Israel (Joel 3:2; Amos 9:9; Zech 12:3; 14:2). Asaph and the other prophets such as Amos, Joel, and Zechariah were prophetically envisioning very different situations.

Israel is surrounded by several circles of enemies. Why does Psalm 83 only focus on the innermost circle of enemies if the psalm is fulfilled in the context of Armageddon which entails the largest circle of enemies? This is also an issue in comparing Psalm 83 to the Gog and Magog invasion of Israel in Ezekiel 38–39. Ezekiel describes a detailed alliance of enemies surrounding Israel; however, none of those identified actually border Israel. Gog does not directly control the inner circle. Gog's alliance is an outer circle of enemies, and yet it is still limited in scope. Gog does not control all of the armies of the world. Gog does not lead all nations against Jerusalem.

Psalm 83 describes a coordinated confederacy in conspiracy or "crafty counsel" against Israel, but there is no reference to an all out satanic war against Israel and God as there is in Revelation 16:13-14 and 19:11-21. There is no reference to any specific leader as "supreme commander" wielding supernatural powers such as the Antichrist and the False Prophet. Asaph makes no specific reference to God's Day of the LORD. There is no indication that Asaph has been given any vision of the catastrophic state of Israel or the world at large as it will be during the end of the Great Tribulation after being bombarded by God's judgments in wrath (7 Seals; 7 Trumpets; 7 Bowls) for at least seven years before the Campaign of Armageddon is in full swing.

Asaph's prayer to God in Psalm 83 is not a response to a vision of either the invasion of Gog and Magog or the War of Armageddon. It is a separate and distinct prophecy pertaining to a serious but limited regional war. This observation is not intended to diminish the importance of Asaph's plea to God in Psalm 83. If the intention of this Psalm 83 confederacy in wiping Israel off the map was successful, then God's plan for Israel would be thwarted. What purpose after that would there be for either the Gog and Magog invasion or for all nations to come against Jerusalem? God will not let that happen.

It should also be noted that once either larger war, Gog and Magog or Armageddon, erupts and runs its prophetic course, the conditions for the fulfillment of the Psalm 83 confederacy will no longer exist. Since Psalm 83 cannot be fulfilled after either of the wars comprising a larger circle of enemies, it must take place at an earlier point in time. Unfortunately, Psalm 83 does not tell the entire story.

## God's Response

Psalm 83 does not reveal God's answer to Asaph's prayer. We must look to other prophecies to see the form that God's intervention will take in His defense of Israel.

Prophecies against the Confederates of Psalm 83:

- Edom (Mt. Seir, Idumea, Teman): Num 24:17-19; Ps 60:8-9; 108:9-10; 137:7; Isa 11:14; 34:5-6; 63:1; Jer 49:7-22; Lam 4:21-22; Ezek 25:12-14; 35:2-15; 36:5; Joel 3:19; Amos 1:11-12; 9:12; Obad 1:1-21; Mal 1:3-4. The territory of Edom shall become a possession of Israel and ultimately a perpetual desolation like Sodom and Gomorrah. The descendants of Esau (Edom) will be made small among the nations and despised among men (Jer 49:15; Obad 1:2). The sins of Edom (Mt. Seir) will never escape God's judgment. Her chief sin is her perpetual hatred against Israel, and God decrees the curse of blood for blood against Edom (Ezek 35:5). Edom will be conquered by Israel (Ezek 25:14). Obadiah plainly states that the united houses of Israel will burn the house of Esau until "there shall not be *any* remaining of the house of Esau" (Obad 1:18). Esau is such an enemy of his brother Jacob, whose perpetual hatred for Israel was passed down to his descendants throughout the ages to such an extent, that God declared through the prophet Malachi that He actually hated Esau (Mal 1:3).
- Ammon: Isa 11:14; Jer 49:1-6; Ezek 25:1-7; Amos 1:13-15; Zeph 2:8-11. While in the past Ammon was conquered by the Babylonians, in the future Israel (a united Ephraim and Judah) will conquer Ammon (modern Jordan) and subject her people (Isa 11:13-14). Israel will become heir of the Ammonites when their capital is a desolate heap (Rabbah = modern Amman) as a result of war (Jer 49:2). Ammon will become a perpetual desolation like Gomorrah. It shall be spoiled and possessed by Israel (Zeph 2:8-9).
- Moab: Num 24:17; Ps 60:8; 108:9; Isa 11:14; 15:1-16:14; 25:10-11; Jer 48:1-47; Ezek 25:8-11; Amos 2:1-3; Zeph 2:8-11. The prophetic future of Moab's descendants is often intertwined with those descended from his brother Ammon. Moab will become a perpetual

desolation like Sodom. It shall be spoiled and possessed by Israel (Zeph 2:8-9). "And Moab shall be destroyed from *being* a people, because he hath magnified *himself* against the LORD" (Jer 48:42).

- Ishmaelites (Arabs): The Ishmaelites are Arabs descended from Ishmael, whose father was Abraham and whose mother was Hagar. Both Ishmael's mother and wife were Egyptians. The twelve tribes of Ishmaelites are generally associated with the northern and central regions of the Arabian Desert; however, they dwelt throughout the expanse of territory extending from the Euphrates River all the way down to Egypt. One of the primary tribes was Kedar. Ezekiel mentions "Arabia, and all of the princes of Kedar" (Ezek 27:21), and Isaiah connects an ancient prophetic burden against Arabia with the failing glory of Kedar (Isa 21:13-17). Jeremiah chapter 49, which contains prophecies against several of the peoples included in the confederacy of Psalm 83, also has a focus on Kedar and the kingdoms of Hazor (Jer 49:28-33). Where this prophecy begins with the now past military action of the king of Babylon against Kedar and Hazor (Arabia), it reaches into the future with conditions unfulfilled in ancient times. The Arabians will be defeated militarily and scattered throughout the world ("into all winds"). Ultimately Hazor will become "a dwelling for dragons, *and* a desolation for ever: there shall be no man abide there, nor *any* son of man dwell in it."
- Hagarenes (Hagarites, Hagerites, or Hagrites): Isa 19:1-25; Ezek 29:1-16; Joel 3:19. Generally considered to be Arabs and the descendants of Hagar (the Egyptian mother of Ishmael), from whom this name seems to be derived. Hagarenes shows up only one time in the KJV in Psalm 83:6; however, the same Hebrew word is also variously translated as Hagarites, Hagerites, and Hagrites. Some associate the Hagarenes with Egypt because of Hagar's Egyptian origin, also noting that Hagar took an Egyptian to be Ishmael's wife. However, the Hagarites, along with some Ishmaelites, appear as a group of Arabs who fought against the tribes of Reuben, Gad, and Manasseh in the territory of Gilead east of the Jordan River during the days of King Saul (1 Chr 5:10, 18-22). As such the Hagarites could be either associated with the Arabian Desert or with Aram (Syria) to the north.
    - If we associate the Hagarenes with Egypt then we look to Isaiah 19:1-25; Ezekiel 29:1-16; 30:2-8; and Joel 3:19 to find that Egypt will undergo a time of civil war and internal strife that leads into events resulting in extreme desolation. Where

God gave Egypt over to the king of Babylon for judgment in ancient times, Israel will be God's instrument against Egypt in the future. It is likely that we are witnessing the beginning of these events with the Arab Spring turmoil that has engulfed Egypt, the ascendency of the Muslim Brotherhood to power, and the backlash intervention of Egypt's military. It is also likely that Egypt will break its peace treaty with Israel, probably in support of the Psalm 83 confederacy, and Israel will be forced to take strong military action against Egypt. Egypt will undergo a series of conflicts during the End Times. Isaiah 19 describes the beginning of these troubled times and directly attributes Israel (Judah) as becoming a terror to Egypt as a judgment from God.

- If we associate the Hagarenes with the Arabs related to the Ishmaelites, then we look to the prophetic fate of the Ishmaelites noted above.
- If the Hagarenes are Arabs from the area of Aram (Syria), then they are connected to the fate of Assur noted below.

- Amalek (Amalekites): Ex 17:14-16; Num 24:20; Deut 25:19; 1 Sam 15:2-3. God declared to Moses, "I will utterly put out the remembrance of Amalek from under heaven" (Ex 17:14). God then expanded on His condemnation of Amalek by claiming that God had sworn to have war against Amalek "from generation to generation" (Ex 17:16). It seems that the goal of the Psalm 83 confederacy – "that the name of Israel may be no more in remembrance" – will backfire on the Amalekites to the extent that the name of Amalek will no longer be remembered. When Moab hired the prophet Balaam to curse the tribes of Israel during the time of their wanderings before entering the Promised Land, Balaam's curse backfired in several ways. One of the backfires applied to Amalek. "And when he [Balaam] looked on Amalek he took up his parable, and said, Amalek *was* the first of the nations; but his latter end *shall be* that he perish for ever" (Num 24:20). The Amalekites were the first of the nations to attack the Israelites following their escape from Egypt during the Exodus. This early hatred against Israel sealed Amalek's fate (Ex 17:14-16; 1 Sam 15:2-3). However, it is interesting that the full blotting out of the memory of Amalek does not come until the very end, after Israel is finally dwelling at peace in the Promised Land given to it for an inheritance (Deut 25:19).
- Philistines (Philistia, Gaza): Ps 60:8; 108:9; Isa 11:14; Jer 47:4-7; Ezek 25:15-17; Amos 1:6-8; Obad 1:19; Zeph 2:4-7; Zech 9:5-6. The

ancient coastal territory of the Philistines is the modern Gaza Strip of the Palestinians. In 135 A.D. the Romans renamed the territory of Judah as Palaestina (Palestine) in an attempt to erase the name and memory of Israel from the land. The name Palestine was chosen because of the ancient and long standing conflict between the Philistines and Israel and to associate the land with the Philistines instead of Israel. While the modern Arabic Palestinians are not the direct descendants of the Philistines, the future prophetic reference to the Philistines directly targets the peoples inhabiting the specific coastal territory of ancient Philistia situated between Israel and the Sinai Peninsula. King David prayed to God for victory over the Philistines. Jeremiah prophesied that God would cause the Philistines to be defeated and spoiled and cut off from the land (Jer 47:1-7). After many conflicts and defeats to Israel, the Philistines were finally defeated by Nebuchadnezzar (the King of Babylon) and deported. However, some prophetic passages against the Philistines are seemingly unfulfilled.

- Ezekiel 25:15-17 – In a chapter that also focuses on God's enmity against Ammon, Moab, and Edom, all confederates in Psalm 83, God gives Ezekiel a prophecy aimed at the Philistines. The attitude attributed to the Philistines is precisely characteristic of the modern Arabic Palestinians living in Gaza: "Because the Philistines have dealt by revenge, and have taken vengeance with a despiteful heart, to destroy *it* for the old hatred" (Ezek 25:15). The modern Palestinians desire to destroy Israel because of the "old hatred," or the longstanding enmity that existed between Philistia and Israel and between Edom and Israel. God will stretch out His hand and "destroy the remnant of the sea coast." The modern Palestinians in Gaza are the remnant of the sea coast.
- Isaiah 11:11-15 – Isaiah 11 is another prophecy that focuses on several of the Psalm 83 confederates including: Edom, Moab, Ammon, the Philistines, and the area down to the Nile River in Egypt. At a time after the outcasts of Israel are regathered from the nations and Judah and Ephraim are reunited as one, Israel "shall fly upon the shoulders of the Philistines toward the west" (v. 14). The fulfillment of this prophecy has only been possible since the rebirth of the modern nation of Israel. Israel's army and air forces will defeat the area of Gaza at a time when Israel will

simultaneously defeat the territories of Ammon, Moab, and Edom.
    - Amos 1:8 – The remnant of the Philistines shall perish.
    - Obadiah 1:19 – Israel will possess the plain of the Philistines at the same time that Israel expands its territory to encompass the mount of Esau (Edom), the fields of Ephraim and the fields of Samaria (West Bank), and Gilead (territory east of the Jordan River in northern modern Jordan).
    - Zephaniah 2:7 – The coast of the Philistines (Gaza) will be a possession for the remnant of the house of Judah (Israel).
- Gebal: What geographic area and what people is Asaph pointing to in his inclusion of Gebal in his list of Psalm 83 confederates? There are two possible choices.
    - In the context of the enemies identified in this psalm, many scholars take Gebal to be a mountainous area between Petra (in Edom) and the Dead Sea. It is said to be Gibal in modern Jordan. As such it is easily associated with Edom, Moab, and Ammon. This area would share the prophetic fate of Moab and Edom.
    - The second choice is a better known and more easily identified Gebal. Gebal was a very important Phoenician seaport on the Lebanese coast north of modern Beirut. Gebal is also known by its Greek name Byblos and is depicted on Bible maps by either or both names. Gebal (Byblos) is depicted on modern maps as Jubayl, Jbail, or Jubeil. In this context Gebal is easily seen associated with another ancient Phoenician seaport and Psalm 83 confederate, Tyre.
- Tyre (Tyrus): Isa 23:1-18; Jer 47:4; Ezek 26:2-21; 28:1-12; Amos 1:9-10; Zech 9:2-4. Tyre was a Phoenician seaport on the coast of southern Lebanon comprising two cities, one on the mainland and one situated on a small island nearby. The primary prophecies directed against Tyre predicted its complete destruction, although not permanently. The mainland city of Tyre was conquered by Nebuchadnezzar, King of Babylon. The island city was later destroyed by Alexander the Great. Jeremiah connects Tyrus and the Philistines in a common judgment from the north that was likely fulfilled by the conquering armies from Babylon. Zechariah also links Tyre, Gaza and the area of the Philistines, along with portions of Syria into a common prophetic judgment. Tyre was conquered and rebuilt several times. However, through the prophet Ezekiel God proclaims against Tyrus, “I will bring terrors on you and you will be

no more; though you will be sought, you will never be found again" (Ezek 26:21 NASB). This condition regarding the complete and final destruction of Tyre in Ezekiel's prophecy has yet to be fulfilled as the city of Tyre still exists in modern Lebanon and is known as Sur.

- Obadiah 1:20 – In the closely associated prophecy of Obadiah against Edom and its confederates, it states that "the children of Israel *shall possess* that of the Canaanites, *even* unto Zarephath." Zarephath was a Phoenician city on the coast of Lebanon north of Tyre, located between Tyre and Gebal (Byblos). This linkage of Tyre, Zarephath, and Gebal seems to connect the entire Lebanese seacoast as falling under the control of Israel.
- Ezekiel 28:1-19 – Interestingly, Ezekiel uses a prophecy against the prince of Tyre, and type of Antichrist, as a springboard into a prophecy against Satan as the king of Tyre (Ezek 28:12-19). Where the prince of Tyre (type of Antichrist) considers himself to be a god, he is a man who will not outwit death by the depth of his wisdom. Where the king of Tyre (Satan) was an anointed cherub who had access to the holy mountain of God and God's Garden of Eden and was created as a perfect being, he corrupted himself and brought himself under the condemnation of God. This close association between Tyre and Satan's corrupting influence may be the reason that God has declared that Tyre will be completely destroyed forever.

- Assur (Asshur, Assyria, Syria, Damascus, Northern Iraq): Isa 17:1-14; Jer 49:23-27; Amos 1:3-5; Zech 9:1-2. Asshur was a descendant of Shem and the builder of Nineveh the capital of Assyria. Asshur was also the chief god of the Assyrians. Asaph's reference to Assur joining in the confederacy of Psalm 83 points to the people of the territory of Assyria. In modern terms that indicates Syria, with Damascus as its capital. This area would also include a portion of northern Iraq, which was part of Assyria. Nineveh, the capital of Assyria is located in the territory of northern Iraq. Jeremiah, Amos, and Zechariah all link Damascus and Syria into common judgments with other elements of the Psalm 83 confederacy. Damascus seems to be the heart of this territory prophetically. Isaiah 17 is the primary prophecy directed at Damascus that is yet unfulfilled. While many scholars do not look for the future fulfillment of Isaiah 17 and do not cover it in their prophecy books or scenarios, I consider this to be very shortsighted. Isaiah 17:1 states clearly that Damascus must become a ruinous heap and must cease to be a city. That has never been completely fulfilled, and thus awaits a future dynamic event. As a result of some type of military action or weapons of mass destruction several cities in Syria and northern Jordan will be abandoned. Verse nine attributes the destruction of Damascus and its surrounding territories as taking place "because of the children of Israel." The reader is directed to the chapter titled "The Burden of Damascus" for a more detailed examination of Isaiah 17.

God used the prophet Jeremiah to target prophecies against several of these enemies of Israel that are or may be included in the confederacy of Psalm 83. Jeremiah, as most prophets, intermingled shorter term and longer term prophecies so that they run together. The prophets did not completely understand the timing of God's plan for Israel and the nations surrounding it. Jeremiah 46 is focused against Egypt. This is part history but reaches out into the far future with a reference to the "day of the Lord GOD of hosts" when God has a day of vengeance and a sacrifice planned "in the north country by the river Euphrates." This could relate to the future destruction of Damascus, but more likely relates to God's supernatural destruction of the forces of Gog and Magog. Jeremiah 47 is focused against the Philistines and Gaza, and also includes Tyrus (Tyre) and Zidon (Sidon) and Ashkelon along the coast of Israel and Lebanon. Jeremiah 48 is focused against Moab. Jeremiah 49 then focuses on several other enemies of God and Israel: Ammon, Edom, Damascus, Kedar and Hazor (Saudi Arabia), and Elam.

Of these enemies in Jeremiah 49, Elam is the only one that seems to be out of place for the confederacy of Psalm 83. Elam was a territory east of Babylon and the Tigris River at the north end of the Persian Gulf. Elam had its capital at Sushan (Susa). Elam was eventually incorporated into the Persian Empire and in modern times forms a portion of the nation of Iran. Iran is one of the specific enemies included in the alliance of Gog and Magog.

> Thus saith the LORD of hosts; Behold, I will break the bow of Elam, the chief of their might. And upon Elam will I bring the **four winds from the four quarters of heaven**, and will scatter them toward all those winds; and there shall be no nation whither the outcasts of Elam shall not come. For I will cause Elam to be dismayed before their enemies, and before them that seek their life: and I will bring evil upon them, *even* my fierce anger, saith the LORD; and I will send the sword after them, till I have consumed them: And **I will set my throne in Elam**, and will destroy from thence the king and the princes, saith the LORD. But it shall come to

> pass in the latter days, *that* I will bring again the captivity of Elam, saith the LORD. (Jer 49:35-39 bold added)

The timing of the fulfillment of the prophecy of Jeremiah 49:34-39 against Elam is difficult to assess. It is an unfulfilled prophecy. Will it occur before the Day of the LORD in association with Psalm 83 and the destruction of Damascus? Or will Elam be hit by a different military strike initiated by Israel or the United States before Psalm 83 is fulfilled? Or will this prophecy play out in conjunction with the beginning of the Day of the LORD and the War of Gog and Magog? Bill Salus examines these options in his book *Psalm 83*. He weighs some arguments regarding the possibility of God utilizing a natural disaster such as an earthquake against Iran causing serious damage to a nuclear facility. Iran has been impacted by several earthquakes during the first half of 2013, and Iran has been quick to deny any such damage. The involvement of an earthquake is a real possibility, and we know that a very big one is coming in conjunction with the beginning of the Day of the LORD. The prophecy also implicates a military option. If that military action takes place before, or in conjunction with, the war involving the Psalm 83 confederacy, it will be a limited strike involving only a portion of Iran – leaving much of Iran intact to participate as a major player in the invasion of Israel by Gog and Magog.

The reference to the four winds from the four quarters of heaven in this passage is the first such reference to the four winds in the Bible that I am aware of. It is a focus on the scattering of the Elamites (Iranians) in all of the four primary directions of the compass. References to the four winds are used in this manner several times in the Bible. The last Biblical reference to the four winds appears in Revelation 7:1, where four angels are instructed to restrain the four winds of the earth from causing harm to the earth until the 144,000 Jewish servants to God can be sealed. Is there a connection between Jeremiah's reference to the four winds coming against Elam and the four winds of the earth that will be unleashed as a form of God's wrath during the opening of the seven seal judgments? If so, then this prophecy against Elam will likely be fulfilled by Iran's participation in the War of Gog and Magog. God mentions "my fierce anger" (Jer 49:37) which is comparable to God's fury and wrath at the time of Gog and Magog. Also, God's reference to "I will set my throne in Elam" is difficult to envision prior to God initiating His Day of the LORD. Israel is not going to gain control over Elam prior to the complete destruction of Gog and Magog.

In the panorama of Bible prophecy, it is observed that several of the enemies of Israel and God that Asaph identifies in Psalm 83 are closely associated in terms of judgments brought on by God both historically and pointing towards the future. Several of the prophets including: Isaiah,

Jeremiah, Ezekiel, Amos, Obadiah, Zephaniah, and Zechariah, make these associations. The requirement for Psalm 83 is that they all must unite and come together against Israel at the same time. The target of this assault is a unified Israel, which has only been possible in its modern history since 1948. Several of the relevant prophecies point to Israel as being God's instrument for bringing destruction upon these enemies.

## Israel's Expanded Borders

Israel clearly gains control over most of these territories for either expansion of its borders and occupation, or for military and political control. This has happened as a result of past Arab-Israeli wars. Israel gained control of the Golan Heights from Syria during the Six-Day War in 1967 and subsequently annexed the Golan Heights. The territory gained as a result of the military defeat of the Psalm 83 Confederacy by the Israeli Defense Forces will be the greatest real estate acquisition by Israel yet. It will literally give Israel control over a vast majority of the Promised Land (Isa 11:13-14; 19:17-18; Jer 49:2; Obad 1:18-20; Zeph 2:4-9).

In support of this understanding, a literal interpretation of prophetic scripture demands that Israel's borders be expanded at some point in the future. Ultimately, all of Israel's tribes will be allocated their allotted territory during the Messianic Kingdom (Ezek 45:1-8; 47:13-21; 48:1-29). While many people do not believe that this expansion of Israel will ever occur, others see it taking place only after the War of Armageddon and the second coming of Christ.

However, scripture points to Israel's people (military forces) as being responsible for much of this expansion of territory. When Jesus returns at the time of His revelation, He will do the fighting and the defeating of Israel's and God's enemies all by Himself (Isa 63:3-6; Rev 19:15, 19-21). While Jesus will be accompanied by armies from heaven, He alone wields the sword (from His mouth) that brings victory over Satan's and the Antichrist's armies. The War of Armageddon will not be the time when Israel will expand her borders as a result of her own military success. Nor will this expansion be possible at any time during the second half of the Tribulation. Israel will be mostly fleeing and hiding from the forces of the Antichrist for its very survival during the second half of the Tribulation.

During the first half of the Tribulation Israel will be under the conditions of a covenant of peace with the Antichrist, or will have imposed the conditions of the covenant upon others. The confirmation of the covenant is the event that actually initiates Daniel's 70th Week of the last seven prophetic years of Daniel's vision (Dan 9:24-27). This timeframe is not conducive for Israel militarily expanding its borders through military victories. Israel will be engaged in the restoration of its system of temple worship during this time.

Obadiah gives us a framework for understanding the probable timing of the Promised Land War of Psalm 83. The prophet Obadiah points God's accusing finger at Edom (v. 1) and those who are confederate with Edom (v. 7), because of their plan to attack Israel (v. 1), as well as their historical and perpetual hatred and violence against Israel. In verse 15, Obadiah observes that this crisis takes place as God's Day of the LORD is drawing near upon all nations. From this observation we can draw the conclusion that shortly before God supernaturally intervenes to initiate His Day of the LORD judgments and wrath upon the nations of the earth, which He will do with the Ezekiel 38–39 Gog and Magog War, the confederacy of Psalm 83 will take action to fulfill its joint decision to wipe Israel off the map. A united Israel then rises up to destroy Edom and its confederates. This inner circle war for the Promised Land coming from Israel's borders on all sides will have serious repercussions for the West Bank, Gaza, Lebanon, Syria, Jordan, and the Sinai Peninsula. It could also easily include portions of Iraq, Saudi Arabia, and Egypt.

The best time for Israel to expand its borders is actually before Daniel's 70th Week even begins. That is the least problematic timeframe for the fulfillment of Psalm 83, Isaiah 17, Obadiah's vision, as well as Ezekiel 38–39, and these prophetic events will directly result in Israel increasing its territorial control in the Middle East. This is an argument for Psalm 83 to be a pretribulational event.

## Surrounding Desolation

It is also quite possible that in the aftermath of Psalm 83, Isaiah 17, Obadiah, and any of the other prophecies that become fulfilled in the same time frame, several areas or regions of these enemies' territories may be contaminated or destroyed in such a way that they will be uninhabitable or unsafe for habitation for a number of years. I make this observation and yet distinguish this from the worst series of destructions that will desolate some of these areas such as Edom that will only take place at the time of the Campaign of Armageddon and the full revelation of Christ.

Portions of Syria, and northern and central Jordan are the most likely areas to see this type of destruction or contamination during the activities envisioned and outlined in Psalm 83, Isaiah 17, and others.

- Zephaniah points to this condition for the northern and central portions of Jordan. "Therefore *as* I live, saith the LORD of hosts, the God of Israel, Surely Moab shall be as Sodom, and the children of Ammon as Gomorrah, *even* the breeding of nettles, and saltpits, and a perpetual desolation: the residue of my people shall spoil them, and the remnant of my people shall possess them" (Zeph 2:9).
- The prophecy of Isaiah 17 reveals that Damascus ceases to be a city; the cities of Aroer are forsaken (probably located in Gilead = northern Jordan); other cities in Syria are abandoned; and these areas see desolation because of the children of Israel.
- Jeremiah 49 indicates that Rabbah of the Ammonites will become a desolate heap because of Israel. Rabbah is Amman the capital of modern Jordan (Jer 49:2).

This desolation could easily be the result of chemical or biological weapons of mass destruction, or even tactical nuclear weapons. These areas will come under the control of Israel, yet later invading armies may shun passing through them because of the contamination. This might be one of the reasons that the "glorious land" (greater expanded Israel approximating the Promised Land) can be invaded a few years later, "but these shall escape out of his hand, even Edom, and Moab, and the chief of the children of Ammon" (Dan 11:41). It may also be a reason why the remnant of Israel has the opportunity to escape to and take refuge in the area of Petra (Mt. Seir, Edom) in Jordan during the great tribulation of the last half of Daniel's 70$^{th}$ Week.

# 9

# The Burden of Damascus

**Isaiah 17:1** The burden of Damascus. Behold, Damascus is taken away from *being* a city, and it shall be a ruinous heap.

Bashar al-Assad, the dictatorial president of Syria, and his regime have been struggling to maintain power over Syria in the throws of an uprising resulting in a bloody civil war. The domino effect of the “Arab Spring” threatens Syria’s top leaders as it has in Egypt, Yemen, and other Middle Eastern nations. The violence of the Syrian civil war also threatens to spill over its borders, posing a serious risk to Israel, Jordan, and Turkey. Many thousands of Syrian refugees have fled into Turkey and Jordan seeking safety. While Assad is blatantly supported by Iran and Russia and has so far managed to hang on to his position of power, his fate is uncertain.

Damascus has certainly experienced explosions, fighting, bloodshed, assassinations, and terror in this struggle for control over Syria. Will this Syrian civil war result in significant outside military intervention by Israel or any other nation, or will it spark a larger regional war in the Middle East? What are the biblical prophetic implications for Syria and the city of Damascus?

Damascus (Dimashq in Arabic) is the capital of the modern nation of Syria. Damascus was the chief city of the ancient area known as Aram (the Arameans). The names Aram and Syria essentially refer to the same territory, and the translators of the KJV sometimes used Syria in reference to Aram. From the area of Aram and greater Mesopotamia we get the Aramaic or Syriac dialect. Aramaic is a Semitic dialect related to Hebrew that was adopted by the Israelites during their exiles to Assyria and Babylon, and which appears in portions of the Bible.

The territory of Aram extended from the mountains of Lebanon on its western border to the Euphrates River along its eastern border and from the Taurus Mountains on the north to the territory of Ammon (modern northern Jordan) on the south. Syria, in the present geo-political world, is situated between Lebanon and the Mediterranean Sea to the west, Turkey to the north, Iraq to the east, and Israel and Jordan to the south.

Damascus is commonly referred to as the oldest continually-inhabited city in the world. This claim to longevity is part of the mystique and reputation of Damascus. Ancient kings of Aram who ruled from Damascus included Hadad and Hazael, and so we encounter prophetic references to Damascus in connection to these names (Jer 49:27; Amos 1:4).

The Assyrian King Tiglath-Pileser conquered Syria (Aram) and to some extent destroyed Damascus in 732 B.C. This is mentioned in 2 Kings 16:5-9. It is claimed by some historians and scholars that when King Tiglath-Pileser conquered Syria in 732 B.C. the defeat and destruction of Damascus at that time served as complete fulfillment of the prophecies of Isaiah 8:4; 17:1-14; Jeremiah 49:23-27; and Amos 1:3-5. Because of this presupposition some modern scholars relegate Isaiah chapter 17 to the dustbin of history and do not look for any future prophetic fulfillment of its message directed at the city of Damascus. In his book, *Every Prophecy of the Bible*, John F. Walvoord claimed, "The destruction of Damascus was fulfilled in history and prophecy."

Damascus has been controlled by many different peoples who have impacted the history of the Middle East: Arameans, Assyrians, Babylonians, Persians, Greeks, Armenians, Nabateans, Romans, the Byzantine Empire, Arabs (Omayyad caliphate dynasty), Mongols, Egyptians, Ottoman Turks, and the French prior to the city becoming the capital of the independent nation known as the Syrian Arab Republic. While Damascus has been attacked, besieged, and sacked several times during its long history, it has never been destroyed to the point of merely becoming a heap of ruins (as has happened to Babylon), nor has it ever ceased to be a city. Damascus is somewhat like the famous phoenix of mythology. Damascus keeps rising from the ashes of its defeats to continue playing a role in the history of the Middle East. In fact, the fame of Damascus as the oldest continually-inhabited city stands in direct conflict with the plain sense meaning of Isaiah 17.

Where the prophecies of Isaiah 8:4; Jeremiah 49:23-27; and Amos 1:4-5 have definitely seen partial fulfillment and possibly complete fulfillment, the prophecy of Isaiah 17 stands as a beacon pointing to an event that is yet to take place. The language of Isaiah 17 is not the language of complete historical fulfillment.

As an ancient city, Damascus impacted the kingdoms of both Israel and Judah. The modern city of Damascus continues to impact the land and nation of Israel. Syria has participated in three Arab-Israeli wars (1948, 1967, and 1973) since Israel's rebirth as a nation in 1948. Some students of prophecy believe these three wars point to the "three transgressions of Damascus" mentioned by the prophet Amos (Amos 1:3). They believe that the next war between Syria and Israel will constitute the fourth transgression, which will result in God's bringing punishment against Damascus (Amos 1:3-4).

The Assad regime in Syria has been an active sponsor of Islamic terrorism by providing military support for groups like Hezbollah and Hamas. Syria has sought to regain possession of the Golan Heights, that Israel captured during the Six-Day war in 1967, and has threatened war to get it back. Syria has stockpiled a large amount of chemical weapons and has the capability to deliver them in the warheads of missiles. Syria is allied with Iran, a very outspoken enemy of Israel. The current civil war for control of Syria has not improved any of these conditions. Damascus has not ceased its role of prophetic importance from a biblical perspective.

**Isaiah 17:1-11**

> 1 The burden of Damascus. Behold, Damascus is taken away from *being* a city, and it shall be a ruinous heap.
> 2 The cities of Aroer *are* forsaken: they shall be for flocks, which shall lie down, and none shall make *them* afraid.
> 3 The fortress also shall cease from Ephraim, and the kingdom from Damascus, and the remnant of Syria: they shall be as the glory of the children of Israel, saith the LORD of hosts.
> 4 And in that day it shall come to pass, *that* the glory of Jacob shall be made thin, and the fatness of his flesh shall wax lean.
> 5 And it shall be as when the harvestman gathereth the corn, and reapeth the ears with his arm; and it shall be as he that gathereth ears in the valley of Rephaim.
> 6 Yet gleaning grapes shall be left in it, as the shaking of an olive tree, two *or* three berries in the top of the uppermost bough, four *or* five in the outmost fruitful branches thereof, saith the LORD God of Israel.
> 7 At that day shall a man look to his Maker, and his eyes shall have respect to the Holy One of Israel.
> 8 And he shall not look to the altars, the work of his hands, neither shall respect *that* which his fingers have made, either the groves, or the images.

> 9 In that day shall his strong cities be as a forsaken bough, and an uppermost branch, which they left **because of the children of Israel**: and there shall be desolation. (bold added)
> 10 Because thou hast forgotten the God of thy salvation, and hast not been mindful of the rock of thy strength, therefore shalt thou plant pleasant plants, and shalt set it with strange slips:
> 11 In the day shalt thou make thy plant to grow, and in the morning shalt thou make thy seed to flourish: *but* the harvest *shall be* a heap in the day of grief and of desperate sorrow.

The prophecy of Isaiah 17 foresees the day when Damascus, and the territory over which it rules (Syria), will be catastrophically overthrown. This will not be caused by a slow, gradual deterioration, but a sudden, dynamic intervention imposed upon Damascus. The time frame for this event is stated to be "that day" in verses 4 and 7, and as "the day of grief and of desperate sorrow" in verse 11. These references are consistent with God's future prophetic Day of the LORD when He will intervene in judgment. Jesus specifically refers to the wars and catastrophic events that begin the Day of the LORD as the "beginning of sorrows" (Mt 24:8). There will be a series of traumatic events (the beginning of sorrows) that lead into and initiate God's Day of the LORD time of judgment. The destruction of Damascus will likely be one of these early events.

1. Damascus will cease to be a city (v. 1).
2. Damascus will be a ruinous heap – leveled to rubble (v. 1).
3. The cities of Aroer (central Jordan) will be forsaken (abandoned) (v. 2).
4. The fortress shall cease from Ephraim (northern kingdom of Israel) (v. 3).
5. The kingdom will cease from Damascus (v. 3).
6. The remnant of Syria shall be as the glory of the children of Israel (Syria will become part of the territory of Israel) (v. 3).
7. The glory of Jacob shall be made thin – his fatness shall wax lean (v. 4).
8. There will be few people left in the land (v. 5-6).
9. Men will turn to God the Holy One of Israel (v. 7). This is a specific reference to the awakening of people in Syria and Israel to God as the God of Abraham, Isaac, and Jacob, not necessarily to Jesus Christ as the Messiah.
10. The strong cities shall be forsaken (v. 9).

While this prophecy is titled "The Burden of Damascus," it must be realized that this complete destruction of Damascus is placed within a larger context, both geographically and in time. At the same time that Damascus and Syria are ruined, a larger territory is also impacted negatively. This territory includes the modern nations of Jordan and Israel. The cities of Aroer (the area of central Jordan east of the Dead Sea) are "forsaken," which means they may be abandoned instead of being completely destroyed. "The fortress shall cease from Ephraim" is a reference to the territory of the ancient northern kingdom of Israel that is currently part of the area known today as the West Bank, and which is largely populated by Arab Palestinians. Israel is not destroyed, but it does not escape without serious consequences. The "glory of Jacob shall be made thin, and the fatness of his flesh shall wax lean" (Isa 17:4). The prophecy seems to portray this as a condition resulting from a common war or catastrophe. This is a simultaneous event.

Bible scholars and historians tend to attribute the full focus of this prophecy regarding the destruction of Damascus and the desolation of the territory of Ephraim and the area of ancient Ammon and Moab (northern and central Jordan) to the invasion of the Assyrians. By design there seems to be a logical connection to those historical events. However, is that all there is to this prophecy?

Assyria conquered Aram and Damascus in 732 B.C. Assyria later conquered Samaria (Ephraim) in 722 B.C. Later yet, the Assyrians invaded the southern kingdom of Judah. Sennacherib, the King of Assyria (705-681 B.C.), conducted a siege against Jerusalem during the reign of King Hezekiah and the ministry of the prophet Isaiah. However, the conquest of Jerusalem was unsuccessful as God intervened supernaturally by having an angel destroy 185,000 Assyrian soldiers in one night and Sennacherib had to return to Assyria where he was later assassinated by two of his own sons (2 Kings 19:32-36). Some scholars apply the passage of Isaiah 17:12-14 to this event involving Sennacherib's army, but Sennacherib came from Nineveh, capital of Assyria, not from Damascus. The Assyrian conquest over Damascus took place decades before Sennacherib's siege of Jerusalem. Jerusalem and the kingdom of Judah did not actually fall until a hundred years later, and then it was to the Babylonians under the leadership of Nebuchadnezzar.

Isaiah's ministry as a prophet of God lasted a long time (about 740-680 B.C.) Several of these events took place during Isaiah's lifetime. However, there are problems with the completely historical fulfillment perspective.

1. Damascus never ceased to be a city!

2. The prophet Isaiah does not actually name the Assyrians, or the later Babylonians, as the cause of the destruction of Damascus or to the surrounding territories.
3. The desolation of Samaria (Ephraim) by Assyria took place ten years after Assyria conquered and supposedly destroyed Damascus.
4. The siege of Jerusalem by Sennacherib took place more than thirty years after Damascus fell to Assyria, and more than twenty years after the fall of Samaria.
5. The southern kingdom of Judah and its capital Jerusalem did not fall to the Babylonians until 605-586 B.C.
6. The context of Isaiah 17 places the fulfillment of the destruction as a single event in time, not a series of events spread out over a number of decades.
7. The context of Isaiah 17 places the focus of the event upon Damascus, as well as the territories of both the northern and southern kingdoms of the Israelites. All of Israel is in view. Ephraim (Isa 17:3) points to the area of the northern kingdom. The "valley of Rephaim" (Isa 17:5) points to the area of the southern kingdom of Judah near Jerusalem. The valley of Rephaim lay between Jerusalem and Bethlehem (2 Sam 23:13). The reference to Jacob (Isa 17:4) points to all of Israel. Jacob represents all of the tribes of Israel, not just the ten tribes of the northern kingdom of Israel, or the southern kingdom of Judah (Judah, Benjamin, and half the tribe of Levi).
8. Babylon conquered Assyria and then Judah and Jerusalem. Babylon did not conquer the northern kingdom of Israel. Israel had previously fallen to Assyria. The reference to Jacob points to an impact upon all of national Israel that was not caused by the Babylonian conquest of the southern kingdom of Judah.
9. There is also the problem with who Isaiah hints is responsible for the destruction. Isaiah points the finger towards Israel.

Isaiah states that the strong cities will be forsaken (Isa 17:9) "which they left **because of the children of Israel**: and there will be desolation." One common view is that because Israel fell into idolatry and rebelled against God, this calamity fell upon the people as a judgment by God (Isa 17:10-11). While this is true for Israel and Judah over a long period of time, it does not follow as the reason that Damascus would be destroyed, or that the cities of central Jordan would be abandoned, particularly in the context of a single prophecy relating them all together. Events of history loosely fit the prophecy, but not entirely, thus requiring a future ultimate fulfillment. This specific finger-pointing allows for Israel to be the direct cause of the destruction at the time of the ultimate fulfillment of Isaiah 17.

Damascus will be completely destroyed. The destruction will likely be caused by Israel. The cities of Syria, the West Bank (the Palestinians), and northern and central Jordan will see desolation and abandonment. This may partly be a result of the type of weapons used against Damascus, but that is a speculative observation. It may equally be caused by weapons intentionally or accidently deployed by the Syrians themselves. It is believed that Syria has a very significant and dangerous stockpile of chemical weapons. It has also been reported that during the recent civil war, some of these chemical weapons have been removed from their storage facilities and possibly even armed for use. It has been claimed that some type of chemical weapons have been actively deployed, yet it is disputed which side actually utilized them. Did Syria cross a "red line" by using chemical weapons against the rebels? The United States says it has – to a small extent. The security of these chemical weapons is a great concern for Israel and the other countries bordering on Syria such as Jordan and Turkey. Yet Russia is doing everything it can to prop up the Syrian regime and prevent Israel or the West from intervening effectively against Syria. Russia is being very true to its character and assigned role as the Magog of Ezekiel 38, who is tasked by God to arm and prepare the nations of the Middle East for a future invasion of Israel.

The nation of Israel will be injured but will survive in victory. People throughout the afflicted territory will begin to turn to the true God – the God of Israel (Isa 17:7). The context of Isaiah's prophecy does not limit this to the Jews of Israel. It will logically include Muslims and those of other religions.

What takes place in the larger picture of Isaiah's prophecy? Damascus faces a day of prophetic destiny. Regardless of whether the Assad regime is successful in withstanding the attempt to oust it through civil war, or falls as the next victim of the "Arab Spring," the support for Islamic terrorism and hostility against Israel by Damascus will come to a tragic end. The reward for Damascus will be a harvest, "*but* the harvest *shall be* a heap in the day of grief and of desperate sorrow" (Isa 17:11).

**Isaiah 17:12-14**

> Woe to the multitude of many people, *which* make a noise like the noise of the seas; and to the rushing of nations, *that* make a rushing like the rushing of mighty waters! The nations shall rush like the rushing of many waters: but *God* shall rebuke them, and they shall flee far off, and shall be chased as the chaff of the mountains before the wind, and like a rolling thing before the whirlwind. And behold at eveningtide trouble; *and* before the morning he *is* not. This *is*

the portion of them that spoil us, and the lot of them that rob us.

Some authors view this passage of Isaiah 17:12-14 as describing the overall condition that leads into the sudden destruction of Damascus. However, I view this as a description of the world's (many nations) reaction to the destruction of Damascus and the events that quickly follow. In the aftermath of the destruction of Damascus by Israel, many nations will make a tumultuous uproar. The world body will hear a great outcry demanding retribution and vengeance against Israel. It takes very little provocation for the body of the United Nations to denounce Israel openly. The nations will "rush" (invade Israel), but God shall intervene to silence them. God will rebuke (destroy) the invading armies. Very suddenly, in the space of a single night, (just as God's intervention against Sennacherib's army), the invading forces will cease to be a threat. Some of the invading forces will then flee away.

This passage is not describing the massing of armies against Israel at the time of Armageddon. This is not the intervention of God in the form of the second coming of Christ. There will be no allowance of any invading forces fleeing away in the final confrontation known as Armageddon, when Christ arrives to slay His enemies with the sword that comes from his mouth (Rev 19:15, 19-21).

There are two types of wars when God intervenes during the End Times. The first is an invasion of Israel by multiple (but not all) nations where the enemies are suddenly and decisively defeated and destroyed by God, but some of the invaders are allowed to flee away. The second is an invasion by all nations, who are assembled by the power of Satan, against Israel and against God. This invasion will be completely destroyed by the coming of Christ. No enemy soldiers will survive this confrontation. There will be no fleeing away to fight another day from this battle. See the parallel to this in Isaiah 41:9-16.

The descriptive language that Isaiah uses points to two related unfulfilled prophecies: Psalm 83 and Ezekiel 38–39.

- Psalm 83:13 O my God, make them like a wheel; as the stubble before the wind.
- Ezekiel 39:10 b … and they shall spoil those that spoiled them, and rob those that robbed them, saith the Lord GOD.

Psalm 83 is a prophetic prayer seeking God's intervention to thwart a conspiracy by the innermost enemies surrounding Israel to destroy her as a nation. The alliance of conspirators includes Syria, the Palestinians, and Jordan. Psalm 83 does not depict a conspiracy leading to the final war of Armageddon, as that will entail all of the nations of the earth, not just these innermost enemies. While God's answer to the prayer is not included in Psalm 83, part of the answer may be included in Isaiah 17. These enemies of Israel and of God will be treated as the chaff before the wind (Ps 83:13; Isa 17:13).

Ezekiel 38–39 depicts the war of Gog and Magog, an alliance of nations, forming an outer ring surrounding but not directly bordering Israel, who will invade Israel and be immediately destroyed by God's direct intervention. The KJV translates part of Ezekiel 39:2 as God will "leave but the sixth part of thee." Many scholars interpret this to mean that God will destroy five-sixths of the invading forces and leave one-sixth to flee away. The alliance of Gog and Magog invades partly to take a spoil of Israel (Ezek 38:12-13), but these invading armies will be spoiled by Israel instead (Ezek 39:9-10). This reference to the enemy goal of spoiling and robbing, that is thwarted, seemingly parallels Isaiah 17:14.

At the time of the invasion of Gog and Magog, Israel will be a nation recovered from war ("the land brought back from the sword" Ezek 38:8). This could actually indicate that part of the land of Israel prior to the invasion was recently regained by an act of war. As in the past Arab-Israeli wars, Israel could expand its territory to take in parts of Syria, Jordan, and Lebanon. All of these areas are within the original land grant promised by God to Abraham, Isaac, and Jacob.

Either the boiling over of the civil war festering Syria, or Syria's involvement in the larger conspiracy of Psalm 83 may lead to the eruption of another Arab-Israeli War in the Middle East, which forces Israel to use conventional or even unconventional weapons to destroy Damascus. The loud outcry put up by the remaining Islamic nations and other nations of the world who are hostile to Israel could easily give the alliance of Gog and Magog the excuse to invade Israel. Israel weakened by its recent war would be no match against the mass of invading forces. God intervenes on Israel's behalf and destroys the invading armies.

It seems that the "Burden of Damascus" forecast by Isaiah not only threatens Damascus as a city, but the entire Middle East. At the point that the nations make their uproar and rush to invade Israel, the entire world falls into God's arena of judgment. God's intervention will result in global destruction (Ezek 38:18-22; 39:2-6). The "Burden of Damascus" is literally a "Sword of Damocles" hanging by a thread over the Middle East, ready to ignite a prophetic chain of events that will engulf many nations.

# 10

# Ezekiel 38–39: The War of Gog and Magog

## Synopsis:

**A Mystery:** Ezekiel 38 presents us with a prophetic enigma. A bit of mystery emerges – like a classic "whodunit," except in this case who is going to commit a future crime is more the issue. While God's prophets have been compelled to cast oracles of judgment at a number of Israel's neighbors and known enemies, God commanded Ezekiel to "set thy face against Gog, the land of Magog … and prophesy against him." Ezekiel points the finger of warning at Gog. Who is Gog? Gog represents a previously unidentified enemy to whom God declares "Behold, I *am* against thee, O Gog" (Ezek 38:2-3; 39:1). This prophecy is primarily directed against Gog, as the leader of a future alliance or coalition of nations, instead of a single nation.

**Why? – The Overall Situation:** God has the need to sanctify, glorify, and magnify Himself, and His holy name, to Israel and to the nations of the world (Ezek 38:16, 23; 39:7, 13, 21-29). This is a global situation. All nations are in denial and derision of God. Not one nation is noted as being holy, on God's side, or not needing God's demonstration of His supernatural intervention and presence. Israel is characterized as polluting God's holy name. Israel becomes the focal point of God's intervention, but the message is for the entire world. God uses Gog, and his alliance, as a bloody sacrifice to get the attention of the world. The times have changed – God's silence is broken! – God has intervened! – God's "Day of the LORD" judgments have begun.

God uses the evilness in the hearts of Gog and his allies for His own purpose. Just as God used Assyria and Babylon as instruments of His indignation against Israel and Samaria, and Judah and Jerusalem, God has plans for Gog and his forces. However, God has no victory planned for Gog. God will set His hooks in Gog's jaws and instigate this invasion at the time of God's choosing. God is in complete control and Gog has a date with his own destruction (Ezek 38:4, 8; 39:2, 11).

**What? – The Crime:** Gog and his alliance will commit the unpardonable crime of invading the land of Israel and attacking: God's land, God's people, and God's holy name. The alliance will prepare its armies over a period of time and then suddenly "ascend and come like a storm," "like a cloud to cover the land" (Ezek 38:9, 16), and attempt to spoil the land and the people by taking a great spoil (Ezek 38:12-13). They will attack from all directions, but the primary thrust will be from the north.

**When? – The Timing:** "After many days," "in the latter years," "in the latter days," "this *is* the day whereof I have spoken," (Ezek 38:8, 16; 39:8). The day that God has spoken of repeatedly through His prophets is the Day of the LORD. The question then becomes when does this invasion take place within the context of the Day of the LORD? That question is examined in a following section: Gog & Magog in the Chronology of the End Times.

**Where? – The Target:** The victim is clearly identified as Israel, God's land, God's people – "my people of Israel," a land brought back from the sword, mountains reclaimed from a long period of waste, a people gathered out of many nations, dwelling without walls, and dwelling "safely" (carelessly, under a false sense of security) (Ezek 38:8, 11, 14, 16, 18). This is a good description of the present day nation of Israel. Modern Israeli settlements, towns, and cities are not defended by walls, as in ancient times, as walls provide no security against rockets and missiles. In spite of the everyday threat of rocket and missile attacks, Israel's politicians dwell carelessly, under a false sense of security. How else could Israel's politicians talk the language of appeasement and discuss the possibility of giving up more land, including the Golan Heights, as they did as recently as 2006 following their ill resolved war against Hezbollah in Lebanon?

**Who? – The Adversary:** Gog is a title for the supreme leader of an alliance of nations (Ezek 38:2-6).

- Gog is from the land of Magog and is identified as the "chief prince of Meshech and Tubal" (KJV), or as the "prince of Rosh, Meshech and Tubal" (NASB). Rosh in Hebrew often carries the meaning of head or chief. However, many translators understand Rosh in the context of this verse as a proper noun indicating that Rosh is a designation for a place. Scholars argue the pros and cons of whether Rosh is a designator for the nation of Russia. The larger picture of this prophecy in consideration with the present nature of world dynamics, particularly Russia's diplomatic, economic, and military alliances with Iran and the other nations mentioned in Ezekiel 38, strongly argues in favor of Rosh being Russia. God warns Gog to be prepared for this invasion (Ezek 38:7). Gog is to arm his armies militarily and those of his alliance and to be a "guard unto them." Russia is the only nation on the world scene today that has been and is consistently and aggressively fulfilling this role.
- Magog, Meshech, and Tubal – Identified as three of the sons of Japheth (grandsons of Noah) in the table of nations in Genesis 10:2. They originally settled in portions of Anatolia or Asia Minor (areas of modern Turkey), but later migrated northward where they were largely involved in the population of the expanse of modern Russia and Central Asia. They can be identified with the "north parts" (Ezek 38:15; 39:2 KJV) or the "remote" or "remotest parts of the north" (NASB) from which much of the invasion will originate.
- Persia – Modern Iran. Persia changed its name to Iran in 1935, and since the revolution of 1979, it is known as the Islamic Republic of Iran. Iran is one of the most blatant and outspoken enemies of Israel on the world stage. Iran is an active supporter and weapons supplier of Syria, and Hezbollah in Lebanon, and has promoted violence and terrorism against Israel from the Palestinians in Gaza and the West Bank and from the Sinai Peninsula.
- Ethiopia (Cush) – The territory in Africa south of Egypt, probably including the area from Sudan to Somalia. These areas are predominantly controlled by Islam.
- Libya (Put) – The territory of North Africa to the west of Egypt dominated by modern Libya.
- Gomer – Another of the sons of Japheth. Originally located in the area of Turkey, Gomer was the ancestor of a migratory people called the Cimmerians. The territory of Gomer in modern times is contested. Jewish scholars have identified it to be Germany. However, others have linked Gomer to the Balkans, Ukraine, southern Russia, or other Celtic peoples. The Ukraine and southern

Russia are the most probable locations. Gomer is noted for having "all his bands," which likely indicates the territory overlaps more than one modern country.

- Togarmah – A son of Gomer, identified in this prophecy as the house of Togarmah. Togarmah is another extended family group associated as being from the "north quarters, and all his bands" (Ezek 38:6). Originally associated with the territory of Armenia, in the modern sense it would likely incorporate eastern Turkey, Armenia, and northwestern Iran.
- Many people with thee – Not likely to be the large scale armies of additional nations, but may indicate the support of a larger body of nations, such as the United Nations, or the inclusion of fighters such as the interconnected network of Islamic terrorist groups who come from other nations.
- In summary, the alliance of Gog and Magog will likely include: Russia, Iran, Turkey, Ukraine, Georgia, the Islamic nations of Central Asia, Libya, Sudan, Ethiopia, and Somalia.

**World's Reaction:** How does the world react to this sudden invasion of Israel? Sheba and Dedan (Saudi Arabia, Jordan, and other nations of the Arabian Peninsula), along with "the merchants of Tarshish, with all the young lions thereof," (which most likely represents the nations of the Western world – Britain, Spain, and their former colonies including the U.S.A.) make a mild diplomatic protest (Ezek 38:13). There is no indication of any military intervention or assistance to Israel by any nation. Saudi Arabia would be naturally fearful of the threat that this invasion would pose to the security of its own oil fields and to its control over the Islamic centers of Mecca and Medina.

**God's Reaction and Intervention:**

- My Fury; My Jealousy; My Wrath – "My fury shall come up in my face. For in my jealousy and in the fire of my wrath have I spoken" (Ezek 38:19).
- My Presence; My Judgment; My Hand – "All the men that *are* upon the face of the earth, shall shake at my presence," … "and all the heathen shall see my judgment that I have executed, and my hand that I have laid upon them" (Ezek 38:20; 39:21).
- A great earthquake – a global earthquake! "Surely in that day there shall be a great shaking in the land of Israel." All of nature – all of mankind will shake at God's intervening presence (Ezek 38:19-20).

Compare this to the information revealed in the prophecies of Revelation 6:12, 15-17; and Isaiah 2:10-21. This earthquake likely begins in or near Israel and ripples throughout the entire planet. God shakes all nations to get their attention.

- God turns the invaders against themselves, brother against brother (Ezek 38:21).
- God sends pestilence, blood, torrential rain, great hailstones, fire, and brimstone upon the invading armies (Ezek 38:22).
- God makes the weapons of the invaders ineffective (Ezek 39:3).
- God causes the destruction of the invaders upon the mountains and open fields of Israel (Ezek 39:2, 4-5).
- God will send fire upon the land of Magog, and upon those who dwell carelessly in the isles (continents) (Ezek 39:6). This may be a supernatural judgment of fire from God, or it may be that God removes any divine restraint from the outbreak of global warfare and the use of nuclear weapons.
- God gives the bodies of the invaders as a sacrifice to the birds and the beasts to feast upon (Ezek 39:4, 17-20).
- My glory – God will magnify and sanctify Himself. God will make His holy name known. God will be glorified (Ezek 38:16, 23; 39:7, 13, 21).

## The Aftermath:

- Israel will be protected from the invasion through God's supernatural intervention.
- The invading armies of Gog and Magog are completely defeated and destroyed.
- Israel's territory, power, and influence will have greatly expanded. Israel will completely control the Promised Land and largely dominate the Middle East.
- The world will go through a recovery phase in the aftermath of global destruction. Although God's intervention focuses on the military invasion of Israel, there will be considerable destruction worldwide from the global earthquake and the fire that God sends upon Magog (probably representative of all of the nations of Gog's alliance), and other nations (the coastlands) that are not part of the invading alliance. It is quite possible that there will have been some form of global warfare. Nuclear war between Russia and the United States is possible during the Gog and Magog crisis. War between North and South Korea, between Pakistan and India, or between

China and Taiwan or Japan is also very likely to erupt during this global upheaval of events.

- The people of Israel will burn the invader's weapons of war for fuel for a period of seven years. Israel will plunder and spoil the invaders who thought to plunder and spoil Israel (Ezek 39:9-10).
- The people of Israel will bury Gog and the multitude of dead invaders in a mass grave in a valley east of the Dead Sea. This burial process, while Israel cleanses and purifies the land, lasts for a period of at least seven months (Ezek 39:11-16).
- God's destruction of Gog and Magog will leave a geo-political-military power vacuum in Russia, Iran, and much of Central Asia and the Middle East. This will be the perfect opportunity for a world leader to step forward and propose solutions to the world's many problems.
- Islam will suffer a tremendous defeat directly from the hand of God. The vast majority of invading forces will be Islamic, and their destruction and whatever destruction occurs in their homelands may be the catalyst to draw many people away from submission to Islam and into belief in the God of the Bible.
- Israel and many other peoples of the nations will be awakened to the reality of God – as the God of the Old Testament – the God of Abraham, Isaac, and Jacob. Some people will come to know and accept the Lord Jesus Christ as their Savior. However, as a nation, Israel will not yet be ready to accept Jesus as their Messiah. Instead, Israel will be reawakened to the worship of God practiced in the Old Testament.
- Israel will seek to rebuild the Jewish Temple in Jerusalem and reinstate the Old Testament system of sacrifices and offerings.
- Israel will step forward as a major power to be reckoned with. It will likely be the superpower of the Middle East and possibly much of the world. A covenant of peace is a likely eventual outcome in the aftermath of Gog and Magog. However, Israel is the one who will likely impose the conditions of the covenant.
- Both Russia and the U.S.A. will have ceased to be superpowers. Both nations will have sustained considerable destruction from the effects of war (probably nuclear), earthquakes, meteors, fire, and hail. The United States will have been impacted greatly by the loss of many Christians because of the rapture of the church. The ability of the United States to recover and rebuild will be severely diminished. Its ability and willingness to sacrifice to assist other nations recover, as it has so often in the past, will be a thing of the past.

- Many Jews in the U.S.A. and throughout the world will decide to emigrate to Israel. Greater Israel will be a more attractive place to live than the United States or other nations. They will take their wealth with them. Israel will become a major economic powerhouse.
- Israel and the nations will see God's intervention and the supernatural destruction of Gog and Magog as the fulfillment of the final prophetic war – Armageddon. They will think that all of the prophecies regarding God's judgments have been fulfilled. Israel will believe it is now entering its Golden Age in the Messianic Kingdom. Israel must now become the head of the nations with a king on David's throne.
- Now that Armageddon, the war to end all wars, is perceived to be over, and weapons of mass destruction have been unleashed upon a number of nations on a horrific scale, it will be widely viewed by world leaders as the perfect time to push for world disarmament. The nations of the world must beat their "swords into plowshares." The military conflicts that do take place throughout the next several years in the inevitable power struggles for world domination may largely be about who gives up and who retains weapons of mass destruction in the aftermath of this global cataclysm.
- God, through His intervention by instigating and destroying the invasion of Gog and Magog at the beginning of His Day of the LORD, pushes Israel towards making a national decision – Who is Israel's Messiah?

| **The War of Gog & Magog** |
| --- |
| God's Silence is Broken!<br>God's Face is turned toward Israel<br>Israel is God's People; God's Land<br>God supernaturally intervenes: God's Fury; God's Wrath<br>Global Earthquake<br>War: Invading armies turn against each other<br>Pestilence; Blood; Fire and Brimstone<br>Overflowing Rain; Great Hailstorm<br>God destroys the forces of Gog & Magog<br>God sends fire down upon Magog and other nations<br>God's Holy Name is magnified<br>The Birds and the Beasts feed on God's Sacrifice<br>Israel buries the dead for 7 months<br>Israel burns the weapons and equipment for fuel for 7 years<br>Israel is reawakened to God |

**Key Questions:**

- Dwelling Safely: A False Sense of Security – How safely is Israel dwelling in the land before the invasion of Gog and Magog?
- Gog & Magog in the Chronology of the End Times – When in the timeline of the End Times does the invasion of Gog and Magog take place?
- Gog vs. Antichrist – Is Gog the Antichrist?
- Gog & Magog vs. Armageddon – Is the invasion of Gog and Magog the same war as Armageddon?
- Ezekiel 38 & 39 vs. Revelation 20 – Is the invasion of Gog and Magog in Ezekiel 38–39 the same confrontation as Satan's final rebellion in Revelation 20:7-10?

## Dwelling Safely: A False Sense of Security

The King James Version of Ezekiel 38 describes Israel as dwelling "safely" in the land as a precondition to the invasion of Gog and Magog (38:8, 11, 14). The nature of Israel's "dwelling safely" is a key issue that needs to be understood in the context of this prophecy. Some scholars argue that Israel is dwelling safely because it is living under the conditions created by a seven-year covenant of peace that Israel has entered into with a strong world leader. It has also been proposed that Israel is dwelling safely because it has first won a major military victory over its immediate enemies, expanded its borders, thus making its territory and people secure. Others interpret this dwelling safely as Israel being in the Messianic or Millennial Kingdom. However, all of these arguments miss the true nature of Ezekiel's description of Israel at the time of Gog's "evil thought" (38:10).

> After many days thou shall be visited: in the latter years thou shalt come up into the land that is brought back from the sword, and is gathered out of many people, against the mountains of Israel, which have been always waste: but it is brought forth out of the nations, and they shall dwell **safely** all of them. …. And thou shalt say, I will go up to the land of unwalled villages; I will go to them that are at rest, that dwell **safely**, all of them dwelling without walls, and having neither bars nor gates, …. Therefore, son of man, prophesy and say unto Gog, Thus saith the Lord GOD; In that day when my people of Israel dwelleth **safely**, shalt thou not know it?" (Ezekiel 38:8, 11, 14 KJV – bold added)

This description of Israel as being at rest, dwelling safely, in unwalled villages, without bars and gates, has led many interpreters of Ezekiel 38 to conclude that the people of Israel will be living in a unique state of peace and security before Gog's invasion. Most authors who take this view argue that the seven-year covenant of peace described by the prophet Daniel (Dan 9:27) must be in effect to create this condition of security. They see Israel living under the covenant protection of a world leader who guarantees Israel's safety. As a result they conclude that Ezekiel's prophecy of Gog and Magog will be fulfilled during the first half of the seven-year Tribulation or near its midpoint.

Is this view warranted? Will the people of Israel be living in a unique period of peace and security at the time Gog and Magog erupts upon them? Does Ezekiel's description of Israel indicate that Israel will have entered into the protection of a strong covenant of peace? I don't think so. I believe there is a better interpretation and explanation of Ezekiel's description that is more consistent with the current conditions in Israel and the characteristics exhibited by Israel's leaders today.

The significant factor in this prophecy is how Ezekiel describes Israel and how Gog and his allies view Israel – as a vulnerable target. Is this because Israel is under the protection of a covenant of peace from a strong world leader, or because Israel has won a decisive military victory? Or is something completely different going on here?

In Ezekiel's time villages were surrounded by rock walls for protection from enemies. However, modern Israel is a nation consisting of unwalled settlements and cities. This is true in spite of the security checkpoints that control access to most settlements. It is also true in spite of the large security fence that Israel is constructing between certain Jewish and Palestinian controlled areas. Walls, bars, and gates still exist, but they do not play the same first-line-of-defense role that they did in ancient times. To a large extent modern weapons have made the ancient protection provided by walls, bars, and gates obsolete. They do not provide any protection from rockets, missiles, or mortars.

While Ezekiel does state that Israel will be "at rest," he does not actually state that Israel will be completely at peace or without enemies. The very fact that Gog leads a very large alliance of armies against Israel is evidence that Israel will have many enemies and will not be completely at peace. I believe the reference to being "at rest" simply indicates that Israel will not be engaged in a state of war at the time Gog decides to invade.

More important to our understanding of this issue is the Hebrew word that Ezekiel uses several times in this prophecy, and which is translated as "safely" in verses 38:8, 38:11, and 38:14 as noted in boldface in the above quotation. This key word is the Hebrew word "betach" בטח. Some sources render this word as "betah." Many students of prophecy and authors who write opinions regarding Ezekiel's prophecy of Gog and Magog take the King James translation of "betach" as safely, or other similar translations, at face value without really examining the deeper implications of the Hebrew word "betach."

Our understanding of this key conditional characteristic of Israel must be based upon the underlying use and meaning of the Hebrew word *betach* by Ezekiel and other passages in the Old testament and upon its application within the context of Ezekiel 38–39, and not upon the impression that its rendering into English gives to the western mind. The KJV has technically not mistranslated the Hebrew word *betach*; however, a casual reading of the prophecy in English easily leads to a misconception. Unfortunately, the translations of the KJV as well as others like the NIV and NASB do not reflect the true meaning of Ezekiel's statements.

**Betach בטח in Ezekiel 38 & 39**

| Bible Version | Ezekiel 38:8 | Ezekiel 38:11 | Ezekiel 38:14 | Ezekiel 39:6 |
|---|---|---|---|---|
| KJV | safely | safely | safely | carelessly |
| RSV | securely | securely | securely | securely |
| NASB | securely | securely | securely | in safety |
| NIV | in safety | peaceful and unsuspecting | in safety | in safety |
| Septuagint | securely | in peace | securely | securely |
| The Jerusalem Bible | safely | in safety | safely | securely |
| ArtScroll Yechezkel | confidently | confidently | confidently | confidently |

## Betach or betah

Strong's Concordance shows that the KJV has translated this word "betach" in various ways throughout the scriptures of the Old Testament. It is variously taken to mean: safely, safe, safety, secure, securely, boldly, confidence, assurance, and hope. In the majority of instances, the word is taken to mean safely or safety. The context of how "betach" is used in scripture indicates that the word can imply safety in either a physical sense or in a mental sense as relating to a state of mind.

However, there is another side to the word "betach." It is also understood to sometimes mean: without care, careless, or carelessly. In this context "betach" describes a group of people, or a place such as a city, in a mental state of assumed security where they are unsuspecting and confident in their safety and security, while that is in reality a false perception. Thus, "betach" can mean having a false sense of security.

We will take a look at several examples concerning how the word "betach" is utilized in scripture. Several passages will emphasize the importance of the mental state of mind associated with "betach" and how dangerous dwelling under a false sense of security can be. Although many scholars equate "betach" with safety, we will see that "betach" can actually mean just the opposite.

**1 Kings 4:25**

"And Judah and Israel dwelt **safely**, every man under his vine and under his fig tree, from Dan even to Beer-sheba, all the days of Solomon." The KJV renders "betach" as *safely* in 1 Kings 4:25 and clearly that is exactly what it means. The context of the surrounding passage indicates that Solomon had established peace on all of his borders.

**Genesis 34:25**

"And it came to pass on the third day, when they were sore, that two of the sons of Jacob, Simeon and Levi, Dinah's brethren, took each man his sword, and came upon the city **boldly**, and slew all the males." In this KJV translation of Genesis 34:25, "betach" is rendered as *boldly*. This is the first use of the word "betach" in the Bible. It is interesting to examine how this use of "betach" is rendered by other translations. Instead of boldly, *The Living Torah* states "without arousing suspicion."[1] *The Jerusalem Bible* uses the word "unresisted."[2] The NASB utilizes "unawares," while the NIV employs the word "unsuspecting."

Where the KJV translation of "betach" as boldly seems to point to the frame of mind of Simeon and Levi, the other translations point to the unsuspecting frame of mind of the men of the city of Shechem. The occupants of Shechem suffered from a false sense of security. The city was unsuspecting, which resulted in all of the males being killed. While the Hebrew word "betach" relates to the concept of safety or security, we can see in this example that the people of Shechem were, in reality, anything but safe or secure.

**Judges 8:11**

"And Gideon went up by the way of them that dwelt in tents on the east of Nobah and Jogbehah, and smote the host: for the host was **secure**." In Judges 8:11, the KJV translates "betach" as *secure*. In this case, *The Jerusalem Bible* also interprets "betach" as *secure* but does so by stating "for the camp thought itself secure."[3] Yaakov Elman translates this passage in *The Living Nach*, to the effect that the camp was "off guard."[4] The NASB renders this as "when the camp was unsuspecting." The NIV also utilizes the word *unsuspecting* for "betach" in this verse.

"Unsuspecting" is the best understanding of "betach" in this example. The very wording of Judges 8:11 implies that the security of these people was an illusion because Gideon was able to attack the camp successfully. These people had a false sense of security. They certainly were not secure or safe in any real sense.

**Judges 18:7**

"Then the five men departed, and came to Laish, and saw the people that were therein, how they dwelt **careless**, after the manner of the Zidonians, quiet and **secure**; and there was no magistrate in the land, that might put them to shame in any thing; and they were far from the Zidonians, and had no business with any man." In Judges 18:7 the KJV translates "betach" as *careless* in the first part of the verse. The word translated as *secure* later in this verse is the Hebrew word "bâtach" which is related to "betach." Instead of careless, both the NASB and *The Living Nach* render "betach" as "in security," while both the NIV and *The Jerusalem Bible* understand it as "in safety."

The five men were spies from the tribe of Dan, who were spying out the land. Ultimately, in Judges 18:27, the Danites attacked and destroyed the city of Laish. Thus, the occupants of Laish were not dwelling in any real condition of safety or security, but were living under a false sense of security.

**Jeremiah 49:31**

"Arise, get you up unto the wealthy nation, that dwelleth without **care**, saith the LORD, which have neither gates nor bars, which dwell alone." The KJV translates "betach" in Jeremiah 49:31 as *care* in the sense of being without care or carefree. *The Jerusalem Bible* renders this as "dwells in security." The NASB has this as "which lives securely" while the NIV translates it as "lives in confidence."

Can the concept of living in safety or security or dwelling securely relate to one's mental sense of confidence? Can having a false sense of security lead people to live seemingly without care, carefree, or carelessly?

**Ezekiel 30:9**

"In that day shall messengers go forth from me in ships to make the **careless** Ethiopians afraid, and great pain shall come upon them, as in the day of Egypt: for, lo, it cometh." In Ezekiel 30:9 the KJV translates "betach" as *careless*. The NASB renders this as "to frighten **secure** Ethiopia" while the NIV translates it as "to frighten Cush out of her **complacency**." *The Jerusalem Bible* renders this passage as "to terrify the **confident** men of Kush."

We see that the concept of "betach" as *secure*, in this example of its use, is really about the mental state of mind of the Ethiopians. The prophet Ezekiel is describing a pending judgment from God which reveals that the Ethiopians were not really safe or secure. The Ethiopians were living under a false sense of security.

**Isaiah 47:8**

"Therefore hear now this, thou that art given to pleasures, that dwellest **carelessly**, that sayest in thine heart, I am, and none else beside me; I shall not sit as a widow, neither shall I know the loss of children." The KJV translates "betach" in Isaiah 47:8 as *carelessly*. The NASB and *The Jerusalem Bible* both translate this use of "betach" as *securely*, while the NIV renders it as *security* in the sense of "lounging in your security."

The context of Isaiah 47:9-11 makes it clear that these people are neither secure nor safe. Both the loss of children and widowhood will suddenly fall upon them. These people are not only dwelling under a false sense of confidence or security, they are living in denial of the true circumstances they face. Thus, in this example of "betach," they are dwelling carelessly.

**Zephaniah 2:15**

"This is the rejoicing city that dwelt **carelessly**, that said in her heart, I am, and there is none beside me: how is she become a desolation, a place for beasts to lie down in! every one that passeth by her shall hiss, and wag his hand." Zephaniah 2:15 provides another instance where the KJV translates "betach" as *carelessly*. The NASB and *The Jerusalem Bible* both render this as *securely*, while the NIV translates it as *in safety*.

This is another example of the Hebrew word "betach" being used to demonstrate that a false sense of confidence or security can lead to disaster.

**Ezekiel 39:6**

"And I will send fire on Magog, and among them that dwell **carelessly** in the isles: and they shall know that I am the LORD." This is the fourth instance that the word "betach" shows up in the prophecy of Gog and Magog. Instead of safely, the KJV translates this occurrence of "betach" in Ezekiel 39:6 as *carelessly. The Jerusalem Bible* renders this use of "betach" as *securely*, while both the NASB and the NIV translations have it as *in safety*.

Since God is promising to send a judgment of fire upon these peoples who dwell in the isles or coastlands, they are obviously not living in true safety or security. They just think that they are safe. They are living carelessly, unsuspecting, dwelling under a false sense of confidence or security. They are also living in denial of God's promise to send a judgment of fire upon them. This is another form of carelessness – discounting the literalness of God's prophetic scriptures.

## Observations regarding Ezekiel 38–39

Israel's true security does not depend upon walls, bars, fences, and gates, or even upon its own military defense forces. It is not reliant upon a security barrier wall separating Israeli and Palestinian populated areas. The security that Israel needs lies in a faithful relationship with God. The only source of protection that really makes a difference is God. Without God's divine blessing and hedge of protection, the best defense forces, walls, and gates, are merely stop gap measures that enhance a false sense of security.

Until Israel enters into a national faithful relationship with God, it cannot be considered to be dwelling securely. Israel must return to the God of Abraham, Isaac, and Jacob in trust and reliance upon Him for their protection. Israel must awaken to the identity of and accept the genuine Messiah of God – Yeshua (Jesus Christ). Until that happens, Israel will not have an authentic faithful relationship with God and cannot have true security or realistically dwell in safety.

One of the important characteristics of Ezekiel 38–39, as it relates to this issue, that is often not considered, is that God is adamant that Israel is profaning God's holy name at the time of Gog's invasion. The nation of Israel is not in a faithful spiritual relationship with God, even though it has largely returned to the land and is blessed with wealth. This is a key underlying reason that God initiates the invasion of Gog and Magog – to protect and magnify His holy name.

How does Israel profane God's holy name? How does Israel cause God's name to be profaned by others? Israel has a long history of turning its back on God in spite of God's many blessings. When Israel rejected Jesus as God's Messiah, God placed Israel under the prophesied curses of Deuteronomy 28. God used the Romans to destroy the Temple in Jerusalem and to eject Israel from the land. God hid His face from Israel and imposed a shroud of silence in His relationship to Israel, as if Israel was dead. Israel became: "Not my people." Israel was both separated and divorced from God. Yet God kept Israel and its unique identity alive. This heaven-imposed blackout buffeted Israel through a murky haze: between life and death, between the world and God, between its tumultuous past and its glorious prophetic future, between total darkness and God's light at the end of a very long tunnel. This estrangement from God resulted in Israel's long Diaspora of wanderings throughout the nations of the world under the curses imposed by God. As a consequence the nations are able:

- To deny that the God of Israel even exists.
- To deny that God still loves Israel.
- To deny that Israel is still the apple of God's eye.
- To claim that God cannot or will not protect Israel.
- To claim that the church has replaced Israel as the true Israel.
- To claim that Islam has replaced Judaism and the Koran has replaced the Bible.

Since God largely created this situation with Israel, He bears a lot of responsibility for these consequences, unintended or not. God foresaw and timed the results of these consequences – so that He would have the opportunity and obligation to intervene in defense of His own holy name at just the right prophetic time. God created the prophecy of the War of Gog and Magog for the very same reason.

Throughout Israel's history, whenever Israel remained in faithful observance of the conditions of the covenants that God specifically gave to it as a nation, Israel dwelt in genuine safety. However, when Israel violated the conditions of God's covenants, Israel lost the condition of security that God provided. Therefore, by God's own principles, Israel cannot truly be dwelling in safety until Israel is fully restored in its faithful spiritual relationship to God. That complete spiritual restoration cannot come until Israel accepts Jesus Christ as God's Messiah. That cannot happen before the fulfillment of Ezekiel's prophecy of Gog and Magog because Israel would then not be profaning God's holy name. In this context, a covenant of peace guaranteed to Israel by any world leader will not bring a condition of dwelling safely. It would still be a condition of dwelling under a false sense of security.

## Dwelling Safely Conclusion

These are only a few examples of the use of the Hebrew word "betach" in scripture. Some other uses of "betach" focus on God's protection of Israel as the defining characteristic which brings safety to Israel. This is how the word is used in Deuteronomy 12:10; Psalm 4:8; and Psalm 78:53. In Leviticus "betach" is used in the context of Israel dwelling in the land safely or in safety, but only if they keep God's statutes and commandments (Lev 25:18-19; 26:5). Many other verses that incorporate the word "betach" look forward to the time when God will give Israel rest from all of her enemies so that Israel will dwell in genuine safety in the Messianic Kingdom. These uses of "betach" point to the future safety of Israel following the Day-of-the-LORD judgments (Deut 33:28; Jer 23:6, 32:37, 33:16; Ezek 28:26, 34:25, 34:27-28, and 39:26; Hos 2:18; and Zech 14:11). Ezekiel 39:26 is the last use of "betach" in the prophecy of Gog and Magog and specifically points to a state that will exist during a time of safety after the invasion and after all the people of Israel are regathered to the land by God.

However, it should be clear from the lessons of the cited examples that the surface interpretation of "betach" as: safe, safely, safety, secure, or securely may not present the actual condition of the people who are being written about. The state of mind of the people must be considered in the context of their larger surroundings. Are they truly dwelling safely, or are they harboring a false sense of security? Are they dwelling carelessly when they should know better?

The context of Ezekiel 38 has Israel looked upon as a vulnerable prey by a number of enemy nations. This is not the characteristic of a nation that is under the strong protection of a covenant of peace, but the characteristic of a nation that has left itself vulnerable by placing its trust in the wrong places. This is the characteristic of a nation that harbors a false sense of security. Israel will be dwelling carelessly in regards to its own real security interests.

Does this sound familiar?

For a number of years Israel has been dwelling under a false sense of security. Israel entered into the Oslo Accords under the false sense that trading land to the Palestinians, allowing the formation of the Palestinian Authority, and arming a Palestinian security force would bring peace to Israel. "Land for peace" did not bring peace. Israel further compromised and entered into the "Road Map" for Middle East peace by giving up more land and concessions to the Palestinians. It did not bring peace. Israel pulled its forces out of southern Lebanon, allowing Hezbollah to have free reign over that territory to the north of Israel. It did not bring peace. Israel unilaterally withdrew from Gaza and acceded control of Jewish settlements, greenhouses, and synagogues to the Palestinians. Israel's leaders claimed it would foster peace. It did not bring peace to Israel. Instead, Israel's actions fostered chaos, increased terrorism, and placed Israeli citizens at greater risk.

Israel has placed a very strong reliance upon its military and security forces. Israeli's have a right to be proud of their military. The Israeli Defense Forces are technologically advanced, extremely motivated, and generally highly innovative in their approach to dealing with tactical problems. The size and reach of Israel's military greatly exceeds the capability that could reasonably be expected of such a small nation.

However, the Israeli people have placed a false level of confidence in the ability of their military forces and their political leaders to protect them. They have also placed a false sense of security in their relationships to larger nations to act as a support mechanism and buffer between Israel and the Arab-Muslim nations of North Africa, the Middle East, and Central Asia. Israel relies too heavily upon the political support of the United States, the European Union, the United Nations, and Russia. Israel is gambling that these nations, and groups of nations, will not turn against her or abandon her to her more openly declared foes. The recent events of the Arab Spring and the temporary rise of the Muslim Brotherhood to power in Egypt give evidence against Israel's misplaced reliance that the United States or other nations either can, or will, control events or nations in the Middle East by putting Israel's security first.

Israel's present misplaced false sense of security is quickly catching up to her place in God's prophetic scripture. The prophecy of Ezekiel 38–39 reveals that a massive invasion by an alliance of nations will suddenly strike Israel to take advantage of her apparent weakness or vulnerability.

If we realize that Ezekiel's use of "betach" in the three verses of Ezekiel 38 is more reflective of Israel's dwelling carelessly under a false sense of security, as opposed to an actual condition of safety, then we can understand the prophecy of Gog and Magog as an event unrelated to Daniel's seven-year covenant of peace. Nowhere in Ezekiel 38 or 39 does the prophet Ezekiel mention or make any reference to a strong world leader who protects Israel, to a covenant of peace, or to the period of time known as Daniel's 70th Week. The invasion of Gog and Magog can come suddenly upon an Israel dwelling carelessly under a false sense of security, at any time. In fact, Ezekiel's invasion scenario can create the perfect environment for the rise of the Antichrist and the implementation of Daniel's strong covenant. This allows for a pretribulational fulfillment of Gog and Magog.

## Gog & Magog in the Chronology of the End Times

When does the invasion of Israel by the alliance of Gog and Magog take place during the End Times? There is much confusion and controversy regarding this issue. There are several theories presented by prophecy scholars as to when this event occurs. The prophetic chronology of the time of the end reveals several key time frames during which the War of Gog and Magog could possibly occur. These include:

A. Some time shortly before to several years before the beginning of the seven-year Tribulation.
B. At the very beginning of the Tribulation.
C. During the first half of the Tribulation after the seven-year Covenant of Peace is confirmed with Israel by the Antichrist, to just before the middle of the Tribulation.
D. At the Midpoint of the Tribulation.
E. Near the end of the tribulation during the War of Armageddon.
F. After the War of Armageddon, during the interval between the Tribulation and the Millennium, or at the very beginning of the Millennium.
G. At the very end of the Millennium.

### Key Factors:

Several details of specific information, provided by Ezekiel in chapters 38 and 39, are critical for properly analyzing the time frame of Gog and Magog, and making an accurate determination as to when it is possible or impossible, or probable or improbable, for this war to take place. The determining factors given by Ezekiel include:

- Israel is dwelling "safely" in the land (under a false sense of security) at the time of the invasion. It is a land brought back from war, a people gathered out of many nations, and mountains that have been a continual waste for a long time.
- The invasion of Gog and Magog is instigated by God to have the invading armies serve His purpose by rousing the fury of His jealousy for His people Israel. God gives Himself the reason to supernaturally intervene to protect Israel and to judge the nations of

this alliance by destroying the invading armies and much of their homelands in a supernatural display of His wrath.

- Israel is polluting the holy name of God, and God instigates the invasion for the specific purpose of sanctifying His holy name among the people of Israel, and among the nations of the world.
- Israel undergoes a partial spiritual rebirth following the destruction of Gog and Magog. Israel recognizes that God has intervened in its defense and has returned His face towards Israel after many long years of being focused elsewhere.
- Israel is given a specific period of seven months for cleansing the land and the burial of Gog's dead soldiers immediately following the war.
- Israel is given a specific period of seven years for burning the weapons left by Gog's armies following the war.

## Missing Pieces of the Puzzle:

What is missing in the content of this prophecy?

Some authors approach the prophecy of Ezekiel 38–39 with preconceived notions about what it is about and when it will take place, and as a result they unfortunately read into the prophecy conditions that are not actually described by Ezekiel. It is important to note what the prophecy does not specifically tell us. As objective students of prophecy, we should not read into the prophecy, or draw unwarranted conclusions based upon information that is not present. Therefore, it is observed that there is absolutely no mention made by Ezekiel in chapters 38 or 39 of the following:

- There is no description of Israel's form of government or spiritual worship. There is no king, high priest, priesthood, temple, or temple sacrifices.
- There is no seven-year covenant of peace mentioned as being in place, or being broken.
- There is no antichrist, false prophet, abomination of desolation, or mark of the Beast.
- While it can be easy to confuse Gog with the king of the North, there is no specific mention of the king of the North, king of the South, Babylon, Egypt, the drying up of the Euphrates River, the kings of the East, or the massing of armies at Megiddo.
- There is no Jewish remnant holed up in the area of Bozrah (Petra), or war being waged against the saints.

- There is no direct mention of any of Israel's immediate neighbors: Lebanon, Syria, Jordan, Egypt, or Gaza, or even of adversaries within the midst of Israel (the Palestinians in the West Bank).
- There is no reference to the Jewish Messiah, Jesus Christ, the Second Coming, the armies of the invaders being destroyed by the brightness of God or the Messiah, or by the sword from His mouth, or of the people seeing the Messiah whom they had pierced.
- There is no final judgment of the Gentile nations by God or Christ, the resurrection of the dead, or of Gog or any other leader of his alliance being cast into the Lake of Fire.

## Prime Times for Gog & Magog

This section lays out seven major possible placements for the War of Gog and Magog and highlights pros and cons applying to each of these time frames. The letters designating each placement on the prophetic timeline correlate to the lettered bullets noted in the list below. For the purposes of this section, the Tribulation is considered to be Daniel's 70th Week, which is a period of seven years.

**Prime Times for Gog & Magog**

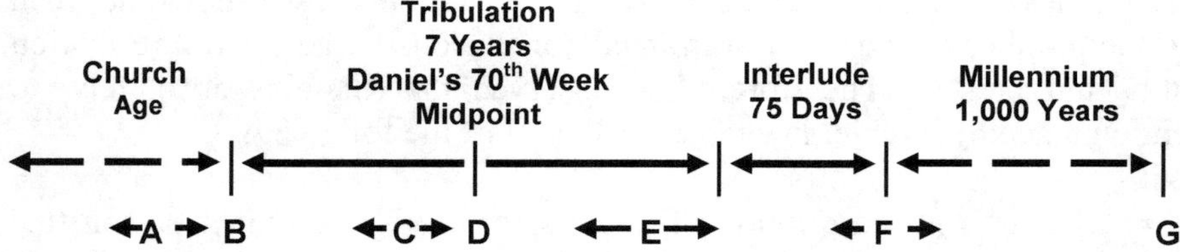


**A) Prior to the beginning of the 7 years of Tribulation**
**B) At the very beginning of the Tribulation**
**C) Before the middle of the Tribulation**
**D) At the midpoint of the Tribulation**
**E) Near the end of the Tribulation during the War of Armageddon**
**F) During the 75 Day Interlude, or at the beginning of the Millennium**
**G) At the very end of the Millennium**

**A) Prior to the beginning of the Tribulation**

Arguments For:

- Israel can be considered to be a land brought back from war, a people gathered out of many nations, and mountains that have been a continual waste until the recent rebirth of the nation.
- Although Israel is not completely living safely or peacefully, as it is subject to frequent deadly acts of terrorism, Israel is a land of unwalled villages and does have a false sense of security based upon an overconfidence or false confidence in the power of its military. This confidence could be further bolstered if Israel takes a decisive and successful military stand against the terrorist threat of Hamas in Gaza, Hezbollah in Lebanon, or the support provided to Islamic terrorism by Syria or Iran. An Israeli victory over the Psalm 83 confederacy would also enhance this mind-set.
- Israel can be considered to be dwelling in the land in spiritual unbelief and polluting the holy name of God (Ezek 39:7). God initiates the invasion of Gog and Magog to sanctify His name and to make it known among Israel and the nations. This time frame lays the groundwork for a partial spiritual awakening by Israel, for Israel to accept an emerging leader as the Messiah, and for the rebuilding of the Jewish Temple.
- The alliance of invading armies are destroyed by God before the Tribulation, creating a power vacuum, that allows the Antichrist to emerge and begin his rise to global power, and may set the stage for the seven-year covenant of peace with Israel.
- The seven months of cleansing the land and the burial of the dead occurs prior to the breaking of the peace covenant by the Antichrist at the midpoint of the Tribulation during a time when Israel is in complete control of its land.
- The seven years of burning the weapons can be substantially or entirely completed before the Antichrist takes over the Temple at the Midpoint and begins massive persecution of the Jews who reject him. This would be especially true if Gog's invasion takes place 3 ½ years or more prior to the confirmation of the seven-year covenant of peace.
- The pretribulational fulfillment of Gog and Magog is the only timing view that does not conflict with any of the conditional requirements described by Ezekiel. Nor does this timing for Gog's invasion

unnecessarily insert any other end-time characters or events that are not mentioned or revealed in Ezekiel's prophecy.

Arguments Against:

- Some argue that Israel is not dwelling safely in the land prior to the seven-year covenant of peace being confirmed by the Antichrist. However, as we have seen, Ezekiel is really describing the people of Israel as dwelling under a false sense of security – not true safety.
- Some argue that Israel could not reject or misinterpret God's miraculous intervention and enter into rebellion against God by turning to and accepting the claims of a False Prophet or Antichrist soon after the destruction of Gog and Magog. However, Israel's history is riddled with a pattern of this type of rebellious behavior going all the way back to the Exodus.
- Some argue that Gog and Magog must take place within the context of Daniel's 70$^{th}$ Week (the seven-year Tribulation) because the prophecy places it within Israel's "latter years" and "last days." However, scripture never defines these terms in this limited manner. This objection ignores the possibility, and probability, that Ezekiel 38–39 is the very event that marks the beginning point of Israel's latter years or last days, or that Israel's latter years began with its rebirth in 1948.

**B) At the beginning of the Tribulation**

Arguments For:

- The beginning of the Tribulation is marked by the confirmation of a seven-year covenant of peace between Israel and an emerging world leader who will become the Antichrist. The invasion of Gog and Magog can either be the event that produces the covenant in its immediate aftermath, or a rebellious event as an immediate and direct result of the signing of the covenant. The alliance of invading armies are destroyed at the very beginning of the Tribulation, creating a power vacuum, that allows the Antichrist to accelerate his rise to global power.
- Israel can be considered to be a land brought back from war, a people gathered out of many nations, and mountains that have been a continual waste until the recent rebirth of the nation.

- Although Israel is not completely dwelling safely or peacefully, as it is subject to frequent deadly acts of terrorism, Israel is a land of unwalled villages and does have a false sense of security or false confidence in the power of its military.
- Israel can be considered to be dwelling in the land in spiritual unbelief and polluting the holy name of God (Ezek 39:7). God initiates the invasion of Gog and Magog to sanctify His name and to make it known among Israel and the nations. This time frame lays the groundwork for a partial spiritual rebirth by Israel, and for Israel to accept an emerging leader as the Messiah, and for the rebuilding of the Jewish Temple.
- The seven months of cleansing the land and the burial of the dead occurs prior to the breaking of the peace covenant by the Antichrist at the midpoint of the Tribulation during a time when Israel is in complete control of its land. The seven months cleansing of the land and burial of the dead could coincide with the time of rebuilding of the Jewish Temple.
- It has been argued that the seven-year period for burning the weapons for fuel and the seven-year Tribulation being the same length of time is not a coincidence. This view believes these two periods run concurrently, and thus are one and the same.
- 3 ½ years of the 7 years for burning the weapons can be completed before the Antichrist takes over the Temple at the midpoint of Daniel's 70th Week and begins massive persecution of the Jews who reject him. It is then argued that there will be apostate Jews in Israel who will accept the Antichrist who can continue to burn the weapons during the second half of the Tribulation. Also, some of the weapons (fuel) may be taken into hiding (refuge) with the remnant of Israel when it flees from the Antichrist.

Arguments Against:

- The invasion of Gog and Magog cannot be the event that begins the Tribulation or Daniel's 70th Week. That distinction is the confirmation of a seven-year covenant of peace between Israel and a world leader. Gog and Magog either (and most likely) precedes this event by some period of time or follows after it by some period of time.
- Some argue that Israel is not dwelling safely in the land prior to the seven-year covenant of peace being confirmed by the Antichrist. However, if the invasion of Israel by Gog and Magog is the result of

an immediate direct challenge against the covenant of peace, then the covenant does not really add any measure of safety to Israel.

- While some believe that we are given the information of a seven-year period for burning the weapons so that we can directly associate it with the seven-year period of the Tribulation, perhaps God gives us this information so that we can do just the opposite. Perhaps we are to use this information wisely, as a means of testing the character of the time period that is indicated. Since Gog and Magog is not the event that begins Daniel's 70th Week, the seven years for burning the weapons cannot exactly match the seven years of the Tribulation. There would be at least a short but significant inherent conflict between these two time periods.
- It will be very difficult for Israel to be burning the weapons of Gog and Magog in compliance with this prophecy during the second half of the Tribulation when the Antichrist and False Prophet are waging a war of persecution against the Jews and Christians who reject them. "And they that dwell in the cities of Israel shall go forth, and shall set on fire and burn the weapons … and they shall burn them with fire seven years: So that they shall take no wood out of the field, neither cut down *any* out of the forests; for they shall burn the weapons with fire: and they shall spoil those that spoiled them, and rob those that robbed them, saith the Lord GOD" (Ezek 39:9-10). The language of Ezekiel 39 is such that the people of Israel come out from dwelling in their own cities to spoil the armies that intended to spoil them by burning the weapons for fuel. Israel will not have to cut any firewood (or use other natural resources) for fuel during that period of seven years. This language strongly points to Israel living freely in its own cities and being in control of its own land the entire time of this process, as opposed to fleeing and being in hiding from the armies of the Antichrist. Israel will perform these tasks while basking in the glow of God's miraculous intervention to save Israel from total destruction. A divided and subjugated Israel, with only some left in the land, does not conform to the character of God's prophecy. Israel's reaction to the destruction of Gog and Magog will be that it is entering its promised Golden Age when its needs are to be met by God supernaturally. The plundering of the battlefield and the burning of the weapons for fuel symbolizes the providence of God during Israel's Golden Age. However, this is just a taste. God is not finished testing or refining Israel. Israel will not truly enter its Golden Age until it completely comes to terms with God by repenting of its national iniquity and accepting Jesus Christ as its Messiah. The Antichrist will be God's Messianic test for Israel. The

entire seven-year period of burning must precede the betrayal of Israel by the Antichrist. From that moment on Israel will be a perilous place. Any timing view for the fulfillment of Gog and Magog that places any part of the burning of the weapons for fuel during any part of the second half of Daniel's $70^{th}$ Week is in conflict with God's character portrayal of this prophecy.

**C) During the first half to just before the middle of the Tribulation**

Arguments For:

- Israel is described as dwelling safely in the land, which some argue places this event in the first half of the Tribulation when Israel is under the covenant of peace before it is violated by the Antichrist at the Midpoint.
- The invasion of Gog and Magog is viewed by some as a direct challenge against the Antichrist and his covenant of peace by invading Israel.
- The seven months of cleansing the land and burying the dead can be completed before the Antichrist takes over the Temple at the Midpoint, during a time when Israel is in control of its territory.

Arguments Against:

- It is highly significant that **none** of the end-time leaders, events, or conditions that are generally considered to be so characteristic of the first half of the Tribulation are directly mentioned or alluded to in Ezekiel's description of Gog and Magog.
- It is argued that dwelling safely means dwelling under a false sense of security – confidently in the sense of false confidence or overconfidence and does not mean that Israel is living under the conditions of a covenant of peace. There is no mention of any peace covenant or protector of Israel in either Ezekiel 38 or 39.
- The first half timing places the war and the cleansing of the land and burying the dead during a time when the Temple and system of daily animal sacrifices will be in service. There is no mention of the Temple in Ezekiel 38 and 39 or of the Temple being in service before the war, during the war, or during the cleanup. It is specifically mentioned that God instigates the invasion to sanctify his holy name among the midst of His people (Ezek 38:23; 39:7). This

stated objective points to a time frame prior to the Temple being rebuilt and the temple services being reinstated.

- o How can Israel enter into any phase of restoration and begin to rebuild its Temple if Russia, Iran, Islamic terrorism, and Islamic hatred of Israel are not dealt a serious blow first? No world leader has the power to allow Israel to rebuild its Temple under the present conditions of the Middle East or those of the foreseeable future. It will take the direct intervention of God to change this situation temporarily. That is exactly the intervention that Ezekiel's prophecy describes. The destruction of Gog and his Islamic allies by God precedes the rebuilding of the Jewish Temple, which must be rebuilt and in service during the first half of the Tribulation. This argues for an earlier fulfillment of Ezekiel's prophecy.
- o The seven years required for burning the weapons for fuel will cause the period of burning to extend through the War of Armageddon and into the Millennial Kingdom of God. This places the burning of the weapons throughout the entire second half of the Tribulation, throughout the final plagues of God's wrath, and into the Millennium, which conflicts with the massive renovation of the land that will occur immediately or shortly after the second coming of Christ when the earth itself will be freed from the curse on creation (Rom 8:19-23).

**D) At the Midpoint of the Tribulation**

Arguments For:

- Israel is viewed as dwelling in peace and safety in the land under a covenant of peace up to this point.
- Some view the invasion of Gog and Magog as a direct result of the Antichrist's declaration the he is God and his initiation of the Abomination of Desolation in the Jewish Temple in Jerusalem.
- Some view Gog as the king of the North of Daniel 11:40 and see the kings of the North and South attacking Israel at this point in the form of Gog and Magog.
- Some view Gog and Magog as the breaking of the false peace of the first half of the Tribulation, giving the Antichrist a reason to break the conditions of his covenant of peace with Israel, and thus initiating the events of the Great Tribulation of the second half of Daniel's $70^{th}$ Week.

Arguments Against:

- The events at the Midpoint initiated by the Antichrist are so dramatic and so important in their impact upon Israel that it is highly significant that **none** of these events are referenced in Ezekiel's description of Gog and Magog. Neither the Antichrist, the covenant of peace, God's two witnesses, the Temple, the stopping of the daily sacrifices, the abomination of desolation, the miracles and deception propagated by the Antichrist and the False Prophet, nor the persecution of Israel is referenced in any way in Ezekiel 38 or 39. Why would God ignore mentioning these conditions if Gog and Magog had any direct relationship to any of them?
- During the first half of the Tribulation, Israel will undergo a partial spiritual revival to God and will rebuild the Temple. It does not logically follow that God would instigate this invasion for the purpose of magnifying and sanctifying His holy name among Israel and the nations only to have this be immediately followed by the Antichrist blaspheming God and declaring himself to be God in the Temple in Jerusalem. Nor does it logically follow that God would use Gog and Magog to attack the Antichrist because of his desecration of the Temple and his blasphemy against God and then supernaturally destroy Gog and his forces while leaving the Antichrist in place with supernatural authority for 3 ½ more years. What would be the point of God's intervention against Gog at the midpoint of the Tribulation? How would that magnify God's holy name?
- Israel cannot be considered to be dwelling safely in the land at, or immediately after, the time the Antichrist betrays Israel by violating the seven-year covenant of peace, forcibly taking over the Temple and declaring himself to be God.
- This places the seven months of cleansing the land and burial of the dead at a time when Israel is warned to flee in haste from Jerusalem and Judea into a place of refuge in the wilderness. The Antichrist and False Prophet will begin a massive campaign of persecution against those who reject him. It will be impossible for Israel to undertake the clean-up process described by Ezekiel during this time of major persecution. The cleansing of the land and burial process must be completed prior to the midpoint of the Tribulation.
- The seven years required for burning the invaders weapons for fuel will cause the period of burning to extend through the War of Armageddon and about 3 ½ years into the Millennial Kingdom of God. This places the burning of the weapons throughout the entire

second half of the Tribulation, throughout the final plagues of God's wrath, and into the Millennium, which conflicts with the massive renovation of the land that will occur immediately or shortly after the second coming of Christ when the earth itself will be freed from the curse on creation (Rom 8:19-23).

**E) Near the end of the Tribulation during the War of Armageddon**

Arguments For:

- Gog is viewed as either Daniel's king of the North, or the Antichrist, or both, in his attack against Israel.
- Gog and Magog is a phase of the war of Armageddon or is considered to be symbolic of all nations coming against Jerusalem.
- God's supernatural intervention to defeat Gog and Magog is viewed, by some, as the second coming of Jesus Christ.
- The feast of the birds and beasts in Ezekiel 39 is taken as the same feast of the birds in Revelation 19, immediately following the end of the War of Armageddon.
- The restoration language of Ezekiel 39:21-29 is interpreted as the Messianic Kingdom being initiated immediately following the destruction of Gog and Magog.

Arguments Against:

- Gog is not the Antichrist. Their characteristics, roles, authority, and deaths are very different. This is examined in greater detail in the next section: Gog & Magog vs. Antichrist & Armageddon, and the table: Gog vs. Antichrist.
- Gog and Magog is a significant but limited alliance that invades Israel with no success. The War of Armageddon is characterized by all nations coming to war against Israel and against God. The armies of the Antichrist are much more successful in their efforts against Israel for a time, and the war lasts much longer than that of Gog and Magog.
- Israel will be dwelling "at rest" and safely (under a false sense of security) at the time of Gog's invasion. However, Israel will not have any rest and no security, nor will it have any pretense of security, throughout the entire second half of the Tribulation until after the end of the War of Armageddon. It is a time of intense persecution

during which a remnant of Israel will flee into hiding in the wilderness (Bozrah – Petra).

- Israel will be polluting the name of God at the time of Gog and Magog, as it will still be in spiritual rebellion against God and Jesus Christ as God's Messiah. By the time of Armageddon, the remnant of Israel will have repented to God and accepted Jesus as Messiah.
- God specifically leads Gog and Magog against Israel for His own purpose. The armies of the world are gathered at Megiddo specifically by the demonic influence of Satan, the Antichrist, and the False Prophet (Rev 16:13-14).
- Ezekiel 38:13 describes a protest by a few nations, including Arab-Muslim nations (Sheba and Dedan), as a result of the invasion. However, there is no scriptural evidence of any diplomatic protest or defense of Israel by these nations at the time of Armageddon.
- Ezekiel describes God's initial judgments following a long period of silence when He intervenes against Gog and Magog in wrath. However, Armageddon does not come until after a long series of God's supernatural judgments and wrath that have devastated much of the earth.
- While Gog and Magog are immediately followed by overlapping time periods of seven months for burying the dead and seven years for burning the weapons for fuel, Armageddon is immediately followed by only a period of seventy-five days which precedes the 1,000 year Messianic Kingdom (Dan 12:12).

Additional observations and arguments regarding this time frame are provided in the later table: War of Gog & Magog vs. War of Armageddon.

**F) After the War of Armageddon, during the interval between the Tribulation and the Millennium, or at the very beginning of the Millennium**

Arguments For:

- Israel will truly be dwelling in peace and safety in the land.
- Israel will be a land recently restored from the sword of war.
- Israel will be a people regathered to the land from many nations.
- The defeat of Gog and Magog results in Gentile nations coming to know God.

Arguments Against:

- Revelation 15:1 presents seven angels with the last seven plagues of God's wrath. These are the last plagues in which God's anger (wrath) is "filled up" or completed. Yet God's anger and wrath arises against Gog and Magog. Gog and Magog must come earlier in the End Times before God's wrath is expended.
- The enemies of God and Israel are completely defeated by Jesus Christ at His second coming. The Antichrist, the False Prophet, the Kings of the earth and their armies are destroyed (Rev 17:14; 19:19-21). What armies are left to attack Israel?
- Satan is bound and confined in the Abyss for 1,000 years. He is not deceiving the nations or provoking them to war.
- The character of this time frame after Armageddon is one of restoration and renovation, not war. Israel is completely regathered. The land is completely restored. The topography is significantly changed.
- Weapons of war will be destroyed or converted into agricultural implements and all warfare and training for war will cease (Isa 2:4; Hos 2:18; Mic 4:3).
- God's purpose for the invasion of Gog and Magog – to magnify His holy name – is completely purposeless at this point in time soon after the second coming of Christ.
- Israel will be spiritually restored as a nation under the New Covenant and will not be profaning God's name at this point in time. Israel will have recently come to terms with God and accepted Jesus Christ as God's and Israel's Messiah.
- Some scholars believe that the time periods of seven months for cleansing the land and burying the dead and the seven years for plundering the weapons of war and burning the weapons for fuel are uncharacteristic of this time frame at the beginning of the Millennium when there will be large scale supernatural restoration of the land (restoration of all things – Act 3:20-21 NASB, RV).
- The very characteristic in Ezekiel 38 of Israel being surrounded by a ring of enemy nations, who are well armed by a common source and who coordinate an attack against Israel, begs for fulfillment in a different time frame.

**G) At the very end of the Millennium**

Arguments For:

- Revelation 20:8 mentions "Gog and Magog" in association with the nations that Satan deceives and gathers into his rebellion.
- Israel will truly be dwelling in peace and safety in the land.
- God supernaturally destroys the rebellion by fire from heaven.

Arguments Against:

- The characteristics of the Millennium, and the events and circumstances at the end of the Millennial Kingdom of Christ, that introduce the Eternal Kingdom when God will institute a New Heaven and a New Earth, are completely inconsistent with many specific details of Ezekiel's prophecy.
- Israel has not been profaning God's holy name for 1,000 years.
- God has no need to magnify Himself or make His name known to Israel or the Gentile nations at the end of the 1,000 year reign of Christ during the Messianic Kingdom.
- Israel has been a renovated land for 1,000 years – it is not a land recently brought back from war, a people recently gathered out of many nations, and mountains that have been a continual waste.
- The period of 7 months for cleansing the land and burial of the dead is inconsistent with this time frame since it is going to immediately be followed by the resurrection of the dead to stand in judgment before the Great White Throne of God.
- The period of 7 years for burning the weapons of war is inconsistent with this time frame.
- God's feast for the birds and beasts of the field is completely inconsistent with this time frame. God will restore peace and harmony between man, nature, and the animal kingdom during the Millennium.

Additional observations and arguments regarding this time frame are provided in the later table: Ezekiel 38 & 39 vs. Revelation 20.

## Chronology Conclusion

The only timing for the fulfillment of Ezekiel 38–39 that does not have a major conflict with one or more of Ezekiel's critical conditions imbedded within the prophecy is the pretribulational time frame. It is also the only perspective that does not insert end-time characters, conditions, or events which are not directly present within the wording of this prophecy. A pretribulational fulfillment also best serves the purpose of God for this prophecy. God instigates and destroys Gog and the Magog alliance at the very beginning of His Day of the LORD judgments. This allows for God to magnify His holy name to Israel and the nations as He begins Israel's "last days" and sets Israel up for its final period of testing. God's supernatural intervention to save Israel from destruction promotes Israel's reawakening to God and the return of the Jews in much greater numbers to the land of Israel. It serves to break down the internal barriers within Israel's Jewish society and secular government to the rebuilding of their Temple, as well as the external barriers to a Jewish Temple created by the hatred and conflicting interests of Islam, Roman Catholicism, Replacement Theology, Anti-Zionism, the land-for-peace process, and any world economic interests that are dependent upon Middle Eastern oil. It gives Israel the motivation and time to build the Jewish Temple in Jerusalem and enter it into service before Satan and the Antichrist initiate their final campaign of destruction against Israel.

**The Timing of the War of Gog and Magog**

God's destruction of Gog and Magog creates a political and military power vacuum, both in the Middle East and globally. This power vacuum could be very instrumental in allowing for the emergence and rise to power of the Antichrist. It could create the conditions that bring about the confirmation of the seven-year covenant of peace which has been so elusive to date. God's intervention not only neutralizes the barriers to the Jews reclaiming their presence on the Temple Mount and building their Temple, but God also neutralizes the barriers to the present peace process while He completely demolishes the entire "land-for-peace" concept by expanding Israel's present borders and sphere of influence considerably.

## Gog & Magog vs. Antichrist & Armageddon

Gog: Are You the One?
Gog: Are You the Antichrist?
Is Gog & Magog the War of Armageddon?

These are three strongly related questions that require a certain amount of more detailed analysis. Who is the prophetic end-time leader referred to in Ezekiel 38:17? Is Gog that leader? Is Gog the same end-time leader known as the Antichrist? If Gog is the Antichrist, then the War of Gog and Magog must be the War of Armageddon ending with the second coming of Christ. Is the invasion of Gog and Magog the same war as Armageddon? Is God's revealed presence in Ezekiel 38–39 the same as the second coming of Christ? Scholars are divided in their answers to these questions.

### Gog: Are You the One?

> Thus saith the Lord GOD; Art thou he of whom I have spoken in old time by my servants the prophets of Israel, which prophesied in those days many years that I would bring thee against them? (Ezek 38:17)

Why does God include this verse in His prophecy regarding Gog and Magog in chapters 38 and 39 of the book of Ezekiel? In verses 38:2-3 and 39:1, God establishes that the prophecy is directed towards a future leader, Gog, of the land of Magog, and that God, Himself, is specifically against this leader Gog. Ezekiel tells us that God declares, "Behold, I am against thee, O Gog," at the beginning of both chapters.

God is focused on Gog in a very unfavorable manner. Gog is asked if he thinks he is the one whom God has spoken about through the prophets. Is Gog the one who will successfully invade Israel and bring destruction to the land? Is Gog the prophetic end-time leader referred to in Ezekiel 38:17?

This is a verse that has caused some confusion and misunderstanding for many readers of the prophecy of Ezekiel 38–39. Most readers and scholars conclude that God is telling us that Gog and his invasion were already predicted by the prophets, prior to Ezekiel's time, and that Gog will be the fulfillment of those prophecies. However, I believe that conclusion is a misunderstanding of the character of this passage.

Scholars, who interpret Gog as the fulfillment of previous prophecies, struggle with identifying which prophecies were written about Gog. This is an inevitable result of not having any prophecies in the Old Testament that specifically name Gog. The only exception to this lack of identification of Gog is in the Septuagint translation of Numbers 24:7 and Amos 7:1. In the Septuagint, Gog replaces Agag in Numbers 24:7, and in Amos 7:1 Gog is mentioned as a king of the locusts. Neither of these translations is consistent with the Masoretic text and neither helps us in the identification of Ezekiel's Gog, as neither of these passages contains any prophetic information directly relating to Ezekiel 38–39.

Some scholars point out that there are books mentioned in the Bible that we no longer have access to that could contain the prophecies referred to in Ezekiel 38:17. These books include: the book of the wars of the LORD (Num 21:14), the book of Jasher (Josh 10:13 and 2 Sam 1:18), and the book of Nathan the Prophet (1 Chr 29:29). There are multiple versions of the book of Jasher available. I have one titled, *Sefer Hayashar: The Book of the Generations of Adam.* Whether this is the same book referred to in scripture is uncertain and probably unlikely. Regardless, this book does not contain prophecies regarding a leader called Gog.

It cannot be completely ruled out that prophecies regarding Gog were made and then lost, and thus not recorded in the canon of the Old Testament. However, that would indicate that the Holy Spirit lost control of some of God's important prophetic messages, and I have difficulty reconciling that with the status of the Bible as the supernatural word of God. I do not believe the answer to Gog's prophetic status lies in lost prophecies.

In Ezekiel 38:17, God is making a point by asking a question. But why is this statement raised in the form of a question? What is the message that we are to take from this passage? We need to understand that the prophet Ezekiel is not asking this question. It is God who is asking this question. God is pointing this question directly at Gog, "Are you the one?"

Ezekiel was called by God to become a prophet during Israel's seventy year period of exile to Babylon. God is insinuating that in the historical time preceding Ezekiel's day, He had instructed the Israelites through the prophets regarding a future leader who would come against them (invade Israel militarily) as a form of judgment or chastisement by the sanction of God. God used Nebuchadnezzar and Babylon for that very purpose during

Ezekiel's lifetime, but God is not referring to Babylon in this prophecy. He is referring to a future event following Israel's return to the Land from their exile to Babylon. In fact, God makes it clear that He is referring to a time following the return of Israel to the Land from an exile that includes not just Babylon but the many nations of the world (Ezek 38:8). God also makes it clear that this prophecy will be fulfilled in the "latter years" and "latter days" of Israel's history (Ezek 38:8, 16).

When we study the character of this prophecy and God's relationship to it, the fact that God raised this verse in the form of a question becomes highly significant. God is taunting Gog with a question regarding both his identity and his authority.

What leader is God referring to when He mentions "the one about whom I spoke" in this passage? He can only be referring to the future Antichrist. That future leader will invade Israel and will be used by God as the final world leader who comes against Israel in the form of a divinely sanctioned judgment or chastisement. God has a purpose for the Antichrist to fulfill, which is to act as an instrument of God's indignation by pushing Israel to the brink of total destruction, and thus forcing the Jewish people to acknowledge God's Son, Jesus Christ, as their true Messiah. God has specifically allocated a period of three and one-half years for the Antichrist to be empowered by Satan and to impose his will over Israel. The Antichrist will ultimately come to power, not because Satan mandates his coming, but because God mandates it.

We should ask whether God allows any such comparable role for the Gog of Ezekiel 38–39. Does Gog get any supernaturally mandated time to impose his own will over Israel?

Absolutely not! The very next verse (Ezek 38:18) makes this clear when Ezekiel declares, "And it shall come to pass at the same time when Gog shall come against the land of Israel, saith the Lord GOD, that my fury shall come up in my face." God reveals His reaction to Gog's invasion of Israel by announcing an immediate divine intervention against Gog and his armies. God will decisively intervene to cause the supernatural destruction of all of the invading forces in Gog's alliance. When will God intervene? At the very beginning of the invasion before it has a chance of succeeding, not three and a half years later.

What purpose does the question that God has raised in this verse serve God in the context of the prophecy of Ezekiel 38–39 if Gog is really the final world leader prophesied by God's prophets? I think the answer is none. If Gog really is the one, then the verse is superfluous. But what if Gog is not the one? Then the verse in question form makes perfect sense, both from God's perspective and ours.

Why does God throw such a challenging question in Gog's face? "Are you the one …?" God seems to be plainly declaring: "Gog: You are not the one! You are not the final world dictator. You are not the Antichrist who will come against the land and the people of Israel. You are not the one who will enter the Jewish Temple in Jerusalem and who will declare himself to be the god of gods."

Thus, we can see and understand God's immediate and supernatural reaction to Gog's invasion of Israel. Gog believes he will have a sudden and decisive victory over Israel. But God sees it differently. Gog has no sanction from heaven for his invasion, and it will end just as quickly as it begins. God is against Gog because Gog has ill intentions against Israel for his own purposes without any authorization from God. Gog is not the Antichrist. Gog is not the one!

## Gog vs. Antichrist – Is Gog the Antichrist?

There is a considerable focus in prophetic circles on Armageddon. Many authors are closely following the events in the Middle East and warning of the impending approach of a major war. The question is frequently asked, "How close are we to the End Times and the Tribulation?" In this context most authors immediately focus on the Antichrist, his seven-year covenant of peace with Israel, and the war of Armageddon. Some authors mention the prophecy of Ezekiel 38–39 and note that it could come before the war of Armageddon. A few, such as Arnold Fruchtenbaum, Peter Goodgame, Grant Jeffrey, Randall Price, and I have argued that the invasion of Gog and Magog will occur as a pretribulational event, and thus could be fulfilled in the near future. Other authors, such as Arthur E. Bloomfield, Michael Heiser, Robert Van Kampen, and Walid Shoebat equate Ezekiel's main character Gog with the Antichrist and the invasion of Israel by Gog and Magog with the war or campaign of Armageddon.

Let's examine some of the primary characteristics revealed by scripture regarding the end-time leaders of Gog and the Antichrist, and the prophetic wars of Gog and Magog and Armageddon to determine the accuracy of the claim that they are the same leaders and the same wars.

### Is Gog another name for the Antichrist?

In his comprehensive examination of the Antichrist, Arthur W. Pink makes one passing reference to Ezekiel 38 in his introduction, where he mentions titles for the Antichrist given by the prophets. Pink includes, without comment, 'the chief Prince of Meshech and Tubal' from Ezekiel 38:2 in his introductory list, which is a reference to Gog. Yet when Pink examines the references to the Antichrist in his chapter "Antichrist in the Prophets," he completely omits any reference to Gog or the prophecy of Ezekiel 38–39. Under Ezekiel, Pink notes the references in 21:25-27 to the 'wicked Prince of Israel' and in chapter 28 to the Prince or King of Tyre as titles for the Antichrist, but he makes no reference to Gog. I find it very curious that Arthur Pink did not make more of the prophecy of Gog and Magog, with God's clear and repeated declaration "I am against you, O Gog" in Ezekiel 38:3 and 39:1, if he was entirely convinced that Gog is the Antichrist.[5]

Nonetheless, several authors do clearly associate Gog with the Antichrist. Walid Shoebat is an ex-Muslim and a former member of the Palestinian Liberation Organization. He has converted to Christianity and has written an interesting book, *Why I Left Jihad*. In this book Walid Shoebat argues that Gog and the Antichrist are the same person and that he will come out of Islam. Shoebat claims, "Once we understand that Gog is Satan incarnate, we will see that Ezekiel 38 is the same Gog of Revelation 20:8, unleashed in the world twice, once at Armageddon and once after the Millennium. … Gog is simply another word for the Antichrist, the Assyrian, the Son of Perdition, and Lucifer."[6]

In his book, *Before the Last Battle – Armageddon*, Arthur E. Bloomfield, draws a similar conclusion. "When Satan operates in person on the earth, he is known as Gog and Magog. … Gog is not the name of any man in the Bible. It is the name of Satan when he becomes a man in Antichrist. After the Rapture, Antichrist is Satan in the flesh: then he is Gog."[7] Other authors have equated Gog with the Antichrist including: Robert Van Kampen, *The Sign*; and Michael S. Heiser, *Islam and Armageddon.*

**What do we know from scripture about the Antichrist?**

1. The Antichrist will be an end-time leader who will uproot three leaders in his rise to power over ten kings (Dan 7:8, 24).
2. The Antichrist is restrained from rising to power and being revealed as the man of lawlessness, the son of destruction (perdition) until God's restraining force is removed out of the way (2 Thes 2:3, 6-8).
3. The Antichrist will confirm a strong covenant (peace covenant) with Israel for a period of seven years (Dan 9:27).
4. The Antichrist will break the covenant in the middle of the seven years (Dan 9:27).
5. The Antichrist will enter a rebuilt temple in Jerusalem and declare himself to be God, exalting himself above all gods (2 Thes 2:4).
6. The Antichrist will demand to be worshipped as God and will seek to kill all who refuse to worship him and his image (Rev 13:15).

7. The Antichrist will be empowered by Satan (and given authority by God) over every tribe and nation and will be worshipped by everyone on earth whose name is not recorded in Christ's book of life (Rev 13:7-8).
8. In his satanically possessed form, the Antichrist is referred to as "the beast." He is the beast out of the abyss, and the beast out of the sea (Rev 11:7; Rev 13). This title is in direct opposition to Christ's role as the "lamb" of God (Rev 5:6-13).
9. Supernatural authority is granted to the Antichrist to act (to do his own will and the will of Satan) for a specific period of forty-two months or 3 ½ years (Rev 13:5).
10. The Antichrist will be killed by Jesus Christ at His second coming at the end of the War of Armageddon (2 Thes 2:8; Rev 19:19-20).
11. The Antichrist will be killed but then cast alive (resurrected) into the Lake of Fire (Rev 19:20).

This is not intended to be a comprehensive list of characteristics or titles by which the person of the Antichrist will be known. However, it does give us several certain specific characteristics that must be identifiable in an end-time leader before we can seriously entertain the notion that he is the Antichrist.

## What do we know from Ezekiel 38–39 about Gog?

1. Gog is an end-time leader of a large, but limited, alliance of geographic territories which include: Rosh, Magog, Meshech, Tubal, Persia, Cush, Put, Gomer, Beth-togarmah, and many other peoples with them. (Ezek 38:2-6).
2. Gog and his alliance will invade Israel in Israel's "latter years" or its "last days" (Ezek 38:8, 16).
3. Gog will invade Israel when God Himself summons Gog, at the specific time of God's choosing (Ezek 38:4, 8; 39:2).
4. Gog's armies will be supernaturally destroyed almost immediately by God. God Himself rises up in divine fury to intercede for Israel through a combination of judgments: global earthquake, turning Gog's forces against themselves, pestilence, blood, torrential rain, hailstones, fire, and brimstone (Ezek 38:18-22).
5. Gog will be killed and buried in a mass grave with his troops in Israel (Ezek 39:11).
6. The destruction of Gog's invading forces is recognized by Israel and many nations as the intervention of God, and God's holy name will be magnified and made known (Ezek 38:15, 23; 39:7, 21-22).

There are some characteristics of similarity between the Antichrist and Gog:

1. Both the Antichrist and Gog will lead alliances that will fight against and invade Israel.
2. Both the Antichrist and Gog will be killed by the direct intervention of God.
3. The timing of the destruction of both the Antichrist and Gog will be linked to a demonstration of God's presence revealed to the world.
4. Both the War of Gog and Magog and the War of Armageddon will be followed by birds feasting on the bodies of dead soldiers (Ezek 39:4, 17-20 birds and beasts; Rev 19:17-18, 21 birds only).

Are these similarities enough to positively assert that Gog is the Antichrist, and thus the invasion of Gog and Magog is the war of Armageddon? In spite of the similarities, we need to consider some very important questions:

1. What supernatural authority is granted to each leader by God, or by Satan?
2. What relationship does each leader have to the nation of Israel?
3. What is the fate of each leader upon his defeat by God and his physical death?
4. What is the spiritual relationship of each leader – his relationship to God?
5. What supernatural powers are manifested by each leader's actions?
6. What relationship does each leader have to Satan? Is Gog possessed or indwelt by Satan? Is Gog Satan incarnate?

## 1. What supernatural authority is granted to each leader by God, or by Satan?

The Antichrist is specifically granted authority by God and supernatural power by Satan to rule for a period of forty-two months (Rev 13:5-7). He will have authority "to make war with the saints and to overcome them, and authority over every tribe and people and tongue and nation was given to him."

Are we told that Gog will be granted any supernatural power or authority by God or Satan? The answer is – No! Gog will have an evil thought and will invade the land of Israel, but on the very day that Gog invades God rises up in fury against Gog and his forces and destroys them. Gog is given no opportunity by God to overcome either Israel or the saints, much less every people group and nation. Gog does not have 3 ½ years to dominate Israel. His invasion is completely doomed from its very start and it is a very short and one-sided war. God is absolutely clear that Gog's invasion will not be the least bit successful.

**2. What relationship does each leader have to the nation of Israel?**

The Antichrist will establish a seven-year covenant of peace with Israel, which he will break during the middle of the seven-year period. Israel will have placed its trust in the leadership of the Antichrist, either as a strong leader of Israel itself, or as a strong ally of Israel, but the Antichrist will turn against Israel and betray that trust. The Antichrist will do everything in his power to destroy Israel.

Ezekiel makes no reference to the making or breaking of any peace covenant between Gog and Israel. The context of the prophecy makes one all but impossible. Gog will form and equip an alliance and invade Israel, to take a spoil and to plunder Israel. However, Gog is not successful for any period of time and will never gain any control over Israel or Jerusalem. Instead, God reveals that Gog's forces will be turned into a spoil and plundered by Israel, who will burn Gog's weapons for a period of seven years.

**3. What is the fate of each leader upon his defeat by God and his physical death?**

The Antichrist is killed, immediately resurrected, and thrown (alive) into the Lake of Fire by Jesus Christ upon His second coming at the end of the Tribulation (Dan 11:7; Isa 14:19-20; 2 Thes 2:8; Rev 19:20). He is not buried in a tomb or a mass grave with his troops.

Gog will be killed during his invasion of Israel and will be buried in a mass grave with his troops in a valley that will then be known as the valley of Hamon-gog (Ezek 39:11). Israel will undergo a process of cleansing the land and burying the dead forces of Gog and Magog that will last for at least a period of seven months. God does not reveal exactly how Gog will be killed, and there is no reference to Gog being killed by Jesus Christ. Gog will not be resurrected until the White Throne Judgment at the end of the Millennium and will not be cast into the Lake of Fire before that time.

**4. What is the spiritual relationship of each leader – his relationship to God?**

The Antichrist is against God. He will speak monstrous things against the God of Israel. He will honor a god of fortresses or war (Satan). He will exalt himself above all gods (Dan 11:36-38; Rev 13:6). He will enter the temple in Jerusalem and declare himself to be God (2 Thes 2:3-4). He demands to be worshipped as God. Ultimately, the Antichrist's target is God, as he attempts to replace God as the supreme spiritual being. He will make war with God and attempt to defeat Jesus Christ at His second coming.

God declares that He is against Gog. We do not know who Gog's god will be. Is he an atheist from Russia? Is he a Muslim who worships Allah? Does he worship Satan? Scripture does not answer these questions. Gog will be against the God of Israel in that he will be in denial of the power of God to save Israel from the overwhelming might of Gog's alliance. However, Gog's primary target is Israel, not God. Gog is given no spiritual power or authority in Ezekiel's prophecy. There is no reference to the Jewish Temple, or to Gog making any declarations of his own deity, or to any demands that he is to be worshipped by his troops or any other peoples.

**5. What supernatural powers are manifested by each leader's actions?**

The Antichrist becomes a supernatural figure empowered by Satan. He comes "after the working of Satan with all power and signs and lying wonders" (2 Thes 2:9). He is associated with the beast out of the earth (false prophet) who will perform great signs and miracles such as calling fire down from heaven. The false prophet will make an image of the Antichrist seemingly come to life (breathing and speaking) which will then be worshipped by many people (Rev 13:11-15).

Gog is not identified as having any supernatural power at all. He is not described as performing any great signs, wonders, or miracles. He is instructed in Ezekiel's prophecy to be prepared, to prepare his alliance for the invasion of Israel, and to be a guard for his forces and allies. Gog undergoes a lengthy preparation of equipping and arming all of the armies that will invade Israel under his command. This is the exact role that Russia is playing out in the dynamics of the world today. Gog's strength is in planning, preparation, and strength of arms, not supernatural might (Ezek 38:7).

**6. What relationship does each leader have to Satan? Is Gog possessed or indwelt by Satan? Is Gog Satan incarnate?**

The Antichrist is clearly empowered by Satan, the dragon (Rev 13:2, 4). Most Bible prophecy scholars interpret the Antichrist as originating as a human leader (beast out of the sea) who becomes entirely possessed or indwelt by Satan when Satan is completely cast out of heaven, and thus becomes the beast out of the Abyss. Thus, the Antichrist becomes Satan incarnate, or at the very least indwelt by a fallen satanic spirit that rises out of the Abyss.

Gog is not identified with Satan or the dragon in any way in Ezekiel's prophecy. It is logical to understand that Gog will be a pawn of Satan since Gog is going to have an evil thought and invade Israel. Gog will be an evil, power hungry leader, and those are Satan's kind of leaders. However, Gog is not characterized as having the full power of Satan controlling him.

The following table summarizes the characteristics presented by asking these six questions regarding the nature of Gog and the Antichrist.

**Gog vs. Antichrist**

| Characteristic | Gog | Antichrist |
|---|---|---|
| Supernatural Authority | None! | 3 ½ Years – Authority to make war with the saints and over all peoples and nations. |
| Relationship to Israel | Invader to take a spoil. Very short unsuccessful war. | Makes and later breaks seven-year Covenant of Peace. Lengthy war against Israel. |
| Fate at death | Buried in a mass grave. | Immediately resurrected and cast into the Lake of Fire. |
| Spiritual Relationship | Against the God of Israel, but makes no claims of deity. | Enters the Temple and claims to be God. Exalts himself above all gods. Demands to be worshipped. |
| Supernatural Powers | None! | Signs, Wonders, and Miracles. |
| Relationship to Satan | An evil human leader, but not indwelt or possessed by Satan. Completely controlled by God. | Possessed by Satan. Satan incarnate, or possessed by a satanic spirit. |

In fact, the picture portrayed concerning Gog is quite the opposite as opposed to the Antichrist. Gog is a puppet on a string controlled by God, not Satan. God commands Gog at every step and turn of the prophecy. God repeatedly tells Gog exactly what Gog is going to do and what God is going to do to Gog and his forces. God says that He is going to place hooks in Gog's jaws and turn him around and drive or lead him against Israel. God tells Gog that after many days (in the future from Ezekiel's time) Gog will be summoned by God to fulfill his role in this prophecy (Ezek 38:4, 8; 39:2).

Ezekiel gives us no reason to view Gog as possessed by Satan or to be Satan incarnate. The portrayal of Gog by Ezekiel really does not say very much for the power or role of Satan when it comes to his relationship with Gog. This is one of the characteristics that is poorly analyzed by authors who equate Gog with Satan because of the passing mention of "Gog and Magog" in Revelation 20:8, which describes Satan's final rebellion against God.

## Gog & Magog vs. Armageddon – Is the invasion of Gog & Magog the same war as Armageddon?

The following table summarizes similarities and differences between the wars of Gog and Magog and Armageddon.

### War of Gog & Magog vs. War of Armageddon

| Gog & Magog | Armageddon |
|---|---|
| Invasion of Gog & Magog Ezek 38 & 39 | Battle of the great day of God Almighty Rev 16:14 |
| Israel dwelling safely (in false confidence) in the land Ezek 38:8, 11, 14 | No safety! It is a time of much persecution and troubles. The remnant of Israel has fled Jerusalem and Judaea and is dwelling in exile, in refuge in the wilderness of Bozrah (Petra). Rev 12:6, 13-16; Mt 24:15-21 |
| Surprise invasion of Israel by an alliance of a few nations: Magog (Russia); Persia (Iran); Cush (Sudan, Ethiopia); Put (Libya); Gomer (southern regions of old U.S.S.R.); Togarmah (Armenia, Turkey). Ezek 38:2-6 | All Kings of the world are gathered to Israel to do battle. Rev 16:14; 19:19<br>No mention of Gog or any of Gog's specific allies in the book of Revelation. |
| Invasion from the far north – | Armies come from all over the |

| Gog & Magog | Armageddon |
|---|---|
| Ezek 38:6, 15. No mention is made of the Kings of the east or of the Euphrates River. | world and the Kings of the east cross the dried up Euphrates River. Rev 16:12 |
| Invasion is made to take a great spoil in the land of Israel. Ezek 38:12-13; 39:10 | Demonic gathering of armies to Megiddo to crush Israel and unite in war against Christ. Rev 16:12-16; 19:19 |
| Gog is the leader from the far north but is not said to be any of: the World Dictator, the Antichrist, the Beast, the Little Horn, the Assyrian, the King of Assyria, the King of Babylon, or the King of the North. | Antichrist is Satanically possessed and is the World Dictator. The Antichrist, The False Prophet, and Satan are working together. |
| God declares that He Himself will turn Gog around and drive him and his forces to invade Israel. Ezek 38:4 | Demons from Satan, the Antichrist, and the False Prophet gather the armies to Megiddo in Israel. Rev 16:13-14 |
| No mention of Megiddo, Jerusalem, or Babylon. | Armies are gathered at Megiddo; Battle against Jerusalem; and Babylon is destroyed in the same time frame. |
| No mention of seven-year Peace Covenant | Peace Covenant has been violated and Israel betrayed. Dan 9:27 |
| No stated expectation by Israel for any nation or leader to protect Israel from invasion. Does not describe Israel calling upon God in repentance. | Israel is being persecuted by the Antichrist and the False Prophet. Israel calls upon God in repentance for deliverance. Zech 13:9 |
| Diplomatic protest by Sheba and Dedan, the merchants of Tarshish, and the young lions thereof: Possibly Saudi Arabia and Western World (England and U.S.A.) Ezek 38:13 | No diplomatic protest – the assembling of the armies is demonically guided and there are no nations allied with Israel against the Antichrist. |
| No mention of any of the end-time plagues or judgments of God taking place before the invasion is judged by God's intervention. | The War of Armageddon will be preceded by a number of devastating plagues and judgments from God – 7 Seals, 7 Trumpets, and 6 Bowls. |

| Gog & Magog | Armageddon |
|---|---|
| Invaders are destroyed by the supernatural intervention of God but no mention of Jesus Christ or 2nd Coming. Destruction is descriptive of the 6th Seal Judgment – Rev 6:12-17 | Armies are destroyed supernaturally by Jesus Christ at His Revelation (2nd Coming) – Rev 19:19-21<br>The 7th Bowl Judgment of God's Wrath – Rev 16:17-21 |
| Homelands of invading armies are also destroyed by fire<br>Ezek 39:6 | No mention of homelands – except all cities will fall<br>Rev 16:19 |
| Invaders do not reach Jerusalem – no mention of Jerusalem. Invaders fall on the mountains and open fields of Israel. Very likely they fall in northern Israel, Lebanon, and possibly Syria.<br>Ezek 39:4-5 | Jerusalem is a primary target – All nations come against Jerusalem. Battles extend from Megiddo south to Petra / Bozrah in Jordan (about 200 miles)<br>Zech 12:1-8; 14:1-3; Rev 14:20 |
| Gog and his multitude are buried in the Valley of Gog's Horde<br>Ezek 39:11 | Antichrist and False Prophet are not buried, but cast into the Lake of Fire (Rev 19:20). The slain armies are not buried – Jer 25:33 |
| The birds and beasts of the field feast upon Gog's dead soldiers. God refers to this as "My sacrifice" and "My table"<br>Ezek 39:4, 17-20 | Birds feast upon the dead soldiers (beasts not mentioned). God refers to this as "the great supper of God"<br>Rev 19:17-18, 21 |
| Invasion is followed by 7 months of cleansing of the land and burying the dead and 7 years of burning the weapons. Israel will spoil and rob those who came to spoil and rob her.<br>Ezek 39:9-16 | Armageddon is followed by an interim interval of 75 days which will include cleansing the land and the Temple after which the Millennial Kingdom of God will begin. Dan 12:11-12; Rev 20:6; Dan 7:14, 27 |
| Spiritual wake up call to the world – God has intervened! Leads to spiritual revival of faith – a national reawakening of Israel to God (but not Christ) and many nations of the world will know God is the Lord, the Holy One in Israel. Ezek 38:23; 39:21-22 | Leads to the National spiritual regeneration of Israel under the New Covenant with their acceptance of Christ.<br>Jer 31:31-34; Zech 12:10<br>Israel will become the head of the nations. |

| Gog & Magog | Armageddon |
|---|---|
| Leads to an increased regathering of Jews in Jerusalem and Israel in preparation for judgment by God. | Results in the final worldwide regathering of all Jews to Israel with the supernatural assistance of angels – Mt 24:31 |
| War of Gog and Magog similar enough to Armageddon to confuse the world – Israel will view this war as the last war (Armageddon) and will accept an emerging leader as Messiah! | Messiah will return in the clouds from heaven and will be visible to all with the brightness of his coming – the sign of the Son of Man will be in the sky. Mt 24:30; Rev 19:11-16 |

We can readily see that there are several major differences between Ezekiel's prophecy of Gog and Magog and the prophecies that reveal the characteristics of the Antichrist and the war of Armageddon. Some of the extremely important characteristics that are revealed about the Antichrist are either not revealed regarding Gog or are completely impossible for him to fulfill.

## God's Presence Revealed

Another issue that is related to the question concerning the relationship of Gog and the Antichrist and the direct association of the War of Gog and Magog with the War of Armageddon has to do with the revealed presence of God. In both prophecies, God will reveal Himself to Israel and the nations of the world. Are these the same manifestations of God, and thus the same event?

There are three sub-questions that fall under this inquiry.

1. Is the earthquake in Ezekiel 38:19 the same as the earthquake in Revelation 16:18 or the earthquake in Zechariah 14:4?
2. Is the reference in Ezekiel 38:18 to God's fury coming up in His face a direct reference to Jesus Christ at His second coming?
3. Is God's reference to being the Holy One in Israel in Ezekiel 39:7 a confirmation of the timing of Gog and Magog at Christ's second coming?

In his book, *Why I Left Jihad*, Walid Shoebat claims that these references to God's presence are all connected and that they are representations of Jesus Christ when He descends upon the Mount of Olives at His second coming. "In Ezekiel 38:19, the earthquake is the greatest in history and matches Zechariah 14:4. This earthquake is definitely the mark of the Messiah's presence on earth at the moment of His touch-down. He will descend from heaven to fight the enemy, Gog … This '*presence*' can be demonstrated further within Christian theology to prove that Ezekiel 38-39 is the showdown between Christ and Antichrist (Gog). … "[8]

**1. Is the earthquake in Ezekiel 38:19 the same as the earthquake in Revelation 16:18 or the earthquake in Zechariah 14:4?**

> In My zeal and in My blazing wrath I declare that on that day [the day Gog invades Israel] there will surely be a great earthquake in the land of Israel. The fish of the sea, the birds of the heavens, the beasts of the field, all the creeping things that creep on the earth, and all the men who are on the face of the earth will shake at My presence; the mountains also will be thrown down, the steep pathways will collapse and every wall will fall to the ground. (Ezek 38:19-20)

> And there were flashes of lightning and sounds and peals of thunder; and there was a great earthquake, such as there had not been since man came to be upon the earth, so great an earthquake was it, and so mighty. The great city was split into three parts, and the cities of the nations fell. Babylon the great was remembered before God, to give her the cup of the wine of His fierce wrath. And every island fled away, and the mountains were not found. And huge hailstones, about one hundred pounds each, came down from heaven upon men; and men blasphemed God because of the plague of the hail, because its plague was extremely severe. (Rev 16:18-21)

> In that day His feet will stand on the Mount of Olives, which is in front of Jerusalem on the east; and the Mount of Olives will be split in its middle from east to west by a very large valley, so that half of the mountain will move toward the north and the other half toward the south. (Zech 14:4)

There is strong similarity between the earthquake in Ezekiel 38 and the one in Revelation 16, but similarity does not make for equality. What we know about the earthquake in Revelation 16 is that it is the result of the seventh angel pouring out the seventh bowl of God's wrath at the end of the Tribulation. It is the last manifestation of God's wrath cast upon the earth, and it is associated with God's final judgment upon Babylon. This earthquake will be the greatest, most severe, earthquake in the history of mankind. Contrary to Shoebat's claim, while the earthquake in Ezekiel 38 is said to be great, it is not specifically identified as being the greatest in history. Scripturally, that distinction is reserved for the earthquake in Revelation 16.

Is the earthquake in Revelation 16 the same earthquake that Zechariah predicts will split the Mount of Olives at Christ's presence? We cannot say for certain, but it is quite possible. There are multiple earthquakes mentioned in the book of Revelation, and of those this is the most likely candidate for Zechariah's earthquake.

However, is the seventh bowl earthquake the same earthquake revealed in Ezekiel 38? I argue that it is not. Ezekiel's earthquake will be extremely severe, and it will be a global event, but will it be part of the manifestation of God's final judgment of divine wrath? Absolutely not! Let's take God at His own word for our proof. God adamantly declares that the reason that He will bring Gog against Israel is that God is going to use the event of Gog's invasion and destruction as an opportunity to reveal Himself to Israel and the nations who profane His holy name. God is going to make Himself known by His supernatural intervention to save Israel and as a result Israel and many nations will recognize that intervention. Many nations, not all nations, will recognize God's intervention.

> It will come about in the last days that I will bring you against My land, so that the nations will know Me when I am sanctified through you before their eyes, O Gog. … I will magnify Myself, sanctify Myself, and make Myself known in the sight of many nations; and they will know that I am the LORD. … My holy name I will make known in the midst of My people Israel; and I will not let My holy name be profaned anymore. And the nations will know that I am the LORD, the Holy One in Israel. (Ezekiel 38:16, 23; 39:7)

Is this the second coming of Christ and Christ's continued presence within Israel? At first glance these verses might seem to indicate just that. However, what is the point that God is really making? At the time of Gog's invasion, not only are the nations of the world profaning God's name, but Israel is also profaning God's holy name. Christ's second coming will not take place until Israel turns to both God and Jesus Christ in repentance and calls upon Him to save them. So, at the time of Christ's second coming,

Israel will not be profaning God's holy name. Israel, as a national people, will have gotten past that form of rebellion against God and Jesus Christ. The invasion of Israel by Gog and Magog must come before the national conversion of Israel to Jesus Christ, not after. God's destruction of Gog will not awaken the nation of Israel to the reality of Jesus Christ as God's true Messiah. Instead, it will reawaken Israel to the Old Testament God of their ancestors. It will cause a spiritual rebirth within Israel to the God of Abraham, Isaac, and Jacob. Israel's conversion to accept Jesus Christ as the Messiah comes later, after Israel is betrayed by the Antichrist. This is another reason why Gog and the Antichrist cannot be the same end-time leader.

This argues for a much earlier fulfillment of Gog and Magog than Armageddon. Since a devastating global earthquake is so characteristically linked to the destruction of Gog and Magog, where God rattles the entire world and causes all people to shake at His presence, what other end-time earthquake can we identify that fits this description of events? We find this earthquake in Revelation 6, when Christ opens the sixth seal.

> I looked when He broke the sixth seal, and there was a great earthquake .... and every mountain and island were moved out of their places. Then the kings of the earth and the great men and the commanders and the rich and the strong and every slave and free man hid themselves in the caves and among the rocks of the mountains; and they said to the mountains and to the rocks, 'Fall on us and hide us from the presence of Him who sits on the throne, and from the wrath of the Lamb; for the great day of their wrath has come, and who is able to stand?' (Rev 6:12a, 14b-17 NASB).

This is the great earthquake that equates to Ezekiel's earthquake that comes with the invasion of Gog and Magog. The passages in Isaiah 2:10-21 and 13:6-8 also correspond to this event. The sixth seal describes seven categories of men (symbolism of totality) from all walks of life, and thus from all over the planet. This is a global earthquake. All people are shaken by the revealed presence of God and Christ in judgment against a rebellious world. However, this is not the second coming of Christ. This occurs at the beginning of God's judgments in Revelation. Note that the people realize that "the great day of their wrath has come."

This great day is the beginning of God's Day of the LORD judgments, which comes in the form of sudden destruction (1 Thes 5:2-3), not the final day of wrath at the second coming of Christ. Many students of prophecy get this confused. The similarity between the sixth seal and the seventh bowl judgments cause some to claim that they portray the same events. But that is not possible. The great earthquake of Revelation 6:12 cannot be the same event as the greatest earthquake of Revelation 16:18.

## Global Earthquake

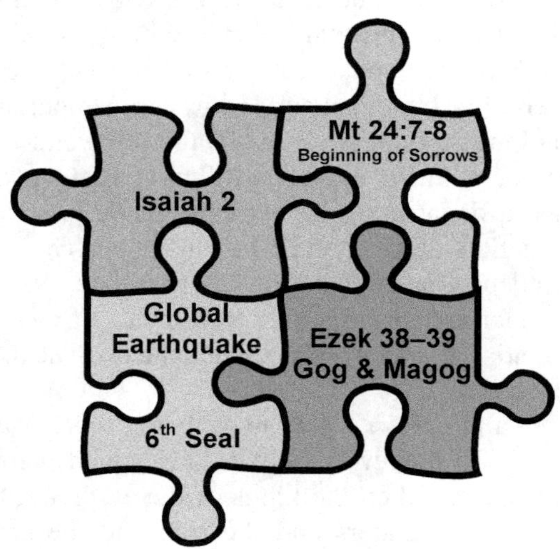


All seven seals must be opened before the scroll can be read – before the entire message of God's judgment is revealed in heaven and on earth. The seventh seal must be opened before the seven angels with the trumpets can reveal God's trumpet judgments (Rev 8:1-2, 6-7), and the seventh trumpet must sound before the seven angels pour out the bowls of God's greatest wrath (Rev 11:15; 15:1, 6-8; 16:1-2). The progression of these three series of events is consecutive, not concurrent. This point is emphasized by Revelation 15:1, "Then I saw another sign in heaven, great and marvelous, seven angels who had seven plagues, which are the last, because in them the wrath of God is finished." These seven angels with the bowls of God's wrath are the last of his judgments. This clearly differentiates them from the series of seven seals and seven trumpet judgments. They cannot be simultaneous.

What is important to observe is that God is going to reveal Himself to the world more than once during the End Times. He is going to reveal Himself at the very beginning of the Day of the LORD, and then He is going to reveal Himself again at the very end. The latter revelation will be manifested as the second coming of Christ and will be accompanied by the greatest earthquake in the history of mankind. The beginning of the Day of the LORD will be characterized by the events of the seven seals, with particular correspondence between the second, fourth, and sixth seals to the invasion of Gog and Magog, when God breaks His silence and returns His hidden face towards Israel. Men will attempt to hide from God's revealed presence, which is described in the portrayal of the sixth seal and also by the prophet Isaiah (Isa 2:10-21). This is true in part because Satan has not yet been cast out of heaven and the Antichrist is not in power as Satan incarnate when the Day of the LORD begins. However, at the time of Armageddon and Christ's second coming, Satan and the Antichrist will be supervising the war against God and Christ, and we see no description of people hiding from God in fear. Instead they are blaspheming God for the severity of His judgments.

**2. Is the reference in Ezekiel 38:18 to God's fury coming up in His face a direct reference to Jesus Christ at His second coming?**

> And it shall come to pass at the same time when Gog shall come against the land of Israel, saith the Lord GOD, that my fury shall come up in my face. (Ezek 38:18 KJV)

Ezekiel 38–39 is an Old Testament prophecy. It needs to be evaluated in the context of the Old Testament scriptures. The important characteristic that we should remember when it comes to references to God's face is that God uses His face as an indication of His relationship to the nation of Israel. In the Old Testament, scripture repeatedly describes God as having His face turned toward Israel or away from Israel. When He turns His face away from Israel, God is said to be hiding His face from Israel. This is the silence of God. The long period of Israel's exile from the land of Israel (the Diaspora) has been characterized by God hiding His face from Israel.

This description in Ezekiel 38 of God's fury mounting up in His face relates directly to the pent up anger that God has against Israel's enemies. When that anger reaches the boiling point, which it does with Gog's invasion of Israel, God will return His face back to Israel and unleash His pent up fury on Israel's enemies. God's silence will be broken. God is describing a serious form of divine intervention to save Israel from utter destruction, but this intervention is not manifested in the form of the bodily second coming of Christ to the earth. This is an Old Testament manifestation of God which comes at the very beginning of God's Day of the LORD judgments.

New Testament scripture describes Christ as treading the wine press of God's wrath. His eyes are described as flames of fire. From His mouth comes a sharp sword (the word of God). But we are not given a description of Him displaying an angry face full of pent up fury when He comes at His second coming to stand on the Mount of Olives.

**3. Is God's reference to being the Holy One in Israel in Ezekiel 39: 7 a confirmation of the timing of Gog and Magog at Christ's second coming?**

> My holy name I will make known in the midst of My people Israel; and I will not let My holy name be profaned anymore. And the nations will know that I am the LORD, the Holy One in Israel. (Ezek 39:7)

Walid Shoebat examines this verse and draws the conclusion, "Note that the Holy One is *in* Israel; the rest of Scripture uses the phrase 'Holy One of Israel,' hence Messiah will be found on Earth."[9]

Again, Ezekiel 38–39 is an Old Testament prophecy. All throughout the Old Testament the holy name of God is יהוה which is Yahweh (sometimes rendered as Jehovah) and is translated "LORD" by the KJV and other versions of the Bible. "God then said to Moses, 'You must [then] say to the Israelites, "YHVH, the God of your fathers, the God of Abraham, Isaac and Jacob, sent me to you." This is My eternal name, and this is how I am to be recalled for all generations.'" (Ex 3:15 The Living Torah).[10]

God is going to use Gog's invasion of Israel to make known His holy name to Israel and the nations of the world. Is that the name of Jesus (Yeshua) or is it God's eternal name of YHVH? It is His eternal name. Israel is a predominantly secular nation in denial of the Old Testament God of Israel, in addition to being in denial of and rebellion to Jesus Christ. While God calls individuals to Christ, from both Jews and Gentiles, to become "One New Man" in the body of Christ, He deals with the nation of Israel as an entirely different corporate body.

How can Israel jump into an immediate acceptance of Jesus Christ as God when they are, as a nation, in active denial of God Himself? They cannot. And that is why God has prophetically and systematically planned out the Day of the LORD. It is the period of time that God will use to refine Israel and bring it to salvation as a nation. The nation of Israel, as a body of people, must be returned to the God of their fathers before they will be made ready to make the transition to a full recognition and acceptance of Jesus Christ as their promised Messiah. That is what God is telling Israel. God uses Gog's invasion as the mechanism for revealing Himself to Israel and reawakening them spiritually to Him as [יהוה] YHVH.

The church, the body of Christ, must be removed from the earth, and God will supernaturally seal the 144,000 Jewish servants of God as His true remnant of believers on earth. When does God accomplish that sealing? In Revelation 7, exactly when the great multitude of saved believers shows up in heaven standing with Christ before God's throne. God interjects this between the opening of the sixth and seventh seals, which is the time of the invasion of Gog and Magog and the global earthquake. Where is Christ? He is in heaven with the raptured church, not on earth in the midst of Israel.

These 144,000 Jewish evangelists will take up the message of the Kingdom of God and Jesus Christ as the Messiah. However, the corporate body of Israel, will first turn to a renewed belief in God [יהוה] and rebuild their temple in Jerusalem. "And the nations will know that I am the LORD [יהוה], the Holy One in Israel." While God had His face turned away (hidden) from Israel He was the God (Holy One) **of** Israel who allowed all of the tragedies of the Diaspora and the Holocaust to be perpetrated against Israel. Following His intervention to save Israel from Gog and Magog, God will have His face turned back to Israel and will be the God (Holy One) **in** Israel. However, God is setting Israel up to be the sacrificial Passover lamb. Just as God sacrificed His Son Jesus Christ as a Passover lamb, Israel will be sacrificed and purged (refined) through the period of time known as the Day of the LORD until the final purified remnant of Israel turns completely to an acceptance of Jesus Christ as their Messiah and God.

How do the Antichrist and the False Prophet rise to power? Israel and the nations (including Islam) who are reawakened to the knowledge of the eternal God YHVH as the Holy One **in** Israel must look for God's Messiah, and one will come. But he will not be the real Jesus Christ. He will come in the form of either the False Prophet or the Antichrist.

## Gog & Magog vs. Antichrist & Armageddon Conclusion

If one compares the most dynamic characteristics of Gog and the Antichrist, it is easy to see that these two end-time leaders cannot be the same person. Gog does not have any of the supernatural power and authority that is the hallmark of the Antichrist. In spite of some similarities, there are irreconcilable differences between the wars of Gog and Magog and Armageddon. Israel must be at rest and dwelling under a sense of security (albeit false) at the time of Gog's invasion. That is an absolutely impossible characteristic for Israel during any part of the second half of Daniel's 70th Week, after the Antichrist enters the temple and declares himself to be God.

Instead, Gog and the Antichrist are two different leaders, and Gog and Magog and Armageddon are two completely different wars, which take place at different times. The War of Gog and Magog comes first and begins God's Day of the LORD judgments. It is accompanied by a global earthquake and the revealed presence of God at the opening of the sixth seal. The similarities between Gog and Magog and Armageddon will actually foster the worldwide belief that the destruction of Gog and Magog by God will be the fulfillment of Armageddon. In a partial way Gog serves as a false antichrist – whose destruction by God makes it appear to Israel, to the apostate Christian church, and to the nations of the world, that the Antichrist has been defeated – Peace has come at last! The invasion of Gog and Magog will serve as a false Armageddon. Thus, Israel and the world will be primed for the coming of a false Messiah and a false Messianic Kingdom. The actual War of Armageddon with the defeat of Antichrist comes several years later, after his 3 ½ year period of supernatural empowerment. This event takes place in conjunction with the seventh bowl judgment, the greatest earthquake in the history of mankind, and the revealed presence of God in the visible form of the second coming of Jesus Christ. Jesus Christ is then manifested as not only God, the Holy One in Israel, but also God Almighty, the Holy One in the World! In the words of the apostle John, Jesus Christ is "the Lamb of God, who takes away the sin of the world!" (Jn 1:29 NASB).

## Ezekiel 38 & 39 vs. Revelation 20

This table highlights characteristics of the War of Gog and Magog described by the prophet Ezekiel in chapters 38 and 39 as compared to characteristics of the rebellion mentioning Gog and Magog, which are revealed by the apostle John in chapter 20 of the book of Revelation. Some people argue that these two characterizations describe the same event. John's portrayal in Revelation is very brief. However, from the information that we are provided, there is almost no similarity between these two events. My conclusion is that Ezekiel describes an event that takes place prior to the War of Armageddon, and most likely prior to the Tribulation period itself. The rebellion revealed by John is situated after the Millennial Kingdom of God. Therefore, these are two distinct events which are separated by a time span of more than 1,000 years. I refer to the latter event as Satan's Final Rebellion, to give it a distinction in title from Gog and Magog.

**Ezekiel 38 & 39 vs. Revelation 20**

| **Gog & Magog<br>(Ezekiel 38 & 39)<br>War of Gog & Magog** | **Gog & Magog<br>(Revelation 20:7-10)<br>Satan's Final Rebellion** |
|---|---|
| Instigated by God himself who puts hooks in the jaws of Gog and drives Gog and his alliance of a few nations to invade Israel. | Instigated by Satan, who, when released from the Abyss after a confinement of 1,000 years, goes out to deceive all the nations. |

| **Gog & Magog (Ezekiel 38 & 39) War of Gog & Magog** | **Gog & Magog (Revelation 20:7-10) Satan's Final Rebellion** |
|---|---|
| A specific alliance of nations is named: Gog, the overall leader; Rosh, Magog, Meshech, Tubal, Persia, Gomer, Togarmah, Cush, and Put. | Satan is specifically identified as the leader. Gog and Magog are mentioned with no detail. No other leaders or nations are named. Proponents of these being different conflicts argue that the reference to "Gog and Magog" in Revelation 20 is like making a reference to a classic military defeat such as Napoleon's Waterloo. In this context the words "Gog and Magog" should carry a similar if not even greatly magnified mental image of God's supernatural defeat of an enemy to the knowledgeable reader. |
| The alliance comes primarily from the far quarters of the north as well as from the Middle East and Africa. | Satan goes out in all directions to deceive the nations which are in the four quarters of the earth. |
| There is a specific alliance of nations, whose armies are large but not numbered. | The number of whom *is* as the sand of the sea. |
| The invasion comes against the land of Israel described as being a land brought back from war, a people gathered out of many nations, and mountains that have been a continual waste. | Israel will have been a totally renovated and productive land without warfare for 1,000 years. The people of Israel will not be scattered in exile throughout the nations during the Millennium. |
| The invasion comes against the people of Israel who are dwelling "safely" in villages without walls, bars of gates. In spite of this dwelling "safely" under a false sense of security, Israel is surrounded by enemies instead of a supernatural "wall of fire." Nor does Israel have the glory of God | Israel will truly be dwelling safely without walls during the Millennium. "Jerusalem shall be inhabited *as* towns without walls for the multitude of men and cattle therein: For I, saith the LORD, will be unto her a wall of fire round about, and will be the glory in the midst of her" (Zech 2:4-5). |

| Gog & Magog<br>(Ezekiel 38 & 39)<br>War of Gog & Magog | Gog & Magog<br>(Revelation 20:7-10)<br>Satan's Final Rebellion |
|---|---|
| in its midst. | |
| The invading forces are described as being heavily armed and equipped for war. Gog is commanded by God to prepare his armies – to arm, equip, and train them. Ezekiel places a strong emphasis on the weapons. | No weapons of warfare are mentioned at all. Weapons will be beaten into agricultural implements during the Millennium. War will cease and warfare will not be learned by anymore (Isa 2:4; Mic 4:3). This seems to be more like an invasion of zombies – the real Zombie Apocalypse. |
| The invasion comes against the mountains of Israel where the invading armies fall (are destroyed) upon the mountains and the open fields. There is no mention of Jerusalem or any reference to saints or a camp of the saints. | No mention is made of the mountains of Israel. They went up on the breadth of the earth, and compassed the camp of the saints about, and the beloved city (Jerusalem). |
| The invasion comes to take a prey and to take a great spoil (wealth) from Israel. | The nations are deceived to gather to battle (against God and the saints). |
| Gog and Magog are destroyed by God by turning the invading armies against each other; a massive earthquake; pestilence and blood; an overflowing rain, with great hail, fire and brimstone. The lands of Gog and Magog are destroyed by fire. | Fire simply comes down from God out of heaven and destroys the rebellion.<br>No global earthquake.<br>No overflowing rain.<br>No blood.<br>No hail.<br>No pestilence. |
| Gog and his armies are slain. God provides a feast for the birds and the beasts of the field on the fallen armies. | There is no mention of any feast for the birds or beasts. This dynamic of the birds feasting on the slain armies, as described in the prophecy of Ezekiel 38–39 and the War of Armageddon in Revelation 19, is completely out of character for the supernaturally renovated nature of the Earth during the |

| **Gog & Magog (Ezekiel 38 & 39) War of Gog & Magog** | **Gog & Magog (Revelation 20:7-10) Satan's Final Rebellion** |
|---|---|
| | Millennium. God promises to restore harmony between man and the animal kingdom during the Messianic Kingdom. |
| Gog and his dead soldiers are buried in a mass grave in the Valley of Hamon-Gog (Gog's Horde). Ezekiel specifically states that Gog is killed and put in a grave. The burial of the dead lasts for 7 months. There is no mention of the Lake of Fire. | Satan is cast into the Lake of Fire, where the Beast and the False Prophet already are in torment. The rebellion is devoured by fire. There is no mention of any burial of the dead. Also, this event is followed by the Great White Throne Judgment, where all unbelievers are resurrected and judged. There would be absolutely no point in any burial activity lasting for 7 months, even if there are any bodies left to bury, after God's divine destruction. |
| The weapons (fuel) of Gog and Magog are burned for 7 years. | There is no mention of any subsequent burning of weapons, but it would be inconsistent with the time at the end of the Millennial Kingdom of God when the old heaven and earth pass away and are replaced by a new heaven and a new earth and New Jerusalem descends to the new earth from heaven. |
| God causes this invasion to sanctify His holy name before Israel and the nations, so that God will be known and magnified in the eyes of many nations. Israel is to undergo a spiritual rebirth and return to a faithful relationship with God as a result of God's supernatural intervention. | Satan does this in direct rebellion against God. There is no need for a demonstration by God to the house of Israel or to the nations on earth at this point to make them aware of God because they have been living in the Millennial Kingdom of God and serving Christ for 1,000 years. |

For a much more in-depth examination of the prophecy of Ezekiel 38–39, and the various interpretations put forth by scholars, the reader is referred to my book: *The Silence is Broken! God Hook's Ezekiel's Gog & Magog.* www.thesilenceisbroken.us.

## Notes: Ezekiel 38–39: The War of Gog and Magog

1. Rabbi Aryeh Kaplan, *The Living Torah,* (New York: Maznaim Publishing Corporation, 1981), p. 165.
2. Harold Fisch, ed., *The Jerusalem Bible,* (Jerusalem: Koren Publishers Ltd., 1992), p. 40.
3. Harold Fisch, ed., *The Jerusalem Bible*, p. 303.
4. Yaakov Elman, *The Living Nach*, (Jerusalem: Moznaim Publishing Corporation, 1994), p.126.
5. Arthur W. Pink, *The Antichrist*, (Grand Rapids, MI: Kregel Publications, 1988, reprint of 1923 original), p. 11.
6. Walid Shoebat, *Why I Left Jihad: The Root of Terrorism and the Rise of Islam*, (USA: Top Executive Media, 2005), p. 229.
7. Arthur E. Bloomfield, *Before the Last Battle—Armageddon*, (Minneapolis: Bethany Fellowship, Inc. 1971), p. 89.
8. Shoebat, *Why I Left Jihad*, pp. 227-228.
9. Shoebat, *Why I Left Jihad*, p. 228.
10. Kaplan, *The Living Torah,* p. 271.

# 11

# The End of the Beginning

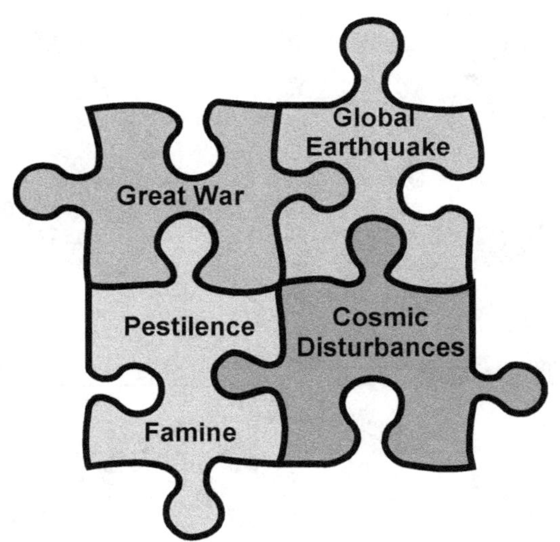


**The Beginning of Sorrows**

## Pieces of the Prophetic Puzzle

A number of passages of Bible prophecy are relevant to the time and nexus of events that comprise the beginning of the End Times and the Day of the LORD. We have seen several key pieces of the puzzle come together to intersect and interconnect very well. While we can envision this as a puzzle with neatly fitting pieces, or a tapestry with intricately interwoven details, we can also perceive our picture of the Beginning of the End as the central intersecting hub of a large number of passages coming together at a grand monument or historical landmark. It will be the grand junction of six thousand years of man's history intersecting with God's prophetic Day of the LORD. There are several categories of events within the context of this nexus that can be identified, and each category has interconnecting pieces of the puzzle from the Old Testament as well as the New Testament. It is almost like the multiple prongs or tines of several forks coming together to form an interconnected linkage.

**The Prophetic Intersection of the Beginning of the End**

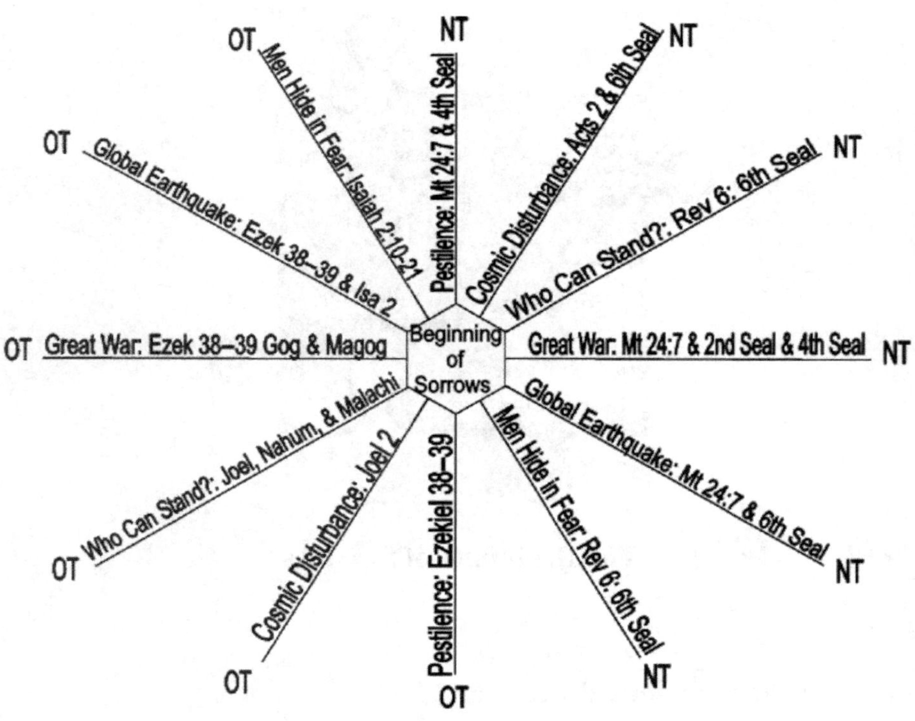


[Note: OT = Old Testament; NT = New Testament]

The major events and conditions that come together at the time of the end of the Church Age and the Beginning of Sorrows with the opening of the seals include:

- The Rapture of the Church
- Cosmic Disturbances
- Great War
- Global Earthquake
- Famine
- Pestilence
- Men Hiding Underground in Fear
- God's Question – Who Can Stand?

**Interconnecting Puzzle Pieces of Beginning Events**

| **Category of Beginning Events** | **Prophetic Puzzle Pieces** |
|---|---|
| The Rapture of the Church | OT: Isa 26:19-21; Isa 57:1; Zeph 2:3<br>NT: Jn 14:1-3; 1 Cor 15:51-55;<br>1 Thes 4:13-18; Rev 7:9-17; 19:7-8 |
| Cosmic Disturbances –<br>Sun Dark; Blood Red Moon<br>Heaven Shaken; Stars Fall | OT: Joel 2:30-31; Act 2:19-20;<br>NT: 6th Seal Rev 6:12-17 |
| Great War | OT: Ezek 38–39;<br>NT: Mt 24:7-8; 2nd Seal Rev 6:3-4;<br>4th Seal Rev 6:7-8 |
| God Rises to Shake the Earth –<br>Global Earthquake | OT: Isa 2:19, 21; Ezek 38:19-20;<br>NT: Mt 24:7-8; 6th Seal Rev 6:12-17 |
| Famine | NT: Mt 24:7-8; 3rd Seal Rev 6:5-6;<br>4th Seal Rev 6:7-8 |
| Pestilence | OT: Ezek 38:22;<br>NT: Mt 24:7-8; 4th Seal Rev 6:7-8 |
| Men Hiding Underground in Fear | OT: Isa 2:10, 19, 21;<br>NT: Rev 6:15-16 |
| God's Question –<br>Who Can Stand? | OT: Joel 2:11; Nah 1:6; Mal 3:2;<br>NT: 6th Seal Rev 6:17 |

## The End of the Beginning

As I pointed out in the first chapter, "The Beginning of the End," there are many different approaches to interpreting the beginning of the End Times. A number of different models have been proposed by different scholars to account for the sequence of events that will make up the time of the end. There are a number of issues that directly or indirectly relate to the beginning of the End for which there is no overall consensus. The timing and character of the rapture of the church is highly contested. The timing and length of the Day of the LORD is disputed. The relationship of the rapture to the Day of the LORD is questioned. The time that God's wrath begins is challenged. The timing and character of the War of Gog and Magog is a source of contention between certain camps of interpretation. The identity of the leader Gog is disputed. The Beginning of Sorrows is viewed in various ways regarding its length, timing, and character. The time period through which the seven seals are opened is also disputed. While many scholars link the opening of the first seal to the very beginning of Daniel's 70$^{th}$ Week as the seven-year Tribulation, what follows with the rest of the seals varies considerably. Many scholars link the beginning of birth pangs to at least the first four seals, while others separate the birth pangs from the seals and begin the birth pangs earlier in time. The student of Bible prophecy is left to try to make sense out of the various approaches and interpretations.

This book examines a number of these issues. In places it reinforces traditional pretribulational interpretations. In others, it challenges conventional thinking. I have attempted to follow as literal an approach to interpreting the prophetic passages as possible. Pieces of the prophetic puzzle have been linked based upon exact sameness, as well as similarity, while keeping an eye out for any distinguishing details. Information has been included in various formats to make it easier for different students to take in the larger picture meaningfully and to use this book as a reference. The student is challenged to question the assumptions made by authors and scholars, even mine. Think for yourself. Let the Bible interpret the Bible. Work at assembling the prophetic puzzle – repeatedly over time. God never intended it to be easy.

No one has the prophetic puzzle completely figured out. Solving a forensic puzzle can be difficult. Ask questions. Follow the trail of the evidence. God will reward the committed and diligent student. Jesus says, "And I say unto you, Ask, and it shall be given you; seek and ye shall find; knock, and it shall be opened unto you. For every one that asketh receiveth; and he that seeketh findeth; and to him that knocketh it shall be opened" (Mt 7:7-8; Lk 11:9-10). We knock on the door to God's Word seeking solutions to His prophetic scriptures. We knock on a door because it is closed, instead of finding it wide open. We seek and the Holy Spirit guides. We knock and the Holy Spirit answers, a little bit at a time. Seek with persistence and patience. It never comes all at once. It will never come completely in all of its puzzling details. In the end, expect to be surprised by God's completed masterpiece.

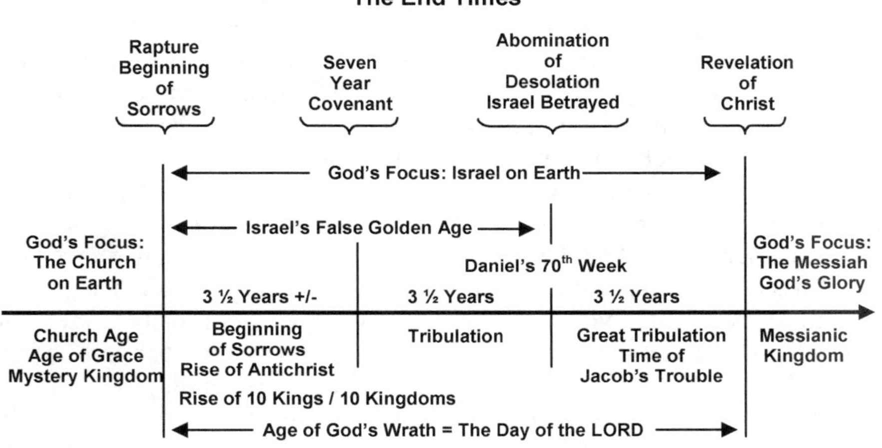


Christians also knock on the door to heaven. While the door to heaven is currently closed, the door to salvation that Jesus represents is open (Jn 10:9). One day the door to heaven will also be opened – not a little bit, but opened wide! Christ will shout, and the church will be raptured. The church will go through that door into heaven, and in an instant everything will change.

We are presently in the last days of the Age of the Church. The world is in a time of transition. Israel has been reborn as a nation and has taken center stage regarding the issue of "peace and safety," not only for the Palestinians and the nations of the Middle East, but the entire world. Israel sits, physically and prophetically, at the center of the world, as the bull's-eye of target earth. The nations of the world are going to launch a series of wars against Israel. These will come in the form of progressive stages.

First, the inner circle of nations that immediately border Israel, described as the confederacy of Psalm 83, will attack Israel. This will unleash a war involving the territory of the Promised Land. Israel will win that war, but be weakened. Israel's successful defense against the Psalm 83 Confederacy will likely include the destruction of Damascus and fulfill the prophecy of Isaiah 17. Israel's victory and increase in territory within the Promised Land will very likely result in an immediate condemnation of Israel on the world stage and within the body of the United Nations. This condemnation could easily include additional UN Resolutions against Israel as well as sanctions. There will quite likely be demands for the demilitarization of Israel – particularly an effort to remove Israel's nuclear weapons arsenal and capability. This international outrage could lead to a United Nations authorized invasion force led by Russia to seize Israel's nuclear weapons and long range missiles (to seize a spoil). This could account for the tumultuous rushing of the nations against Israel described in Isaiah 17:13 and God's rebuke of those nations. If that turns out to be the case, then the rushing of the nations will be the set up for the next phase of attack targeting Israel – the outer circle of nations.

At some point the inner circle war for the Promised Land will be followed by the outer circle of nations comprising the alliance of Gog and Magog suddenly invading Israel. That will embroil the swath of territory from Russia down through Central Asia and the entire Middle East into northern Africa. God will supernaturally intervene to protect Israel and destroy the invaders and their homelands. These and many other areas of the world will be affected at this time by war, a global earthquake, cosmic disturbances, famine, and pestilence. This is the Beginning of Sorrows. The Grand Finale invasion will entail all of the nations of the world who are left on the world stage at the end of the Tribulation being gathered against Israel for the Campaign of Armageddon. Jesus Christ will physically return to destroy all of these armies and their nefarious leaders under the control of Satan, the Antichrist, the False Prophet, and the ten kings.

Of these wars that target Israel, the inner circle of the Psalm 83 confederacy is the most probable for taking place next in the timeline of Bible prophecy. It is also quite probably going to take place during the last days of the Church Age before the Day of the LORD actually begins. This is a very likely time for the prophecy of the destruction of Damascus in Isaiah 17 to be fulfilled. These events could be used by God to set up the final dynamics for the cascading events of the Beginning of Sorrows, which will begin with the rapture of the church and the invasion of Gog and Magog.

God is transitioning His focus from the church back to Israel. Currently, God is silent on the prophetic global stage. He has His face turned towards the church as His representative body of salt and light to the world. As the church reaches the fullness of its ranks, God will break His silence and fully return His face to Israel, while snatching the church out of this world. God will yank on the supernatural hooks in the jaws of Gog and Magog, and that invasion of Israel will erupt with devastating consequences for the world.

The beginning of the End marks the end of the world as we know it. It will be a time of shock and awe, both on earth and in heaven. Who can stand in the time of God's judgment and wrath? It will be an end of the believing church on earth. All Christians born again by the power of the Holy Spirit will be raptured. The church will cross the threshold to heaven and enter the Day of Christ. The great multitude of the church will stand with Christ before the throne of God. The time of God's judgment has come. The church will be judged at the Bema – the Judgment Seat of Christ. Christians will be rewarded for their faithful walk in Christ. Crowns and roles of rulership are in store for many Christians. Some Christians will be shocked that their lives are not rewarded to the extent of others. The apostate church left behind will be judged on earth. A group of 144,000 Jews from the tribes of Israel will be chosen by God and supernaturally sealed to Him to stand as servants to God on earth. The nations will enter the time of God's wrath identified in the Bible as the Day of the LORD. That wrath will come as sudden destruction. It will be the Beginning of Sorrows – the time of travail initiated by the very first birth pang.

The Beginning of Sorrows is a time of cataclysmic cosmic disturbances, great warfare, earthquake, pestilence, and famine, simultaneously on a global scale. It is the time of the opening of the seven seals on the heavenly scroll by Jesus. The first seal releases the supernatural restraint that withholds the Antichrist from rising to power as a global political and military leader, and then as a False Christ. This is symbolic. This is not the physical person of the Antichrist riding out from heaven. It is the sanctioned authority granted to the person of the Antichrist by God that rides out from heaven. This is not the signing of the seven-year covenant of peace with Israel. The rider of the first seal goes out to conquer. The second seal takes peace from the earth and unleashes warfare on a horrific scale. The third seal initiates widespread famine as a result of natural disaster, war, economic collapse, and inflation. The fourth seal gives authority to Death and Hades to kill one-fourth of the world's population. The fifth seal reveals the souls of Christian martyrs under the altar in heaven and their being given the white robes of righteousness, which marks their resurrection during the rapture of the church. The sixth seal reveals the cosmic disturbances – the sign of the end of the age, the effects of the global earthquake, and men hiding in fear of God. The seventh seal unleashes God's declaration of war against all of the sinners left on earth.

Great warfare begins with Israel being invaded by the alliance of Gog and Magog with catastrophic results for the invading forces. God rises in indignation to defeat these enemies on His own. He does not need any help. Nation will rise against nation, and kingdom against kingdom. Much of the world will become embroiled in war. Nuclear war is likely unleashed with tragic consequences. The animal kingdom will turn against mankind. Birds and beasts will feast on the carcasses of the armies sacrificed on the battlefield of Gog and Magog. God's global earthquake will shake every person – every form of life on earth. All of the islands and mountains are moved out of their places. The planet has likely experienced a cataclysmic pole shift.

It will begin as a time of great cosmic disturbances. The sun turns dark, very dark – actually black. Yet it does not go out. The sun continues to give its light throughout the years to come. The moon turns to a blood red color, for awhile. The atmosphere of the earth is rent apart. Phenomenally, stars fall to earth in some manner, like a large and violent meteor shower. People hide underground in fear of what is happening and in fear of the realization that the God that they have long denied has risen in judgment of the earth. There are great clouds and gloominess, great hailstorms and overflowing rain, fire and brimstone raining down from the sky. The blood red moon will be reflected on earth as blood will be spilled – one-fourth of the people on earth will be killed.

It will be a time of thunderous noise. God has broken His long period of silence. Christ has shouted for His church. The trumpet of God has sounded. The wailing of mighty men on earth has begun. As the judgments of God continue, this wailing will later turn into blatant shouts of blasphemy against the name of God. As terrible as this time on earth is – it is just the beginning. The Day of the LORD has just begun!

This beginning of the Time of the End – the beginning of the Day of the LORD; the Beginning of Sorrows; the opening of the seven seals; the War of Gog and Magog – is a nexus of events. It comprises a series of events that are all related and which take place over a very short period of time. Exactly how long the initial cascading series of events lasts is anyone's guess.

Most scholars extend the opening of the seven seals over several years. This is usually projected over the first few years of the Tribulation. Some extend them over a much longer period of time. It has been suggested that Christ began to open the seals in the first century following His ascension to heaven in conjunction with the giving of the Holy Spirit to the church (John Abent, David Lowe).[1,2] This view sees the seals being opened throughout the Church Age as the Beginning of Sorrows or birth pangs culminating with the rapture of the church at the time of the sixth seal. Others have argued that the seals began to be broken or the birth pangs started at the time of World War I, or Adolf Hitler and World War II (Peter Goodgame),[3] or some other time in the 20th Century. In *Footsteps of the Messiah*, Arnold Fruchtenbaum has argued that the birth pangs started with World War I, while the seals begin to be opened at the beginning of the Tribulation.[4] Tim LaHaye has taken the same stand in his book *The Beginning of the End*, where he directly links the birth pangs and beginning of sorrows of Matthew 24:7-8 to World War I, specifically as the sign of the beginning of the end.[5]

The point of view that I have presented in this book is that Jesus revealed the Beginning of Sorrows as a group of interconnecting, simultaneous conditions that collectively denote the sign of the end of the Church Age and the very first birth pang, which begins the Day of the LORD. The conditions of: Great War, Famine, Pestilence, Global Earthquake, along with the specific cosmic disturbances of the sixth seal, cannot be separated from each other in their time of occurrence and still denote the sign of the End and the first birth pang. The Beginning of Sorrows of Matthew 24:7-8 is inherently connected to the opening of the first six seals and the War of Gog and Magog. Both the Beginning of Sorrows and the opening of the seven seals are inherently connected to the rapture of the church. All four dynamic prophetic arrows: the Beginning of Sorrows, the opening of the seven seals, the War of Gog and Magog, and the rapture of the church intersect, overlap, and intertwine to mark the very beginning of the Day of the LORD. These are all events which are so connected in their prophetic timing and impact that they cannot be separated in time without seriously ripping apart the fabric of God's majestic tapestry.

In addition, this intertwining, cascading, nexus of events that so suddenly inundates the world at the very beginning of the Day of the LORD is so overwhelming that it mimics, almost as a downsized mirror image, the very end of the Day of the LORD and the War of Armageddon. God will have intervened to destroy Gog and Magog. The earth will have experienced upheaval to an extent that is practically unimaginable. As the dust begins to settle the world will be upside down, figuratively, and quite possibly literally.

The cascading cataclysmic series of events that comprise the Beginning of Sorrows comes to an end and the extended period of the aftermath of the Beginning of Sorrows begins. I refer to this period of aftermath also as the Beginning of Sorrows. This is the time period between the rapture and the beginning of Daniel's 70th Week or the Tribulation. This time will see the rise to power of the person who will become the Antichrist. The False Prophet will also rise to power. Ten kings and ten kingdoms will emerge onto the global stage. Instead of just the territory of the ancient Roman Empire being represented, I believe the entire world will be divided into ten kingdoms.

While planet earth has gone through terrible turmoil and many nations have experienced horrific devastation, Israel will be entering its False Golden Age. The perception will be that the war to end all wars has ended. God has intervened. Israel has survived and been sanctioned by God to lead the world. This period will last at least seven years as a false peace and Renaissance for Israel. Israel will burn the weapons of Gog and Magog for fuel throughout the next seven years. Israel will flourish in its regeneration.

Israel and the world will expect the arrival of a Messiah and one will be presented on the world stage. At some point Israel and some global world leader will enter into a seven-year covenant of peace. Many believe that Israel will be forced into this covenant by a strong world leader who will guarantee Israel's safety. I see that scenario as completely unrealistic in the aftermath of God's intervention against Gog and Magog. Rather, Israel will be the strong nation – possibly the strongest. Israel is likely to be the nation imposing the conditions of the seven-year covenant. Israel will not need any nation's or world leader's permission or guarantee to rebuild its Temple in Jerusalem. The covenant will likely be the creation and collaboration between Israel's False Prophet and a unique world leader. The ratification of this covenant will initiate the countdown of Daniel's 70th Week. The Beginning of the End will have ended – the time of the seven-year Tribulation begins.

Many scholars believe this original Messianic figure to Israel will be a gentile Antichrist. I tend to believe this Messiah will be Israel's False Prophet who will be a puppet of Satan. In the middle of Daniel's 70th Week, Israel's Messianic False Prophet will betray Israel and endorse a world leader controlled or indwelt by Satan who will then enter the Jewish Temple and declare himself to be the god of the world. Israel will accept a False Messiah, who will be Jewish, but the final Antichrist will be a Gentile leader endorsed by Israel's False Messiah. This act will be the great betrayal of Israel and will send many in Israel into panic and turmoil. The people of Israel will not see this coming. It will catch them by surprise. The False Prophet then erects whatever entity entails the Abomination of Desolation in the Temple and demands worship of this abomination as worship of the Antichrist god of the earth.

## Notes: The End of the Beginning


1. John A. Abent, *Signs in the Heavens: Biblical Prophecy and Astronomy*, (Shippensburg, PA: Treasure House, Destiny Image Publishers, Inc., 1995), pp. 73, 109-110, 112, 120.
2. David W. Lowe, *Earthquake Resurrection: Supernatural Catalyst for the Coming Global Catastrophe*, (www.earthquakeresurrection.com, and www.lulu.com, 2005), pp. 198, 203, 206, 211, 215.
3. Peter Goodgame, *Red Moon Rising – The Rapture and the Timeline of the Apocalypse*, (Xulon Press, 2005), pp. 171-172, 231. See also (www.redmoonrising.com).
4. Arnold G. Fruchtenbaum, *Footsteps of the Messiah: A Study in the Sequence of Prophetic Events*, (Tustin, CA: Ariel Ministries, 1982, revised 2003), pp. 91-97.
5. Tim LaHaye, *The Beginning of the End*, (Wheaton, IL: Tyndale House Publishers, 1972, Living Books edition 1981), pp. 35-40, 166.

# Appendix 1

## Cosmic Disturbances

This book places a significant emphasis on the interconnection between the prophetic passages of Joel 2:30-31, Acts 2:19-20, and Revelation 6:12-17. These passages highlight a combination of cosmic disturbances associated with the Day of the LORD: the sun turning very dark, the moon becoming a blood red color, stars falling from heaven, and the atmosphere seemingly splitting apart. All of these are accompanied by a global earthquake, or series of related earthquakes rippling throughout the entire planet. It is stated in Isaiah 2:19 and Isaiah 2:21 that God arises to terribly shake the entire earth. It has been suggested that the earth could be moved on its axis or undergo a pole shift and even change its orbit during these initial events (Isa 13:13). While many look to conditions on the earth for the cause and effect of these combined phenomena, there is another possible explanation that lies in the realm of the cosmos.

What happens if an astronomical body such as a comet passes between the earth and the sun, causing the sun to become black when observed from the earth, without stopping it from giving off light? What if the comet is too close to the earth's atmosphere? Can the proximity of the comet cause significant effects to the earth? Can the earth cause significant effects to the comet resulting in other catastrophic conditions?

Immanuel Velikovsky examined passages of the Bible pertaining to Israel's Exodus from Egypt, other events recorded in the Old Testament, mythology and folklore from around the entire world, along with geological and astronomical evidence of past catastrophes and concluded that the earth has experienced similar or identical cosmic disturbances in its historical past. In his books, *Worlds in Collision* (1950), and *Earth in Upheaval* (1955), Velikovsky postulated that cataclysmic encounters between astronomical bodies were involved and responsible for much of the unusual or supernatural phenomena experienced on earth during certain periods of great physical upheaval. Velikovsky described astronomical wars in the celestial sphere between Venus (as a comet originating out of Jupiter), Mars, and the earth.

Velikovsky believed that electricity and magnetism play significant roles in celestial mechanics in addition to the traditional views of gravitation. He observes, "A thunderbolt, on striking a magnet, reverses the poles of the magnet. The terrestrial globe is a huge magnet. A short circuit between it and another celestial body could result in the north and the south magnetic poles of the earth exchanging places." He concluded "that electrical discharges took place between Venus, Mars, and the earth when, in very close contacts, their atmospheres touched each other" resulting in a reversal of the poles, in conjunction with: a change in the speed of the earth's rotation, a change in the earth's orbit, meteorites, hurricanes, the inundation of coastal areas and continents by great waves, volcanic activity, and earthquakes. He referred to this as the "theory of cosmic catastrophism."[1]

While describing the past celestial war, Velikovsky postulates, "the tail of the comet and its head, having become entangled with each other by their close contact with the earth, exchanged violent discharges of electricity. It looked like a battle between the brilliant globe and the dark column of smoke. In the exchange of electrical potentials, the tail and the head were attracted one to the other and repelled one from the other. … The discharges tore the column to pieces, a process that was accompanied by a rain of meteorites upon the earth." This electrical interaction was not limited to just between portions of the comet. He adds, "The head of the comet did not crash into the earth, but exchanged major electrical discharges with it. A tremendous spark sprang forth at the moment of the nearest approach of the comet."[2]

Remember the prophetic references to the noise of the Day of the LORD – to the sound of God's voice and the trumpet of God. Velikovsky notes, "The approach of two charged globes toward each other could also produce trumpetlike sounds, varying as the distance between them increased or lessened. … The sound probably had the same pitch all over the world as it came from the deep interior of the earth, all of whose strata were dislocated when it was thrown from its orbit and forced from its axis."[3]

**Notes: Cosmic Disturbances**

1. Immanuel Velikovsky, *Worlds in Collision*, (New York, NY: Dell Publishing Co., Inc., 1950, Twelfth Laurel Edition July, 1973), pp. 126-127, 379-380, 384, 387.
2. Velikovsky, *Worlds in Collision*, pp. 92, 100.
3. Velikovsky, *Worlds in Collision*, pp. 111-112.

# Appendix 2

## Earth's Population

**Isaiah 13:12** I will make mortal man scarcer than pure gold. And mankind than the gold of Ophir. (NASB)

It has been estimated that the population of the world passed the seven billion (7,000,000,000) mark sometime between October 31, 2011 (United Nations) and March 12, 2012 (United States Census Bureau). It has also been estimated that in 2011 there were 134 million births and 56 million deaths worldwide. This leaves a net gain of about 78 million persons for the year of 2011. That gain has been characterized as a 1.1 percent growth rate for 2011 by the U.S. Census Bureau. It is estimated that there is a birth every eight seconds and a death every twelve seconds for a net gain of one person every thirteen seconds. Obviously, these numbers are estimates and projections. No one can know with certainty the exact population of the entire world. This uncertainty leads to some variability in the estimates and projections by different organizations dealing with the size of the world's population, such as the United Nations and the U.S. Census Bureau.[1]

In spite of the absolute uncertainty, the U.S. Census Bureau maintains a World Population Clock on the internet.[2] This World Population Clock projected a population for the planet in excess of seven billion, ninety-one million in June 2013. Using the estimated 78 million net gain of births per year from the 2011 estimated data and assuming a relative constancy of that data for the next decade, we could project an additional increase to the world's population of about 780 million people over the next ten years. That would be our normal logical projection for the population. But what if something drastically changes?

**Estimated World Population Milestones**

| Estimated World Population | Year Reached | Time Span to Add 1 Billion |
|---|---|---|
| 1 Billion | 1804 | |
| 2 Billion | 1927 | 123 Years |
| 3 Billion | 1960 | 33 Years |
| 4 Billion | 1974 | 14 Years |
| 5 Billion | 1987 | 13 Years |
| 6 Billion | 1999 | 12 Years |
| 7 Billion | 2011 to 2012 | 12 to 13 Years |

It has been noted that the population of the world did not increase very rapidly until the time of the Industrial Revolution. At that point the population began to explode. Some of the primary factors that have impacted the growth rate of the world's population historically have been: plague, disease epidemics (such as influenza, smallpox, and measles), and war. At times, the world has experienced high fertility rates, varied between different nations and regions of the planet. Presently the overall rate of population growth has slowed due to decreasing birth rates.

Issues that complicate an accurate projection of the earth's population in the future include: the current trend of an aging population due to increased longevity, advances in medicine, medical treatment, and the potential for a continued decrease in fertility rates, particularly in the nations of the West. Modern society still faces the traditional variables that have affected population growth throughout history. The threats of wars, disease epidemics (including the modern HIV/AIDS epidemic), and pandemics complicated by faster means of global travel, and increased mass casualty events due to natural disasters impacting larger density population centers than in the past, make these variables as relevant as ever. The risk of famine is increasingly becoming a major threat to larger portions of the world.

Nonetheless, the population continues to steadily increase. Many people are concerned that an increase of one billion people every 12 to 14 years is going to, sooner or later, have a tremendous and possibly devastating impact upon the available resources for food, water, and energy. What is the Biblical outlook for the world's population growth in the near future?

At some point several factors are going to impact the future population of the world during the End Times. First, the rapture of the church will remove a great multitude of believers from the earth. We cannot know how many believers will comprise the completed body of the church at the time of the rapture, but it can easily be projected into the millions. Second, since Revelation 6:8 reveals that God grants power to Death and Hades to kill one-fourth of the world's population with the opening of the fourth seal judgment, the world is looking at a loss of at least 1.75 billion people during the combined events of just the Beginning of Sorrows. Following the opening of the seven seals, there will be a number of events: wars, natural disasters, judgments associated with God's wrath, and acts of Satan's wrath that will result in the deaths of many more people. The prophetic passage of the sixth trumpet judgment (Rev 9:15 and 9:18) reveals that when the angel blows the trumpet four angels are released who have been prepared in advance for this specific time for the purpose of overseeing the slaying of a third of the population of mankind. That will be a third of the surviving population after the loss of a fourth of the population during the Beginning of Sorrows and any additional people killed during the interim period of time.

**The Reduction of Earth's Population**

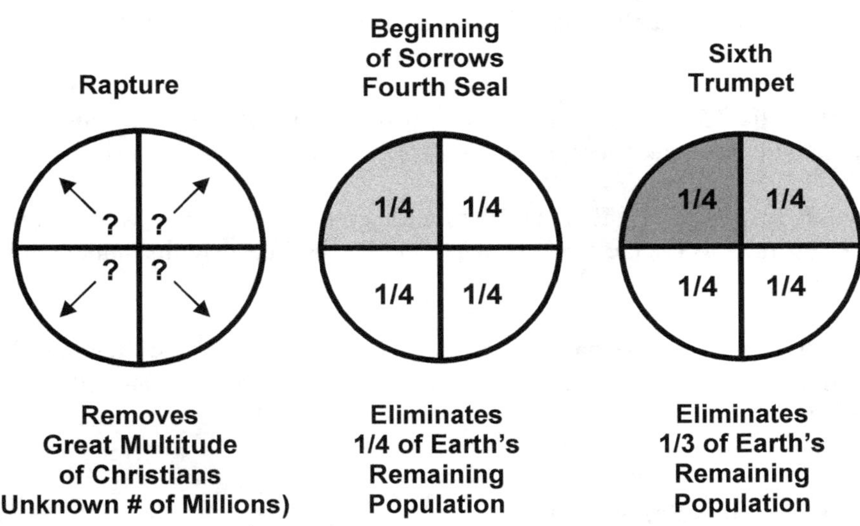


When we project this loss of the world's population in terms of a simplified picture we see that one-fourth (25%) of the world is killed during the opening of the seals. That leaves about three-fourths or 75% remaining. The sixth trumpet then results in the death of one-third of those remaining. One-third of the surviving 75% is an additional 25% of the **original** population, resulting in a combined loss of one-half or 50% of the original post-rapture population of the world. The book of Revelation plainly states that as a direct result of the combined effects of the fourth seal judgment and the sixth trumpet judgment half of the world's population will be wiped out. That is a staggering loss of in excess of three billion, five hundred forty-five million, five hundred thousand people over the course of just a few years (3,545,500,000). That is not even counting all of the other wars, disasters, and judgments that take place between and after these two devastating events. That is not counting any of the seven bowl judgments, the War of Armageddon, and the Revelation of Christ.

This picture gives the image of splitting a pill of bitter medicine and swallowing it in partial but devastating doses. Some medicines are poisons (such as chemotherapy used to treat cancer). These forms of medical treatment can play havoc with the patient's body during the course of the treatment. God is treating a form of cancer and that cancer is – sin! God's prescription is a bitter one. When God says He is going to remove sinners from the face of the earth, He is not to be taken lightly.

**Psalm 37:20** But the wicked shall perish, and the enemies of the LORD *shall be* as the fat of lambs: they shall consume; into smoke shall they consume away.

**Psalm 104:35** Let the sinners be consumed out of the earth, and let the wicked be no more. Bless thou the LORD, O my soul. Praise ye the LORD.

**Isaiah 13:9** Behold, the day of the LORD cometh, cruel both with wrath and fierce anger, to lay the land desolate: and he shall destroy the sinners thereof out of it.

**Isaiah 24:6** Therefore hath the curse devoured the earth, and they that dwell therein are desolate: therefore the inhabitants of the earth are burned, and few men left.

**Notes: Earth's Population**

1. Wikipedia (the free encyclopedia on the internet), *World Population Milestones*, http://en.wikipedia.org/wiki/World_population, accessed June 2013.
2. World Population Clock, The United States Census Bureau, www.census.gov/popclock/, accessed June 2013.

# Appendix 3

## Satan's Little Season

And I saw an angel come down from heaven, having the key of the bottomless pit and a great chain in his hand. And he laid hold on the dragon, that old serpent, which is the Devil, and Satan, and bound him a thousand years, And cast him into the bottomless pit, and shut him up, and set a seal upon him, that he should deceive the nations no more, till the thousand years should be fulfilled: and after that he must be loosed a little season. (Revelation 20:1-3)

When Jesus Christ triumphantly returns, at the time known as His second coming, He will conquer and destroy the armed forces of the Antichrist, the False Prophet, and the kings of the earth (Rev 19:11-21). The Antichrist and the False Prophet will be slain, resurrected, and then cast alive into the Lake of Fire. The kings of the earth and their armies will be killed by Christ. All of the military forces that assemble to do battle with Christ and Christ's armies from heaven are cursed to become carnage for the birds. Birds are called to assemble to feast upon the carnage of the battlefield. This invitation to the birds to assemble for the "great supper of God" in verse 17 should be contrasted with the blessing that is bestowed upon all people who are invited to attend the marriage supper of the Lamb in verse 9. The blessing of the marriage supper will follow on earth sometime after the cursing of the great supper of God is finished.

Immediately following this portrayal of Christ's triumphant victory in Revelation 19, we are shown the helplessness of Satan in Revelation 20. Satan – the Dragon – the Old Serpent – the Devil is chained by an angel and cast into the Abyss. For some reason Satan is designated by four titles. Four is the number for the earth. According to E. W. Bullinger in his book *Numbers in Scripture*, four is the number of Creation. Thus, we may have a symbolical characterization of Satan in Revelation 20:2 as the ultimate created being who attempts to wrestle control of the earth and creation away from God.

This four-fold characterization of Satan is a continuation of essentially the same description applied to him in Revelation 12:9. Thus, this section of the book of Revelation forms an inclusio (a section of scripture bracketed in this manner for emphasis). This inclusio begins with the casting of Satan out of heaven to the surface of the earth, where he deceives the world and vents his wrath because his time is short. The inclusio ends with the casting of Satan from the surface of the earth into the Abyss, where he is confined for a specific period of one thousand years during which he can no longer deceive the nations.

However, we are informed that immediately after Satan's one thousand year prison sentence is fulfilled, he will be released (loosed) for "a little season" (Rev 20:3). As soon as he is released from the Abyss, Satan goes out to deceive the nations and instigates his final rebellion against God. Revelation 20:8 makes an unexplained reference to "Gog and Magog." This is a cryptic manner of inserting a flashback to the Gog and Magog prophecy of Ezekiel 38 and 39, as a form of rebellion against God through an invasion against God's chosen people and God's chosen land, which is completely terminated by God's supernatural intervention. That is exactly what happens to Satan's final rebellion.

Satan's little season is the period of time during which he has to deceive the nations and make his final attack against God. When does Satan's little season begin, and how long can it last? A superficial reading of Revelation 19 and 20 can leave a person with the impression that at the end of the one thousand year reign of Christ's Messianic Kingdom, Satan is then released to instigate his rebellion. However, the prophetic timeline at the end of the Tribulation is more complicated than that.

Daniel 9:24-27 gives us the vision of the Seventy Weeks which applies to Daniels' people, the Jews, and to the holy city Jerusalem. The 70th Week of this prophecy has commonly become known as the Tribulation. "And he [the Antichrist] shall confirm the covenant with many for one week: and in the midst of the week he shall cause the sacrifice and the oblation to cease," (Dan 9:27). "And from the time *that* the daily *sacrifice* shall be taken away, and the abomination that maketh desolate set up, *there shall be* a thousand two hundred and ninety days. Blessed *is* he that waiteth, and cometh to the thousand three hundred and five and thirty days" (Dan 12:11-12).

Daniel's 70th Week is evenly divided into two halves of **1,260** days or 42 months each. Daniel 9:27 and 12:11 inform us that the process of sacrifices in the rebuilt Jewish Temple in Jerusalem will be stopped in the middle of the Tribulation. This will be when the Antichrist takes over the Temple and sits in the Temple declaring himself to be God (2 Thes 2:4). An image of the Antichrist is created at the direction of the False Prophet and erected in the Temple. People are commanded to worship the Antichrist and his image. This is the Abomination of Desolation that Jesus referred to in His Olivet discourse (Mt 24:15; Rev 13:14-15).

In chapter 12, Daniel makes reference to three periods of time: *First*, there is the time of greatest trouble when the Antichrist has power to scatter the Jews. This is the second half of Daniel's 70th Week. It is the same 42 months that the Antichrist is supernaturally empowered (Dan 12:7; Rev 11:2; 12:14; 13:5). It begins in the middle of Daniels 70th Week with the desecration of the Temple. *Second*, a period of time begins with the interruption of the sacrifices and the erection of the abomination of desolation in the middle of the Tribulation, and lasts for **1,290** days (Dan 12:11). This is thirty days longer than the second half of the Tribulation. This period of 30 days could be a time of mourning (Zech 12:10-14; Mt 24:30; Rev 1:7). It is also believed by some scholars that the Abomination of Desolation will be removed from the Temple at the end of the 1,290 days (i.e. Arnold Fruchtenbaum, *Footsteps of the Messiah*). *Third*, there is a period of **1,335** days (Dan 12:12). This period is 45 days longer than the 1,290 days, and both these periods must be immediately sequential – 30 days followed by 45 days. Daniel's wording specifically designates a point in time as "the" 1,335 days. This implies that people must endure the time of the

1,260 days, plus the 30 days, plus an additional 45 days, before reaching the special blessing point of the 1,335 days. The 1,335 days is generally considered to mark the advent of the Messianic Kingdom. Thus, the 1,335 days is inclusive of both the 1,260 and 1,290 day periods. This creates a 75 day interval of time between the second coming of Christ at the end of the Tribulation and the beginning of the Millennial Kingdom.

How does the 75 day interval revealed to us by Daniel relate to the timing of Satan's little season? The Antichrist is empowered to rule the earth for 1,260 days and not a single day longer. Thus, Jesus Christ should return to earth with His armies from heaven on the last day of Daniel's 70$^{th}$ Week. This is His triumphant Revelation known as His second coming. Jesus can easily destroy the armies of the Antichrist, cast the Antichrist and the False Prophet into the Lake of Fire, and have Satan bound and cast into the Abyss on that very day. This is "the battle of that great day of God Almighty" referred to in Revelation 16:14, that Satan and his minions have assembled their armies to fight. If this climax of the Tribulation does take place in one day, then the battle will not extend into any portion of the 75 day interval. Satan's one thousand year countdown to his release from confinement begins immediately upon his being cast into the Abyss.

At the same time, the 75 day interval will begin and precede the one thousand year Messianic Kingdom. There will be 1,000 years plus 75 days until the end of the Sabbath Millennium. Thus, the surviving people on earth have one thousand years without the deceiving influence of Satan. However, Satan's release comes 75 days before the end of the Millennium and his acts of deception are renewed. This 75 day interval for Christ and the earth, at the beginning of the Millennial Kingdom, foreshadows an equal period of 75 days at the very end of the Millennium. The last 75 days of the Millennium immediately follow Satan's release from the Abyss and directly equate with Satan's little season of rebellion.

If Jesus Christ delays the binding and casting of Satan into the Abyss for a day or two into the 75 day interval preceding the Millennium, then the corresponding period for Satan's little season will be shortened by the same number of days. Satan will be confined for exactly one thousand years to the day. The Millennial Kingdom will last for exactly one thousand years to the day. Daniel's 75 day interval teaches us that the period of Satan's confinement and the period of the Millennial Kingdom overlap, but are not identical periods on God's prophetic timeline.

# Subject and Author Index

## B



## C

## D



## E

## H



## I

## J



## K



## L



## M

## N



## O



## P

## Q



## R



## S

# T

## U



## V



## W



## Y



## Z

# Scripture Index

**Jeremiah**



**Lamentations**



**Ezekiel**

**Daniel**



**Hosea**



**Joel**



**Amos**



**Obadiah**



**Micah**

**1 Corinthians**



**2 Corinthians**



**Galatians**



**Ephesians**



**Philippians**



**Colossians**



**1 Thessalonians**



**2 Thessalonians**

# About the Author

Douglas Berner is a retired police Detective Sergeant with a background in Criminal Investigations, police S.W.A.T. team training, and edged weapons. Mr. Berner applies skills of criminal case analysis and the evaluation of criminal evidence to the study of Biblical Scripture and the examination of the prophetic puzzle of the End Times. He believes in utilizing a logic problem approach to solve some of the difficulties in understanding which biblical passages are, or are not, parallel passages of prophecy.

Douglas studied geology and criminology at Florida State University and received B.S. degrees in both fields. He has no theological training but has been a student of the Bible and Bible prophecy for over 30 years. He expanded his interests in the Bible, geology, and archaeology by making four trips to Israel in the 1990's, twice serving as a volunteer involved in archaeological research and field activities. He briefly lived in Israeli settlements in the West Bank during these archaeological trips. Douglas is an active participant of Bible Study Fellowship (www.bsfinternational.org).

Mr. Berner is the author of *The Silence is Broken! God Hooks Ezekiel's Gog & Magog*, an in-depth examination of the War of Gog and Magog prophesied in the $38^{th}$ and $39^{th}$ chapters of Ezekiel.

Website: www.thesilenceisbroken.us

CPSIA information can be obtained
at www.ICGtesting.com
Printed in the USA
BVHW042151250419
546610BV00013B/142/P

9 781490 944883